Essential ASP.NET Web Forms Development

Full Stack Programming with C#, SQL, Ajax, and JavaScript

Robert E. Beasley

Apress®

Essential ASP.NET Web Forms Development: Full Stack Programming with C#, SQL, Ajax, and JavaScript

Robert E. Beasley
Franklin, IN, USA

ISBN-13 (pbk): 978-1-4842-5783-8   ISBN-13 (electronic): 978-1-4842-5784-5
https://doi.org/10.1007/978-1-4842-5784-5

Managing Director, Apress Media LLC: Welmoed Spahr
Acquisitions Editor: Joan Murray
Development Editor: Laura Berendson
Coordinating Editor: Jill Balzano

Cover image designed by Freepik (www.freepik.com)

Distributed to the book trade worldwide by Springer Science+Business Media New York, 233 Spring Street, 6th Floor, New York, NY 10013. Phone 1-800-SPRINGER, fax (201) 348-4505, e-mail orders-ny@springer-sbm.com, or visit www.springeronline.com. Apress Media, LLC is a California LLC and the sole member (owner) is Springer Science + Business Media Finance Inc (SSBM Finance Inc). SSBM Finance Inc is a **Delaware** corporation.

For information on translations, please e-mail rights@apress.com, or visit http://www.apress.com/rights-permissions.

Apress titles may be purchased in bulk for academic, corporate, or promotional use. eBook versions and licenses are also available for most titles. For more information, reference our Print and eBook Bulk Sales web page at http://www.apress.com/bulk-sales.

Any source code or other supplementary material referenced by the author in this book is available to readers on GitHub via the book's product page, located at www.apress.com/9781484257838. For more detailed information, please visit http://www.apress.com/source-code.

Printed on acid-free paper

To Elizabeth, Zachariah, Isaac, Nathanael, and Elijah
I Love You

Table of Contents

About the Author xv

Acknowledgments xvii

Preface xix

Part I: Overview 1

Chapter 1: Web Application Development 3

   1.1 Introduction.. 3

   1.2 Client-Server Model 4

   1.3 .NET Framework 8

   1.4 Object-Orientation Concepts 9

      1.4.1 Classes and Objects 10

      1.4.2 Properties 12

      1.4.3 Methods.. 12

      1.4.4 Events 13

      1.4.5 Encapsulation 13

      1.4.6 Inheritance 14

   1.5 ASP.NET and C# Programming 21

   1.6 Visual Studio 22

   1.7 Starting a New Project.. 23

   1.8 Solution Explorer.. 24

Part II: Single-Page Web Application Development 27

Chapter 2: Page Development 29

2.1 Introduction 29

2.2 Identifier Naming Standards 29

2.3 Page Class 30

2.4 Adding a Page Class 32

Chapter 3: Basic Server Controls 39

3.1 Introduction 39

3.2 Toolbox 39

3.3 Label Class 40

3.4 TextBox Class 43

3.5 Button Class 45

3.6 Table Class 52

3.7 TableRow Class 53

3.8 TableCell Class 54

Chapter 4: More Server Controls 59

4.1 Introduction 59

4.2 Calendar Class 59

4.3 CheckBox Class 63

4.4 RadioButton Class 65

4.5 FileUpload Class 68

4.6 HyperLink Class 71

4.7 Image Class 72

4.8 ImageButton Class 74

4.9 ImageMap Class 77

4.10 RectangleHotSpot Class 78

4.11 LinkButton Class 82

4.12 ListControl Class 87

4.13 ListItem Class 89

4.14 DropDownList Class 90

4.15 ListBox Class 92

4.16 Panel Class 94

Chapter 5: Data Validation Controls.. 99

5.1 Introduction 99

5.2 Script Manager Package 101

5.3 BaseValidator Class 101

5.4 RequiredFieldValidator Class 103

5.5 CompareValidator Class 105

5.6 RangeValidator Class 107

5.7 RegularExpressionValidator Class 110

5.8 CustomValidator Class 114

5.9 ValidationSummary Class 117

Part III: C# Programming 123

Chapter 6: Assignment Operations 125

6.1 Introduction 125

6.2 Types 125

6.3 Variable Declarations 127

6.4 Constant Declarations 130

6.5 Assignment Operators 130

6.6 Enumerations 133

6.7 Exception Handling 134

6.8 Exception Class 135

6.8.1 DivideByZeroException Class 137

6.8.2 FormatException Class 138

6.8.3 IndexOutOfRangeException Class 139

6.8.4 OverflowException Class 141

6.8.5 Multiple Exceptions 142

Chapter 7: Conversion Operations 145

7.1 Introduction 145

7.2 Widening Conversions 145

7.3 Narrowing Conversions 148

7.4 Convert Class 153

Chapter 8: Control Operations 161

8.1 Introduction 161

8.2 Relational Operators 162

8.3 Equality Operators 162

8.4 Logical Operators 163

8.5 Decision Structures 164

    8.5.1 If Structure 164

    8.5.2 If-Else Structure 167

    8.5.3 If-Else-If Structure 168

    8.5.4 Nested-If Structure 169

    8.5.5 Switch Structure 171

    8.5.6 Switch-Through Structure 173

8.6 Iterative Structures 174

    8.6.1 While Structure 174

    8.6.2 Do-While Structure 175

    8.6.3 For Structure 176

    8.6.4 For-Each Structure 178

    8.6.5 Break Statement 180

    8.6.6 Continue Statement 180

Chapter 9: String Operations 183

9.1 Introduction 183

9.2 Concatenations 183

9.3 Escape Sequences 184

9.4 Verbatim Literals 186

9.5 String Class 186

Chapter 10: Arithmetic Operations 193

10.1 Introduction.. 193

10.2 Arithmetic Operators... 194

10.3 Order of Precedence and Associativity 197

10.4 Parentheses 199

10.5 Math Class 201

Chapter 11: Date and Time Operations 207

11.1 Introduction.. 207

11.2 DateTime Structure... 208

11.3 Date-Related Properties... 211

11.4 Date-Related Methods 212

11.5 Date Formatting 213

11.6 Date Parsing.. 214

11.7 Time-Related Properties 216

11.8 Time-Related Methods... 216

11.9 Time Formatting... 218

Chapter 12: Array Operations 221

12.1 Introduction.. 221

12.2 Array Class 222

12.3 One-Dimensional Arrays 224

12.4 Two-Dimensional Arrays 231

Chapter 13: Collection Operations 241

13.1 Introduction.. 241

13.2 Stack Class 242

13.3 Queue Class 244

13.4 LinkedList Class 246

13.5 SortedList Class 250

Chapter 14: File System Operations 253

14.1 Introduction.. 253

14.2 File Class... 254

Chapter 15: Custom C# Classes... 265

15.1 Introduction.. 265

15.2 Class Design 266

15.3 C# Class 267

15.4 Adding a Classes Folder.. 268

15.5 Adding a Non-static C# Class.. 268

15.6 Adding a Static C# Class 273

Part IV: Multiple-Page Web Application Development 279

Chapter 16: State Maintenance 281

16.1 Introduction.. 281

16.2 Client-Based State Maintenance 282

16.2.1 View State... 282

16.2.2 Cookies... 284

16.2.3 Query Strings.. 289

16.3 Server-Based State Maintenance 294

16.3.1 Session State... 294

16.3.2 HttpSessionState Class 296

16.4 Maintaining the State of a Data Structure 301

Chapter 17: Master Pages 303

17.1 Introduction.. 303

17.2 MasterPage Class 303

17.3 Adding a MasterPage Class 305

17.4 Adding a Page Class with a MasterPage.. 309

Chapter 18: Themes..**323**

18.1 Introduction...323

18.2 Adding a Theme 323

18.3 Skin Files 325

18.4 Adding a Skin File 325

18.5 Cascading Style Sheet Files...332

18.6 Adding a Cascading Style Sheet File...333

Chapter 19: Navigation **343**

19.1 Introduction...343

19.2 SiteMap Class 344

19.3 Adding a SiteMap Class 345

19.4 Menu Class 349

19.5 TreeView Class 353

Part V: Database Connectivity **357**

Chapter 20: Database Design, SQL, and Data Binding **359**

20.1 Introduction...359

20.2 Database Schema 360

20.3 Tables..361

20.4 Attributes...362

20.5 Relationships 363

20.6 Structured Query Language 364

20.6.1 Select Statement...366

20.6.2 Insert Statement..374

20.6.3 Update Statement..377

20.6.4 Delete Statement...378

20.7 DataBoundControl Class 379

20.8 SqlDataSource Class...380

20.8.1 Connection Strings 383

20.8.2 Data-Bound Control Population 384

20.8.3 Data-Bound Control Filtering...386

Chapter 21: Single-Row Database Table Maintenance 395

21.1 Introduction 395

21.2 FormView Class 395

Chapter 22: Multiple-Row Database Table Maintenance 419

22.1 Introduction 419

22.2 ListView Class 420

22.3 DataPager Class 441

22.4 NextPreviousPagerField Class 442

22.5 NumericPagerField Class 445

Chapter 23: Code Behind Database Operations 449

23.1 Introduction 449

23.2 SqlConnection Class 450

23.3 WebConfigurationManager Class 452

23.4 SqlCommand Class 453

23.5 SqlDataReader Class 455

23.6 Non-parameterized Queries 458

23.7 Parameterized Queries 463

23.7.1 SqlParameterCollection Class 464

23.7.2 SqlParameter Class 465

23.8 Stored Procedures 471

Part VI: Additional Functionality 487

Chapter 24: Email Messaging 489

24.1 Introduction 489

24.2 Development Machine Email Server 490

24.3 MailMessage Class 490

24.4 SmtpClient Class 492

Chapter 25: Ajax Programming **499**

25.1 Introduction.. 499

25.2 ScriptManager Class... 500

25.3 Extension Classes 501

    25.3.1 UpdatePanel Class... 501

    25.3.2 UpdateProgress Class 504

25.4 Ajax Control Toolkit.. 507

    25.4.1 Installing the Ajax Control Toolkit 507

    25.4.2 Control Classes... 509

    25.4.3 Control Extender Classes.. 517

Chapter 26: JavaScript Programming **533**

26.1 Introduction.. 533

26.2 Browser Compatibility.. 534

26.3 Script Elements.. 535

26.4 Functions 535

26.5 HTML Document Object Model.. 536

26.6 Examples.. 537

    26.6.1 Assignment Operations.. 538

    26.6.2 Confirm Dialogs and Alert Messages.. 544

    26.6.3 Control Property Manipulation.. 547

    26.6.4 Date and Time Display.. 550

    26.6.5 Iterative Operations 553

Index... **559**

About the Author

Robert E. Beasley is Professor of Computing at Franklin College in Franklin, Indiana, USA, where he teaches a variety of software engineering courses. He received both his BS and MS degrees from Illinois State University and his PhD from the University of Illinois at Urbana-Champaign. He has been developing software since 1981, has been an active software consultant in both the public and private sectors since 1987, and has been teaching software engineering since 1995. He has authored three books on software engineering, contributed chapters to two books, published over 50 articles in refereed journals and conference proceedings, and delivered numerous speeches and keynote addresses at international conferences.

Acknowledgments

For any project like this to be successful, input is required from a number of people. I would like to thank David G. Barnette for providing a significant amount of technical feedback on the entire book, Elijah M. Beasley for providing a number of suggestions for improving the flow and continuity of the book, and my other software engineering students for reporting misspellings, typos, and other defects as they were encountered.

Preface

Audience

This book was written for anyone interested in learning the ASP.NET Web Forms, C#.NET, SQL, Ajax, and JavaScript Web application development stack, including novice software developers, professional software developers, and college or university students enrolled in a one-semester course or two-semester sequence of courses in Web application development.

Organization

This book helps you become a pro in one of the most effective and widely used technology stacks for developing highly interactive, professional-grade, database-driven Web applications—ASP.NET Web Forms, C#.NET, SQL, Ajax, and JavaScript. It takes you from beginner to pro in no time. In Part 1, you become familiar with some of the major concepts, methodologies, and technologies associated with .NET Web application development. In this part, you learn about the client-server model, the .NET Framework, the ASP.NET and C# programming languages, and the Visual Studio integrated development environment. In Part 2, you learn how to develop a single-page .NET Web application. In this part, you learn how to create a page and add server and data validation controls to it. The concepts in this part of the book lay the foundation required for learning the C# programming language *in the context of an ASP.NET Web application.* In Part 3, you learn how to program in the C# programming language. In this part, you learn how to perform assignment operations, conversion operations, control operations, string operations, arithmetic operations, date and time operations, array operations, collection operations, and file system operations, as well as create custom C# classes—*in the context of a .NET Web application.* In Part 4, you learn how to develop a multiple-page .NET Web application. In this part, you learn how to maintain state between pages and create master pages, themes, and navigation controls. In Part 5, you learn how to connect a .NET Web application to a SQL Server database. In this part, you learn to read a database schema, program in the SQL programming language, utilize data binding, perform single- and multiple-row database table maintenance, and write code behind database operations. And in Part 6, you learn how to enhance the interactivity of a .NET Web application. In this part, you learn to generate email messages, make use of basic Ajax controls and the Ajax Control Toolkit, and program in the JavaScript programming language.

Features

Class Focus

A class diagram is included for every class discussed in the text. Each class diagram articulates some of the most important properties, methods, and events of the class. For those properties, methods, and events that are not included in the class diagram, a link to the official class reference is provided.

Real-Life Examples

A significant proportion of the examples in the text are drawn from the real-life experiences of the author's own software development practice that began in 1987.

Clear-Minded, Consistent, and Concise Prose

Every effort has been made to present concepts clearly and logically, utilize consistent language and terminology across all chapters and topics, and articulate concepts fully yet concisely.

Accessible Language

Although the subject matter of this book is highly technical and specialized, trendy and/or arcane language that is inaccessible to the average learner is either clearly defined or replaced in favor of clear and generalizable terminology.

PART I

Overview

CHAPTER 1

Web Application Development

1.1 Introduction

The concept of *hypermedia* (i.e., the combination of hypertext and media) was first envisioned in 1945 by American engineer, inventor, and science administrator Vannevar Bush. However, it wasn't until much later that the technology required to support such a concept was mature enough to make hypermedia something most of us take for granted today.

In 1969, the *Advanced Research Projects Agency Network* (ARPANET) became the first computer network to implement *packet switching* using the *Transmission Control Protocol/Internet Protocol* (TCP/IP) suite—the protocol suite that forms the technical foundation of the Internet today. Packet switching is a method of data transmission that requires three basic steps to get data (e.g., remote computer screens, files, email messages, Web pages) from one computer on a network to another. First, at its origin, the data to be transmitted is separated into a sequenced set of relatively small parts called *packets*. Second, the packets are transmitted independently from their origin to their final destination over routes that have been determined to be optimal for each packet. And third, after all the packets have made their way to their final destination, the data is reassembled from its packets. Early TCP/IP *Application Layer* protocols included *Telnet* for logging in to remote computers, *File Transfer Protocol* (FTP) for transmitting files from one computer to another, and *Simple Mail Transfer Protocol* (SMTP) for sending email messages. These protocols are still in heavy use today.

Although the Internet was alive, well, and growing from the late 1960s through the late 1980s, there was no World Wide Web (a.k.a., Web). However, this was about to change. In 1989, development of the *Hypertext Transfer Protocol* (HTTP) was initiated by English scientist Tim Berners-Lee at the European Organization for Nuclear Research (a.k.a., CERN) in Meyrin, Switzerland—a suburb of Geneva. This protocol was to become the standard for

© Robert E. Beasley 2020
R. E. Beasley, *Essential ASP.NET Web Forms Development*, https://doi.org/10.1007/978-1-4842-5784-5_1

governing the communication between distributed hypermedia systems. With the definition of the first official version of HTTP in 1991, the Web, the hypermedia part of the Internet, was born, and HTTP became another TCP/IP Application Layer protocol like its predecessors Telnet, FTP, and SMTP. Shortly thereafter, Berners-Lee created the very first Web browser. This browser became available to other researchers in January 1991 and was released to the public in August 1991.

Early on, the Web was simply a large collection of *static Web pages*. These pages did little more than display formatted text and visual media (i.e., images, graphics, animations, videos) and permit us to download files and play audio recordings. Today, however, the Web is a massive collection of both static and *dynamic Web pages*. And thanks to programming languages like ASP.NET, dynamic Web pages can do much more than static Web pages can. In addition to the things static Web pages allow us to do, dynamic Web pages allow us to *interact* with the items displayed on a Web page. They also permit us to do things like edit the data on a page, check the data for errors, and save the data to a database.

In this chapter, we will begin by looking at the client-server model, which is a computing approach that distributes processing between servers and clients. Next, we will introduce the .NET Framework. The .NET Framework is Microsoft's Windows-based software development and execution framework. Then, we will discuss ASP.NET and C# programming. ASP.NET is a software development framework that includes all of the classes necessary for building modern, sophisticated Web applications, and C# is a general-purpose programming language for building a variety of application types, including Web applications and Windows applications. After that, we will look at Visual Studio, which is Microsoft's flagship integrated development environment (IDE). This development environment permits us to code and test in several different programming languages via a consistent user interface. And finally, we will learn how to start a new ASP.NET Web Application project.

1.2 Client-Server Model

The client-server model is a computing approach that distributes processing between a *server* (i.e., the provider of a resource, service, or application) and its *clients* (i.e., the users of a resource, service, or application). A server is composed of a *server host*, which is a physical computing device connected to a network, and a *server application*, which is a software program that manages multiple, simultaneous client access to the server. Likewise, a client is composed of a *client host*, which is a physical computing device connected to a network, and a *client application*, which is a software program that initiates a *session* with a server so that it can access the server's resources, services, and/or applications. Examples of client-server systems include Web servers and Web clients, email servers and email clients, and FTP servers and FTP clients. Examples of Web server applications include *Internet Information Services* (IIS), *Apache HTTP Server*, and *Oracle iPlanet Web Server*. Examples of Web client applications include *Microsoft Internet Explorer*, *Google Chrome*, and *Mozilla Firefox*. Web client applications are usually called *Web browsers*.

Figure 1-1 shows an example of the client-server model as it applies to a Web application. In the middle of the figure, we see a Web server. As mentioned previously, this server is composed of a server host and a server application that manages client access to the host. Connected to this server via a network (e.g., the Internet) are a number of different clients, including a tablet client, a laptop client, a Mac client, a PC client, and a phone client. The dotted line in the figure indicates that the phone client is connected to the Internet wirelessly. Of course, any server or client can be connected to the Internet wirelessly. Again, each of these clients is composed of a client host and a client application that initiates a session with the server and then accesses the server's resources, services, and/or applications.

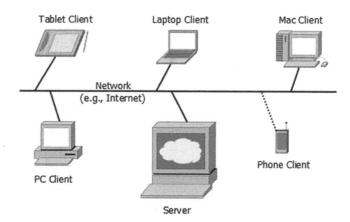

Figure 1-1. *Example of the client-server model as it applies to a Web application*

Recall that Web pages are either static or dynamic. The content and appearance of a static Web page doesn't change each time it is requested. Instead, it always looks the same no matter how many times it is requested or who requests it. It is easy to tell if a Web page is static because it has a file extension of .htm or .html. As we will see in the next figure, this type of Web page only requires the attention of a Web server.

Figure 1-2 shows the processing cycle of a *static* Web page. As can be seen, a Web client (e.g., a laptop computer running Internet Explorer) requests a Web page from a Web server (e.g., a tower computer running IIS) via an *HTTP request*. One important part of this request is the name of the requested Web page (e.g., Display_Products.html). Two other important parts of the request are the *IP addresses* (i.e., the unique Internet addresses) of the server and client. These are necessary so that the HTTP request can make its way to the Web server and so that the requested Web page can make its way back to the requesting Web client. When the Web server receives the HTTP request, it locates the desired Web page file on its hard drive, attaches the file's *Hypertext Markup Language* (HTML) code to an *HTTP response*, and then sends the response to the requesting Web client. When the Web client receives the HTTP response, it uses the attached HTML code to format and display the requested Web page for the end user. If the requested Web page does not exist on the server, the infamous 404 (i.e., Page Not Found) error is passed back to the Web client where it is displayed for the end user.

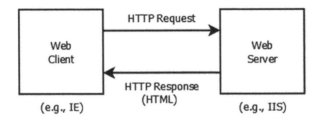

Figure 1-2. *Processing cycle of a static Web page*

Unlike the content and appearance of a static Web page, a dynamic Web page can (and usually does) change each time it is requested. In fact, depending on when it is requested and by whom, it usually contains different information (e.g., different customer information) and can look completely different (e.g., different fields, different images). It is easy to tell if a Web page is dynamic because it has a file extension that is associated with dynamic Web pages. Examples of such file extensions are .aspx (active server page), .php (hypertext preprocessor), and .jsp (java server page). As we will see in the next figure, this type of Web page is processed by both a Web server and an *application server*. When a Web application requires database functionality, a *database server* is required as well.

Figure 1-3 shows the processing cycle of a *dynamic* Web page. As before, a Web client requests a Web page from a Web server via an HTTP request. In this case, however, the request contains the name of a dynamic Web page (e.g., Display_Products.aspx) and the state of any Web page controls (e.g., a name entered into a text box, a check mark placed into a checkbox, a date selected from a calendar). When the Web server receives the HTTP request and sees that the Web page has a file extension of .aspx, it passes processing control to the application server where the *business logic* (e.g., ASP.NET and C# code) of the Web page is executed. If the business logic of the Web page requires the services of a database server (i.e., reading, inserting, updating, or deleting data), the application server passes processing control to the database server (along with any pertinent input parameters) where the database call (usually a Structured Query Language [SQL] call) of the Web page is executed. Once the database call is executed, the response from the database server (e.g., the retrieved data and/or the status of the call) is passed back to the application server where it is processed (e.g., the retrieved data is formatted and/or the status of the call is handled). After this, the application server passes its work back to the Web server, where it locates the desired Web page file on its hard drive, formats the Web page's HTML based on the results of the application server's work, attaches the resulting HTML code to an HTTP response, and then sends the response to the requesting Web client. When the Web client receives the HTTP response, it uses the attached HTML code to format and display the requested Web page for the end user. Again, if the requested Web page does not exist on the server, the infamous 404 (i.e., Page Not Found) error is passed back to the Web client where it is displayed for the end user.

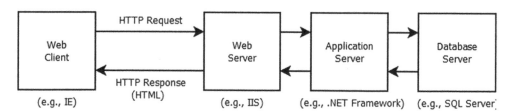

Figure 1-3. *Processing cycle of a dynamic Web page*

Keep in mind that although servers and clients usually run on separate computing devices, they can run on the same device. As an example of the latter, we often use a Web server (e.g., IIS Express), an application server (e.g., .NET Framework), a database server (e.g., SQL Server), and a Web client (e.g., Internet Explorer) all installed on the *same* machine when developing ASP.NET Web applications.

1.3 .NET Framework

The .NET Framework is a Windows-based software development and execution framework from Microsoft. This framework consists of two main parts—the *Framework Class Library* (FCL) and the *Common Language Runtime* (CLR).

The Framework Class Library is a large library of *classes*. These classes perform many of the functions needed to develop modern, state-of-the-art software applications, such as Windows applications and Web applications. The classes in the FCL can be utilized by any of the programming languages associated with the .NET Framework (e.g., Visual Basic, Visual C++, Visual C#, Visual F#) and include user interface classes, file access classes, database access classes, and network communication classes. By combining our own custom programming code with the classes in the FCL, we can develop sophisticated software applications relatively efficiently.

The Common Language Runtime is an environment in which all .NET applications execute. These applications do not interact with the operating system directly like some software applications do. Instead, regardless of the programming language used to develop them, .NET applications are compiled into a *Microsoft Intermediate Language* (MSIL) *assembly* and then executed by the CLR. Thus, it is the CLR that interacts with the operating system, which then interacts with the computer's hardware via device drivers. An important aspect of the CLR is the *Common Type System*. The Common Type System defines how all of the value types, reference types, and other types are declared, used, and managed across all of the programming languages of the .NET Framework. Since the CLR provides for its own security, memory management, and exception handling, code running in the CLR is referred to as *managed code*. Figure 1-4 summarizes the organization of the .NET Framework.

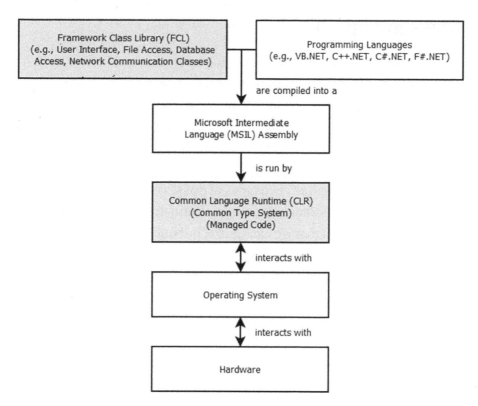

Figure 1-4. *Organization of the .NET Framework*

1.4 Object-Orientation Concepts

Object Orientation is a software development paradigm where virtually everything is viewed in terms of *classes* (e.g., customers, Web pages, buttons on a Web page) and *objects* (e.g., a specific customer, a specific Web page, a specific button on a Web page). A class can contain *properties* (i.e., the data of the class) and *methods* (i.e., the functionality of the class) and can handle *events* (i.e., end-user actions or other things that occur in time). The properties, methods, and events of a class are referred to as its *members.* A class *encapsulates* its properties, methods, and events by bundling them together into a single unit and by hiding the details of those internals from other classes. And finally, a class can *inherit* (i.e., take on and utilize) the properties, methods, and events of other classes. We will learn more about these concepts next.

1.4.1 Classes and Objects

Classes are like "templates" that represent the characteristics and behaviors of things we encounter in the real world. In our professional lives, we would likely encounter things like customers, employees, products, and orders. On a Web page, we would normally interact with things like buttons, checkboxes, calendars, and text boxes. When developing software applications that involve such things, we typically design and/or utilize classes that model their attributes and actions.

In the .NET Framework, there are two types of classes—*non-static classes* and *static classes*. As a general rule, a non-static class contains non-static properties, non-static methods, and non-static events that we can utilize, but only *after* an object has been instantiated from the class.[1] A static class, on the other hand, contains static properties, static methods, and static events that we can utilize *immediately*, without having to instantiate an object from the class.

When describing a class in this book, we will include a *class diagram*. Table 1-1 shows the general format of a class diagram. Such a diagram will always contain the name of the class and the *namespace* in which it resides. A namespace contains *classes* that provide specific functionality (e.g., page functionality, email functionality, database access functionality) or specialized *types* (e.g., interface types, array types, value types, reference types, enumeration types). A class diagram will also list some *selected* properties, methods, and events of the class. The descriptions of these items will be taken directly from Microsoft's official documentation so that they can be trusted as authoritative. And finally, a class diagram will provide a reference to Microsoft's official documentation of the class. To see all of a class's properties, methods, and events, as well as see code samples of how the class can be used, the interested reader can refer to this documentation.

---

[1] A *non-static* class can also contain *static* properties, *static* methods, and *static* events that we can utilize *immediately*, without having to instantiate an object from the class.

Table 1-1. *General format of a class diagram*

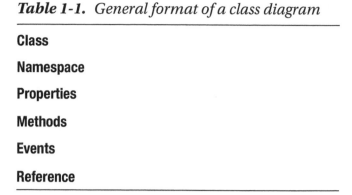

Class
Namespace
Properties
Methods
Events
Reference

There is one more *very* important thing to remember about the class diagrams used in this book. The *event handler methods* used to handle the events of a class will be omitted to conserve space. Event handler methods are those methods that begin with the word "On" and end with an event name. For example, OnInit is an event handler method that is raised by the Init event. If the Init event is already displayed in the Events section of the class diagram, then the OnInit event handler method will be omitted from the Methods section of the class diagram to conserve space.

An object is a single *instance* of a class. For example, say we have an Employee class that serves as the "template" for all employees. In this case, we might have an Employee object that represents Jim J. Jones who has an email address of jjones@mail.com and a password of abc123. We might also have an Employee object that represents Mary M. Morris who has an email address of mmorris@work.com and a password of xyz789. These two distinct objects, both of which are viewed as independent items, were *instantiated* from the Employee class by *constructing* each one and then *setting* their respective Name, EmailAddress, and Password properties. The ability to instantiate multiple objects from a single class is why, for example, we can have several text box and button objects on a single Web page, and each one of them can look and behave similarly yet differently.

1.4.2 Properties

Properties represent the data of a class. Properties are *read from* (via a get method) and *written to* (via a set method). For example, the .NET TextBox class has a Text property. If we wish to retrieve the value entered into a text box object, we would need to *get* this property. As another example, the .NET Button class has a BackgroundColor property, a ForegroundColor property, and a Text property. If we wish to display a gray button with red lettering that says "Submit," we would need to *set* these three properties appropriately. Properties can be non-static or static.

1.4.3 Methods

Methods perform a function (i.e., a task that returns a value) or a procedure (i.e., a task that *does not* return a value) and are *invoked* or *called*. There are two types of methods—non-static methods and static methods.

A non-static method is a method that can be invoked, but only *after* an object has been instantiated from its associated *non-static* class. For example, if we have an Employee object that has been created from a non-static Employee class, and this class includes a non-static ModifyPassword method, then we can invoke the Employee object's ModifyPassword method to update the employee's password, something like this

```
booSuccess = Employee.ModifyPassword("abc123");
```

where Employee is an object of the non-static Employee class and ModifyPassword is a non-static method of the Employee object.

A static method, on the other hand, is a method that can be invoked *immediately*, without having to instantiate an object from a class. For example, if we have a static Math class that includes a static Sqrt method, and we want to take the square root of 100, then we can invoke the Math class's Sqrt method *directly* (i.e., *without* having to instantiate a Math object from the Math class) to get the square root of 100, something like this

```
bytResult = Math.Sqrt(100);
```

where Math is a static class and Sqrt is a static method of the Math class.

1.4.4 Events

Events are things that happen. Events are *raised* by an end-user action or by something else that occurs in time. When an event is raised, and we wish to *handle* that event, we invoke a corresponding method. For example, the .NET Page class raises a Load event every time a Web page loads. If we want to display something for the end user every time the page loads, we would need to handle that event by adding the necessary code to the corresponding OnLoad method. Keep in mind that we need not handle every event that is raised. Events can be non-static or static.

1.4.5 Encapsulation

Encapsulation has two meanings in the context of object orientation. First, it refers to the notion that a class's properties (i.e., data) and methods (i.e., the processing that operates on that data) are bundled together and treated as a single unit. Second, it refers to the notion that a class's properties and methods cannot be directly accessed by code that resides outside of the class itself. Thus, in order to get or set a class's properties or execute a class's methods, a class that requires such operations must *request* them from the class that contains the desired properties or methods. This idea is referred to as *information hiding*. Although the concept of information hiding is an important guideline of object orientation, the .NET programming languages permit us to explicitly relax or enforce such access restrictions by declaring properties and methods as private (i.e., they can only be accessed by code within the same class), protected (i.e., they can be accessed by code within the same class and by any related subclasses), or public (i.e., they can be accessed by code in any other class).

One of the benefits of encapsulation is that it shields the internals of a class from other classes so that they can utilize the class's functionality without concern for how the class actually performs its duties. The only thing the other classes need to know about the class is what inputs it requires and what outputs it produces—that is, knowledge of the class's *interface*. In addition, encapsulation facilitates code refactoring (e.g., making a method more efficient or easier to maintain). This is because we can modify the methods of a class without disrupting the class's use by other classes—as long as the modifications do not affect the class's interface. Another benefit of encapsulation is that it encourages us to think through all of a class's properties and methods and to keep them together in one place. This makes coding, testing, and maintenance much easier.

1.4.6 Inheritance

Inheritance permits a *child class* (a.k.a., subclass, derived class) to take on and utilize the properties, methods, and events of its *parent class* (a.k.a., superclass)—as well as its parent's parent class and so on. A child class inherits all of the properties, methods, and events of its parent class (with the exception of its *constructor methods* and *destructor methods*), but it also contains properties, methods, and/or events of its own. Thus, a child class always extends the attributes and functionality of its parent class. A parent class that does not inherit any of its properties, methods, or events from another class is referred to as a *base class*. In a class inheritance hierarchy, the relationship that exists between a parent class and its child class is an *is-a-type-of* relationship.

As will become apparent, the main benefits of class inheritance are that *code redundancy* is minimized and *code reuse* is maximized. This is because a child class can use all of the properties, methods, and events of its parent class as if they were its own—we need not write that code again. Keep in mind that inherited properties, methods, and events can be *overridden* by a child class when necessary.

Figure 1-5 shows an example of a class inheritance hierarchy for an employee. In the figure, we can see that the base class in the hierarchy is the Employee class. This class contains the most fundamental properties and methods of the class.[2] The Employee class's child classes (i.e., the Salaried class and the Hourly class) not only inherit *all* of the properties and methods of the Employee class, but they each include additional properties and methods that extend the characteristics and functionality of the Employee class. Looking farther down the hierarchy, we can see that the Salaried class's child classes (i.e., the Administrator class and the Faculty class) not only inherit *all* of the properties and methods of the Salaried class and the Employee class, but they each include additional properties and methods that extend the characteristics and functionality of those classes. Thus, we can see, for example, that a faculty member is a type of salaried employee, who is a type of employee, who works in a department, who has a list of degrees, has a title, gets paid a salary, has a name, has an email address, and has a password. The Faculty class also inherits *all* of the methods of the classes above it, so in addition to a ModifyDepartment method, the Faculty class has a ModifyTitle method, a ModifyName method, and so on.

---

[2]No events are shown in this example.

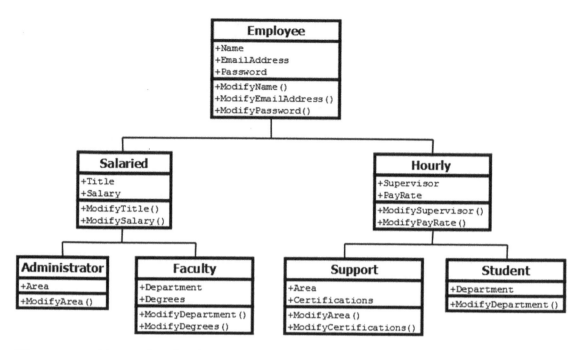

Figure 1-5. *Example of a class inheritance hierarchy for an employee*

Now let us turn our attention to an example of how class inheritance manifests itself within the .NET Framework generally and within the Framework Class Library specifically. A solid understanding of .NET Framework class inheritance is important because it will help us make the most of the classes available to us as we develop ASP.NET Web applications.

Figure 1-6 shows an example of the (partial) class inheritance hierarchy of the Framework Class Library.[3] In the figure, we can see that the base class of the FCL is the Object class. This class, which has no properties or events, contains the most fundamental methods of the class inheritance hierarchy. These methods provide low-level services to *all* of the other classes in the FCL. For example, the ToString method of the Object class can be used to convert *any* object (instantiated from a class in the FCL) to its equivalent string representation. The Object class's child classes (i.e., the Control class and some other classes) not only inherit *all* of the methods of the Object class, but they each include additional properties and methods that extend the characteristics and functionality of the Object class. Looking farther down the hierarchy, we can see that the

---

[3]For brevity, not all of the properties and methods of the classes in the figure are shown, and none of the events of the classes in the figure are shown.

Control class's child classes (i.e., the WebControl class, the FormControl class, and some other classes) not only inherit *all* of the properties and methods of the Control class and the Object class, but they each include additional properties and methods that extend the characteristics and functionality of those classes. Looking even farther down the hierarchy, we can see that the WebControl class's child classes (i.e., the Page class, the Button class, and some other classes) not only inherit *all* of the properties and methods of the WebControl class, the Control class, and the Object class, but they each include additional properties and methods that extend the characteristics and functionality of those classes. Thus, we can see that, for example, a button is a type of Web control, which is a type of control, which is a type of object, that can cause validation, can contain text, has a background color, can be enabled or disabled, has a height, has an ID, has a skin ID, can be made visible or invisible, and can be converted to a string. The Button class also inherits *all* of the methods of the classes above it, so in addition to an OnClick method, the Button class has an ApplyStyle method, a DataBind method, a GetType method, and so on.

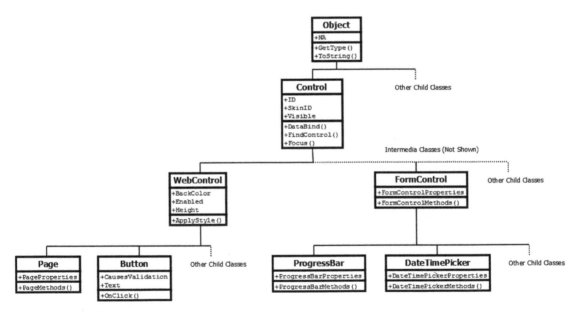

Figure 1-6. *Example of the (partial) class inheritance hierarchy of the Framework Class Library*

We will now take a closer look at the Object, Control, and WebControl classes in more detail. Although we have little context for these at the moment, it is important to at least become familiar with them as we will refer to them later in this book.

1.4.6.1 Object Class

As mentioned previously, the Object class is the base class of the .NET Framework Class Library. As such, it is said to be the *root* of the .NET class inheritance hierarchy, and all of the other classes in the FCL are derived from it. The Object class provides methods that can be used by the Control class, the WebControl class, and *all* of the ASP.NET server control classes (e.g., the Page class, the Button class, the TextBox class). Table 1-2 shows some of the methods of the Object class. As can be seen, this class has no properties or events—just a description of two of its methods.

Table 1-2. *Some of the methods of the Object class*

Class Object[4]

Namespace System

Properties

NA

Methods

GetType()	Gets the type of the current instance.
ToString()	Returns a string that represents the current object.

Events

NA

Reference

https://msdn.microsoft.com/en-us/library/system.object(v=vs.110).aspx

---

[4]All property, method, and event descriptions were taken directly from Microsoft's official documentation. The event handler methods used to handle the events of this class were omitted to conserve space. See the reference for all of the methods of this class.

1.4.6.2 Control Class

The Control class provides properties, methods, and events that can be used by the WebControl class and *all* of the ASP.NET server control classes (e.g., the Page class, the Button class, the TextBox class). Table 1-3 shows some of the properties, methods, and events of the Control class.

Table 1-3. *Some of the properties, methods, and events of the Control class*

Class Control[5]

Namespace System.Web.UI

Properties

ClientID	Gets the control ID for HTML markup that is generated by ASP.NET.
ClientIDMode	Gets or sets the algorithm that is used to generate the value of the ClientID property.
EnableTheming	Gets or sets a value indicating whether themes apply to this control.
ID	Gets or sets the programmatic identifier assigned to the server control.
Page	Gets a reference to the Page instance that contains the server control.
SkinID	Gets or sets the skin to apply to the control.
Visible	Gets or sets a value that indicates whether a server control is rendered as UI on the page.

Methods

DataBind()	Binds a data source to the invoked server control and all its child controls.
FindControl(String)	Searches the current naming container for a server control with the specified ID parameter.
Focus()	Sets input focus to a control.

(continued)

---

[5]All property, method, and event descriptions were taken directly from Microsoft's official documentation. The event handler methods used to handle the events of this class were omitted to conserve space. See the reference for all of the methods of this class.

Table 1-3. (*continued*)

Events

DataBinding	Occurs when the server control binds to a data source.
Disposed	Occurs when a server control is released from memory, which is the last stage of the server control life cycle when an ASP.NET page is requested.
Init	Occurs when the server control is initialized, which is the first step in its life cycle.
Load	Occurs when the server control is loaded into the Page object.
PreRender	Occurs after the Control object is loaded but prior to rendering.
Unload	Occurs when the server control is unloaded from memory.

Reference

https://msdn.microsoft.com/en-us/library/system.web.ui.control(v=vs.110).aspx

1.4.6.3 WebControl Class

The WebControl class provides properties, methods, and events that can be used by *all* of the ASP.NET server controls classes (e.g., the Page class, the Button class, the TextBox class). Table 1-4 shows some of the properties, methods, and events of the WebControl class. Notice that this class has several properties that affect a control's *appearance* (e.g., BackColor property, ForeColor property, Height property) and that it has a number of properties that affect a control's *behavior* (e.g., Enabled property, TabIndex property, ToolTip property).

Table 1-4. *Some of the properties, methods, and events of the WebControl class*

Class WebControl[6]

Namespace System.Web.UI.WebControls

Properties

AccessKey	Gets or sets the access key that allows you to quickly navigate to the Web server control.
BackColor	Gets or sets the background color of the Web server control.
CssClass	Gets or sets the cascading style sheet (CSS) class rendered by the Web server control on the client.
Enabled	Gets or sets a value indicating whether the Web server control is enabled.
Font	Gets the font properties associated with the Web server control.
ForeColor	Gets or sets the foreground color (typically the color of the text) of the Web server control.
Height	Gets or sets the height of the Web server control.
IsEnabled	Gets a value indicating whether the control is enabled.
TabIndex	Gets or sets the tab index of the Web server control.
ToolTip	Gets or sets the text displayed when the mouse pointer hovers over the Web server control.
Width	Gets or sets the width of the Web server control.

Methods

ApplyStyle(Style)	Copies any nonblank elements of the specified style to the Web control, overwriting any existing style elements of the control. This method is primarily used by control developers.

(continued)

---

[6]All property, method, and event descriptions were taken directly from Microsoft's official documentation. The event handler methods used to handle the events of this class were omitted to conserve space. See the reference for all of the methods of this class.

Table 1-4. *(continued)*

Events

(See reference.)

Reference

```
https://msdn.microsoft.com/en-us/library/system.web.ui.webcontrols.
webcontrol(v=vs.110).aspx
```

1.5 ASP.NET and C# Programming

ASP.NET is a software development framework that includes all of the classes necessary for building modern, sophisticated Web applications. Since ASP.NET is part of the .NET Framework, we have access to all of the classes of the .NET Framework when coding ASP. NET Web applications.

When developing in ASP.NET, we can code in any of the programming languages compatible with the .NET Framework. These languages include Visual Basic, Visual C++, Visual C#, and Visual F#. Several other programming languages are compatible with the .NET Framework as well. However, this book focuses on the C# programming language, which is a sophisticated, general-purpose, object-oriented programming language developed by Microsoft for building a variety of application types, including Web Forms applications and Windows Forms applications. It is important to keep in mind that C# is also a *type-safe programming language*, meaning that an invalid computing operation on an object will be detected at *design time* (i.e., when the operation is parsed) instead of at *runtime* (i.e., when the operation is executed). For example, the operation x = "abc" + 123 would throw a type error during coding because *abc* is a string, *123* is a number, and C# *will not* implicitly convert the string to a number (or the number to a string) to perform the addition (or the concatenation) operation. Anyone familiar with C, C++, Java, and/or similar languages will have little difficulty learning C# with its familiar curly bracket style.

1.6 Visual Studio

Visual Studio is Microsoft's flagship *integrated development environment* (IDE). While many available IDEs are dedicated to a specific programming language, Visual Studio permits us to code and test in several different programming languages via a consistent user interface. In this book, we will demonstrate how to use Visual Studio to write and test code in ASP.NET, C#, SQL, Ajax (Asynchronous JavaScript and XML), and JavaScript.

Visual Studio is designed to maximize developer productivity by providing us with an array of interrelated tools with a common user interface. It includes source code editing tools, debugging tools, unit testing tools, compiling tools, class browsing tools, application deployment tools, code management tools (i.e., Team Foundation Server), and so on. Visual Studio also includes a built-in Web server called *Internet Information Services Express* (IIS Express) that permits us to execute and test our ASP.NET Web applications on our own computer. *Visual Studio* can be downloaded for free from microsoft.com.

Figure 1-7 shows the Visual Studio environment. Notice the *Toolbox* tab in the upper left-hand corner of the environment and the *Solution Explorer* tab in the upper right-hand corner of the environment. We will use these tools frequently when developing ASP.NET Web applications. Keep in mind that this environment may look a little different depending on how the environment has been configured or which version of Visual Studio has been installed. If the *Toolbox* tab isn't visible, we can select *View* ➤ *Toolbox* from the main menu. If the *Solution Explorer* tab isn't visible, we can select *View* ➤ *Solution Explorer* from the main menu.

Figure 1-7. *Visual Studio environment*

1.7 Starting a New Project

Now that we have seen a little bit of the Visual Studio environment, it is time to start a brand new project. To start a brand new ASP.NET Web Application project

1. Select *File* ➤ *New* ➤ *Project...* from the main menu.

When the *New Project* dialog appears

1. Select *Installed* ➤ *Templates* ➤ *Visual C#* ➤ *Web* from the left pane of the dialog.

2. Select *ASP.NET Web Application (.NET Framework)* from the middle pane of the dialog.

3. Give the project a *Name* (e.g., SportsPlay) at the bottom of the dialog.

4. Give the project a *Location* by typing in a file path or by browsing to an existing folder.

5. Check the *Create directory for solution* checkbox.

6. Click *OK*.

When the *New ASP.NET Web Application* dialog appears

1. Select *Empty* from the pane of the dialog.

2. Unselect any checkboxes.

3. Click *OK*.

1.8 Solution Explorer

Once we have created a new project, we can view it using the Solution Explorer. The Solution Explorer is used to manage *solutions*, which themselves contain one or more *projects*. Within the Solution Explorer, we can add, modify, and delete projects as well as add, modify, and delete any other items associated with a project (e.g., folders, Web pages, images).

Figure 1-8 shows the Solution Explorer. To open the Solution Explorer, click the *Solution Explorer* tab. Notice that we can auto hide the Solution Explorer by clicking the *pin* icon in the upper right-hand corner of the Solution Explorer. Notice as well that we can close the Solution Explorer by clicking the *Solution Explorer* tab again. If we click the *x* icon, which removes the *Solution Explorer* tab, we can restore it by selecting *View* ➤ *Solution Explorer* from the main menu. We can also drag the Solution Explorer to another location in the Visual Studio environment. To do this, click and hold the top of the Solution Explorer and drag it to the desired location in the Visual Studio environment. Note that all of the other tabs we will see in the Visual Studio environment behave the same way. Thus, it is easy to adjust the Visual Studio environment to the way we want it. By the way, notice that there are a number of other icons at the top of the Solution Explorer. We can ignore these for now.

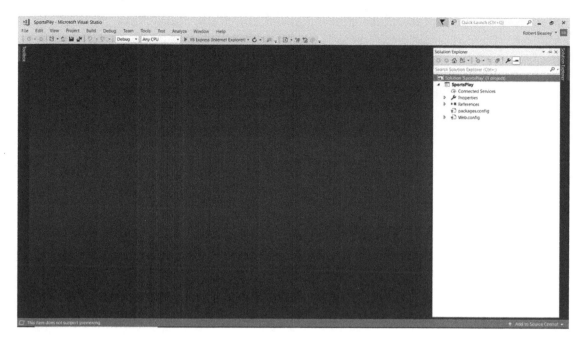

Figure 1-8. *Solution Explorer*

As we make changes to our ASP.NET Web Application project, we will need to save those changes. To do this, we can select *File ➤ Save (name of the project)* from the main menu, or we can just click the *blue disk* icon at the top of the Visual Studio environment. Keep in mind, however, that every time we execute a project in the Visual Studio environment, any changes we have made to the project will be saved automatically first. Thus, it is not necessary to save a project immediately prior to executing it.

PART II

Single-Page Web Application Development

Experiments

CHAPTER 2

Page Development

2.1 Introduction

A Web page is a document with a unique *Uniform Resource Locator* (URL) or *Web address*. This document is served by a Web server and is displayed in a Web client (i.e., browser). Web pages are formatted using the *Hypertext Markup Language* (HTML), which is a standardized coding system that uses *tags* to affect a page's basic display characteristics (e.g., font, color, layout) and create simple functionality (e.g., transitions to other pages). Transitions to other pages are achieved through *hypertext links* (a.k.a., hyperlinks), where a hypertext link is associated with a single URL. When clicked, a hypertext link causes a transition from one Web page to another.

In this chapter, we will begin by looking at the identifier naming standards we will apply throughout this book. These standards will be applied when naming variables, constants, server controls, and other items. Next, we will discuss the Page class (a.k.a., the Web Forms Page class), which is the class we will use to create ASP.NET Web pages. And finally, we will learn how to add a page to an ASP.NET Web Application project using Visual Studio. As we will see throughout this book, we will add a Page class to our project for every Web page we want to display in our ASP.NET Web application.

2.2 Identifier Naming Standards

An *identifier* is the name we give a variable, constant, server control, or other items. Using identifier naming standards makes reading the source code of a class much easier—especially when maintaining the code later.

© Robert E. Beasley 2020
R. E. Beasley, *Essential ASP.NET Web Forms Development*, https://doi.org/10.1007/978-1-4842-5784-5_2

When naming variables and constants, we should use names that make the *content* of the item as obvious as possible. This is accomplished by doing two things. First, it is accomplished by beginning the name of the item with a *three-letter prefix* that reflects the *type of data* the item will contain. And second, it is accomplished by completing the name of the item with a *suffix* that reflects *what data* the item will contain. For example, when declaring a string variable that will hold a person's last name, we would give the variable the name strLastName. This shows the *type of data* the variable will hold (i.e., string data) as well as *what data* the variable will hold (i.e., a person's last name).

When naming server controls, on the other hand, we should use names that make the *use* of the control as obvious as possible. This is also accomplished by doing two things. First, it is accomplished by beginning the name of the control with a *three-letter prefix* that reflects the *type of control* the control is. And second, it is accomplished by completing the name of the control with a *suffix* that reflects *what control* the control is. For example, when creating a text box that will accept a person's last name, we would give the control the name txtLastName. This shows the *type of control* the control is (i.e., TextBox control) as well as *what control* the control is (i.e., the last name text box).

2.3 Page Class

The Page class is a container that holds other ASP.NET server classes, such as Label classes, TextBox classes, and Button classes. Thus, the Page class is the foundation of the user interface of a .NET Web application. Web pages are requested from the server by a client. In the .NET Framework, the first time a Web page is requested by a client, it is compiled on the server, served to the client, and cached in server memory to be used for subsequent client requests. A given Page class is stored on the server in a .aspx file.

Table 2-1 shows some of the properties, methods, and events of the Page class. Although we have little context for these at the moment, it is important to at least become familiar with them as we will refer to them later.

Table 2-1. *Some of the properties, methods, and events of the Page class*

Class Page[1]

Namespace System.Web.UI

Properties

ClientQueryString	Gets the query string portion of the requested URL.
IsPostBack	Gets a value that indicates whether the page is being rendered for the first time or is being loaded in response to a postback.
IsValid	Gets a value indicating whether page validation succeeded.
Master	Gets the master page that determines the overall look of the page.
MasterPageFile	Gets or sets the virtual path of the master page.
Request	Gets the HttpRequest object for the requested page.
Response	Gets the HttpResponse object associated with the Page object. This object allows you to send HTTP response data to a client and contains information about that response.
Server	Gets the Server object, which is an instance of the HttpServerUtility class.
Session	Gets the current Session object provided by ASP.NET.
Theme	Gets or sets the name of the page theme.
Title	Gets or sets the title for the page.

Methods

(See reference.)

Events

InitComplete	Occurs when page initialization is complete.
LoadComplete	Occurs at the end of the load stage of the page's life cycle.

(*continued*)

---

[1]All property, method, and event descriptions were taken directly from Microsoft's official documentation. The event handler methods used to handle the events of this class were omitted to conserve space. See the reference for all of the methods of this class.

Table 2-1. *(continued)*

Class Page[1]

PreInit	Occurs before page initialization.
PreLoad	Occurs before the page Load event.
PreRenderComplete	Occurs before the page content is rendered.
SaveStateComplete	Occurs after the page has completed saving all view state and control state information for the page and controls on the page.

Reference

`https://msdn.microsoft.com/en-us/library/system.web.ui.page(v=vs.110).aspx`

2.4 Adding a Page Class

In the last chapter, we learned how to start a brand new ASP.NET Web Application project. Now, it is time to add a Page class to that project. If not already open, we need to open the ASP.NET Web Application project created in the last chapter. To do this

1. Execute Visual Studio.

2. Select *File ➤ Open ➤ Project/Solution...* from the main menu.

3. When the *Open Project* dialog appears, navigate to the .sln file for the project.

4. Select the .sln file.

5. Click *Open*.

The .sln file, by the way, is the *solution file*. As the name implies, this file contains information about the solution, including the individual projects it contains. This can be a little confusing in Visual Studio because when we create a new ASP.NET Web Application project, we are actually creating a new *solution* that contains a new *project*.

Assuming that the project is open, we can now add a Page class to our project. To add a Page class to an ASP.NET Web Application project

1. Open the Solution Explorer.

2. Right-click the project (not the solution).

3. Select *Add ➤ New Item....*

When the *Add New Item* dialog appears

1. Select *Installed ➤ Visual C# ➤ Web ➤ Web Forms* from the left pane of the dialog.

2. Select *Web Form* from the middle pane of the dialog.

3. Give the Web Form (i.e., Page class) a *Name* (e.g., HelloWorld. aspx) at the bottom of the dialog.

4. Click *Add.*

Figure 2-1 shows the Aspx file of the newly added Page class. Notice the tab between the Visual Studio menu and the top of the code. This tab displays the name of the Page class file just created (i.e., HelloWorld.aspx). It is in this file that we will code the user interface of the page. Now look at the code itself. The very first line of code on this page is a *page directive*. This page directive indicates, among other things, that C# is used as the programming language for the class and that the name of the *code behind file* (i.e., where we will write our server-side ASP.NET and C# code) is HelloWorld.aspx.cs. Notice that the remainder of this file contains a number of basic HTML tags, such as <head>, <title>, <body>, and <div>. And finally, notice in the Solution Explorer that the Page class has been added to the project. Whenever we want to access the code of this Page class in the future, we will simply double-click it in the Solution Explorer.

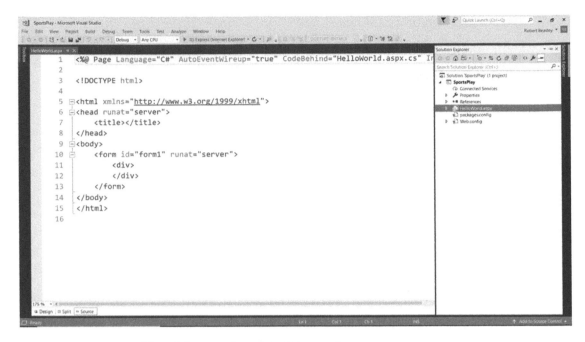

Figure 2-1. *Aspx file of the newly added Page class*

The Page class has two main (and deliberately separate) parts—the user interface part and the code behind part. The .aspx file of a Page class contains the *user interface* part of the class. This part of the class is coded using HTML tags, ASP.NET tags, or a combination of both. The .aspx.cs file of a Page class contains the *code behind* part of the class. This part of the class is coded using ASP.NET and C#. The beauty of this *separation of concerns* is that we can make changes to a page's user interface without affecting its functionality and we can make changes to a page's functionality without affecting its user interface. We will find this separation of concerns extremely beneficial in the future.

To write ASP.NET and C# code, we need to open the code behind file of the class. To access the code behind file

1. Expand the Page class by clicking the *triangle* icon next to the .aspx file in the Solution Explorer.

2. Double-click the associated .aspx.cs file.

Figure 2-2 shows the code behind file of the newly added Page class. Notice the tab between the Visual Studio menu and the top of the code. This tab displays the name of the code behind file of the Page class (i.e., HelloWorld.aspx.cs). It is in this file that we will write the ASP.NET and C# code of our page. Now look at the code itself. Notice at the very top of the code that there are a number of C# directives that begin with the word *using*. These *using directives* refer to the *namespaces* included in the class. Namespaces can contain *classes* that provide the Page class with additional functionality (e.g., email classes, database classes), or they can contain *types* (e.g., interface types, array types, value types, reference types, enumeration types) that provide the Page class with specialized types. As we progress through this book, we will include additional namespaces in our Page classes as the need arises. Now look at the line of code that starts with the word *namespace*. This indicates that the HelloWorld Page class is in the SportsPlay namespace. If for some reason we need to refer to the properties and/or methods of the HelloWorld Page class from some other class in the future, we will need to include the SportsPlay namespace in that class. Next, take a look at the line of code that starts with the phrase *public partial class*. The word *partial* here indicates that this file (i.e., HelloWorld.aspx.cs) contains only a *part* of the HelloWorld Page class. The other files (i.e., HelloWorld.aspx and HelloWorld.aspx.designer. cs) contain the other *parts* of the HelloWorld Page class. And finally, look at the line of code that starts with *protected void*. This line of code identifies the Page_Load event handler method of the class, which is generated automatically when the Page class is added to the project. If there is any ASP.NET and/or C# code that needs to be executed when the page loads (i.e., when the page's Load event is raised), it will be coded here.

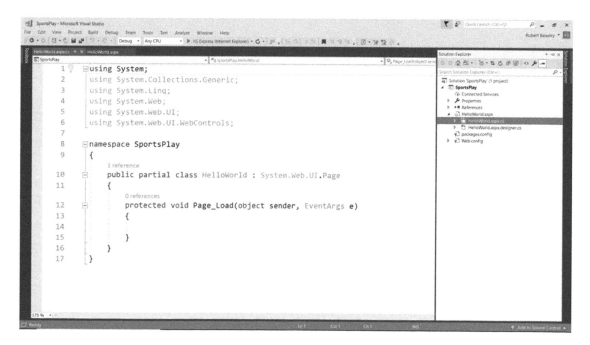

Figure 2-2. *Code behind file of the newly added Page class*

At this point, we are ready to write some code. To begin, let's give our HelloWorld page a title. This title will be displayed at the top of the browser—usually as the title of a browser tab. To give the page a title, type "Hello World!" between the <title> tag and the </title> tag in the HelloWorld.aspx file. Note that these two tags are *HTML tags*. An HTML tag of the form *<something>* is referred to as an *open tag* or *start tag*, whereas an HTML tag of the form *</something>* is referred to as a *close tag* or *end tag*. As we will see later, *ASP.NET server tags* have a similar form. Now, let's display some text in the body of the page. To do this, type the sentence "This is my Hello World page!" between the <div> tag and the </div> tag. Figure 2-3 shows our Aspx code with a page title and text added.

Figure 2-3. *Aspx code with a page title and text added*

Now that we have written some code, it is time to test our Web page. To test our page, we must first set it as the *start page* of our project. To do this

1. Right-click the HelloWorld.aspx file in the Solution Explorer.

2. Select *Set as Start Page*.

Now, when we run our ASP.NET Web Application project in Visual Studio, the HelloWorld.aspx page will be displayed. Keep in mind that if we neglect to set a start page for a project before we run it, we will receive a *403 error*. This error means that the IIS server understood the HTTP request but cannot fulfill it for some reason.

Now that we have set our start page, we are ready to test it. To test the page, click the green *triangle* icon at the top of the Visual Studio environment. The name of the browser next to the green *triangle* icon should default to Internet Explorer. To select a different browser to test the page, click the black *triangle* icon next to the current browser name and select the desired browser. The list of browsers to choose from should contain all of the browsers currently installed on the development machine. Figure 2-4 shows the HelloWorld page displayed in Internet Explorer. Notice the title of the Web page in the browser tab that says "Hello World!" Also notice the sentence "This is my Hello World page!" in the body of the Web page.

Figure 2-4. *HelloWorld page displayed in Internet Explorer*

CHAPTER 3

Basic Server Controls

3.1 Introduction

A server control is an object that is displayed on an ASP.NET Web page. When a Web page is requested from a server via an HTTP request, the server processes the page request (as described in Chapter 1, titled "Web Application Development") and then sends the client the resulting HTML code via an HTTP response. When the Web browser receives the HTTP response, it *renders* the page and displays it for the end user. In the context of an ASP.NET Web application, the term *render* refers to the process of creating a visual representation of the page, including all of its associated server controls, based on the HTML code received from the server in its HTTP response.

In this chapter, we will begin by looking at Visual Studio's Toolbox. This toolbox contains most of the ASP.NET server controls we will be studying in this book. Next, we will discuss six basic server control classes: the Label class, the TextBox class, the Button class, the Table class, the TableRow class, and the TableCell class. As we look at these classes, keep in mind that all of them inherit the properties, methods, and events of their parent classes. Thus, we will focus mostly on the properties, methods, and events of the classes being studied.

3.2 Toolbox

The Visual Studio Toolbox contains most of the ASP.NET server controls we will be studying in this book. To open the Toolbox, click the *Toolbox* tab in the upper left-hand corner of the Visual Studio environment. We can auto hide the Toolbox by clicking the *pin* icon in the upper right-hand corner of the Toolbox. We can also close the Toolbox by clicking the *Toolbox* tab again. If we click the *x* icon in the upper right-hand corner of the Toolbox, which removes the *Toolbox* tab, we can restore it by selecting *View* ➤ *Toolbox* from the main menu.

© Robert E. Beasley 2020
R. E. Beasley, *Essential ASP.NET Web Forms Development*, https://doi.org/10.1007/978-1-4842-5784-5_3

Figure 3-1 shows the standard server control classes in the Toolbox. If the classes displayed in the figure aren't visible, we may need to expand the *Standard* tab by clicking the *triangle* icon. Keep in mind that the classes in the Toolbox will only be displayed when a .aspx file is being viewed. Notice that the Button class, the Label class, the Table class, and the TextBox class are included in this alphabetical listing of classes. We will make use of these four classes in this chapter, and we will explore many of the others in the next chapter.

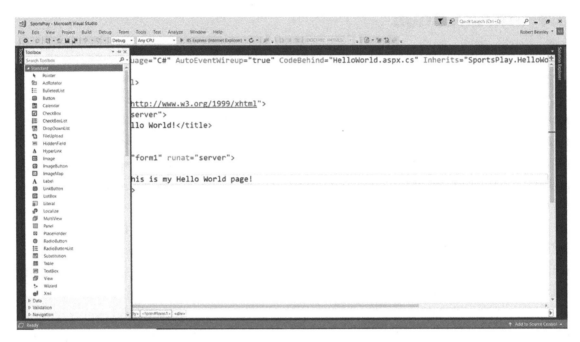

Figure 3-1. *Standard server control classes in the Toolbox*

3.3 Label Class

The Label class displays text. Unlike the text displayed on a static Web page, the text displayed on an ASP.NET Web page using a Label control can change dynamically by modifying the value of the control's Text property in the code behind. Table 3-1 shows some of the properties, methods, and events of the Label class. Although the only member displayed in the table is the Text property, the Label class contains additional members and inherits many other properties, methods, and events from its parent classes.

Table 3-1. *Some of the properties, methods, and events of the Label class*

Class Label[1]

Namespace System.Web.UI.WebControls

Properties

Text	Gets or sets the text content of the Label control.

Methods

(See reference.)

Events

(See reference.)

Reference

```
https://msdn.microsoft.com/en-us/library/system.web.ui.webcontrols.
label(v=vs.110).aspx
```

Figure 3-2 shows an example of the Label class.

Notice at 01 the Label control and its associated properties. As can be seen, the Label control starts with an *ASP.NET server tag*. This tag begins with <asp: and ends with />. As we will see throughout this book, all ASP.NET server tags begin and end this way. Note that this is in stark contrast to HTML tags, which begin with < and end with />.

Also notice that the runat property is set to *server*. This indicates that the control is to be treated as a *dynamic* ASP.NET server control—not a *static* HTML control. The need to specify the value of this property for every ASP.NET server control is tedious and redundant and could probably have been defaulted by Microsoft. Nevertheless, if we don't set this property to *true* in the definition of an ASP.NET server control, a syntax error will occur.

---

[1]All property, method, and event descriptions were taken directly from Microsoft's official documentation. The event handler methods used to handle the events of this class were omitted to conserve space. See the reference for all of the methods of this class.

Notice as well that the Font-Bold property is set to *true*. This indicates that the text in the Text property of the control will be displayed in bold when the control is rendered on the page. Note that this property is *not* part of the Label class itself but is, instead, inherited from the Font class. The default value of the Font-Bold property is *false*.

We can also see that the Text property is set to *Employee*. This indicates that the word "Employee" will be displayed in the label when it is rendered on the page. Of course, since the Label class is a *dynamic* server control class, we can modify the value of its Text property (and most of its other properties) in the code behind at will. Note that this property is not inherited like the Font-Bold property but is, instead, defined in the Label class itself (see Table 3-1).

Also notice that the runat property is coded first followed by the other properties of the class (i.e., Font-Bold and Text), which are coded *in alphabetical order* after the runat property. As a coding standard, we will always code the runat property first, the ID property (to be discussed later) second, and then any other properties and methods next in alphabetical order. We will do this because coding properties and methods in alphabetical order will make it *much* easier to visually reference the properties and methods that have been coded for a control—especially when the list of properties and methods gets long.

And finally, notice that the end of the line contains a <br /> tag. This is an HTML tag that forces a line break on the page. This is one of the few HTML tags we will use to format ASP.NET pages in this book, since most HTML tags have an equivalent ASP.NET server tag. The result of the Aspx code is displayed at the bottom of the figure.

ASPX CODE

```
01   <asp:Label runat="server" Font-Bold="true" Text="Employee" /><br />
     <asp:Label runat="server" Text="Last Name" /><br />
     <asp:Label runat="server" Text="First Name" /><br />
     <asp:Label runat="server" Text="Middle Initial" /><br />
```

RESULT

Employee
Last Name
First Name
Middle Initial

Figure 3-2. *Example of the Label class*

3.4 TextBox Class

The TextBox class displays an input field that can be used by an end user to enter information. A TextBox control contains a number of properties that permit us to control the appearance of the control. For example, we can set the TextMode property of the control to *SingleLine* if we want the text box to permit the entry of one line of end-user data. Or, we can set it to *MultiLine* if we want the text box to permit the entry of multiple lines of end-user data. Or, we can set it to *Password* if we want the characters to be masked as they are typed into the text box. Many other properties are available as well. Table 3-2 shows some of the properties, methods, and events of the TextBox class.

Table 3-2. *Some of the properties, methods, and events of the TextBox class*

Class TextBox[2]

Namespace System.Web.UI.WebControls

Properties

AutoPostBack	Gets or sets a value that indicates whether an automatic postback to the server occurs when the TextBox control loses focus.
CausesValidation	Gets or sets a value indicating whether validation is performed when the TextBox control is set to validate when a postback occurs.
Columns	Gets or sets the display width of the text box in characters.
MaxLength	Gets or sets the maximum number of characters allowed in the text box.
Rows	Gets or sets the number of rows displayed in a multiline text box.
Text	Gets or sets the text content of the TextBox control.
TextMode	Gets or sets the behavior mode (such as single line, multiline, or password) of the TextBox control.

(continued)

---

[2]All property, method, and event descriptions were taken directly from Microsoft's official documentation. The event handler methods used to handle the events of this class were omitted to conserve space. See the reference for all of the methods of this class.

Table 3-2. (*continued*)

ValidationGroup	Gets or sets the group of controls for which the TextBox control causes validation when it posts back to the server.
Wrap	Gets or sets a value indicating whether the text content wraps within a multiline text box.

Methods

(See reference.)

Events

TextChanged	Occurs when the content of the text box changes between posts to the server.

Reference

```
https://msdn.microsoft.com/en-us/library/system.web.ui.webcontrols.
textbox(v=vs.110).aspx
```

Figure 3-3 shows an example of the TextBox class.

Notice at 01 the TextBox control and its associated properties. As can be seen, the Columns property of the control is set to *50*. This indicates that the width of the text box will be 50 characters when it is rendered in the browser. Notice as well that the Rows property is set to *5*. This indicates that five rows will be displayed when the text box is rendered in the browser. We can also see that the TextMode property is set to *MultiLine*, which indicates that the text box will be rendered in the browser as a multiple-line text box that can accept several lines of input from the end user. And finally, notice that the Wrap property is set to *true*. This indicates that the content of the text box will wrap to the next line if it contains more than one line of text. The result of the Aspx code is displayed at the bottom of the figure. As can be seen, several lines of information have been entered into the text box.

ASPX CODE

```
    <asp:Label runat="server" Font-Bold="true" Text="Product Description" />
        <br />
01  <asp:TextBox runat="server" Columns="50" Rows="5" TextMode="MultiLine"
        Wrap="true" />
```

RESULT

Figure 3-3. *Example of the TextBox class*

3.5 Button Class

The Button class displays a button that can be used by an end user to invoke an action. When a Button control is clicked, its Click and Command events are raised. To handle one of these events, we must code the appropriate event handler method. More about that in a moment. A Button control can behave like a Submit button (i.e., a button that posts the page back to the server where we can handle its Click event), or it can behave like a Command button (i.e., a button that posts the page back to the server where we can handle the Click events of several buttons in one event handler method by passing the event handler method a command name and [optionally] a command argument). By default, a Button control behaves like a Submit button. Table 3-3 shows some of the properties, methods, and events of the Button class.

Table 3-3. *Some of the properties, methods, and events of the Button class*

Class Button[3]

Namespace System.Web.UI.WebControls

Properties

CausesValidation	Gets or sets a value indicating whether validation is performed when the Button control is clicked.
CommandArgument	Gets or sets an optional parameter passed to the Command event along with the associated CommandName.
CommandName	Gets or sets the command name associated with the Button control that is passed to the Command event.
Text	Gets or sets the text caption displayed in the Button control.
ValidationGroup	Gets or sets the group of controls for which the Button control causes validation when it posts back to the server.

Methods

(See reference.)

Events

Click	Occurs when the Button control is clicked.
Command	Occurs when the Button control is clicked.

Reference

```
https://msdn.microsoft.com/en-us/library/system.web.ui.webcontrols.
button(v=vs.110).aspx
```

---

[3]All property, method, and event descriptions were taken directly from Microsoft's official documentation. The event handler methods used to handle the events of this class were omitted to conserve space. See the reference for all of the methods of this class.

Figure 3-4 shows how to create a new Click event handler method for a Button control. As can be seen, we have already added a Button control to the .aspx file of a Page class, and this control has its ID property set to *btnSave*. To create the control's Click event handler method in the code behind of the Page class, all we must do is

1. Place the mouse cursor at an appropriate place in the Button control.

2. Type *OnClick*.

3. When the options of the OnClick method appear, select *<Create New Event>*. This will create a new Click event handler method for the btnSave button in the code behind of the Page class.

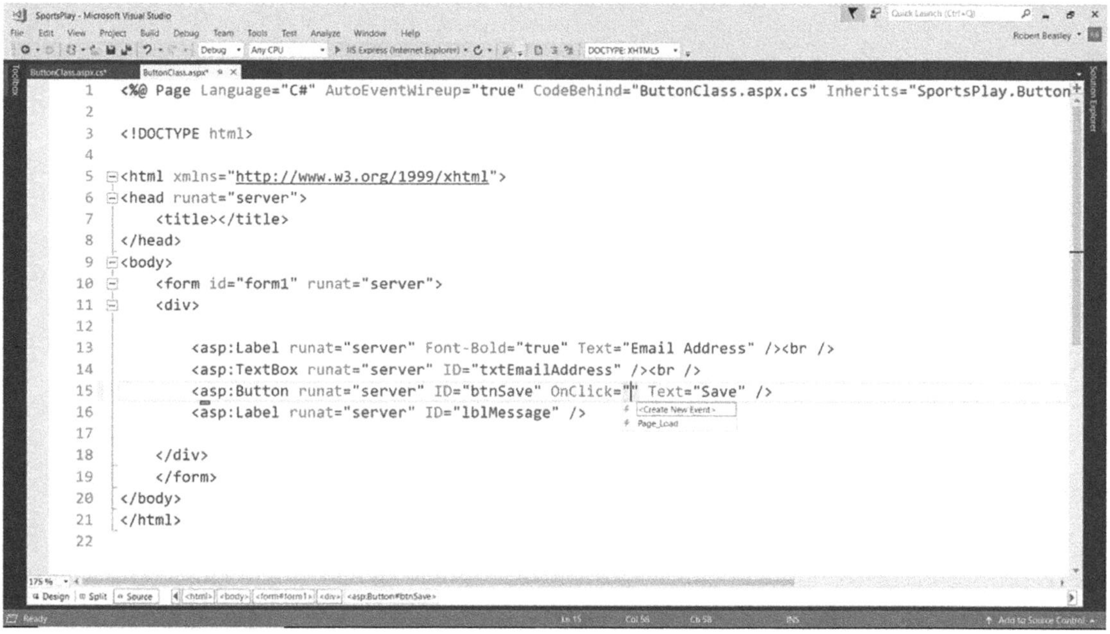

Figure 3-4. *How to create a new Click event handler method for a Button control*

Figure 3-5 shows the newly created Click event handler method for the Button control. Notice that the name of the event handler method is btnSave_Click. This method name reflects both the ID of the Button control (i.e., btnSave) and the event that is being handled in the code behind of the Page class (i.e., Click). Whatever code is written in this event handler method will be executed when the end user clicks the Save button.

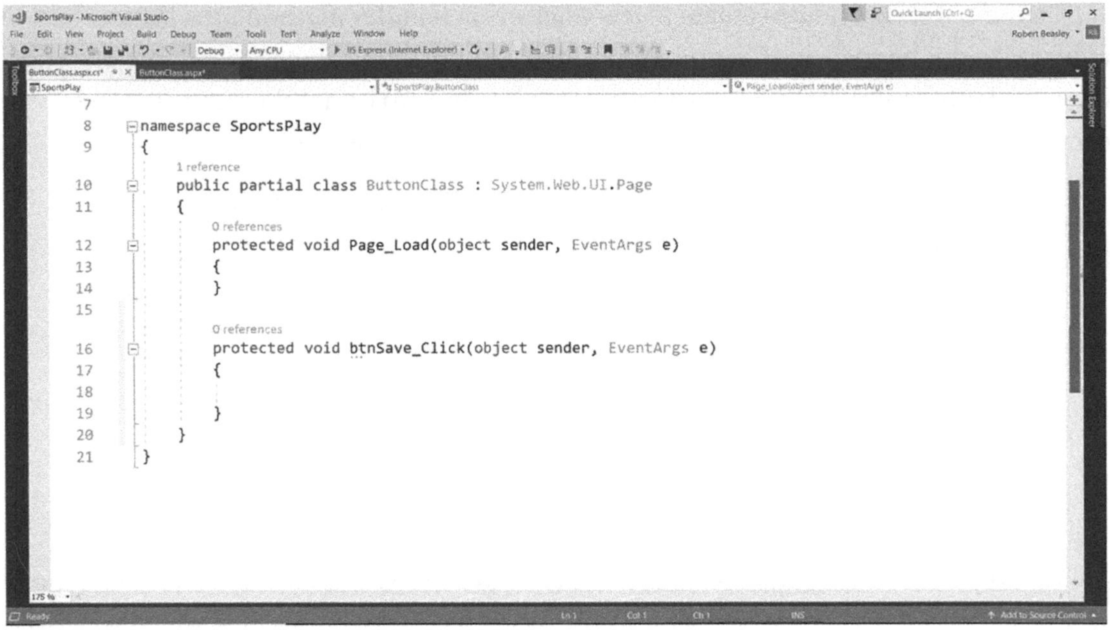

Figure 3-5. *Newly created Click event handler method for the Button class*

Figure 3-6 shows an example of the Button class behaving like a Submit button.

Notice at 01 that the ID property of the TextBox control is set to *txtEmailAddress*. By giving this control an ID, we can reference it in the code behind of the page. If we try to reference a control that has not been given an ID, a syntax error will occur. As can be seen, the ID property of this control begins with the three-letter prefix *txt* to indicate in the code behind that this ID is referring to a text box, and it ends with *EmailAddress* to indicate in the code behind that this control will contain an email address.

Notice at 02 that the ID property of the Button control is set to *btnSave*. As can be seen, the ID property of this control begins with the three-letter prefix *btn* to indicate in the code behind that this ID is referring to a button, and it ends with *Save* to indicate in the code behind that this control will perform a save function. Notice as well that the OnClick method is set to *btnSave_Click*. It is in this event handler method that we will write code to handle the Click event. In addition, we can see that the Text property is set to *Save*. This indicates the text that will be displayed in the button when the button is rendered in the browser.

Notice at 03 that the ID property of the Label control is set to *lblMessage*. As can be seen, the ID property of this control begins with the three-letter prefix *lbl* to indicate in the code behind that this ID is referring to a *label*, and it ends with *Message* to indicate in the code behind that this control will contain a message.

Notice at 04 that two lines of comments have been added to the event handler method. In C#, comments are indicated by two forward slashes (i.e., //).

Notice at 05 that the ForeColor property of the lblMessage control is set to *Green*. The ForeColor property refers to the color of the text displayed in the label.

Notice at 06 that the Text property of the lblMessage control is set to *The email address* concatenated with the value of the Text property of txtEmailAddress control concatenated with *was successfully saved*. Notice that the concatenation character is a plus (+) sign in C#.

The screenshot in the Result section of the figure shows the result of clicking the *Save* button.

ASPX CODE

```
    <asp:Label runat="server" Font-Bold="true" Text="Email Address" /><br />
01  <asp:TextBox runat="server" ID="txtEmailAddress" /><br />
02  <asp:Button runat="server" ID="btnSave" OnClick="btnSave_Click"
        Text="Save" />
03  <asp:Label runat="server" ID="lblMessage" />
```

CODE BEHIND

```
protected void btnSave_Click(object sender, EventArgs e)
{

04  // The database call to save the email address would go here.
    // If successful, the following message would be displayed.
05  lblMessage.ForeColor = System.Drawing.Color.Green;
06  lblMessage.Text = "The email address " + txtEmailAddress.Text +
        " was successfully saved.";

}
```

RESULT

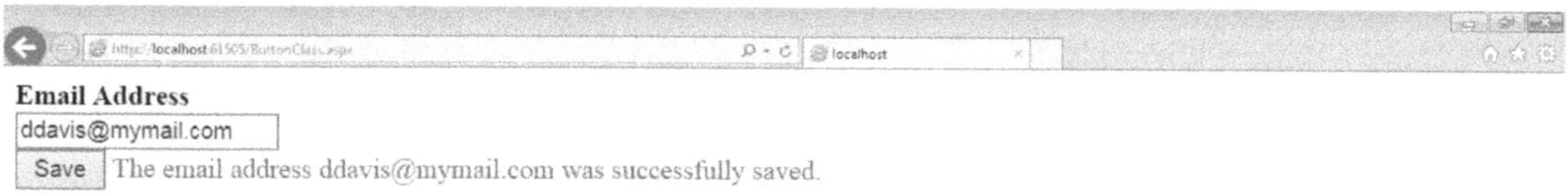

Figure 3-6. *Example of the Button class behaving like a Submit button*

Figure 3-7 shows an example of the Button class behaving like a Command button.

Notice at 01 that the CommandArgument property is set to *Adidas* and the CommandName property is set to *View*. These two properties will be passed to the button's event handler method in the code behind when the button is clicked. Notice as well that the OnCommand property is set to *Button_Command*. This is the name of the event handler method that will handle the Click event of the button. As can be seen, none of the buttons on the page require an ID in this scenario and that the first five buttons have *different* command arguments but have the *same* command name.

Notice at 02 that the last button does *not* have a command argument and has a *different* command name than the other buttons.

Notice at 03 that the command name passed to the event handler method is being tested. If the value of the CommandName property is set to *View*, the block of code inside the If structure will be executed. If not (i.e., the value of the CommandName property is set to *Cancel*), the block of code in the Else part of the If structure will be executed.

Notice at 04 that the command argument passed to the event handler method is being evaluated using a Switch structure to determine which case to execute. If the value of the CommandArgument property is set to *Adidas*, the Text property of the message label will be set appropriately. If it is set to something else, the Text property of the message label will be set to something else.

The screenshot in the Result section of the figure shows the result of clicking the Adidas button.

ASPX CODE

```
    <asp:Label runat="server" Font-Bold="true" Text="View Supplier" />
        <br /><br />
01  <asp:Button runat="server" CommandArgument="Adidas" CommandName="View"
        OnCommand="Button_Command" Text="Adidas" />
    <asp:Button runat="server" CommandArgument="Babolat" CommandName="View"
        OnCommand="Button_Command" Text="Babolat" />
    <asp:Button runat="server" CommandArgument="Head" CommandName="View"
        OnCommand="Button_Command" Text="Head" />
    <asp:Button runat="server" CommandArgument="Nike" CommandName="View"
        OnCommand="Button_Command" Text="Nike" />
    <asp:Button runat="server" CommandArgument="Prince" CommandName="View"
        OnCommand="Button_Command" Text="Prince" />
02  <asp:Button runat="server" CommandName="Cancel"
        OnCommand="Button_Command" Text="Cancel" /><br /><br />
    <asp:Label runat="server" ID="lblMessage" /><br />
```

CODE BEHIND

```
    protected void Button_Command(object sender, CommandEventArgs e)
    {

03      if (e.CommandName == "View")
        {
            lblMessage.ForeColor = System.Drawing.Color.Green;
04          switch (e.CommandArgument.ToString())
            {
                case "Adidas":
                    lblMessage.Text = e.CommandArgument.ToString();
                    break;
                case "Babolat":
                    lblMessage.Text = e.CommandArgument.ToString();
                    break;
                case "Head":
                    lblMessage.Text = e.CommandArgument.ToString();
                    break;
                case "Nike":
                    lblMessage.Text = e.CommandArgument.ToString();
                    break;
                case "Prince":
                    lblMessage.Text = e.CommandArgument.ToString();
                    break;
            }
```

Figure 3-7. *Example of the Button class behaving like a Command button*

```
    }
    else
    {
        lblMessage.ForeColor = System.Drawing.Color.Red;
        lblMessage.Text = "Cancelled";
    }

}
```

RESULT

Figure 3-7. *(continued)*

3.6 Table Class

The Table class displays a table that can be used to organize the layout of a Web page's controls. A Table control consists of one or more table *rows*, and each table row consists of one or more table *cells*. These table rows and table cells, which will be discussed in a moment, are constructed from the TableRow class and the TableCell class, respectively. A table can be created at design time by specifying its format and content in Aspx code, or it can be generated at runtime by writing the necessary code in the code behind. Tables can contain other tables. Table 3-4 shows some of the properties, methods, and events of the Table class.

Table 3-4. *Some of the properties, methods, and events of the Table class*

Class Table[4]

Namespace System.Web.UI.WebControls

Properties

BackImageUrl	Gets or sets the URL of the background image to display behind the Table control.
CellPadding	Gets or sets the amount of space between the contents of a cell and the cell's border.
CellSpacing	Gets or sets the amount of space between cells.
GridLines	Gets or sets the grid line style to display in the Table control.
HorizontalAlign	Gets or sets the horizontal alignment of the Table control on the page.

Methods

(See reference.)

Events

(See reference.)

Reference

https://msdn.microsoft.com/en-us/library/system.web.ui.webcontrols.
table(v=vs.110).aspx

3.7 TableRow Class

The TableRow class defines a row in a table. Each TableRow control consists of one or more table cells, each of which is constructed from the TableCell class (discussed next). The TableRow class permits us to control how the contents of a table row are displayed. For example, the HorizontalAlign property of a TableRow control can be set to *center, left, right,* or some other value depending on how we want to display the contents of the row from left to right. Likewise, the VerticalAlign property of a TableRow control can be set to *bottom, middle, top,* or some other value depending on how we want to display the contents of the row from top to bottom. Table 3-5 shows some of the properties, methods, and events of the TableRow class.

---

[4]All property, method, and event descriptions were taken directly from Microsoft's official documentation. The event handler methods used to handle the events of this class were omitted to conserve space. See the reference for all of the methods of this class.

Table 3-5. *Some of the properties, methods, and events of the TableRow class*

Class TableRow[5]

Namespace System.Web.UI.WebControls

Properties

HorizontalAlign	Gets or sets the horizontal alignment of the contents in the row.
VerticalAlign	Gets or sets the vertical alignment of the contents in the row.

Methods

(See reference.)

Events

(See reference.)

Reference

```
https://msdn.microsoft.com/en-us/library/system.web.ui.webcontrols.
tablerow(v=vs.110).aspx
```

3.8 TableCell Class

The TableCell class defines a cell in a row. This class controls how the contents of a cell are displayed. For example, the HorizontalAlign property of a TableCell control can be set to *center*, *left*, *right*, or some other value depending on how we want to display the contents of the cell from left to right. Similarly, the VerticalAlign property of a TableCell control can be set to *bottom*, *middle*, *top*, or some other value depending on how we want to display the contents of the cell from top to bottom. In addition, the Wrap property of a TableCell control can be set to *true* or *false* depending on whether or not we want the contents of the cell (e.g., text) to wrap to the next line if it contains more than it can contain on a single line. Table 3-6 shows some of the properties, methods, and events of the TableCell class.

---

[5]All property, method, and event descriptions were taken directly from Microsoft's official documentation. The event handler methods used to handle the events of this class were omitted to conserve space. See the reference for all of the methods of this class.

Table 3-6. *Some of the properties, methods, and events of the TableCell class*

Class TableCell[6]

Namespace System.Web.UI.WebControls

Properties

ColumnSpan	Gets or sets the number of columns in the Table control that the cell spans.
HorizontalAlign	Gets or sets the horizontal alignment of the contents in the cell.
RowSpan	Gets or sets the number of rows in the Table control that the cell spans.
VerticalAlign	Gets or sets the vertical alignment of the contents in the cell.
Wrap	Gets or sets a value that indicating whether the contents of the cell wrap.

Methods

(See reference.)

Events

(See reference.)

Reference

```
https://msdn.microsoft.com/en-us/library/system.web.ui.webcontrols.
tablecell(v=vs.110).aspx
```

Figure 3-8 shows an example of the Table, TableRow, and TableCell classes.

Notice at 01 and 06 the Table control's start tag and corresponding end tag, respectively. As can be seen, the Table control's GridLines property is set to *Horizontal*.

Notice at 02 and 05 the TableRow control's start tag and corresponding end tag, respectively.

---

[6]All property, method, and event descriptions were taken directly from Microsoft's official documentation. The event handler methods used to handle the events of this class were omitted to conserve space. See the reference for all of the methods of this class.

Notice at 03 and 04 the TableCell control's start tag and corresponding end tag, respectively.

As we can see in the figure, each TableRow control is indented four spaces within its associated Table control, and each TableCell control is indented four spaces within its associated TableRow control. This coding style for tables makes it clear what table rows are contained within what table and what table cells are contained within what table rows. Thus, this coding style for tables will be the standard we will follow throughout this book. Another thing to notice in the code is that the runat property is only set in the Table control—it is *not* set in the TableRow or TableCell controls.

The screenshot in the Result section of the figure shows the three row by two column table defined in the associated Aspx code. Because this table was used to lay out the controls on the page, the controls are more nicely aligned, which produces a more professional-looking page.

ASPX CODE

```
    <asp:Label runat="server" Font-Bold="true" Text="Employee" />

01  <asp:Table runat="server" GridLines="Horizontal">
02      <asp:TableRow>
03          <asp:TableCell>
                <asp:Label runat="server" Text="Last Name" />
04          </asp:TableCell>
            <asp:TableCell>
                <asp:TextBox runat="server" ID="txtLastName" />
            </asp:TableCell>
05      </asp:TableRow>
        <asp:TableRow>
            <asp:TableCell>
                <asp:Label runat="server" Text="First Name" />
            </asp:TableCell>
            <asp:TableCell>
                <asp:TextBox runat="server" ID="txtFirstName" />
            </asp:TableCell>
        </asp:TableRow>
        <asp:TableRow>
            <asp:TableCell>
                <asp:Label runat="server" Text="Middle Initial" />
            </asp:TableCell>
            <asp:TableCell>
                <asp:TextBox runat="server" ID="txtMiddleInitial"
                    Width="20px" />
            </asp:TableCell>
        </asp:TableRow>
06  </asp:Table>

    <asp:Button runat="server" ID="btnSave" OnClick="btnSave_Click"
        Text="Save" />
```

RESULT

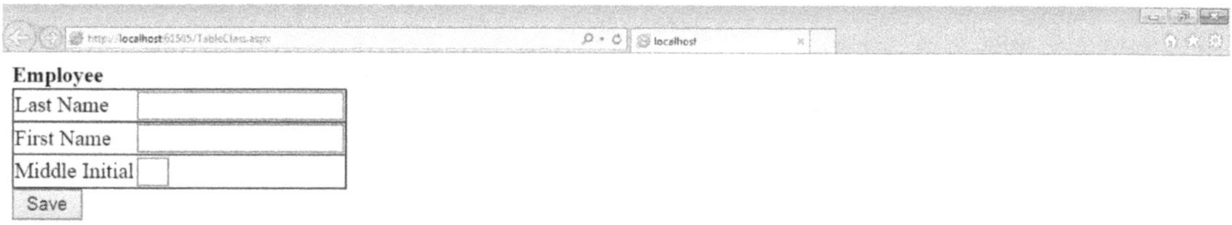

Figure 3-8. *Example of the Table, TableRow, and TableCell classes*

CHAPTER 4

More Server Controls

4.1 Introduction

As mentioned in the previous chapter, a server control is an object that is displayed on an ASP.NET Web page. When a Web page is requested from a server via an HTTP request, the server processes the page request (as described in Chapter 1, titled "Web Application Development") and then sends the client the resulting HTML code via an HTTP response. When the Web browser receives the HTTP response, it *renders* the page and displays it for the end user. In the context of an ASP.NET Web application, the term *render* refers to the process of creating a visual representation of the page, including all of its associated server controls, based on the HTML code received from the server in its HTTP response. In that chapter, we looked at six basic server control classes: the Label class, the TextBox class, the Button class, the Table class, the TableRow class, and the TableCell class. Although these six classes provided us with enough ASP.NET functionality to get started, there are many other server control classes in the .NET Framework Class Library.

In this chapter, we will look at a number of ASP.NET server control classes that can be used to build more interesting and sophisticated Web applications than we have built to this point. The server control classes that will be described in this chapter are the Calendar class, the CheckBox class, the RadioButton class, the FileUpload class, the Hyperlink class, the Image class, the ImageButton class, the ImageMap class, the RectangleHotSpot class, the LinkButton class, the ListControl class, the ListItem class, the DropDownList class, the ListBox class, and the Panel class.

4.2 Calendar Class

The Calendar class displays a monthly calendar that can be used by an end user to select a single date or a range of dates (e.g., an entire week or an entire month). By default, a Calendar control displays a Gregorian calendar, but other calendars can be specified. Also by default, a Calendar control displays the current month of the current year. In

© Robert E. Beasley 2020
R. E. Beasley, *Essential ASP.NET Web Forms Development*, https://doi.org/10.1007/978-1-4842-5784-5_4

terms of appearance, a Calendar control displays a title that includes the month and the year, links for moving backward and forward to previous and future months, headings for the days of the week, and an array of selectable days. The Calendar class contains myriad formatting properties that permit us to customize the appearance of a Calendar control. In addition, there are a number of properties that permit us to show and hide the various parts of a Calendar control. Since there are entirely too many formatting properties to list here, the interested reader should see the reference at the bottom of Table 4-1. Table 4-1 shows some of the properties, methods, and events of the Calendar class.

Table 4-1. *Some of the properties, methods, and events of the Calendar class*

Class Calendar[1]

Namespace System.Web.UI.WebControls

Properties

FirstDayOfWeek	Gets or sets the day of the week to display in the first day column of the Calendar control.
NextMonthText	Gets or sets the text displayed for the next month navigation control.
PrevMonthText	Gets or sets the text displayed for the previous month navigation control.
SelectedDate	Gets or sets the selected date.
VisibleDate	Gets or sets the DateTime value that specifies the month to display on the Calendar control.

Methods

(See reference.)

Events

SelectionChanged	Occurs when the user selects a day, a week, or an entire month by clicking the date selector controls.

Reference

https://msdn.microsoft.com/en-us/library/system.web.ui.webcontrols.calendar(v=vs.110).aspx

---

[1]All property, method, and event descriptions were taken directly from Microsoft's official documentation. The event handler methods used to handle the events of this class were omitted to conserve space. See the reference for all of the methods of this class.

Figure 4-1 shows an example of the Calendar class.

Notice at 01 the Calendar control and its associated properties. Specifically, notice the name of the event handler method that will be executed when its SelectionChanged event is raised.

Notice at 02 that we are setting the SelectedDate property of the Calendar control to the current date when the page loads so that today's date will be highlighted on the calendar.

Notice at 03 that we are setting the Text property of the date label when the date selected on the calendar is changed.

The first screenshot in the Result section of the figure shows the calendar with the default date set to the current date. The second screenshot shows the result of selecting another date on the calendar. Notice the selected date displayed under the calendar.

ASPX CODE

```
    <asp:Label runat="server" Font-Bold="true" Text="Order Date" /><br />
01  <asp:Calendar runat="server" ID="calDate" FirstDayOfWeek="Sunday"
        NextMonthText="Next" OnSelectionChanged="calDate_SelectionChanged"
        PrevMonthText="Prev" />
    <asp:Label runat="server" ID="lblDate" />
```

CODE BEHIND

```
    protected void Page_Load(object sender, EventArgs e)
    {

02      calDate.SelectedDate = DateTime.Today;

    }

    protected void calDate_SelectionChanged(object sender, EventArgs e)
    {

03      lblDate.Text = calDate.SelectedDate.ToShortDateString();

    }
```

RESULT

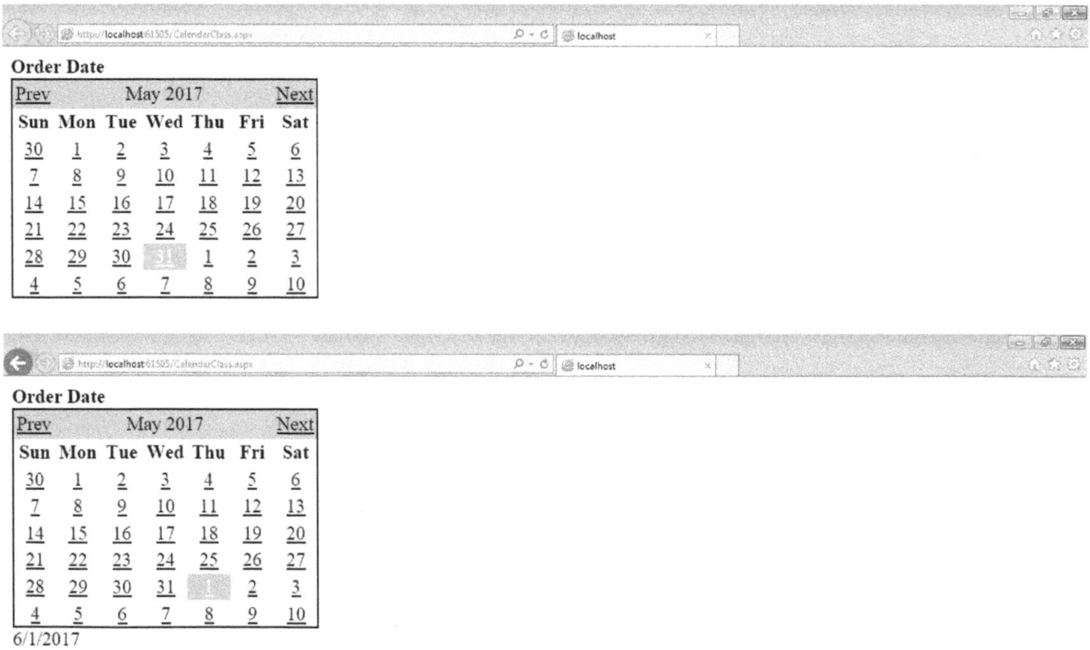

Figure 4-1. *Example of the Calendar class*

4.3 CheckBox Class

The CheckBox class displays a small box that can be used by an end user to check or uncheck an item. When an end user checks a CheckBox control, its Checked property is set to *true*. Conversely, when an end user unchecks a CheckBox control, its Checked property is set to *false*. After an end user has checked or unchecked a CheckBox control, we can evaluate the control's Checked property in the code behind to perform an action based on the truth or falseness of the Checked property. By default, a CheckBox control is unchecked. Also by default, a checkbox doesn't perform an action upon being checked or unchecked. If we want an action to be performed when a checkbox is checked or unchecked, we must set its AutoPostBack property to *true*. Table 4-2 shows some of the properties, methods, and events of the CheckBox class.

Table 4-2. *Some of the properties, methods, and events of the CheckBox class*

Class CheckBox[2]

Namespace System.Web.UI.WebControls

Properties

AutoPostBack	Gets or sets a value indicating whether the CheckBox state automatically posts back to the server when clicked.
CausesValidation	Gets or sets a value indicating whether validation is performed when the CheckBox control is selected.
Checked	Gets or sets a value indicating whether the CheckBox control is checked.
Text	Gets or sets the text label associated with the CheckBox.
ValidationGroup	Gets or sets the group of controls for which the CheckBox control causes validation when it posts back to the server.

Methods

(See reference.)

Events

CheckedChanged	Occurs when the value of the Checked property changes between posts to the server.

Reference

https://msdn.microsoft.com/en-us/library/system.web.ui.webcontrols.
checkbox(v=vs.110).aspx

---

[2]All property, method, and event descriptions were taken directly from Microsoft's official documentation. The event handler methods used to handle the events of this class were omitted to conserve space. See the reference for all of the methods of this class.

Figure 4-2 shows an example of the CheckBox class.

Notice at 01 the CheckBox control and its associated properties.

Notice at 02 the Button control and its associated properties. Specifically, notice the name of the event handler method that will be executed when its Click event is raised.

Notice at 03 that the chkFootwear checkbox is being tested to determine whether or not it has been checked.

The screenshot in the Result section of the figure shows the result of checking the first two checkboxes and clicking the *Set Filter* button.

ASPX CODE

```
    <asp:Label runat="server" Font-Bold="true"
        Text="Filters" /><br />
01  <asp:CheckBox runat="server" ID="chkFootwear"
        Text="Footwear" /><br />
    <asp:CheckBox runat="server" ID="chkClothing"
        Text="Clothing" /><br />
    <asp:CheckBox runat="server" ID="chkTennisEquipment"
        Text="Tennis Equipment" /><br />
    <asp:CheckBox runat="server" ID="chkSoccerEquipment"
        Text="Soccer Equipment" /><br />
02  <asp:Button runat="server" ID="btnSetFilter" OnClick="btnSetFilter_Click"
        Text="Set Filter" />
    <asp:Label runat="server" ID="lblFilters" ForeColor="Green" />
```

CODE BEHIND

```
    protected void btnSetFilter_Click(object sender, EventArgs e)
    {

        String strFilters = "You are filtering your search on: ";
03      if(chkFootwear.Checked)
        {
            strFilters = strFilters + "Footwear ";
        }
        if (chkClothing.Checked)
        {
            strFilters = strFilters + "Clothing ";
        }
        if (chkTennisEquipment.Checked)
        {
            strFilters = strFilters + "Tennis Equipment ";
        }
```

Figure 4-2. *Example of the CheckBox class*

```
    if (chkSoccerEquipment.Checked)
    {
        strFilters = strFilters + "Soccer Equipment ";
    }
    lblFilters.Text = strFilters;

}
```

RESULT

Figure 4-2. *(continued)*

4.4 RadioButton Class

The RadioButton class displays a group of related buttons that can be used by an end user to select an option from a set of *mutually exclusive* options. When an end user clicks a RadioButton control, the Checked property of the control is set to *true*, and the Checked properties of the related controls are set to *false*. When an end user clicks a RadioButton control, we can evaluate the control's Checked property in the code behind and perform an action based on the truth or falseness of the Checked property. By default, a RadioButton control is unselected. Also by default, a radio button doesn't perform an action upon being selected. If we want an action to be performed when a radio button is selected, we must set its AutoPostBack property to *true.* In order for a group of RadioButton controls to be related to one another and thus be treated as a set of mutually exclusive options, we must set their GroupName properties to the same value. Table 4-3 shows some of the properties, methods, and events of the RadioButton class. Note that the RadioButton class is derived from the CheckBox class. Thus, we should see the properties, methods, and events of the CheckBox class in addition to the ones below.

Table 4-3. *Some of the properties, methods, and events of the RadioButton class*

Class RadioButton[3]

Namespace System.Web.UI.WebControls

Properties

GroupName   Gets or sets the name of the group that the radio button belongs to.

Methods

(See reference.)

Events

(See reference.)

Reference

```
https://msdn.microsoft.com/en-us/library/system.web.ui.webcontrols.
radiobutton(v=vs.110).aspx
```

Figure 4-3 shows an example of the RadioButton class.

Notice at 01 the RadioButton control and its associated properties. As can be seen, the GroupName property of this control is set to *Shipper*, which is the same for all three radio buttons. Thus, these radio buttons are treated as a group of mutually exclusive options.

Notice at 02 the Button control and its associated properties. Specifically, notice the name of the event handler method that will be executed when its Click event is raised.

Notice at 03 that each radio button (except the last one) is being tested to determine whether or not it has been checked.

The first screenshot in the Result section of the figure shows that the first radio button is the default option in the group of options. The second screenshot shows the result of selecting the third option and clicking the *Select Shipper* button.

---

[3]All property, method, and event descriptions were taken directly from Microsoft's official documentation. The event handler methods used to handle the events of this class were omitted to conserve space. See the reference for all of the methods of this class.

ASPX CODE

```
    <asp:Label runat="server" Font-Bold="true" Text="Shipper" /><br />
01  <asp:RadioButton runat="server" ID="radUSPS" Checked="true"
        GroupName="Shipper" Text="USPS" /><br />
    <asp:RadioButton runat="server" ID="radUPS"
        GroupName="Shipper" Text="UPS" /><br />
    <asp:RadioButton runat="server" ID="radFedEx"
        GroupName="Shipper" Text="FedEx" /><br />
02  <asp:Button runat="server" ID="btnSelectShipper"
        OnClick="btnSelectShipper_Click" Text="Select Shipper" />
    <asp:Label runat="server" ID="lblShipper" ForeColor="Green" />
```

CODE BEHIND

```
    protected void btnSelectShipper_Click(object sender, EventArgs e)
    {

        String strShipper = "You have selected ";
03      if(radUSPS.Checked)
        {
            strShipper = strShipper + "USPS ";
        }
        else if(radUPS.Checked)
        {
            strShipper = strShipper + "UPS ";
        }
        else
        {
            strShipper = strShipper + "FedEx ";
        }
        strShipper = strShipper + "as your shipper.";
        lblShipper.Text = strShipper;

    }
```

RESULT

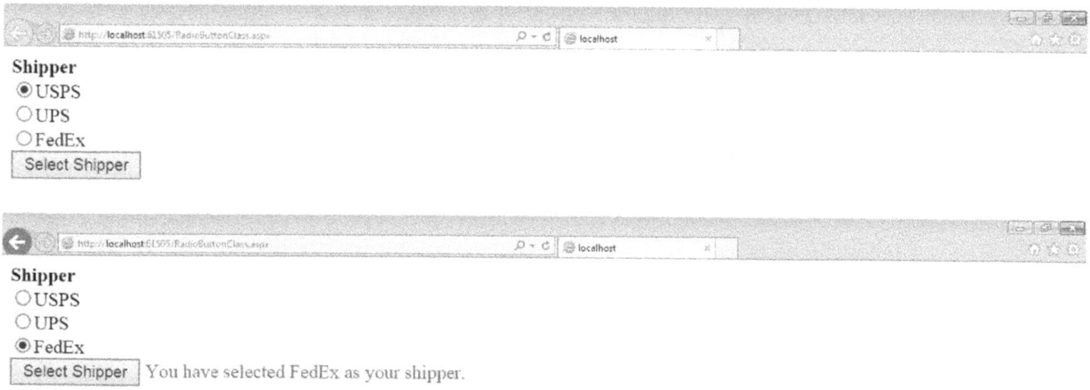

Figure 4-3. *Example of the RadioButton class*

4.5 FileUpload Class

The FileUpload class displays a text box and browse button that can be used by an end user to enter or select a file (or files) to be uploaded to the server. To *enter* the name of a file to be uploaded, the end user must enter the *full* path of the file in the text box. To *select* the name of a file to be uploaded, the end user must click the browse button, use the *Choose File to Upload* dialog to locate the file, and then select the file. A FileUpload control does *not* automatically upload a file to the server when a file name is entered or selected. Instead, a separate mechanism that performs the actual upload must be employed. One way to do this is to use a Button control with an event handler method that contains the code necessary to upload the file to the server. Such a method would invoke the SaveAs method of the FileUpload control after setting the target location for the file on the server. Before attempting to upload a file to the server, we typically check the HasFile property of the FileUpload control to make sure that a file has been entered or selected for upload. By default, the size limit of a file to be uploaded is 4MB. However, larger files can be uploaded as well. To upload larger files, see the reference at the bottom of Table 4-4. Table 4-4 shows some of the properties, methods, and events of the FileUpload class.

Table 4-4. *Some of the properties, methods, and events of the FileUpload class*

Class FileUpload[4]	
Namespace System.Web.UI.WebControls	
Properties	
AllowMultiple	Gets or sets a value that specifies whether multiple files can be selected for upload.
FileName	Gets the name of a file on a client to upload using the FileUpload control.
HasFile	Gets a value indicating whether the FileUpload control contains a file.
HasFiles	Gets a value that indicates whether any files have been uploaded.
Methods	
SaveAs(String)	Saves the contents of an uploaded file to a specified path on the Web server.
Events	
(See reference.)	
Reference	
https://msdn.microsoft.com/en-us/library/system.web.ui.webcontrols. fileupload(v=vs.110).aspx	

[4]All property, method, and event descriptions were taken directly from Microsoft's official documentation. The event handler methods used to handle the events of this class were omitted to conserve space. See the reference for all of the methods of this class.

Figure 4-4 shows an example of the FileUpload class. In this example, a FileUpload control is being used to upload images to an *Images* folder. We will assume that this folder has already been added to the project. Keeping our images together in such a folder will help us keep our Web application organized.

Notice at 01 the FileUpload control and its associated properties.

Notice at 02 the Button control that will be used by the end user to actually upload the file to the server. Specifically, notice the name of the event handler method that will be executed when its Click event is raised.

Notice at 03 that we are using the HasFile property of the FileUpload control to confirm that a file has been entered or selected for upload before performing the upload.

Notice at 04 that we are constructing the *full* path of the file to be uploaded using the physical path of the application on the server, the Images directory of the application, and the FileName property of the FileUpload control.

Notice at 05 that we are using the SaveAs method of the FileUpload control to perform the actual upload of the file.

The first screenshot in the Result section of the figure shows the FileUpload control after the end user has clicked the *Browse...* button and selected a file for upload. The second screenshot shows the result of uploading the file to the server.

ASPX CODE

```
   <asp:Label runat="server" Font-Bold="true" Text="Product Image" /><br />
   <asp:Label runat="server" Text="Please select a product image and click
       Upload." /><br />
01 <asp:FileUpload runat="server" ID="fiuImage" /><br />
02 <asp:Button runat="server" ID="btnUpload" OnClick="btnUpload_Click"
       Text="Upload" />
   <asp:Label runat="server" ID="lblMessage" />
```

CODE BEHIND

```
   protected void btnUpload_Click(object sender, EventArgs e)
   {

03     if (fiuImage.HasFile)
       {
04         String strPath = Request.PhysicalApplicationPath + "Images\\" +
               fiuImage.FileName;
05         fiuImage.SaveAs(strPath);
           lblMessage.ForeColor = System.Drawing.Color.Green;
           lblMessage.Text = "Product image was successfully uploaded.";
       }
       else
       {
           lblMessage.ForeColor = System.Drawing.Color.Red;
           lblMessage.Text = "No product image was selected. Please select
               a file and try again.";
       }

   }
```

RESULT

Figure 4-4. *Example of the FileUpload class*

4.6 HyperLink Class

The HyperLink class displays a link that can be used by an end user to navigate from one Web page to another. The Web page to navigate to is specified in the NavigateUrl property of a HyperLink control. By default, a HyperLink control is displayed as clickable *text*. The content of that text is specified in the Text property of the HyperLink control. However, a HyperLink control can also be displayed as a clickable *image* by specifying an image using the ImageUrl property of the HyperLink control. If for some reason the image is not available for display at runtime, the text in the Text property of the HyperLink control will be displayed. Also by default, the Web page that is navigated to is displayed in the current browser tab. If we want the new Web page to be displayed in a new browser tab, we must set the Target property of the HyperLink control to *_blank*. Table 4-5 shows some of the properties, methods, and events of the HyperLink class.

Table 4-5. *Some of the properties, methods, and events of the HyperLink class*

Class HyperLink[5]

Namespace System.Web.UI.WebControls

Properties

ImageHeight	Gets or sets the height of the hyperlink when the hyperlink is an image.
ImageUrl	Gets or sets the path to an image to display for the HyperLink control.
ImageWidth	Gets or sets the width of the hyperlink when the hyperlink is an image.
NavigateUrl	Gets or sets the URL to link to when the HyperLink control is clicked.
Target	Gets or sets the target window or frame in which to display the Web page content linked to when the HyperLink control is clicked.
Text	Gets or sets the text caption for the HyperLink control.

Methods

(See reference.)

Events

(See reference.)

Reference

https://msdn.microsoft.com/en-us/library/system.web.ui.webcontrols.
hyperlink(v=vs.110).aspx

---

[5]All property, method, and event descriptions were taken directly from Microsoft's official documentation. The event handler methods used to handle the events of this class were omitted to conserve space. See the reference for all of the methods of this class.

Figure 4-5 shows some examples of the HyperLink class. Note that no code behind code is required to utilize a HyperLink control.

Notice at 01 the first HyperLink control and its associated properties. As can be seen, the NavigateUrl property of the control is set to *http://google.com*, the Target property of the control is set to *_blank*, and the Text property of the control is set to *Go to Google*.

Notice at 02 the second HyperLink control and its associated properties. As we can see, this control displays an image. Notice that the ImageUrl property of the control is set to *~/Images/Google.png*, which indicates that the Google.png image resides in the Images folder of the application. When the end user clicks either of these HyperLink controls, google.com will be displayed in a *new* Web browser tab.

The screenshot in the Result section of the figure shows the first HyperLink control, which is being displayed in the form of clickable text, and the second HyperLink control, which is being displayed in the form of a clickable image.

ASPX CODE

```
01   <asp:HyperLink runat="server" NavigateUrl=http://google.com
         Target="_blank" Text="Go to Google" /><br />
02   <asp:HyperLink runat="server" ImageHeight="35"
         ImageUrl="~/Images/Google.png" ImageWidth="100"
         NavigateUrl="http://google.com" Target="_blank" Text="Go to Google" />
```

RESULT

Figure 4-5. *Examples of the HyperLink class*

4.7 Image Class

The Image class displays an image that can be used by an end user to view a photograph, drawing, chart, graph, or other two-dimensional visual aid. Any type of image can be displayed using an Image control as long as the image type (e.g., .bmp, .gif, .jpg, .png) is supported by the end user's browser. The image to be displayed in an Image control is specified in its ImageUrl property. If for some reason the image is not available for display at runtime, the text in the AlternateText property of the control will be displayed. Table 4-6 shows some of the properties, methods, and events of the Image class.

Table 4-6. *Some of the properties, methods, and events of the Image class*

Class Image[6]

Namespace System.Web.UI.WebControls

Properties

AlternateText	Gets or sets the alternate text displayed in the Image control when the image is unavailable. Browsers that support the ToolTips feature display this text as a ToolTip.
ImageAlign	Gets or sets the alignment of the Image control in relation to other elements on the Web page.
ImageUrl	Gets or sets the URL that provides the path to an image to display in the Image control.

Methods

(See reference.)

Events

(See reference.)

Reference

```
https://msdn.microsoft.com/en-us/library/system.web.ui.webcontrols.
image(v=vs.110).aspx
```

Figure 4-6 shows an example of the Image class. Note that no code behind code is required to utilize an Image control.

Notice at 01 the Image control and its associated properties. As can be seen, the ImageUrl property of the Image control is set to *~/Images/NZV9.5T.jpg*, which indicates that the NZV9.5T.jpg image resides in the Images folder of the application.

The screenshot in the Result section of the figure shows the image being displayed.

---

[6]All property, method, and event descriptions were taken directly from Microsoft's official documentation. The event handler methods used to handle the events of this class were omitted to conserve space. See the reference for all of the methods of this class.

ASPX CODE

```
    <asp:Label runat="server" Font-Bold="true" Text="Product" /><br />
01  <asp:Image runat="server" AlternateText="Nike Zoom Vapor 9.5 Tour"
        ImageUrl="~/Images/NZV9.5T.jpg" />
```

RESULT

Figure 4-6. *Example of the Image class*

4.8 ImageButton Class

The ImageButton class displays an image that can be used by an end user to perform
an action. When an ImageButton control is clicked, its Click and Command events
are raised. To handle one of these events, we must code the appropriate event handler
method. When handling the Click event of an ImageButton control, we can identify
where on the image button the end user has clicked. This permits us to perform different
actions depending on the location of the click. To see how this is done, see the reference
at the bottom of Table 4-7. Table 4-7 shows some of the properties, methods, and events
of the ImageButton class.

Table 4-7. *Some of the properties, methods, and events of the ImageButton class*

Class ImageButton[7]

Namespace System.Web.UI.WebControls

Properties

CausesValidation	Gets or sets a value indicating whether validation is performed when the ImageButton control is clicked.
CommandArgument	Gets or sets an optional argument that provides additional information about the CommandName property.
CommandName	Gets or sets the command name associated with the ImageButton control.
OnClientClick	Gets or sets the client-side script that executes when an ImageButton control's Click event is raised.
PostBackUrl	Gets or sets the URL of the page to post to from the current page when the ImageButton control is clicked.
ValidationGroup	Gets or sets the group of controls for which the ImageButton control causes validation when it posts back to the server.

Methods

(See reference.)

Events

Click	Occurs when the ImageButton is clicked.
Command	Occurs when the ImageButton is clicked.

Reference

```
https://msdn.microsoft.com/en-us/library/system.web.ui.webcontrols.
imagebutton(v=vs.110).aspx
```

Figure 4-7 shows an example of the ImageButton class.

---

[7]All property, method, and event descriptions were taken directly from Microsoft's official documentation. The event handler methods used to handle the events of this class were omitted to conserve space. See the reference for all of the methods of this class.

Notice at 01 the ImageButton control and its associated properties. Specifically, notice the name of the event handler method that will be executed when its Click event is raised. As can be seen, the ImageUrl property of the ImageButton control is set to ~/ *Images/PTW100.jpg*, which indicates that the PTW100.jpg image resides in the Images folder of the application.

Notice at 02 that we are setting the Text property of the description label when the end user clicks the image button.

The screenshot in the Result section of the figure shows the image button and the result of clicking it.

ASPX CODE

```
    <asp:Label runat="server" Font-Bold="true" Text="Product" /><br />
01  <asp:ImageButton runat="server" ID="btnDisplayDescription"
        ImageUrl="~/Images/PTW100.jpg"
        OnClick="btnDisplayDescription_Click" /><br />
    <asp:Label runat="server" ID="lblDescription" />
```

CODE BEHIND

```
    protected void btnDisplayDescription_Click(object sender,
        ImageClickEventArgs e)
    {

02      lblDescription.Text = "Prince Textreme Warrior 100";

    }
```

RESULT

Product

Prince Textreme Warrior 100

Figure 4-7. *Example of the ImageButton class*

4.9 ImageMap Class

The ImageMap class displays an Image with discrete *hot spot regions* that can be used by an end user to invoke an action based on where on the Image he or she clicks. The ImageUrl property of an ImageMap control indicates the image to be displayed in the control. The HotSpotMode property of an ImageMap control indicates the behavior of the control when it is clicked by the end user (i.e., do nothing, navigate to another URL, or post back to the server). Hot spot regions are defined using a hot spot class, such as the RectangleHotSpot class, the CircleHotSpot class, or the PolygonHotSpot class. Custom hot spot classes can also be defined and used as hot spot regions on an ImageMap control. We will only discuss the RectangleHotSpot class in this chapter since the other hot spot classes behave similarly. Table 4-8 shows some of the properties, methods, and events of the ImageMap class.

Table 4-8. *Some of the properties, methods, and events of the ImageMap class*

Class ImageMap[8]

Namespace System.Web.UI.WebControls

Properties

HotSpotMode	Gets or sets the default behavior for the HotSpot objects of an ImageMap control when the HotSpot objects are clicked.
ImageUrl	Gets or sets the URL that provides the path to an image to display in the Image control. (Inherited from Image.)
Target	Gets or sets the target window or frame that displays the Web page content linked to when the ImageMap control is clicked.

Methods

(See reference.)

Events

Click	Occurs when a HotSpot object in an ImageMap control is clicked.

Reference

```
https://msdn.microsoft.com/en-us/library/system.web.ui.webcontrols.
imagemap(v=vs.110).aspx
```

---

[8]All property, method, and event descriptions were taken directly from Microsoft's official documentation. The event handler methods used to handle the events of this class were omitted to conserve space. See the reference for all of the methods of this class.

4.10 RectangleHotSpot Class

The RectangleHotSpot class defines a four-sided *hot spot region* within an ImageMap control that can be used by an end user to invoke an action. When a RectangleHotSpot control is clicked, one of three things can happen depending on the value of the associated ImageMap control's HotSpotMode property—the current Web page can do nothing, the current Web page can transition to the Web page specified in the RectangleHotSpot control's NavigateUrl property, or the current Web page can post back to the server where the Click event of the ImageMap control can be handled. The region of a RectangleHotSpot control within an ImageMap control is defined by setting its Top property (i.e., the y-coordinate of the top side of the rectangular region in pixels), Left property (i.e., the x-coordinate of the left side of the rectangular region in pixels), Bottom property (i.e., the y-coordinate of the bottom side of the rectangular region in pixels), and Right property (i.e., the x-coordinate of the right side of the rectangular region in pixels). Table 4-9 shows some of the properties, methods, and events of the RectangleHotSpot class.

Table 4-9. *Some of the properties, methods, and events of the RectangleHotSpot class*

Class RectangleHotSpot[9]

Namespace System.Web.UI.WebControls

Properties

Bottom	Gets or sets the y-coordinate of the bottom side of the rectangular region defined by this RectangleHotSpot object.
HotSpotMode	Gets or sets the behavior of a HotSpot object in an ImageMap control when the HotSpot is clicked. (Inherited from HotSpot.)
Left	Gets or sets the x-coordinate of the left side of the rectangular region defined by this RectangleHotSpot object.
NavigateUrl	Gets or sets the URL to navigate to when a HotSpot object is clicked. (Inherited from HotSpot.)

(*continued*)

---

[9]All property, method, and event descriptions were taken directly from Microsoft's official documentation. The event handler methods used to handle the events of this class were omitted to conserve space. See the reference for all of the methods of this class.

Table 4-9. (*continued*)

PostBackValue	Gets or sets the name of the HotSpot object to pass in the event data when the HotSpot is clicked. (Inherited from HotSpot.)
Right	Gets or sets the x-coordinate of the right side of the rectangular region defined by this RectangleHotSpot object.
Top	Gets or sets the y-coordinate of the top side of the rectangular region defined by this RectangleHotSpot object.

Methods

(See reference.)

Events

(See reference.)

Reference

```
https://msdn.microsoft.com/en-us/library/system.web.ui.webcontrols.
rectanglehotspot(v=vs.110).aspx
```

Figure 4-8 shows an example of the ImageMap and RectangleHotSpot classes that cause a transition to another URL. Note that no code behind code is required to utilize an ImageMap and RectangleHotSpot control.

Notice at 01 the ImageMap control and its associated properties. As can be seen, the ImageUrl property of the control is set to *~/Images/ShipperMap.jpg*, which indicates that the ShipperMap.jpg image resides in the Images folder of the application. Also notice that the HotSpotMode property of the ImageMap control is set to *Navigate*. This indicates that clicking the control will cause a transition to another Web page. Notice as well that the Target property of the control is set to *_Blank*, which indicates that a new browser tab will be opened when the end user clicks one of the rectangle hot spots on the image.

Notice at 02 the RectangleHotSpot control and its associated properties. As we can see, the Top, Left, Bottom, and Right properties of the control are set to reflect the desired dimensions of the rectangle hot spot, and the NavigateUrl property is set to *http://usps.com*.

The screenshot in the Result section of the figure shows the result of clicking the second rectangle hot spot. Notice that a new browser tab has been opened for ups.com.

ASPX CODE

```
    <asp:Label runat="server" Font-Bold="true" Text="Shipper" /><br />
01  <asp:ImageMap runat="server" ID="imgShipperMap" Height="100"
        ImageUrl="~/Images/ShipperMap.jpg" HotSpotMode="Navigate"
        Target="_Blank">
02      <asp:RectangleHotSpot Top="0" Left="0" Bottom="25" Right="158"
            NavigateUrl="http://usps.com" />
        <asp:RectangleHotSpot Top="26" Left="0" Bottom="67" Right="158"
            NavigateUrl="http://ups.com" />
        <asp:RectangleHotSpot Top="68" Left="0" Bottom="99" Right="158"
            NavigateUrl="http://fedex.com" />
    </asp:ImageMap>
```

RESULT

Figure 4-8. *Example of the ImageMap and RectangleHotSpot classes that cause a transition to another URL*

Figure 4-9 shows an example of the ImageMap and RectangleHotSpot classes that cause a postback to the server.

Notice at 01 the ImageMap control and its associated properties. Specifically, notice the name of the event handler method that will be executed when its Click event is raised. As can be seen, the ImageUrl property of the ImageMap control is set to ~/ *Images/ShipperMap.jpg*, which indicates that the ShipperMap.jpg image resides in the Images folder of the application. Also notice that the HotSpotMode property of the ImageMap control is set to *PostBack*. This indicates that clicking the control will cause a postback to the server.

Notice at 02 the RectangleHotSpot control and its associated properties. As we can see, the Top, Left, Bottom, and Right properties of the control are set to reflect the desired dimensions of the rectangle hot spot, and the PostBackValue property of the control is set differently for each rectangle hot spot.

Notice at 03 that we are checking the PostBackValue passed to the event handler method to determine which RectangleHotSpot control was clicked by the end user.

The screenshot in the Result section of the figure shows the result of clicking the second rectangle hot spot.

ASPX CODE

```
    <asp:Label runat="server" Font-Bold="true" Text="Shipper" /><br />
01  <asp:ImageMap runat="server" ID="imgShipperMap" Height="100"
        ImageUrl="~/Images/ShipperMap.jpg" HotSpotMode="PostBack"
        OnClick="imgShipperMap_Click">
02      <asp:RectangleHotSpot Top="0" Left="0" Bottom="25" Right="158"
            PostBackValue="USPS" />
        <asp:RectangleHotSpot Top="26" Left="0" Bottom="67" Right="158"
            PostBackValue="UPS" />
        <asp:RectangleHotSpot Top="68" Left="0" Bottom="99" Right="158"
            PostBackValue="FedEx" />
    </asp:ImageMap><br />
    <asp:Label runat="server" ID="lblShipper" ForeColor="Green" />
```

CODE BEHIND

```
    protected void imgShipperMap_Click(object sender, ImageMapEventArgs e)
    {

        String strShipper = "You have selected ";
03      switch (e.PostBackValue)
        {
            case "USPS":
                strShipper = strShipper + "USPS ";
                break;
            case "UPS":
                strShipper = strShipper + "UPS ";
                break;
            case "FedEx":
                strShipper = strShipper + "FedEx ";
                break;
        }
        strShipper = strShipper + "as your shipper.";
        lblShipper.Text = strShipper;

    }
```

RESULT

Figure 4-9. *Example of the ImageMap and RectangleHotSpot classes that cause a postback to the server*

4.11 LinkButton Class

The LinkButton class displays a hyperlink-style button that can be used by an end user to invoke an action. Although a LinkButton control looks like a HyperLink control, it behaves like a Button control. (A HyperLink control should be used when we simply want to navigate from one Web page to another.) Since a LinkButton control is rendered in a browser with some associated JavaScript code, the end user's browser must be script enabled for this control to work. When a LinkButton control is clicked, its Click and Command events are raised. To handle one of these events, we must code the appropriate event handler method. A LinkButton control can behave like a Submit button (i.e., a button that posts the page back to the server where we can handle its Click event), or it can behave like a Command button (i.e., a button that posts the page back to the server where we can handle the Click events of several buttons in one event handler method by passing the event handler method a command name and [optionally] a command argument). By default, a LinkButton control behaves like a Submit button. Table 4-10 shows some of the properties, methods, and events of the LinkButton class.

Table 4-10. *Some of the properties, methods, and events of the LinkButton class*

Class LinkButton[10]

Namespace System.Web.UI.WebControls

Properties

CausesValidation	Gets or sets a value indicating whether validation is performed when the LinkButton control is clicked.
CommandArgument	Gets or sets an optional argument passed to the Command event handler along with the associated CommandName property.
CommandName	Gets or sets the command name associated with the LinkButton control. This value is passed to the Command event handler along with the CommandArgument property.

(*continued*)

---

[10]All property, method, and event descriptions were taken directly from Microsoft's official documentation. The event handler methods used to handle the events of this class were omitted to conserve space. See the reference for all of the methods of this class.

Table 4-10. (*continued*)

OnClientClick	Gets or sets the client-side script that executes when a LinkButton control's Click event is raised.
PostBackUrl	Gets or sets the URL of the page to post to from the current page when the LinkButton control is clicked.
Text	Gets or sets the text caption displayed on the LinkButton control.
ValidationGroup	Gets or sets the group of controls for which the LinkButton control causes validation when it posts back to the server.

Methods

(See reference.)

Events

Click	Occurs when the LinkButton control is clicked.
Command	Occurs when the LinkButton control is clicked.

Reference

```
https://msdn.microsoft.com/en-us/library/system.web.ui.webcontrols.
linkbutton(v=vs.110).aspx
```

Figure 4-10 shows an example of the LinkButton class behaving like a Submit button.

Notice at 01 the LinkButton control and its associated properties. More specifically, notice the name of the event handler method that will be executed when the control's Click event is raised.

Notice at 02 and 03 the code that will be executed when the associated event handler method is executed.

The screenshot in the Result section of the figure shows the result of clicking the *Modify* link button.

ASPX CODE

```
    <asp:Label runat="server" Font-Bold="true" Text="Email Address" /><br />
    <asp:TextBox runat="server" ID="txtEmailAddress" /><br />
01  <asp:LinkButton runat="server" ID="btnModify" OnClick="btnModify_Click"
        Text="Modify" />
    <asp:Label runat="server" ID="lblMessage" /><br />
```

CODE BEHIND

```
    protected void btnModify_Click(object sender, EventArgs e)
    {

        // The database call to update the email address would go here.
        // If successful, the following message would be displayed.
02      lblMessage.ForeColor = System.Drawing.Color.Green;
03      lblMessage.Text = "The email address was successfully modified.";

    }
```

RESULT

Figure 4-10. *Example of the LinkButton class behaving like a Submit button*

Figure 4-11 shows an example of the LinkButton class behaving like a Command button.

Notice at 01 the LinkButton control and its associated properties. More specifically, notice the name of the event handler method that will be executed when the control's Command event is raised. As can be seen, the CommandArgument property is set to *Adidas,* and the CommandName property is set to *View.* These two properties will be passed to the link button's event handler method in the code behind when the link button is clicked. As can be seen, none of the link buttons on the page require an ID in this scenario and that the first five link buttons have *different* command arguments but have the *same* command name.

Notice at 02 that the last link button does *not* have a command argument and has a *different* command name than the other buttons.

Notice at 03 that the command name passed to the event handler method is being tested. If the value of the CommandName property is set to *View*, the block of code inside the If structure will be executed. If not (i.e., the value of the CommandName property is set to *Cancel*), the block of code in the Else part of the If structure will be executed.

Notice at 04 that the command argument passed to the event handler method is being evaluated using a Switch structure to determine which case to execute. If the value of the CommandArgument property is set to *Adidas*, the Text property of the message label will be set appropriately. If it is set to something else, the Text property of the message label will be set to something else.

The screenshot in the Result section of the figure shows the result of clicking the Adidas button.

ASPX CODE

```
    <asp:Label runat="server" Font-Bold="true" Text="View Supplier" />
        <br /><br />
01  <asp:LinkButton runat="server" CommandArgument="Adidas"
        CommandName="View" OnCommand="LinkButton_Command" Text="Adidas" />
    <asp:LinkButton runat="server" CommandArgument="Babolat"
        CommandName="View" OnCommand="LinkButton_Command" Text="Babolat" />
    <asp:LinkButton runat="server" CommandArgument="Head"
        CommandName="View" OnCommand="LinkButton_Command" Text="Head" />
    <asp:LinkButton runat="server" CommandArgument="Nike"
        CommandName="View" OnCommand="LinkButton_Command" Text="Nike" />
    <asp:LinkButton runat="server" CommandArgument="Prince"
        CommandName="View" OnCommand="LinkButton_Command" Text="Prince" />
02  <asp:LinkButton runat="server"
        CommandName="Cancel" OnCommand="LinkButton_Command" Text="Cancel" />
    <br /><br />
    <asp:Label runat="server" ID="lblMessage" /><br />
```

CODE BEHIND

```
    protected void LinkButton_Command(object sender, CommandEventArgs e)
    {

03      if(e.CommandName == "View")
        {
            lblMessage.ForeColor = System.Drawing.Color.Green;
04          switch (e.CommandArgument.ToString())
            {
                case "Adidas":
                    lblMessage.Text = e.CommandArgument.ToString();
                    break;
                case "Babolat":
                    lblMessage.Text = e.CommandArgument.ToString();
                    break;
                case "Head":
                    lblMessage.Text = e.CommandArgument.ToString();
                    break;
                case "Nike":
                    lblMessage.Text = e.CommandArgument.ToString();
                    break;
                case "Prince":
                    lblMessage.Text = e.CommandArgument.ToString();
                    break;
            }
```

Figure 4-11. *Example of the LinkButton class behaving like a Command button*

```
        }
        else
        {
            lblMessage.ForeColor = System.Drawing.Color.Red;
            lblMessage.Text = "Cancelled";
        }

    }
```

RESULT

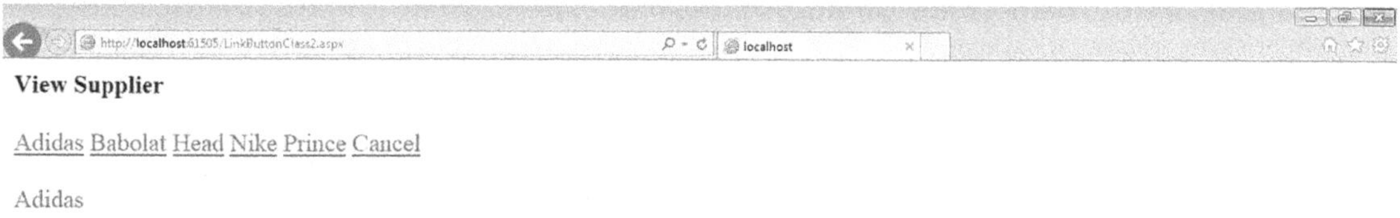

View Supplier

Adidas Babolat Head Nike Prince Cancel

Adidas

Figure 4-11. *(continued)*

4.12 ListControl Class

The ListControl class serves as the base class for all list-type classes. As such, all list-type classes inherit properties, methods, and events from this class. The ListControl classes include the BulletedList class, the CheckBoxList class, the DropDownList class, the ListBox class, and the RadioButtonList class. In this chapter, we will limit our discussion to the DropDownList class and ListBox class. The items displayed in a list-type control are stored in its Items collection.

To access the *zero-based* index of the selected item in a list-type control, we get or set the SelectedIndex property of the control. To retrieve the selected item from a list-type control, we get the SelectedItem property of the control. The SelectedIndexChanged event is raised when the end user selects a different item in a list-type control. The TextChanged event is raised when the Text or SelectedValue property changes in a list-type control. If we want a postback to the server to occur so that we can handle these events when they happen, we must set the AutoPostBack property of the list-type control to *true*. Table 4-11 shows some of the properties, methods, and events of the ListControl class.

Table 4-11. *Some of the properties, methods, and events of the ListControl class*

Class ListControl[11]

Namespace System.Web.UI.WebControls

Properties

AutoPostBack	Gets or sets a value indicating whether a postback to the server automatically occurs when the user changes the list selection.
CausesValidation	Gets or sets a value indicating whether validation is performed when a control that is derived from the ListControl class is clicked.
DataSourceID	Gets or sets the ID of the control from which the data-bound control retrieves its list of data items. (Inherited from DataBoundControl.)
DataTextField	Gets or sets the field of the data source that provides the text content of the list items.
DataValueField	Gets or sets the field of the data source that provides the value of each list item.
Items	Gets the collection of items in the list control.
SelectedIndex	Gets or sets the lowest ordinal index of the selected items in the list.
SelectedItem	Gets the selected item with the lowest index in the list control.
SelectedValue	Gets the value of the selected item in the list control, or selects the item in the list control that contains the specified value.
Text	Gets or sets the SelectedValue property of the ListControl control.
ValidationGroup	Gets or sets the group of controls for which the control that is derived from the ListControl class causes validation when it posts back to the server.

Methods

(See reference.)

Events

SelectedIndexChanged	Occurs when the selection from the list control changes between posts to the server.
TextChanged	Occurs when the Text and SelectedValue properties change.

Reference

```
https://msdn.microsoft.com/en-us/library/system.web.ui.webcontrols.
listcontrol(v=vs.110).aspx
```

---

[11]All property, method, and event descriptions were taken directly from Microsoft's official documentation. The event handler methods used to handle the events of this class were omitted to conserve space. See the reference for all of the methods of this class.

4.13 ListItem Class

The ListItem class represents an individual item in a list-type control. To specify the *text* that is displayed in a ListItem control, we set its Text property. To specify the *value* that is associated with a ListItem control, we set its Value property. To indicate that a list item should be selected upon display of the page, we set its Selected property to *true*. To indicate that a list item should be disabled upon display of the page, we set its Enabled property to *false*. Setting the Enabled property of a list item to *false* will result in the list item not being displayed in the list-type control. We can define any number of ListItem controls in a list-type control. Table 4-12 shows some of the properties, methods, and events of the ListItem class.

Table 4-12. *Some of the properties, methods, and events of the ListItem class*

Class ListItem[12]

Namespace System.Web.UI.WebControls

Properties

Enabled	Gets or sets a value indicating whether the list item is enabled.
Selected	Gets or sets a value indicating whether the item is selected.
Text	Gets or sets the text displayed in a list control for the item represented by the ListItem.
Value	Gets or sets the value associated with the ListItem.

Methods

(See reference.)

Events

(See reference.)

Reference

https://msdn.microsoft.com/en-us/library/system.web.ui.webcontrols.
listitem(v=vs.110).aspx

---

[12]All property, method, and event descriptions were taken directly from Microsoft's official documentation. The event handler methods used to handle the events of this class were omitted to conserve space. See the reference for all of the methods of this class.

4.14 DropDownList Class

The DropDownList class displays a collection of items that can be used by an end user to select a single option. To specify the items that should be displayed in a DropDownList control, we add the necessary ListItem controls between the opening and closing tags of the DropDownList control. Since the DropDownList class inherits many of its properties, methods, and events from the ListControl class, we can see that class for more details. Table 4-13 shows some of the properties, methods, and events of the DropDownList class.

Table 4-13. *Some of the properties, methods, and events of the DropDownList class*

Class DropDownList[13]
Namespace System.Web.UI.WebControls
Properties
(See reference.)
Methods
(See reference.)
Events
(See reference.)
Reference
https://msdn.microsoft.com/en-us/library/system.web.ui.webcontrols. dropdownlist(v=vs.110).aspx

Figure 4-12 shows an example of the DropDownList and ListItem classes.

Notice at 01 the DropDownList control and its associated properties. More specifically, notice the name of the event handler method that will be executed when the control's SelectedIndexChanged event is raised. As can be seen, the AutoPostBack property of the control is set to *true*. Thus, the page will automatically post back to the server when the value of the SelectedIndex property changes.

Notice at 02 the ListItem control and its associated properties. As can be seen, the Text property of the control is set to *Adidas*, and the Value property of the control is set to *A*. The other ListItem controls have different Text and Value properties.

---

[13]All property, method, and event descriptions were taken directly from Microsoft's official documentation. The event handler methods used to handle the events of this class were omitted to conserve space. See the reference for all of the methods of this class.

Notice at 03, 04, and 05 that the *zero-based* SelectedIndex property, the *value* of the SelectedItem property, and the *text* of the SelectedItem property will be displayed whenever the SelectedIndex changes.

The first screenshot in the Result section of the figure shows the drop-down list before it has been clicked. The second screenshot shows the result of clicking the drop-down list. The third screenshot shows the result of selecting the third option in the list. Notice that the SelectedIndex property, the *value* of the SelectedItem property, and the *text* of the SelectedItem property are displayed.

ASPX CODE

```
    <asp:Label runat="server" Font-Bold="true" Text="Supplier" /><br />
01  <asp:DropDownList runat="server" ID="ddlSupplier" AutoPostBack="true"
        OnSelectedIndexChanged="ddlSupplier_SelectedIndexChanged">
02      <asp:ListItem Text="Adidas" Value="A" />
        <asp:ListItem Text="Nike" Value="N" />
        <asp:ListItem Text="Prince" Value="P" />
    </asp:DropDownList>
    <asp:Label runat="server" ID="lblSupplierIndex" />
    <asp:Label runat="server" ID="lblSupplierValue" />
    <asp:Label runat="server" ID="lblSupplierText" />
```

CODE BEHIND

```
    protected void ddlSupplier_SelectedIndexChanged(object sender,
        EventArgs e)
    {

03      lblSupplierIndex.Text = ddlSupplier.SelectedIndex.ToString();
04      lblSupplierValue.Text = ddlSupplier.SelectedItem.Value;
05      lblSupplierText.Text = ddlSupplier.SelectedItem.Text;

    }
```

Figure 4-12. *Example of the DropDownList and ListItem classes*

RESULT

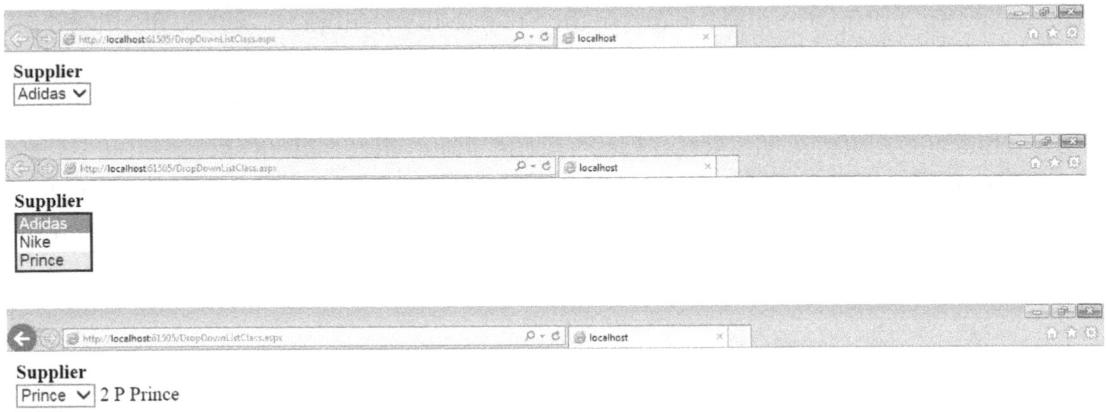

Figure 4-12. *(continued)*

4.15 ListBox Class

The ListBox class displays a collection of items that can be used by an end user to select one or more options. To specify the items that should be displayed in a ListBox control, we add the necessary ListItem controls between the opening and closing tags of the ListBox control. To permit the end user to select more than one option in a ListBox control, we set its SelectionMode to *Multiple*. Since the ListBox class inherits many of its properties, methods, and events from the ListControl class, we can see that class for more details. Table 4-14 shows some of the properties, methods, and events of the ListBox class.

Table 4-14. *Some of the properties, methods, and events of the ListBox class*

Class ListBox[14]	
Namespace System.Web.UI.WebControls	
Properties	
SelectionMode	Gets or sets the selection mode of the ListBox control.
Methods	
(See reference.)	
Events	
(See reference.)	
Reference	
https://msdn.microsoft.com/en-us/library/system.web.ui.webcontrols. listbox(v=vs.110).aspx	

Figure 4-13 shows an example of the ListBox and ListItem classes.

Notice at 01 the ListBox control and its associated properties. More specifically, notice the name of the event handler method that will be executed when the control's SelectedIndexChanged event is raised. As can be seen, the AutoPostBack property of the control is set to *true*. Thus, the page will automatically post back to the server when the value of the SelectedIndex property changes.

Notice at 02 the ListItem control and its associated properties. As can be seen, the Text property of the control is set to *Adidas*, and the Value property of the control is set to *A*. The other ListItem controls have different Text and Value properties.

Notice at 03, 04, and 05 that the *zero-based* SelectedIndex property, the *value* of the SelectedItem property, and the *text* of the SelectedItem property will be displayed whenever the SelectedIndex changes.

The first screenshot in the Result section of the figure shows the list box before it has been clicked. The second screenshot shows the result of selecting the second option in the list. Notice that the SelectedIndex property, the *value* of the SelectedItem property, and the *text* of the SelectedItem property are displayed.

---

[14]All property, method, and event descriptions were taken directly from Microsoft's official documentation. The event handler methods used to handle the events of this class were omitted to conserve space. See the reference for all of the methods of this class.

ASPX CODE

```
     <asp:Label runat="server" Font-Bold="true" Text="Supplier" /><br />
01   <asp:ListBox runat="server" ID="libSupplier" AutoPostBack="true"
         OnSelectedIndexChanged="libSupplier_SelectedIndexChanged">
02         <asp:ListItem Text="Adidas" Value="A" />
           <asp:ListItem Text="Nike" Value="N" />
           <asp:ListItem Text="Prince" Value="P" />
     </asp:ListBox>
     <asp:Label runat="server" ID="lblSupplierIndex" />
     <asp:Label runat="server" ID="lblSupplierValue" />
     <asp:Label runat="server" ID="lblSupplierText" />
```

CODE BEHIND

```
     protected void libSupplier_SelectedIndexChanged(object sender,
         EventArgs e)
     {

03       lblSupplierIndex.Text = libSupplier.SelectedIndex.ToString();
04       lblSupplierValue.Text = libSupplier.SelectedItem.Value;
05       lblSupplierText.Text = libSupplier.SelectedItem.Text;

     }
```

RESULT

Figure 4-13. *Example of the ListBox and ListItem classes*

4.16 Panel Class

The Panel class is a container that holds groups of related ASP.NET server classes, such as Label classes, TextBox classes, and Button classes. Panels are useful when we want to programmatically show and hide groups of related controls without having to show and hide all the related controls individually. We can just show and hide panels.

To display a custom background on a panel, we set its BackImageUrl property to a valid image file path. To identify the default button in a panel, we set its DefaultButton property to the ID of the button that should be "clicked" when the end user hits the *Enter* key on his or her keyboard. To display a descriptive caption for the group of controls in a panel, we specify its GroupingText property. And to display scroll bars on a panel, we set its ScrollBars property to *Horizontal, Vertical, Both*, or *Auto*. By default, scroll bars are not displayed on a panel. Table 4-15 shows some of the properties, methods, and events of the Panel class.

Table 4-15. *Some of the properties, methods, and events of the Panel class*

Class Panel[15]

Namespace System.Web.UI.WebControls

Properties

BackImageUrl	Gets or sets the URL of the background image for the Panel control.
DefaultButton	Gets or sets the identifier for the default button that is contained in the Panel control.
GroupingText	Gets or sets the caption for the group of controls that is contained in the Panel control.
ScrollBars	Gets or sets the visibility and position of scroll bars in a Panel control.

Methods

(See reference.)

Events

(See reference.)

Reference

```
https://msdn.microsoft.com/en-us/library/system.web.ui.webcontrols.
panel(v=vs.110).aspx
```

---

[15]All property, method, and event descriptions were taken directly from Microsoft's official documentation. The event handler methods used to handle the events of this class were omitted to conserve space. See the reference for all of the methods of this class.

Figure 4-14 shows an example of the Panel class.

Notice at 01 the first Panel control and its associated properties. As can be seen, this panel's GroupingText property is set to *Billing Address*. Since this panel's Visible property is set to *true*, it will be rendered in the browser by default.

Notice at 02 the second Panel control and its associated properties. As we can see, this panel's GroupingText property is set to *Shipping Address*. Since this panel's Visible property is set to *false*, it will *not* be rendered in the browser by default.

Notice at 03 the first RadioButton control and its associated properties. More specifically, notice the name of the event handler method that will be executed when the control's CheckedChanged event is raised.

Notice at 04 the second RadioButton control and its associated properties. More specifically, notice the name of the event handler method that will be executed when the control's CheckedChanged event is raised.

Notice at 05 and 06 that the TogglePanel method at 07 will be invoked whenever the billing address radio button or the shipping address radio button is clicked.

The first screenshot in the Result section of the figure shows the billing address panel that has been displayed by default. The second screenshot shows the result of clicking the shipping address radio button.

ASPX CODE

```
   <asp:Label runat="server" Font-Bold="true" Text="Customer" /><br />
01 <asp:Panel runat="server" ID="panBillingAddress"
       GroupingText="Billing Address" Visible="true">
       <asp:Label runat="server" Text="Address " /><br />
       <asp:TextBox runat="server" ID="txtBillingAddress" /><br />
       <asp:Button runat="server" ID="btnSaveBillingAddress"
           OnClick="btnSaveBillingAddress_Click" Text="Save" />
   </asp:Panel>
02 <asp:Panel runat="server" ID="panShippingAddress"
       GroupingText="Shipping Address" Visible="false">
       <asp:Label runat="server" Text="Address " /><br />
       <asp:TextBox runat="server" ID="txtShippingAddress" /><br />
       <asp:Button runat="server" ID="btnSaveShippingAddress"
           OnClick="btnSaveShippingAddress_Click" Text="Save" />
   </asp:Panel>
03 <asp:RadioButton runat="server" ID="radBillingAddress"
       AutoPostBack="true" Checked="true" GroupName="AddressGroup"
       OnCheckedChanged="radBillingAddress_CheckedChanged"
       Text="Billing Address" />
04 <asp:RadioButton runat="server" ID="radShippingAddress"
       AutoPostBack="true" GroupName="AddressGroup"
       OnCheckedChanged="radShippingAddress_CheckedChanged"
       Text="Shipping Address" />
```

CODE BEHIND

```
   protected void radBillingAddress_CheckedChanged(object sender,
       EventArgs e)
   {

05     TogglePanel();

   }

   protected void radShippingAddress_CheckedChanged(object sender,
       EventArgs e)
   {

06     TogglePanel();

   }
```

Figure 4-14. *Example of the Panel class*

```
07   private void TogglePanel()
     {

         if (panBillingAddress.Visible)
         {
             panBillingAddress.Visible = false;
             panShippingAddress.Visible = true;
         }
         else
         {
             panBillingAddress.Visible = true;
             panShippingAddress.Visible = false;
         }

     }
```

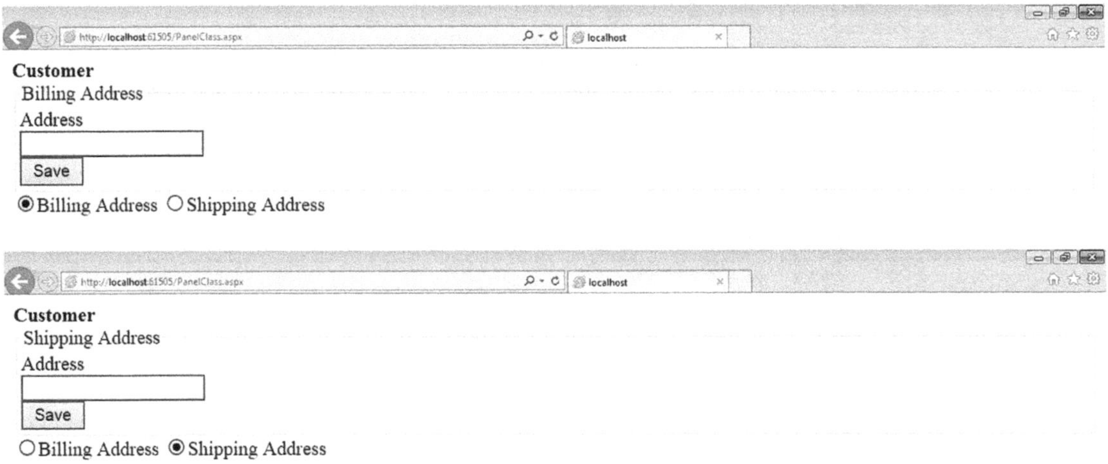

Figure 4-14. *(continued)*

CHAPTER 5

Data Validation Controls

5.1 Introduction

Data validation controls ensure that bad data does not make its way into a software system. If we allow bad *data* into a system, we will get bad *information* out of it. This reflects the age-old principle: garbage in, garbage out (GIGO). The importance of allowing only good data into a software system is that good data leads to good information, good information leads to good decision making, and good decision making leads to organizational stability (in a not-for-profit context) or competitive advantage (in a for-profit context).

Several of the graphical user interface (GUI) controls we discussed in the previous chapter (e.g., the Calendar control, the CheckBox control, the DropDownList control) can be used to help us ensure that only good data is allowed into an ASP.NET Web application. By requiring the end user to select inputs using GUI controls (as opposed to requiring him or her to type the data into a text box or similar control), the problems associated with misspelling, incorrect formatting, and so on are significantly reduced.

There are times, however, when data *must* be entered into a text box or similar control manually. When this is the case, we need to validate the data before it is processed and/or stored in the system. Such validations include existence checks (e.g., ensuring that a customer's last name is entered), data type checks (e.g., ensuring that a monetary value contains only numbers), reasonableness checks (e.g., ensuring that a patient's blood pressure reading makes sense), range checks (e.g., ensuring that a discount rate falls within a valid range), format checks (e.g., ensuring that an email address is in the correct format), combination checks (e.g., ensuring that a pregnant patient's sex is female), and self-checking digit checks (e.g., ensuring that a credit card number is valid). The good news is we can use the data validation classes in the .NET Framework Class Library to perform all of these types of checks.

© Robert E. Beasley 2020
R. E. Beasley, *Essential ASP.NET Web Forms Development*, https://doi.org/10.1007/978-1-4842-5784-5_5

The validation operations described in this chapter can be performed on the client (as long as the browser being used is script enabled) or on the server.[1] When validation is to be performed on the client (like most of the examples in this chapter), JavaScript validation code is generated on the server, embedded in the HTML code of its associated page, returned to the client via an HTTP response, and executed in the browser. In this scenario, the Web application is much more efficient since any end-user inputs must pass browser-side validation *before* the page is posted back to the server for further processing.

In this chapter, we will begin by installing the *Script Manager* package. This package makes available the jQuery (i.e., JavaScript) scripts required for validating data using the validator classes we will be discussing. Next, we will look at the BaseValidator class. This class serves as the base class for all of the validator classes we will be discussing, so familiarity with its properties, methods, and events is important. We will then discuss the RequiredFieldValidator class, which ensures that text has been entered into a TextBox control or FileUpload control or that the text in one of these controls has been changed from some specified initial value. This class also ensures that a selection has been made from a DropDownList control, ListBox control, or RadioButtonList control or that the selection has been changed from some specified initial value. After that, we will consider the CompareValidator class. This class compares the value entered into one input control (e.g., a TextBox control) with the value entered into a second input control. This class also compares the value entered into an input control with a constant (e.g., zero) or ensures that the value entered into an input control is of a specific type (e.g., date). Next, we will look at the RangeValidator class, which ensures that the value entered into an input control (e.g., a TextBox control) lies within a range of acceptable values. We will then discuss the RegularExpressionValidator class. This class ensures that the value entered into an input control (e.g., a TextBox control) matches some predefined pattern. After that, we will consider the CustomValidator class, which ensures that the value entered into an input control (e.g., a TextBox control) passes some custom-defined validation criterion or criteria. And finally, we will look at the ValidationSummary class. This class displays a summary of all the validation errors that occur on an ASP.NET Web page.

---

[1]When a page with validation controls is posted back to the server, validation is performed on the server as well—even if all the validation operations pass on the client. This prevents the end user from bypassing validation by disabling script code execution in his or her browser.

5.2 Script Manager Package

Before the validator classes described in this chapter will work, we must add a *NuGet package* called *AspNet.ScriptManager.jQuery*. Installing this package makes available the jQuery (i.e., JavaScript) scripts required for validating data using the validator classes. If the AspNet.ScriptManager.jQuery package is not installed, an error will occur when a page attempts to validate data. To install the AspNet.ScriptManager.jQuery package

1. Open the Solution Explorer.

2. Right-click the Project.

3. Select *Manage NuGet Packages...*.

4. Search for AspNet.ScriptManager.jQuery.

5. Select *AspNet.ScriptManager.jQuery*.

6. Click *Install*.

7. Click *OK* when asked to review the changes to the project.

8. Close the NuGet Package Manager.

Once this process is complete, notice that a Scripts folder has been added to the project. This folder contains the jQuery scripts required for validating data using the validator classes.

5.3 BaseValidator Class

The BaseValidator class serves as the base class for all validator classes. As such, all validator classes inherit properties, methods, and events from this class. The Validator classes include the RequiredFieldValidator class, the CompareValidator class, the RangeValidator class, the RegularExpressionValidator class, the CustomValidator class, and the ValidationSummary class. As we consider these validator classes individually, keep in mind that multiple validation controls can be used to validate the data in a single input control. This permits us to validate an individual end-user input according to more than one criterion.

Table 5-1 shows some of the properties, methods, and events of the BaseValidator class. Notice in the table the Display property of the BaseValidator class. This property indicates the display behavior of the error message in a validation control. When this property is set to *None*, a generated validation message will not be displayed in the Web page. When the property is set to *Static*, space for a validation message will be set aside in the Web page—even if no validation message is generated. And when the property is set to *Dynamic*, space for a validation message will *not* be set aside in the Web page but will be added to the page when a validation message is generated.

Table 5-1. *Some of the properties, methods, and events of the BaseValidator class*

Class BaseValidator[2]

Namespace System.Web.UI.WebControls

Properties

ControlToValidate	Gets or sets the input control to validate.
Display	Gets or sets the display behavior of the error message in a validation control.
ErrorMessage	Gets or sets the text for the error message displayed in a ValidationSummary control when validation fails.
IsValid	Gets or sets a value that indicates whether the associated input control passes validation.
SetFocusOnError	Gets or sets a value that indicates whether focus is set to the control specified by the ControlToValidate property when validation fails.
Text	Gets or sets the text displayed in the validation control when validation fails.
ValidationGroup	Gets or sets the name of the validation group to which this validation control belongs.

Methods

(See reference.)

Events

(See reference.)

Reference

```
https://msdn.microsoft.com/en-us/library/system.web.ui.webcontrols.
basevalidator(v=vs.110).aspx
```

---

[2]All property, method, and event descriptions were taken directly from Microsoft's official documentation. The event handler methods used to handle the events of this class were omitted to conserve space. See the reference for all of the methods of this class.

5.4 RequiredFieldValidator Class

The RequiredFieldValidator class ensures that text has been entered into a TextBox control or FileUpload control or that the text in one of these controls has been changed from some specified initial value. It also ensures that a selection has been made from a DropDownList control, ListBox control, or RadioButtonList control or that the selection has been changed from some specified initial value. The InitialValue property of a RequiredFieldValidator control indicates the text or selection that we do *not* want the end user to enter into or select from an input control. Thus, an error message will be displayed when an input control contains the same value as its associated RequiredFieldValidator control's InitialValue property. By default, the initial value of a TextBox control is blank. Table 5-2 shows some of the properties, methods, and events of the RequiredFieldValidator class.

Table 5-2. *Some of the properties, methods, and events of the RequiredFieldValidator class*

Class RequiredFieldValidator[3]	
Namespace System.Web.UI.WebControls	
Properties	
InitialValue	Gets or sets the initial value of the associated input control.
Methods	
(See reference.)	
Events	
(See reference.)	
Reference	
https://msdn.microsoft.com/en-us/library/system.web.ui.webcontrols.require dfieldvalidator(v=vs.110).aspx	

---

[3]All property, method, and event descriptions were taken directly from Microsoft's official documentation. The event handler methods used to handle the events of this class were omitted to conserve space. See the reference for all of the methods of this class.

Figure 5-1 shows an example of the RequiredFieldValidator class.

Notice at 01 the RequiredFieldValidator control and its associated properties. As can be seen, the ControlToValidate property of the control is set to *txtPrice*, which identifies the TextBox control to validate. Notice that the Display property of the control is set to *Dynamic*. This indicates that space for the validation message will *not* be set aside in the Web page but will only be added to the page when the control's validation message is generated. Notice as well that the SetFocusOnError property of the control is set to *true*. Thus, when validation fails, the focus of the page will be set to the associated text box to make it easier for the end user to correct the problem. And finally, notice the Text property of the control that contains the error message that will be displayed if the validation fails.

The screenshot in the Result section of the figure shows the result of clicking the *Save* button without entering anything into the Price field on the Web page. Notice that the error message describes both the nature of the problem and what the end user must do to correct it.

ASPX CODE

```
     <asp:Label runat="server" Font-Bold="true" Text="Price" /><br />
     <asp:TextBox runat="server" ID="txtPrice" />
01   <asp:RequiredFieldValidator runat="server" ControlToValidate="txtPrice"
         Display="Dynamic" ForeColor="Red" SetFocusOnError="true"
         Text=" * Price is a required field. Please enter a price." /><br />
     <asp:Button runat="server" ID="btnSave" OnClick="btnSave_Click"
         Text="Save" />
```

RESULT

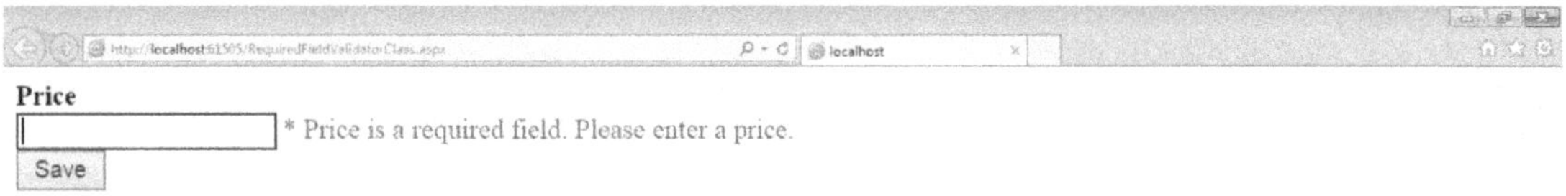

Price

| | * Price is a required field. Please enter a price.

Save

Figure 5-1. *Example of the RequiredFieldValidator class*

5.5 CompareValidator Class

The CompareValidator class compares the value entered into one input control (e.g., a TextBox control) with the value entered into a second input control. It also compares the value entered into an input control with a constant (e.g., zero) or ensures that the value entered into an input control is of a specific type (e.g., date). The ControlToCompare property of a CompareValidator control indicates the input control to be compared to the input control being validated. The Operator property indicates the *type* of comparison operation to be performed (i.e., equal to, not equal to, greater than, greater than or equal to, less than, less than or equal to, or data type check). The Type property indicates the *kind* of values being compared (i.e., currency, date, double, integer, or string). And the ValueToCompare property indicates the value to be compared to the input control being validated. A CompareValidator control displays an error message when the value in its associated input control does not pass the validation criteria specified in the Operator property of the control *and* the ControlToCompare property or the ValueToCompare property of the control. Note that if the input control associated with a CompareValidator control is left empty, no validation will occur, the validation will be considered a success, and no message will be displayed. Thus, if leaving the associated input control empty is not acceptable, we must pair up the CompareValidator control with a RequiredFieldValidator control. Table 5-3 shows some of the properties, methods, and events of the CompareValidator class.

Table 5-3. *Some of the properties, methods, and events of the CompareValidator class*

Class CompareValidator[4]

Namespace System.Web.UI.WebControls

Properties

ControlToCompare	Gets or sets the input control to compare with the input control being validated.
Operator	Gets or sets the comparison operation to perform.
Type	Gets or sets the data type that the values being compared are converted to before the comparison is made. (Inherited from BaseCompareValidator.)
ValueToCompare	Gets or sets a constant value to compare with the value entered by the user in the input control being validated.

Methods

(See reference.)

Events

(See reference.)

Reference

```
https://msdn.microsoft.com/en-us/library/system.web.ui.webcontrols.
comparevalidator(v=vs.110).aspx
```

Figure 5-2 shows an example of the CompareValidator class.

Notice at 01 the CompareValidator control and its associated properties. As can be seen, the ControlToValidate property of the control is set to *txtReorderLevel*, which identifies the TextBox control to validate. Notice that the Display property of the control is set to *Dynamic*. This indicates that space for the validation message will *not* be set aside in the Web page but will only be added to the page when the control's validation message is generated. Also notice that the SetFocusOnError property of the control is set to *true*. Thus, when validation fails, the focus of the page will be set to the associated

---

[4]All property, method, and event descriptions were taken directly from Microsoft's official documentation. The event handler methods used to handle the events of this class were omitted to conserve space. See the reference for all of the methods of this class.

text box to make it easier for the end user to correct the problem. Notice as well the Text property of the control that contains the error message that will be displayed if the validation fails. And finally, notice that the Operator property of the control is set to *GreaterThanEqual*, the Type property of the control is set to *Integer*, and the ValueToCompare property of the control is set to *0*. Thus, for validation to pass, the value in the associated text box must be greater than or equal to zero when an integer comparison is performed.

The screenshot in the Result section of the figure shows the result of clicking the *Save* button without having entered a valid value into the Reorder Level field on the Web page. Notice that the error message describes both the nature of the problem and what the end user must do to correct it.

ASPX CODE

```
    <asp:Label runat="server" Font-Bold="true" Text="Reorder Level " /><br />
    <asp:TextBox runat="server" ID="txtReorderLevel" />
01  <asp:CompareValidator runat="server" ControlToValidate="txtReorderLevel"
        Display="Dynamic" ForeColor="Red" Operator="GreaterThanEqual"
        SetFocusOnError="true" Text=" * Reorder level must be greater than or
        equal to 0. Please enter a valid reorder level." Type="Integer"
        ValueToCompare="0" /><br />
    <asp:Button runat="server" ID="btnSave" OnClick="btnSave_Click"
        Text="Save" />
```

RESULT

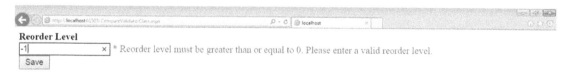

Figure 5-2. *Example of the CompareValidator class*

5.6 RangeValidator Class

The RangeValidator class ensures that the value entered into an input control (e.g., a TextBox control) lies within a range of acceptable values. The MinimumValue property of a RangeValidator control indicates the *minimum* acceptable value that can be entered into an input control. The MaximumValue property indicates the *maximum* acceptable value that can be entered into an input control. Note that the acceptable range of values is *inclusive* of the values specified in the MinimumValue property and the MaximumValue property of the RangeValidator control. The Type property indicates the *kind* of values being compared (i.e., currency, date, double, integer, or string). A RangeValidator control displays an error message when the value in its associated input control does not pass the validation criteria specified in its MinimumValue property, MaximumValue property, and Type property. Note that if the input control associated with a RangeValidator control is left empty, no validation will occur, the validation will be considered a success, and no message will be displayed. Thus, if leaving the associated input control empty is not acceptable, we must pair up the RangeValidator control with a RequiredFieldValidator control. Table 5-4 shows some of the properties, methods, and events of the RangeValidator class.

Table 5-4. *Some of the properties, methods, and events of the RangeValidator class*

Class RangeValidator[5]

Namespace System.Web.UI.WebControls

Properties

MaximumValue	Gets or sets the maximum value of the validation range.
MinimumValue	Gets or sets the minimum value of the validation range.
Type	Gets or sets the data type that the values being compared are converted to before the comparison is made. (Inherited from BaseCompareValidator.)

Methods

(See reference.)

Events

(See reference.)

Reference

```
https://msdn.microsoft.com/en-us/library/system.web.ui.webcontrols.
rangevalidator(v=vs.110).aspx
```

[5]All property, method, and event descriptions were taken directly from Microsoft's official documentation. The event handler methods used to handle the events of this class were omitted to conserve space. See the reference for all of the methods of this class.

Figure 5-3 shows an example of the RangeValidator class.

Notice at 01 the RangeValidator control and its associated properties. As can be seen, the ControlToValidate property of the control is set to *txtReorderLevel*, which identifies the TextBox control to validate. Notice that the Display property of the control is set to *Dynamic*. This indicates that space for the validation message will *not* be set aside in the Web page but will only be added to the page when the control's validation message is generated. Also notice that the SetFocusOnError property of the control is set to *true*. Thus, when validation fails, the focus of the page will be set to the associated text box to make it easier for the end user to correct the problem. Notice as well the Text property of the control that contains the error message that will be displayed if the validation fails. And finally, notice that the MinimumValue property of the control is set to *0*, the MaximumValue property of the control is set to *10*, and the Type property of the control is set to *Integer*. Thus, for validation to pass, the value in the associated text box must be an integer between 0 and 10, inclusive.

The screenshot in the Result section of the figure shows the result of clicking the Save button without having entered a valid value into the Reorder Level field on the Web page. Notice that the error message describes both the nature of the problem and what the end user must do to correct it.

ASPX CODE

```
     <asp:Label runat="server" Font-Bold="true" Text="Reorder Level" /><br />
     <asp:TextBox runat="server" ID="txtReorderLevel" />
01   <asp:RangeValidator runat="server" ControlToValidate="txtReorderLevel"
         Display="Dynamic" ForeColor="Red" MinimumValue="0" MaximumValue="10"
         SetFocusOnError="true" Text=" * Reorder level is invalid. Please enter
         a reorder level between 0 and 10." Type="Integer" /><br />
     <asp:Button runat="server" ID="btnSave" OnClick="btnSave_Click"
         Text="Save" />
```

RESULT

Figure 5-3. *Example of the RangeValidator class*

5.7 RegularExpressionValidator Class

The RegularExpressionValidator class ensures that the value entered into an input control (e.g., a TextBox control) matches a pattern defined by a regular expression. This class is helpful when we want to check an input control for a predictable sequence of characters like those found in postal codes, phone numbers, and email addresses. The ValidationExpression property of a RegularExpressionValidator control indicates the regular expression to be matched. A RegularExpressionValidator control displays an error message when the value in its associated input control does not match the pattern specified in the ValidationExpression property of the control. Note that if the input control associated with a RegularExpressionValidator control is left empty, no validation will occur, the validation will be considered a success, and no message will be displayed. Thus, if leaving the associated input control empty is not acceptable, we must pair up the RegularExpressionValidator control with a RequiredFieldValidator control. Table 5-5 shows some of the properties, methods, and events of the RegularExpressionValidator class.

Table 5-5. *Some of the properties, methods, and events of the RegularExpressionValidator class*

Class RegularExpressionValidator[6]

Namespace System.Web.UI.WebControls

Properties

ValidationExpression	Gets or sets the regular expression that determines the pattern used to validate a field.

Methods

(See reference.)

Events

(See reference.)

Reference

https://msdn.microsoft.com/en-us/library/system.web.ui.webcontrols.regular
expressionvalidator(v=vs.110).aspx

---

[6]All property, method, and event descriptions were taken directly from Microsoft's official documentation. The event handler methods used to handle the events of this class were omitted to conserve space. See the reference for all of the methods of this class.

Table 5-6 shows some of the .NET regular expressions. These expressions can be used in isolation, or they can be combined to form more complex validation expressions.

Table 5-6. *Some of the .NET regular expressions*

Expression	Description
[set]	Matches any character in the set.
[^set]	Matches any character not in the set.
[a–z]	Matches any character in the a–z range.
[^a–z]	Matches any character not in the a–z range.
\	Matches the character that follows.
\w	Matches any word character.
\W	Matches any nonword character.
\d	Matches any decimal digit.
\D	Matches any non-decimal digit.
\s	Matches any white-space character.
\S	Matches any non-white-space character.
*	Matches the preceding item 0 or more times.
+	Matches the preceding item 1 or more times.
?	Matches the preceding item 0 or 1 time.
{*n*}	Matches the preceding item exactly n times.
{*n,*}	Matches the preceding item at least n times.
{*n,m*}	Matches the preceding item n to m times.

Reference

https://msdn.microsoft.com/en-us/library/az24scfc(v=vs.110).aspx

Figure 5-4 shows an example of the RegularExpressionValidator class. Notice in the figure that the Display properties of the RegularExpressionValidator controls are set to *Dynamic.* This indicates that spaces for the validation messages will *not* be set aside in the Web page but will only be added to the page when a given control's validation message is generated. Also notice that the SetFocusOnError properties of the controls are set to *true*. Thus, when a particular validation fails, the focus of the page will be set to the associated text box to make it easier for the end user to correct the problem. Notice as well the Text properties of the controls that contain the error messages that will be displayed if a validation fails.

Notice at 01 the first RegularExpressionValidator control and its associated properties. As can be seen, the ControlToValidate property of the control is set to *txtZipCode*, which identifies the TextBox control to validate. Notice as well that the ValidationExpression property of the control is set to *\d{5}*. Thus, for validation to pass, the value in the associated text box must contain exactly five decimal digits.

Notice at 02 the second RegularExpressionValidator control and its associated properties. As can be seen, the ControlToValidate property of the control is set to *txtPhone*, which identifies the TextBox control to validate. Notice as well that the ValidationExpression property of the control is set to *\d{3}\-\d{3}\-\d{4}*. Thus, for validation to pass, the value in the associated text box must contain exactly three digits, followed by a dash, followed by exactly three digits, followed by a dash, followed by exactly four digits.

Notice at 03 the third RegularExpressionValidator control and its associated properties. As can be seen, the ControlToValidate property of the control is set to *txtEmailAddress*, which identifies the TextBox control to validate. Notice as well that the ValidationExpression property of the control is set to *\S+\@\S+\.\S+*. Thus, for validation to pass, the value in the associated text box must contain any non-white-space character (one or more times), followed by an *at* sign, followed by any non-white-space character (one or more times), followed by a period, followed by any non-white-space character (one or more times). Note that this is a relatively primitive pattern check for an email address and that more sophisticated pattern checks are possible.

Notice at 04 the fourth RegularExpressionValidator control and its associated properties. As can be seen, the ControlToValidate property of the control is set to *txtPassword*, which identifies the TextBox control to validate. Notice as well that the ValidationExpression property of the control is set to *\S{5,10}*. Thus, for validation to pass, the value in the associated text box must contain any non-white-space character (five to ten times).

The screenshot in the Result section of the figure shows the result of clicking the Save button without having entered any valid values into the fields on the Web page. Notice that all of the error messages describe both the nature of the problem and what the end user must do to correct it.

ASPX CODE

```
        <asp:Label runat="server" Font-Bold="true" Text="Customer" /><br />
        <asp:Table runat="server" >
            <asp:TableRow>
                <asp:TableCell>
                    <asp:Label runat="server" Text="Zip Code" />
                </asp:TableCell>
                <asp:TableCell>
                    <asp:TextBox runat="server" ID="txtZipCode" />
01                  <asp:RegularExpressionValidator runat="server"
                        ControlToValidate="txtZipCode" Display="Dynamic"
                        ForeColor="Red" SetFocusOnError="true"
                        Text=" * Zip code is invalid. Please
                        enter a zip code of the form: #####."
                        ValidationExpression="\d{5}" />
                </asp:TableCell>
            </asp:TableRow>
            <asp:TableRow>
                <asp:TableCell>
                    <asp:Label runat="server" Text="Phone" />
                </asp:TableCell>
                <asp:TableCell>
                    <asp:TextBox runat="server" ID="txtPhone" />
02                  <asp:RegularExpressionValidator runat="server"
                        ControlToValidate="txtPhone" Display="Dynamic"
                        ForeColor="Red" SetFocusOnError="true"
                        Text=" * Phone number is invalid. Please
                        enter a phone number of the form: ###-###-####."
                        ValidationExpression="\d{3}\-\d{3}\-\d{4}" />
                </asp:TableCell>
            </asp:TableRow>
            <asp:TableRow>
                <asp:TableCell>
                    <asp:Label runat="server" Text="Email Address" />
                </asp:TableCell>
                <asp:TableCell>
                    <asp:TextBox runat="server" ID="txtEmailAddress" />
03                  <asp:RegularExpressionValidator runat="server"
                        ControlToValidate="txtEmailAddress" Display="Dynamic"
                        ForeColor="Red" SetFocusOnError="true"
                        Text=" * Email address is invalid. Please
                        enter an email address of the form: xxx@yyy.zzz."
                        ValidationExpression="\S+\@\S+\.\S+" />
```

Figure 5-4. *Example of the RegularExpressionValidator class*

```
                    </asp:TableCell>
            </asp:TableRow>
            <asp:TableRow>
                <asp:TableCell>
                    <asp:Label runat="server" Text="Password" />
                </asp:TableCell>
                <asp:TableCell>
                    <asp:TextBox runat="server" ID="txtPassword" />
04                  <asp:RegularExpressionValidator runat="server"
                        ControlToValidate="txtPassword" Display="Dynamic"
                        ForeColor="Red" SetFocusOnError="true"
                        Text=" * Password is invalid. Please
                        enter a password between 5 and 10 characters in length."
                        ValidationExpression="\S{5,10}" />
                </asp:TableCell>
            </asp:TableRow>
        </asp:Table>
        <asp:Button runat="server" ID="btnSave" OnClick="btnSave_Click"
            Text="Save" />
```

RESULT

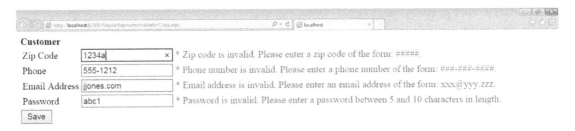

Figure 5-4. *(continued)*

5.8 CustomValidator Class

The CustomValidator class ensures that the value entered into an input control (e.g., a TextBox control) passes some custom-defined validation criterion or criteria. This class is helpful when none of the other validation controls meet our needs. We can define a CustomValidator control that executes on the *client* by writing JavaScript code in our .aspx file, or we can define a CustomValidator control that executes on the *server* by writing C# code in our code behind file.[7] The former is useful when we want to perform the validation on an input control *before* permitting the page to post back to the server.

---

[7]We will learn about JavaScript later in this book.

The latter is useful when we want to perform the validation on an input control *when* the page is posted back to the server, such as when we need to perform a database lookup for the validation. The ClientValidationFunction property of a CustomValidator control indicates the name of the JavaScript function used to perform a *client-side validation*. The ServerValidate method contains the C# validation code used to perform a *server-side validation*. A CustomValidator control displays an error message when the value in its associated input control does not pass the custom-defined validation criterion or criteria. Note that if the input control associated with a CustomValidator control is left empty, no validation will occur, the validation will be considered a success, and no message will be displayed. Thus, if leaving the associated input control empty is not acceptable, we must pair up the CustomValidator control with a RequiredFieldValidator control. Table 5-7 shows some of the properties, methods, and events of the CustomValidator class.

Table 5-7. *Some of the properties, methods, and events of the CustomValidator class*

Class CustomValidator[8]	
Namespace System.Web.UI.WebControls	
Properties	
ClientValidationFunction	Gets or sets the name of the custom client-side script function used for validation.
ValidateEmptyText	Gets or sets a Boolean value indicating whether empty text should be validated.
Methods	
(See reference.)	
Events	
ServerValidate	Occurs when validation is performed on the server.
Reference	
https://msdn.microsoft.com/en-us/library/system.web.ui.webcontrols.customvalidator(v=vs.110).aspx	

---

[8]All property, method, and event descriptions were taken directly from Microsoft's official documentation. The event handler methods used to handle the events of this class were omitted to conserve space. See the reference for all of the methods of this class.

Figure 5-5 shows an example of the CustomValidator class.

Notice at 01 the CustomValidator control and its associated properties. As can be seen, the ID property of the control is set to *cuvCategory*. We must give this control an ID since we will be referring to it in the code behind. We can also see that the ControlToValidate property of the control is set to *txtCategory*, which identifies the TextBox control to validate. Notice that the Display property of the control is set to *Dynamic*. This indicates that space for the validation message will *not* be set aside in the Web page but will only be added to the page when the control's validation message is generated. Also notice that the OnServerValidate property of the control is set to cuvCategory_ServerValidate, which is the name of the event handler method that will be executed when the ServerValidate event is raised. Notice as well that the SetFocusOnError property of the control is set to *true*. Thus, when validation fails, the focus of the page will be set to the associated text box to make it easier for the end user to correct the problem. And finally, notice the Text property of the control that contains the error message that will be displayed if the validation fails.

Notice at 02 the validation event handler method that will be executed when the page is posted back to the server. Notice as well the ServerValidateEventArgs object (and its alias args) that is passed to this event handler method as a parameter. This object provides data for the ServerValidate event handler method. It is the Value property of the ServerValidateEventArgs object that contains the string passed from the input control to validate, and it is the IsValid property of the ServerValidateEventArgs object that is set to indicate the result of the validation.

Notice at 03 that we are testing the Value property of the ServerValidateEventArgs object for a valid input value—*Clothing*, *Footwear*, or *Accessories*. If the input value is one of these, the IsValid property of the ServerValidateEventArgs object will be set to *true*, and the error message will not be displayed. If the input value is not one of these, the IsValid property of the ServerValidateEventArgs object will be set to *false*, and the error message will be displayed.

The screenshot in the Result section of the figure shows the result of clicking the Save button without having entered a valid value into the Category field on the Web page. Notice that the error message describes both the nature of the problem and what the end user must do to correct it.

ASPX CODE

```
    <asp:Label runat="server" Font-Bold="true" Text="Category" /><br />
    <asp:TextBox runat="server" ID="txtCategory" />
01  <asp:CustomValidator runat="server" ID="cuvCategory"
        ControlToValidate="txtCategory" Display="Dynamic" ForeColor="Red"
        OnServerValidate="cuvCategory_ServerValidate" SetFocusOnError="true"
        Text=" * Category is invalid. Please enter Clothing, Footwear, or
        Accessories." /><br />
    <asp:Button runat="server" ID="btnSave" OnClick="btnSave_Click"
        Text="Save" />
```

CODE BEHIND

```
02  protected void cuvCategory_ServerValidate(object source,
        ServerValidateEventArgs args)
    {

03      if(args.Value == "Clothing" | args.Value == "Footwear" |
            args.Value == "Accessories")
        {
            args.IsValid = true;
        }
        else
        {
            args.IsValid = false;
        }

    }
```

RESULT

Category
Footw   × | * Category is invalid. Please enter Clothing, Footwear, or Accessories.
Save

Figure 5-5. *Example of the CustomValidator class*

5.9 ValidationSummary Class

The ValidationSummary class displays a summary of the validation errors that occur on a Web page. A ValidationSummary control can display validation errors in the page itself, or it can display validation errors in a separate message box.[9] A ValidationSummary control is helpful when we want to display all validation errors in one location. The DisplayMode

---

[9]It can display validation errors in both as well.

property of a ValidationSummary control indicates whether the validation summary is to be displayed in the form of a list, a bulleted list, or a paragraph. The HeaderText property indicates the text to be displayed at the top of the validation summary. The ShowMessageBox property indicates whether or not the validation summary is to be displayed in a message box that is separate from the page itself. The ShowSummary property indicates whether or not the validation summary is to be displayed in the page itself. The ShowValidationErrors property indicates whether the validation summary is to be displayed or not displayed. And the ValidationGroup property indicates the group of controls associated with the validation summary. This property permits us to associate one group of validation controls with one validation summary and another group of validation controls with another validation summary. Table 5-8 shows some of the properties, methods, and events of the ValidationSummary class.

Table 5-8. *Some of the properties, methods, and events of the ValidationSummary class*

Class ValidationSummary[10]

Namespace System.Web.UI.WebControls

Properties

DisplayMode	Gets or sets the display mode of the validation summary.
HeaderText	Gets or sets the header text displayed at the top of the summary.
ShowMessageBox	Gets or sets a value indicating whether the validation summary is displayed in a message box.
ShowSummary	Gets or sets a value indicating whether the validation summary is displayed inline.
ShowValidationErrors	Gets or sets a value that specifies whether the validation summary from validator controls should be displayed.
ValidationGroup	Gets or sets the group of controls for which the ValidationSummary object displays validation messages.

(continued)

---

[10]All property, method, and event descriptions were taken directly from Microsoft's official documentation. The event handler methods used to handle the events of this class were omitted to conserve space. See the reference for all of the methods of this class.

Table 5-8. (*continued*)

Methods

(See reference.)

Events

(See reference.)

Reference

`https://msdn.microsoft.com/en-us/library/system.web.ui.webcontrols.`
`validationsummary(v=vs.110).aspx`

Figure 5-6 shows an example of the ValidationSummary class.

Notice at 01 that the ErrorMessage property *and* the Text property of the RequiredFieldValidator control have been set. The ErrorMessage property indicates the message that is to be displayed in the ValidationSummary control, whereas the Text property indicates the message that is to be displayed in the RequiredFieldValidator control itself. Thus, when a validation error occurs, the error message will be displayed in the validation summary, and the asterisk (*) will be displayed directly next the zip code text box. This pattern holds true for the validator controls at 02, 03, and 04 as well.

Notice at 05 the ValidationSummary control and its associated properties. As can be seen, the DisplayMode property of the control is set to *BulletedList*, the HeaderText property contains information about what has occurred and what should be done, the ShowMessageBox property is set to *false*, and the ShowSummary property is set to *true*.

The first screenshot in the Result section of the figure shows the result of clicking the Save button without having entered valid values into the fields on the Web page. In this example, the ShowMessageBox property of the control is set to *false*, and the ShowSummary property is set to *true*. Thus, the validation summary is displayed in the page itself. The second screenshot also shows the result of clicking the Save button without having entered valid values into the fields on the Web page. In this example, the ShowMessageBox property of the control is set to *true*, and the ShowSummary property is set to *false*. Thus, the validation summary is displayed in a message box that is separate from the page.[11] Notice that the error messages in the screenshots describe both the nature of the problems on the page and what the end user must do to correct them.

---

[11]When data is validated in the code behind (e.g., when using a CustomValidator control to perform data validation on the server), errors cannot be displayed in a message box since message boxes are displayed in the client via JavaScript. However, they can be displayed in the page itself.

119

ASPX CODE

```
<asp:Label runat="server" Font-Bold="true" Text="Customer" /><br />
<asp:Table runat="server" >
    <asp:TableRow>
        <asp:TableCell>
            <asp:Label runat="server" Text="Zip Code" />
        </asp:TableCell>
        <asp:TableCell>
            <asp:TextBox runat="server" ID="txtZipCode" />
01          <asp:RequiredFieldValidator runat="server"
                ControlToValidate="txtZipCode" Display="Dynamic"
                ErrorMessage="Zip code is a required field. Please enter
                a zip code." ForeColor="Red" SetFocusOnError="true"
                Text=" *" />
02          <asp:RegularExpressionValidator runat="server"
                ControlToValidate="txtZipCode" Display="Dynamic"
                ErrorMessage="Zip code is invalid. Please enter a zip
                code of the form: #####." ForeColor="Red"
                SetFocusOnError="true" Text=" *"
                ValidationExpression="\d{5}" />
        </asp:TableCell>
    </asp:TableRow>
    <asp:TableRow>
        <asp:TableCell>
            <asp:Label runat="server" Text="Phone" />
        </asp:TableCell>
        <asp:TableCell>
            <asp:TextBox runat="server" ID="txtPhone" />
03          <asp:RequiredFieldValidator runat="server"
                ControlToValidate="txtPhone" Display="Dynamic"
                ErrorMessage="Phone number is a required field. Please
                enter a phone number." ForeColor="Red"
                SetFocusOnError="true" Text=" *" />
04          <asp:RegularExpressionValidator runat="server"
                ControlToValidate="txtPhone" Display="Dynamic"
                ErrorMessage="Phone number is invalid. Please enter a
                phone number of the form: ###-###-####." ForeColor="Red"
                SetFocusOnError="true" Text=" *"
                ValidationExpression="\d{3}\-\d{3}\-\d{4}" />
```

Figure 5-6. *Example of the ValidationSummary class*

```
            </asp:TableCell>
        </asp:TableRow>
    </asp:Table>
    <asp:Button runat="server" ID="btnSave" OnClick="btnSave_Click"
        Text="Save" /><br /><br />
05  <asp:ValidationSummary runat="server" DisplayMode="BulletList"
        ForeColor="Red" HeaderText="The following errors have occurred on
        this page. Please correct them." ShowMessageBox="false"
        ShowSummary="true" />
```

RESULT

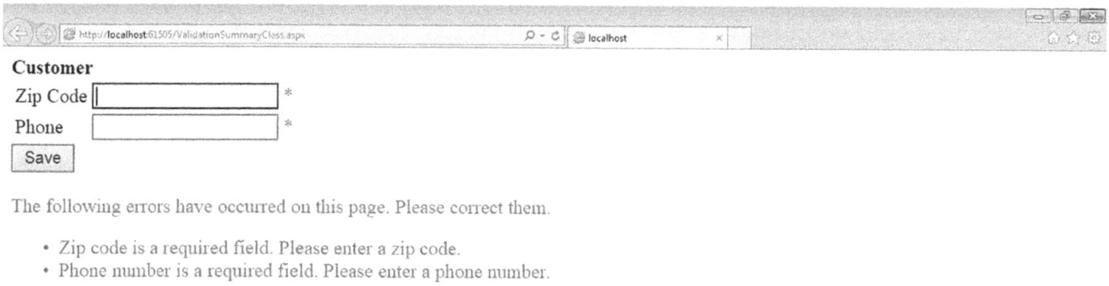

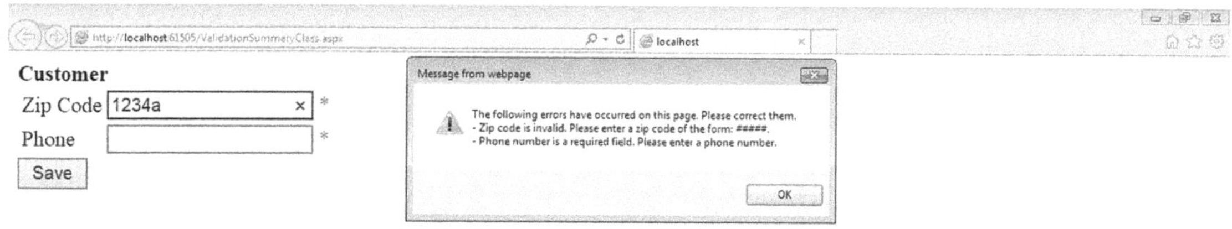

Figure 5-6. *(continued)*

PART III

C# Programming

CHAPTER 6

Assignment Operations

6.1 Introduction

An assignment operation sets the value of a variable, constant, or other item in the code behind of a Page class. The assignment statement is so fundamental to computer programming that every procedural/imperative programming language requires such a statement—regardless of its syntax. The general syntax of an assignment statement in the C# programming language is

```
Operand1 Operator Operand2;
```

where Operand1 is a variable, constant, or other item, Operator is an equal sign (=) or other assignment operator, and Operand2 is the value (or the result of an expression) to be assigned to Operand1.

In this chapter, we will begin by looking at types. A type holds either a value or a pointer to a memory address. We will then describe how to declare variables and constants in the C# programming language. Next, we will discuss the different types of assignment operators—simple and compound—and how they are used. After that, we will look at enumerations, which provide us with a way to declare and use related constants that can be assigned to variables in the code behind. And finally, we will discuss exception handling. Exception handling provides us with a way to catch runtime errors in our code and handle them gracefully.

6.2 Types

In the .NET Framework, there are two important *types*—*value types* and *reference types*. A value type holds a *value* (not a pointer to another memory address) that has a set memory allocation size. For example, a Byte variable is a value type that is allocated exactly one byte in memory and can contain any positive integer between 0 and 255. A reference type, on

R. E. Beasley, *Essential ASP.NET Web Forms Development*, https://doi.org/10.1007/978-1-4842-5784-5_6

the other hand, holds a *pointer* to another memory address (not a value) that does *not* have a set memory allocation size. For example, a String variable is a reference type that can be allocated a different amount of memory depending on the contents of the string.

Table 6-1 shows the some of the types of the .NET Framework and their equivalent generic C# types and code prefixes. In this book, our standard will be to use the .NET type form (e.g., Boolean, Int16, String) as opposed to the generic C# type form (e.g., bool, short, string) when declaring program variables and constants—even though the corresponding types are equivalent. In addition, our standard will be to start all variables and constants with the three-letter prefixes shown in the table. Keep in mind that these particular standards are not universal across all software development organizations. However, the adoption of such standards is essential to good code quality.

Notice that all of the types in the table are value types, except for the String type, which is a reference type. As can be seen, the String type is described as *immutable* (i.e., unchangeable) and *fixed length*. This is because the result of modifying a string in C# is the creation of a *new* string in memory—not the modification of an existing one. The maximum size of a String type is about one billion characters. The String type is also described as a string of *Unicode characters*. The String type represents text as a sequence of *UTF-16* (16-bit Unicode Transformation Format) *code units*, where a code unit is two bytes. The UTF-16 uses one *or* two code units to represent up to 1,114,112 possible Unicode *code points*, where a code point is a sequence of bits (i.e., 16 bits *or* 32 bits) that represents a Unicode character. Although a full discussion of UTF-16 is beyond the scope of this book, the important thing to remember is that *some* Unicode characters are represented using 16 bits, whereas *other* Unicode characters are represented using 32 bits. For example, the Unicode character "A" is represented using the bit pattern

```
0000000001000001 (i.e., hexadecimal 0041)
```

Thus, the English letter "A" requires *one* 16-bit code unit. In fact, all of the characters that make up the English language are represented in one 16-bit code unit and are referenced by one Char object.

The Unicode character "𓃱", on the other hand, is represented using the bit pattern

```
00000000000000010011000011100001 (i.e., hexadecimal 000130E1 surrogate pair)
```

Thus, the Egyptian hieroglyph "𓃱" requires *two* 16-bit code units. Since UTF-16 encoding has only 16 bits, characters that require more than 16 bits are represented using UTF-16 *surrogate pairs*, like that shown in the preceding text. So, we must keep in mind that a single Unicode character might need to be referenced by more than one Char object. Keep in mind that new characters are being added to the Unicode character set all the time, so the Unicode character set should be seen as a work in progress.

Table 6-1. *Some of the types of the .NET Framework and their equivalent generic C# types and code prefixes*

.NET Type	C# Type	Prefix	Description
Boolean	bool	boo	A Boolean value (true or false).
Byte	byte	byt	An 8-bit unsigned integer.
Char	char	cha	A Unicode (16-bit) character.
Decimal	decimal	dec	A decimal (128-bit) value.
Double	double	dbl	A double-precision (64-bit) floating-point number.
Int16	short	i16	A 16-bit signed integer.
Int32	int	i32	A 32-bit signed integer.
Int64	long	i64	A 64-bit signed integer.
SByte	sbyte	sby	An 8-bit signed integer.
Single	float	sin	A single-precision (32-bit) floating-point number.
String	string	str	An immutable, fixed-length string of Unicode characters.
UInt16	ushort	u16	A 16-bit unsigned integer.
UInt32	uint	u32	A 32-bit unsigned integer.
UInt64	ulong	u64	A 64-bit unsigned integer.

6.3 Variable Declarations

To declare a variable in the C# programming language, we define its type (e.g., Boolean, Int16, String) and then give it a name according to the identifier naming standards discussed earlier. We can also give the variable an initial value—as long as that value lies within the *domain* of allowed values for its type. In some programming languages, the value of a variable *is not* automatically set to a default value when the variable is declared. In C#, however, the value of a variable *is* automatically set to a default value when the variable is declared. Thus, if a variable's default value is logically correct already (i.e., the variable's value need not be initialized to something else), there is no need to explicitly state the initial value of the variable in the variable's declaration. However, it is often useful to explicitly state the initial value of the variable in the variable's declaration to improve the clarity of the code—just in case the default initial value of the variable is unclear. So, while it might be *unnecessary* to do so, we will usually assign a default value to a variable when we declare it. Table 6-2 shows some of the .NET types and their respective domains and default values.

Table 6-2. *Some of the .NET types and their respective domains and default values*

.NET Type	Domain	Default Value
Boolean	0 (false) and 1 (true)	0 (false)
Byte	0 to 255	0
Char	Any Unicode symbol used in text	'\0'
Decimal	$\pm 1.0 \times 10e{-}28$ to $\pm 7.9 \times 10e28$	0.0m
Double	$-1.79769313486232e308$ to 1.79769313486232e308	0.0d
Int16	$-32{,}768$ to 32,767	0
Int32	$-2{,}147{,}483{,}648$ to 2,147,483,647	0
Int64	$-9{,}223{,}372{,}036{,}854{,}775{,}808$ to 9,223,372,036,854,775,807	0l
SByte	-128 to 127	0
Single	$-3.402823e38$ to 3.402823e38	0.0f
String	0 to 1,073,741,824 characters	null
UInt16	0 to 65,535	0
UInt32	0 to 4,294,967,295	0
UInt64	0 to 18,446,744,073,709,551,615	0

CODE BEHIND

```
// Declare Booleans.
Boolean booPreferredCustomer = true;
Boolean booOrderShipped = false;
```

Figure 6-1. *Examples of Boolean declarations*

Figure 6-1 shows some examples of Boolean declarations.

Figure 6-2 shows some examples of character declarations. Note that a Char is treated as an array where individual characters are accessible via an index.

CODE BEHIND

```
// Declare characters.
Char[] chaZipCode = new Char[] { '4', '6', '1', '3', '1' };
Char[] chaPrice = new Char[] { '$', '1', '9', '9', '.', '0', '0' };
```

Figure 6-2. *Examples of character declarations*

Figure 6-3 shows some examples of string declarations

CODE BEHIND

```
// Declare strings.
String strSupplier = "";
String strProduct = "Babolat Pure Aero French Open";
```

Figure 6-3. *Examples of string declarations*

Figure 6-4 shows some examples of numeric declarations. The variables assigned negative numbers in these examples illustrate that their types can accommodate signs.

CODE BEHIND

```
// Declare numbers.
Byte bytNumber = 10;
Decimal decNumber = -10.00m;
Double dblNumber = -10.00;
Int16 i16Number = -10;
Int32 i32Number = -10;
Int64 i64Number = -10;
SByte sbyNumber = -10;
Single sinNumber = -10.12345f;
UInt16 u16Number = 10;
UInt32 u32Number = 10;
UInt64 u64Number = 10;
```

Figure 6-4. *Examples of numeric declarations*

6.4 Constant Declarations

A constant is a fixed value that *cannot* be modified during the execution of a program.
A constant can be a value type (e.g., Byte, Decimal, Int32), or it can be a reference type
(e.g., String). The fixed value that a constant takes on is called a *literal* (e.g., 31, 0.07m,
"Last Name:"). To declare a constant in the C# programming language, we specify the
word *const*, define its type, and then give it a name according to the identifier naming
standards discussed earlier in this book. Next, we assign the constant a literal value. We
can assign a constant any value—as long as it lies within the domain of allowed values
for its type. Figure 6-5 shows some examples of constant declarations.

CODE BEHIND

```
// Declare constants.
const Byte bytDaysInJanuary = 31;
const Decimal decSalesTaxRate = 0.07m;
const String strLastNameLabel = "Last Name:";
```

Figure 6-5. *Examples of constant declarations*

6.5 Assignment Operators

An assignment operator assigns a value to a variable, constant (upon declaration only),
or other item in the C# programming language. Recall from earlier that the general
syntax of an assignment statement in C# is

```
Operand1 Operator Operand2;
```

where Operand1 is a variable, constant, or other item, Operator is an equal sign (=) or other assignment operator, and Operand2 is the value (or the result of an expression) to be assigned to Operand1.

There are two kinds of assignment operators—*simple assignment operators* and *compound assignment operators*. A simple assignment operator just stores in Operand1 the value of Operand2. A compound assignment operator, on the other hand, stores in Operand1 the value of Operand2 *after* some kind of arithmetic or logical operation occurs. Table 6-3 shows some commonly used assignment operators, where Operand1 is x and Operand2 is y. Notice that all of the assignment operators in the table are compound assignment operators, except the first one, which is a simple assignment operator. Also, notice the equivalent compound assignment statements in the comments.

Table 6-3. *Some commonly used assignment operators, where Operand1 is x and Operand2 is y*

Operator	Type	Comment
x = y	Simple assignment	
x += y	Compound assignment	Equivalent to x = x + y.
x -= y	Compound assignment	Equivalent to x = x - y.
x *= y	Compound assignment	Equivalent to x = x * y.
x /= y	Compound assignment	Equivalent to x = x / y.
x %= y	Compound assignment	Equivalent to x = x % y.

Figure 6-6 shows some examples of simple and compound assignment operators.

CODE BEHIND

```
// Declare the variables.
Double dblNumber1 = 0;
Double dblNumber2 = 0;

// This is a simple numeric assignment statement.
dblNumber1 = 3;
dblNumber2 = 7;
dblNumber1 = dblNumber2;
// dblNumber1 = 7

// This is a compound numeric assignment statement that is
// equivalent to dblNumber1 = dblNumber1 + dblNumber2.
dblNumber1 = 3;
dblNumber2 = 7;
dblNumber1 += dblNumber2;
// dblNumber1 = 10

// This is a compound numeric assignment statement that is
// equivalent to dblNumber1 = dblNumber1 - dblNumber2.
dblNumber1 = 3;
dblNumber2 = 7;
dblNumber1 -= dblNumber2;
// dblNumber1 = -4

// This is a compound numeric assignment statement that is
// equivalent to dblNumber1 = dblNumber1 * dblNumber2.
dblNumber1 = 3;
dblNumber2 = 7;
dblNumber1 *= dblNumber2;
// dblNumber1 = 21

// This is a compound numeric assignment statement that is
// equivalent to dblNumber1 = dblNumber1 / dblNumber2.
dblNumber1 = 3;
dblNumber2 = 7;
dblNumber1 /= dblNumber2;
// dblNumber1 = 0.42857142857142855

// This is a compound numeric assignment statement that is
// equivalent to dblNumber1 = dblNumber1 % dblNumber2.
dblNumber1 = 3;
dblNumber2 = 7;
dblNumber1 %= dblNumber2;
// dblNumber1 = 3
```

Figure 6-6. *Examples of simple and compound assignment operators*

6.6 Enumerations

An enumeration is a set of *named* constants of a specific type. In the .NET Framework, the Enum class serves as the base class for all enumerations. Enumerations provide a way to declare and use a set of *related* constants that can be assigned to a variable in the code behind. For example, since there are only seven days in a week, where Sunday is day 1, Monday is day 2, and so forth, we can create a DayOfWeek enumeration of type Byte (Int32 is the default Enum type) that permits us to access the *value* of a named (i.e., spelled out) day of the week in the code behind. Figure 6-7 shows an example of an enumeration. In this example, we have a DiscountRate enumeration with three named constants—Standard, Select, and Preferred. Each of these constants refers to a type of customer, and each has a specific discount rate value.

Notice at 01 that the enumeration is declared using the enum keyword, the name of the enumeration is DiscountRate, and the type of enumeration is Byte. Thus, the *literals* associated with each named constant will be of type Byte.

Notice at 02 that we are setting the value of bytCustomerDiscountRate to the value of DiscountRate.Preferred, which we know is *30*. As can be seen, we must *cast* DiscountRate.Preferred to a Byte type even though bytCustomerDiscountRate is already declared as a Byte type. Casting will be discussed in detail in Chapter 7, titled "Conversion Operations."

Notice at 03 that we are setting the value of strCustomerType to DiscountRate. Preferred, which is *Preferred*. As can be seen, the value of DiscountRate.Preferred must be converted to a string before it can be assigned to strCustomerType.

```
CODE BEHIND

01   enum DiscountRate : Byte
     {

          Standard = 10,
          Select = 20,
          Preferred = 30

     }

     protected void Enumerations()
     {

02        Byte bytCustomerDiscountRate = (Byte)DiscountRate.Preferred;
          // bytCustomerDiscountRate = 30

03        String strCustomerType = DiscountRate.Preferred.ToString();
          // strCustomerType = "Preferred"

     }
```

Figure 6-7. *Example of an enumeration*

6.7 Exception Handling

An *exception* occurs in response to a *runtime error*—an error that arises during the execution of a computer program. In C#, *exception handling* permits us to detect these errors and handle them gracefully. The advantage of exception handling is that our Web applications don't crash (i.e., abnormally terminate) when a runtime error occurs but instead behave in a predictable and professional way. When an exception occurs during the execution of a Web application, the .NET Common Language Runtime *throws* an exception of a specified type (e.g., a divide by zero exception, an overflow exception). When testing code in Visual Studio, an exception will result in the display of the *Exception Helper*, which points out the nature of the runtime error for us.

Figure 6-8 shows an example of the Exception Helper. Notice at the very top of the Exception Helper dialog that an exception was thrown that was not handled by us in the code. Notice as well that the type of exception that occurred was a divide by zero exception.

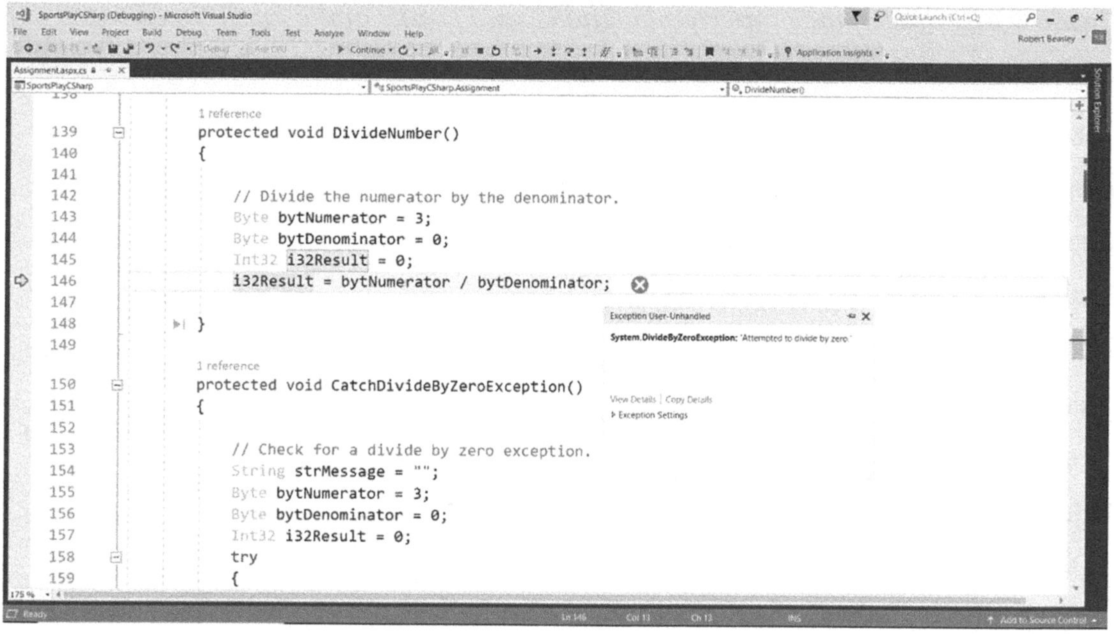

Figure 6-8. *Example of the Exception Helper*

6.8 Exception Class

The Exception class serves as the base class for all exception classes. Table 6-4 shows some of the properties, methods, and events of the Exception class. Notice the Message property in the class. As we will soon see, this property contains the description of a runtime error that has occurred during program execution.

Table 6-4. *Some of the properties, methods, and events of the Exception class*

Class Exception[1]

Namespace System

Properties

Message   Gets a message that describes the current exception.

Methods

(See reference.)

Events

(See reference.)

Reference

`https://msdn.microsoft.com/en-us/library/system.exception(v=vs.113).aspx`

There are currently over 20 exceptions that the .NET Common Language Runtime can throw and that we can handle using the Exception class and its child classes. Table 6-5 shows some common exceptions and the conditions under which they are thrown.

Table 6-5. *Some common exceptions and the conditions under which they are thrown*

Exception	Condition
DivideByZeroException	The denominator in an integer or decimal division operation is zero.
FormatException	A value is not in an appropriate format to be converted from a string by a conversion method such as Parse.
IndexOutOfRangeException	An index is outside the bounds of an array or collection.
OverflowException	An arithmetic, casting, or conversion operation results in an overflow.

---

[1]All property, method, and event descriptions were taken directly from Microsoft's official documentation. The event handler methods used to handle the events of this class were omitted to conserve space. See the reference for all of the methods of this class.

As we will see, exception handling is accomplished via the *Try-Catch-Finally structure*. In the Try part of the structure, we code the statement or statements that can potentially cause an exception in our program. In the Catch part of the structure, we specify what to do if an exception is actually thrown. And in the Finally part of the structure, we specify what to do *whether or not* an exception is thrown. The Finally part of the Try-Catch-Finally structure is optional.

6.8.1 DivideByZeroException Class

As the name implies, a *divide by zero exception* is thrown when we attempt to perform an integer or decimal division operation with a zero in the denominator of a mathematical expression. Figure 6-9 shows an example of using the DivideByZeroException class to catch a divide by zero exception.

Notice at 01 that bytDenominator has been set to *0* to set up our divide by zero exception.

Notice at 02 the Try part of the Try-Catch-Finally structure, which contains the assignment statement that will be tested for a divide by zero exception. If a divide by zero exception is not thrown, processing will continue after the division, and the message will be set to *The division was successful.*

Notice at 03 the Catch part of the Try-Catch-Finally structure. This part of the structure contains a DivideByZeroException object. We have given this object the alias "Exception" so that we can refer to the object in shorthand. As can be seen, if a divide by zero exception is thrown, the message will be set to *The division was NOT successful.* In addition, the Message property of the Exception object, which describes the current exception, will be appended to the end of the message.

Notice at 04 the Finally part of the Try-Catch-Finally structure. The code inside this part of the structure will be executed whether or not an exception is thrown. Thus, the message will always end with *Thank you.* The result of the Try-Catch-Finally code is shown at the bottom of the figure. Notice that a divide by zero exception has been thrown since we cannot perform integer or decimal division with a zero in the denominator of a mathematical expression.

CODE BEHIND

```
    // Check for a divide by zero exception.
    String strMessage = "";
    Byte bytNumerator = 3;
01  Byte bytDenominator = 0;
    Int32 i32Result = 0;
02  try
    {
        i32Result = bytNumerator / bytDenominator;
        strMessage = "The division was successful.";
    }
03  catch (DivideByZeroException Exception)
    {
        strMessage = "The division was NOT successful. " + Exception.Message;
    }
04  finally
    {
        strMessage = strMessage + " Thank you.";
    }
    // strMessage = "The division was NOT successful. Attempted to
    // divide by zero. Thank you."
```

Figure 6-9. *Example of using the DivideByZeroException class to catch a divide by zero exception*

6.8.2 FormatException Class

A *format exception* is thrown when we attempt to convert a string value that is not in an appropriate format to be converted to some other type (e.g., Boolean, Decimal, Int32). Figure 6-10 shows an example of using the FormatException class to catch a format exception.

Notice at 01 that txtNumber.Text (presumably entered by the end user via a TextBox control) has been set to *abc* to set up our format exception.

Notice at 02 the Try part of the Try-Catch-Finally structure, which contains the assignment statement that will be tested for a format exception. If a format exception is not thrown, processing will continue after the conversion, and the message will be set to *The conversion was successful.*

Notice at 03 the Catch part of the Try-Catch-Finally structure. This part of the structure contains a FormatException object. We have given this object the alias "Exception" so that we can refer to the object in shorthand. As can be seen, if a format exception is thrown, the message will be set to *The conversion was NOT successful*. In addition, the Message property of the Exception object, which describes the current exception, will be appended to the end of the message.

Notice at 04 the Finally part of the Try-Catch-Finally structure. The code inside this part of the structure will be executed whether or not an exception is thrown. Thus, the message will always end with *Thank you*. The result of the Try-Catch-Finally code is shown at the bottom of the figure. Notice that a format exception has been thrown since we cannot convert a String type to a Byte type.

```
CODE BEHIND

    // Check for a format exception.
    String strMessage = "";
01  txtNumber.Text = "abc";
02  try
    {
        Byte bytNumber = Convert.ToByte(txtNumber.Text);
        strMessage = "The conversion was successful.";
    }
03  catch (FormatException Exception)
    {
        strMessage = "The conversion was NOT successful. " +
            Exception.Message;
    }
04  finally
    {
        strMessage = strMessage + " Thank you.";
    }
    // strMessage = "The conversion was NOT successful. Input string was
    // not in a correct format. Thank you."
```

Figure 6-10. *Example of using the FormatException class to catch a format exception*

6.8.3 IndexOutOfRangeException Class

An *index out of range exception* is thrown when we attempt to reference an item that is not within the bounds of an array or collection. We will learn more about arrays and collections later in this book. Figure 6-11 shows an example of using the IndexOutOfRangeException class to catch an index out of range exception.

Notice at 01 that an array of strings called strNameArray has been declared that contains three elements. The element at index 0 contains *Bill*, the element at index 1 contains *Mary*, and the element at index 2 contains *Steve*.

Notice at 02 the Try part of the Try-Catch-Finally structure, which contains the assignment statement that will be tested for an index out of range exception. If an index out of range exception is not thrown, processing will continue after the lookup, and the message will be set to *The lookup was successful.*

Notice at 03 the Catch part of the Try-Catch-Finally structure. This part of the structure contains an IndexOutOfRangeException object. We have given this object the alias "Exception" so that we can refer to the object in shorthand. As can be seen, if an index out of range exception is thrown, the message will be set to *The lookup was NOT successful.* In addition, the Message property of the Exception object, which describes the current exception, will be appended to the end of the message.

Notice at 04 the Finally part of the Try-Catch-Finally structure. The code inside this part of the structure will be executed whether or not an exception is thrown. Thus, the message will always end with *Thank you.* The result of the Try-Catch-Finally code is shown at the bottom of the figure. Notice that an index out of range exception has been thrown since we cannot refer to an array element at index 5 when the only valid indexes are 0, 1, and 2.

```
CODE BEHIND

     // Check for an index out of range exception.
     String strMessage = "";
01   String[] strNameArray = new String[] { "Bill", "Mary", "Steve" };
02   try
     {
         String strName = strNameArray[5];
         strMessage = "The lookup was successful.";
     }
03   catch (IndexOutOfRangeException Exception)
     {
         strMessage = "The lookup was NOT successful. " + Exception.Message;
     }
04   finally
     {
         strMessage = strMessage + " Thank you.";
     }
     // strMessage = "The lookup was NOT successful. Index was outside the
     // bounds of the array. Thank you."
```

Figure 6-11. *Example of using the IndexOutOfRangeException class to catch an index out of range exception*

6.8.4 OverflowException Class

An *overflow exception* is thrown when we attempt to perform an arithmetic, casting, or conversion operation that results in a value that is too large or too small to fit into the assigned variable. Figure 6-12 shows an example of using the OverflowException class to catch an overflow exception.

Notice at 01 that i32Number has been set to *256* to set up our overflow exception. An overflow exception will be thrown in this scenario because 256 is *too large* to fit into a variable of type Byte (i.e., an 8-bit unsigned integer). Note that if we set i32Number to -12, an overflow exception would also be thrown because -12 is *too small* to fit into a variable of type Byte.

Notice at 02 the Try part of the Try-Catch-Finally structure, which contains the assignment statement that will be tested for an overflow exception. If an overflow exception is not thrown, processing will continue after the assignment, and the message will be set to *The assignment was successful.*

Notice at 03 the Catch part of the Try-Catch-Finally structure. This part of the structure contains an OverflowException object. We have given this object the alias "Exception" so that we can refer to the object in shorthand. As can be seen, if an overflow exception is thrown, the message will be set to *The assignment was NOT successful.* In addition, the Message property of the Exception object, which describes the current exception, will be appended to the end of the message.

Notice at 04 the Finally part of the Try-Catch-Finally structure. The code inside this part of the structure will be executed whether or not an exception is thrown. Thus, the message will always end with *Thank you.* The result of the Try-Catch-Finally code is shown at the bottom of the figure. Notice that an overflow exception has been thrown since we cannot assign a value to a Byte type that is not between 0 and 255.

CODE BEHIND

```
    // Check for an overflow exception.
    String strMessage = "";
01  Int32 i32Number = 256;
    Byte bytNumber = 0;
02  try
    {
        bytNumber = Convert.ToByte(i32Number);
        strMessage = "The assignment was successful.";
    }
03  catch (OverflowException Exception)
    {
        strMessage = "The assignment was NOT successful. " +
            Exception.Message;
    }
04  finally
    {
        strMessage = strMessage + " Thank you.";
    }
    // strMessage = "The assignment was NOT successful. Value was either
    // too large or too small for an unsigned byte. Thank you."
```

Figure 6-12. Example of using the OverflowException class to catch an overflow exception

6.8.5 Multiple Exceptions

It is also possible to test for multiple exceptions in one Try-Catch-Finally structure—both specific *and* unanticipated exceptions. We have already learned how to catch some specific exceptions (e.g., divide by zero exceptions, format exceptions, index out of range exceptions, overflow exceptions). However, we have not yet discussed how to catch exceptions that we do not anticipate. To do this, we use the Exception class as a "catch all" to catch any unanticipated exceptions. One thing that is important to remember is that the Exceptions class catches *all* exceptions, including *all* of the specific exceptions. Because of this, it is important to test for any specific exceptions first so that when they are thrown, we can catch and handle them in a way that is appropriate for those types of exceptions. Then, if none of the specific exceptions are thrown, we can catch any unanticipated exceptions that are thrown using the Exceptions class. Figure 6-13 shows an example of catching multiple exceptions in a single Try-Catch-Finally structure.

Notice at 01 that txtNumber.Text (presumably entered by the end user via a TextBox control) has been set to *256* to set up an overflow exception. (Had the end user entered *abc* into the TextBox control, a format exception would be thrown.)

Notice at 02 the Try part of the Try-Catch-Finally structure. As can be seen, the value entered into the text box is being converted to a Byte type. If an overflow exception is not thrown, processing will continue after the assignment, and the message will be set to *The conversion and assignment were successful.*

Notice at 03 the first Catch part of the Try-Catch-Finally structure. This part of the structure contains a FormatException object. We have given this object the alias "Exception" so that we can refer to the object in shorthand. As can be seen, if a format exception is thrown, the message will be set to *The conversion was NOT successful.* In addition, the Message property of the Exception object, which describes the current exception, will be appended to the end of the message.

Notice at 04 the second Catch part of the Try-Catch-Finally structure. This part of the structure contains an OverflowException object. We have given this object the alias "Exception" so that we can refer to the object in shorthand. As can be seen, if an overflow exception is thrown, the message will be set to *The assignment was NOT successful.* In addition, the Message property of the Exception object, which describes the current exception, will be appended to the end of the message.

Notice at 05 the third Catch part of the Try-Catch-Finally structure. This part of the structure contains an Exception object. We have given this object the alias "Exception" to be consistent with the aliases of the other Exception objects. This is the "catch all" exception handler that will catch any unanticipated exceptions. Thus, if an exception other than a format exception or an overflow exception is thrown, the message will be set to *Something else was NOT successful.* In addition, the Message property of the Exception object, which describes the current exception, will be appended to the end of the message.

Notice at 06 the Finally part of the Try-Catch-Finally structure. The code inside this part of the structure will be executed whether or not an exception is thrown. Thus, the message will always end with *Thank you.* The result of the Try-Catch-Finally code is shown at the bottom of the figure. Notice that an overflow exception has been thrown since we cannot assign a value to a Byte type that is not between 0 and 255.

CODE BEHIND

```
    // Check for multiple possible exceptions.
    String strMessage = "";
01  txtNumber.Text = "256";
02  try
    {
        Byte bytNumber = Convert.ToByte(txtNumber.Text);
        strMessage = "The conversion and assignment were successful.";
    }
03  catch (FormatException Exception)
    {
        strMessage = "The conversion was NOT successful. " +
            Exception.Message;
    }
04  catch (OverflowException Exception)
    {
        strMessage = "The assignment was NOT successful. " +
            Exception.Message;
    }
05  catch (Exception Exception)
    {
        strMessage = "Something else was NOT successful. " +
            Exception.Message;
    }
06  finally
    {
        strMessage = strMessage + " Thank you.";
    }
    // strMessage = "The assignment was NOT successful. Value was either
    // too large or too small for an unsigned byte. Thank you."
```

Figure 6-13. *Example of catching multiple exceptions in a single Try-Catch-Finally structure*

CHAPTER 7

Conversion Operations

7.1 Introduction

A conversion operation alters the value in a variable of one type so that it can be used in a variable of another type. Conversions can be *widening* or *narrowing*. A widening conversion *always* preserves the value of the source variable since the target variable can fully accommodate the range of possible values of the source variable. Thus, this type of conversion *always* succeeds during program execution because it cannot result in the loss of data. A narrowing conversion, on the other hand, *may not* preserve the value of the source variable since the target variable cannot fully accommodate the entire range of possible values of the source variable. Thus, this type of conversion *may not* succeed during program execution since an OverflowException may occur.

In this chapter, we will begin by looking at widening conversions. As we will see, widening conversions are performed automatically in a C# program since data *cannot* be lost in the conversion. Such conversions are performed *implicitly* (i.e., special syntax *is not* required for the conversion to take place). Next, we will discuss narrowing conversions, which are *not* performed automatically in a C# program since data *can* be lost in the conversion. These conversions are performed *explicitly* (i.e., special syntax *is* required for the conversion to take place). And finally, we will discuss the Convert class. This static class converts the value in a variable of one type so that it can be used in a variable of another type.

7.2 Widening Conversions

A widening conversion (a.k.a., an implicit conversion or coercion) can be performed whenever the target type can fully accommodate the range of possible values of the source type. Thus, widening conversions can always be performed implicitly. For example, a widening conversion can be performed when we want to convert an Int16

© Robert E. Beasley 2020
R. E. Beasley, *Essential ASP.NET Web Forms Development*, https://doi.org/10.1007/978-1-4842-5784-5_7

(i.e., a 16-bit signed integer) to an Int32 (i.e., a 32-bit signed integer) or when we want to convert an Int32 (i.e., a 32-bit signed integer) to a Double (i.e., a 64-bit double-precision floating-point number).

Widening conversions require no special syntax and are automatically performed because no data can be lost in the conversion—that is, no data will be rounded off (in the case of converting from a less precise type to a more precise type) or truncated (in the case of converting from a smaller magnitude type to a larger magnitude type). Such conversions are said to be *type safe*.

Table 7-1 shows the list of widening numeric conversions. Notice in the table that there are no widening conversions to the Char type. Nor are there any widening conversions between the Single and Double types and the Decimal type. Keep in mind that precision (but not magnitude) can be lost when converting from Int32, UInt32, Int64, or UInt64 to Single and from Int64 or UInt64 to Double.

Table 7-1. *List of widening numeric conversions*

.NET Type	Description	Can be implicitly converted to...
Boolean	A Boolean value (true or false).	NA
Byte	An 8-bit unsigned integer.	Int16, UInt16, Int32, UInt32, Int64, UInt64, Single, Double, Decimal
Char	A Unicode (16-bit) character.	UInt16, Int32, UInt32, Int64, UInt64, Single, Double, Decimal
Decimal	A decimal (128-bit) value.	NA
Double	A double-precision (64-bit) floating-point number.	NA
Int16	A 16-bit signed integer.	Int32, Int64, Single, Double, Decimal
Int32	A 32-bit signed integer.	Int64, Single, Double, Decimal
Int64	A 64-bit signed integer.	Single, Double, Decimal
Sbyte	An 8-bit signed integer.	Int16, Int32, Int64, Single, Double, Decimal
Single	A single-precision (32-bit) floating-point number.	Double

(*continued*)

Table 7-1. (*continued*)

.NET Type	Description	Can be implicitly converted to...
UInt16	A 16-bit unsigned integer.	Int32, UInt32, Int64, UInt64, Single, Double, Decimal
UInt32	A 32-bit unsigned integer.	Int64, UInt64, Single, Double, Decimal
UInt64	A 64-bit unsigned integer.	Single, Double, Decimal

Reference

https://docs.microsoft.com/en-us/dotnet/csharp/language-reference/
keywords/implicit-numeric-conversions-table

Widening conversions can also occur when a mathematical expression that contains a mixture of numeric variables of *differing* type precisions and/or magnitudes is evaluated. When this is the case, the operands with less precise types or smaller magnitude types are automatically converted to the most precise type or largest magnitude type used in the expression *before* the expression is evaluated. Figure 7-1 shows some examples of widening conversions.

Notice at 01 and 02 that smaller magnitude types are being implicitly converted to larger magnitude types.

Notice at 03 and 04 that less precise types are being implicitly converted to more precise types. As can be seen at 04, not all floating-point numbers can be represented exactly in binary. This is why the single-precision value 12345.56789f is represented by the double-precision value 12345.568359375, which is a close approximation of 12345.56789f.

Notice at 05 that i16Number2 and i16Number3 (both 16-bit signed integers) are being implicitly converted to the same type as dblNumber1 (a double-precision 64-bit floating-point number) *before* the evaluation of the expression.

CODE BEHIND

```
     // Implicitly convert an 8-bit unsigned integer to a 16-bit unsigned
     // integer.
     Byte bytNumber = 100;
     UInt16 u16Number = 0;
01   u16Number = bytNumber;
     // u16Number = 100

     // Implicitly convert a 32-bit signed integer to a 64-bit signed integer.
     Int32 i32Number = -123;
     Int64 i64Number = 0;
02   i64Number = i32Number;
     // i64Number = -123

     // Implicitly convert an 8-bit signed integer to a single-precision
     // (32-bit) floating-point number.
     SByte sbyNumber = -12;
     Single sinNumber = 0f;
03   sinNumber = sbyNumber;
     // sinNumber = -12

     // Implicitly convert a single-precision (32-bit) floating-point number to
     // a double-precision (64-bit) floating-point number.
     Single sinNumberSmaller = 12345.56789f;
     Double dblNumberLarger = 0;
04   dblNumberLarger = sinNumberSmaller;
     // dblNumberLarger = 12345.568359375

     // Implicitly convert the variable types in the expression before
     // evaluating the expression.
     Double dblNumber1 = 3;
     Int16 i16Number2 = 7;
     Int16 i16Number3 = 12;
     Double dblAverage = 0;
05   dblAverage = (dblNumber1 + i16Number2 + i16Number3)/3;
     // dblAverage = 7.33...
```

Figure 7-1. *Examples of widening conversions*

7.3 Narrowing Conversions

A narrowing conversion (a.k.a., an explicit conversion or cast) must be performed whenever the target type cannot fully accommodate the range of possible values of the source type. Thus, narrowing conversions must always be performed explicitly. For example, a narrowing conversion must be performed when we want to convert an Int32 (i.e., a 32-bit signed integer) to an Int16 (i.e., a 16-bit signed integer) or when we want to convert a Double (i.e., a 64-bit double-precision floating-point number) to an Int32 (i.e., a 32-bit signed integer).

Narrowing conversions require special syntax and are *not* automatically performed since data can be lost in the conversion. To be more specific, data can be rounded toward zero to the nearest integer (e.g., when converting from a decimal type to an integer type), or data can be truncated (e.g., when converting from a double or single type to an integer type). Such conversions are *not* type safe.

In C#, narrowing conversions require the use of a *cast operator*. A cast operator takes the form of a type between two parentheses. For example, to cast a variable of type Single to a variable of type SByte, we would need to include (SByte) immediately before the Single variable to be assigned to the SByte variable like

```
sbyNumber = (SByte)sinNumber;
```

When we use a cast operator, we are telling the compiler that we want to *force* a conversion from a wider type to a narrower type and that we are aware of the fact that data might be lost in the process. When casting one type to another type, keep in mind that

- When a decimal type is cast to an integer type, the decimal value will be *rounded toward zero to the nearest integer*. If the resulting integer value lies outside the range of the integer type, an OverflowException will occur.

- When a double or single type is cast to an integer type, the double or single value will be *truncated*. If the resulting integer value lies outside the range of the integer type, an OverflowException will occur.

- When a double type is cast to a single type, the double value will be *rounded to the nearest single value*. If the double value is too small to fit into the single type, the single value will be zero. If the double value is too large to fit into the single type, the single value will be infinity.

- When a single or double type is cast to a decimal type, the single or double value will be *rounded to the nearest decimal number (after the 28th decimal place if necessary)*. If the single or double value is too small to be represented as a decimal type, the decimal value will be zero. If the single or double value is not a number (NaN), is infinity, or is too large to be represented as a decimal type, an OverflowException will occur.

- When a decimal type is cast to a single or double type, the decimal value will be *rounded to the nearest double or single value*.

Table 7-2 shows the list of narrowing numeric conversions. Notice in the table that the Boolean type cannot be explicitly converted to another type.

Table 7-2. *List of narrowing numeric conversions*

.NET Type	Description	Can be explicitly converted to...
Boolean	A Boolean value (true or false).	NA
Byte	An 8-bit unsigned integer.	SByte, Char
Char	A Unicode (16-bit) character.	SByte, Byte, Int16
Decimal	A decimal (128-bit) value.	SByte, Byte, Int16, UInt16, Int32, UInt32, Int64, UInt64, Char, Single, Double
Double	A double-precision (64-bit) floating-point number.	SByte, Byte, Int16, UInt16, Int32, UInt32, Int64, UInt64, Char, Single, Decimal
Int16	A 16-bit signed integer.	SByte, Byte, UInt16, UInt32, UInt64, Char
Int32	A 32-bit signed integer.	SByte, Byte, Int16, UInt16, UInt32, UInt64, Char
Int64	A 64-bit signed integer.	SByte, Byte, Int16, UInt16, Int32, UInt32, UInt64, Char
Sbyte	An 8-bit signed integer.	Byte, UInt16, UInt32, UInt64, Char
Single	A single-precision (32-bit) floating-point number.	SByte, Byte, Int16, UInt16, Int32, UInt32, Int64, UInt64, Char, Decimal
UInt16	A 16-bit unsigned integer.	SByte, Byte, Int16, Char
UInt32	A 32-bit unsigned integer.	SByte, Byte, Int16, UInt16, Int16, Char
UInt64	A 64-bit unsigned integer.	SByte, Byte, Int16, UInt16, Int32, UInt32, Int64, Char

Reference

https://docs.microsoft.com/en-us/dotnet/csharp/language-reference/
keywords/explicit-numeric-conversions-table

Figure 7-2 shows some examples of narrowing conversions (i.e., casts).

Notice at 01 and 02 that larger magnitude types are being explicitly converted to smaller magnitude types.

Notice at 03 and 04 that larger magnitude and more precise types are being explicitly converted to smaller magnitude and less precise types. As can be seen at 04, the decimal part of the number is truncated.

Notice at 05 that a larger magnitude signed type is being explicitly converted to a smaller magnitude unsigned type. As can be seen, the sign is truncated, and the result is strange. This underscores the importance of carefully testing code that contains casting.

Notice at 06 that a larger magnitude type is being explicitly converted to a smaller magnitude type, but the smaller magnitude type is too small to accommodate the larger magnitude type. Note that no overflow error occurs in this scenario, and the result is strange. Again, this underscores the importance of carefully testing code that contains casting.

CODE BEHIND

```
     // Explicitly convert (i.e., cast) a 16-bit unsigned integer to an 8-bit
     // unsigned integer.
     UInt16 u16Number = 100;
     Byte bytNumber = 0;
01   bytNumber = (Byte)u16Number;
     // bytNumber = 100

     // Explicitly convert (i.e., cast) a 64-bit signed integer to a 32-bit
     // signed integer.
     Int64 i64Number = -123;
     Int32 i32Number = 0;
02   i32Number = (Int32)i64Number;
     // i32Number = -123

     // Explicitly convert (i.e., cast) a decimal (128-bit) value to a
     // double-precision (64-bit) floating-point number.
     Decimal decNumber = 123.45m;
     Double dblNumber = 0;
03   dblNumber = (Double)decNumber;
     // dblNumber = 123.45

     // Explicitly convert (i.e., cast) a single-precision (32-bit)
     // floating-point number to an 8-bit signed integer.
     Single sinNumber = -12.50f;
     SByte sbyNumber = 0;
04   sbyNumber = (SByte)sinNumber;
     // sbyNumber = -12

     // Explicitly convert (i.e., cast) a 16-bit signed integer to an 8-bit
     // unsigned integer.
     Int16 i16NumberSigned = -100;
     Byte bytNumberUnsigned = 0;
05   bytNumberUnsigned = (Byte)i16NumberSigned;
     // bytNumber = 156

     // Explicitly convert (i.e., cast) a 16-bit unsigned integer to an 8-bit
     // unsigned integer that is too large to fit.
     UInt16 u16NumberTooLarge = 65535;
     Byte bytNumberTooSmall = 0;
06   bytNumberTooSmall = (Byte)u16NumberTooLarge;
     // bytNumberTooSmall = 255
```

Figure 7-2. *Examples of narrowing conversions*

7.4 Convert Class

The Convert class is a static class that converts the value in a variable of one type so that it can be used in a variable of another type. Supported types include Boolean, Byte, Char, DateTime, Decimal, Double, Int16, Int32, Int64, SByte, Single, String, UInt16, UInt32, and UInt64. Depending on the value in the source variable and the precision and magnitude of the target value, five things can happen when invoking a method of the Convert class. These are

- No conversion is performed. This occurs when we attempt to convert a variable of one type to a variable of the *same* type (e.g., converting a Double to a Double). In this case, the method simply returns the value of the source variable.

- A successful conversion is performed. This occurs when a widening conversion is performed or when a narrowing conversion is performed without the loss of data. In either case, the method returns a value identical to that in the source variable. A conversion is also considered successful when the conversion only results in the loss of precision (e.g., the loss of decimal points due to rounding).

- A FormatException is thrown. This occurs when we attempt to convert a String type to another type, and the value of the string is not in an appropriate format. A FormatException is thrown when a String type to be converted to a

  - Boolean type does not equal "True" or "False"

  - Char type consists of multiple characters

  - DateTime type is not a valid date and time

  - Numeric type is not a valid number

- An InvalidCastException is thrown. This occurs when we attempt to perform a conversion that doesn't make sense. An InvalidCastException is thrown when we attempt to convert from

  - Char to Boolean, DateTime, Decimal, Double, or Single

  - Boolean, DateTime, Decimal, Double, or Single to Char

- DateTime to any other type (except String)

- Any other type (except String) to DateTime

- An OverflowException is thrown. This occurs when we attempt to perform a narrowing conversion that results in the loss of data (e.g., converting a UInt16 with a value of 256 to a Byte, the latter of which can only store values up to 255).

Table 7-3 shows some of the properties, methods, and events of the Convert class. In the table, the term *Valuetype* represents *any* of the value types supported in .NET. Note that both widening and narrowing conversions are supported.

Table 7-3. *Some of the properties, methods, and events of the Convert class*

Class Convert[1]	
Namespace System	
Properties	
NA	
Methods	
ToBoolean(*Valuetype*)	Converts the value of the specified value type to an equivalent Boolean value.
ToByte(*Valuetype*)	Converts the value of the specified value type to an equivalent 8-bit unsigned integer.
ToChar(*Valuetype*)	Converts the value of the specified value type to an equivalent Unicode character.
ToDateTime(*Valuetype*)	Converts the value of the specified value type to an equivalent date and time value.
ToDecimal(*Valuetype*)	Converts the value of the specified value type to an equivalent decimal number.

(*continued*)

---

[1]All property, method, and event descriptions were taken directly from Microsoft's official documentation. The event handler methods used to handle the events of this class were omitted to conserve space. See the reference for all of the methods of this class.

Table 7-3. (*continued*)

ToDouble(*Valuetype*)	Converts the value of the specified value type to an equivalent double-precision floating-point number.
ToInt16(*Valuetype*)	Converts the value of the specified value type to an equivalent 16-bit signed integer.
ToInt32(*Valuetype*)	Converts the value of the specified value type to an equivalent 32-bit signed integer.
ToInt64(*Valuetype*)	Converts the value of the specified value type to an equivalent 64-bit signed integer.
ToSByte(*Valuetype*)	Converts the value of the specified value type to an equivalent 8-bit signed integer.
ToSingle(*Valuetype*)	Converts the value of the specified value type to an equivalent single-precision floating-point number.
ToString(*Valuetype*)	Converts the value of the specified value type to an equivalent string representation.
ToUInt16(*Valuetype*)	Converts the value of the specified value type to an equivalent 16-bit unsigned integer.
ToUInt32(*Valuetype*)	Converts the value of the specified value type to an equivalent 32-bit unsigned integer.
ToUInt64(*Valuetype*)	Converts the value of the specified value type to an equivalent 64-bit unsigned integer.

Events

NA

Reference

https://msdn.microsoft.com/en-us/library/system.convert(v=vs.110).aspx

It is important to exercise caution when deciding whether to use a narrowing conversion (i.e., a cast) or a seemingly equivalent Convert class method when converting from a more precise numeric type to a less precise numeric type. This is because numeric casts *truncate*, whereas numeric conversions *round to the nearest even number*. In C#, decimal values that end in 5 are, by default, rounded *up or down* to the nearest *even* value during the rounding process *depending on the number being rounded*. For example, the numbers 1.5 and 3.5 would be rounded *up* to 2 and 4, respectively, whereas the numbers 2.5 and 4.5 would be rounded *down* to 2 and 4, respectively. Thus, rounding to an odd value would never occur. This approach follows the standard *banker's rounding* convention. The reason given for using this particular method of rounding is that it avoids roundup bias when rounding a large set of numbers. Figure 7-3 shows some examples of converting one type to another type. As can be seen, there are both widening and narrowing conversions being performed.

Notice at 01–03 that smaller magnitude types are being converted to larger magnitude types.

Notice at 04 that a smaller magnitude type is being converted to a larger magnitude type as well. Note that not all floating-point numbers can be represented exactly in binary. This is why the single-precision value 7.1234f is represented by the double-precision value 7.1234002113342285, which is a close approximation of 7.1234f.

Notice at 05–09 that larger magnitude types are being converted to smaller magnitude types.

Notice at 10 that a larger magnitude type is being converted to a smaller magnitude type as well. Note that the result is rounded according to the rules of banker's rounding.

CODE BEHIND

```
     // Convert the 8-bit unsigned integer to its equivalent Unicode
     // (16-bit) character.
     Byte bytNumber = 65;
     Char[] chaUnicodeCharacter = new Char[1];
01   chaUnicodeCharacter[0] = Convert.ToChar(bytNumber);
     // chaUnicodeCharacter[0] = "A"

     // Convert the DateTime structure to its equivalent immutable,
     // fixed-length string of Unicode characters.
     DateTime datDate = DateTime.Today;
     String strDate = "";
02   strDate = Convert.ToString(datDate);
     // strDate = "7/21/2017 12:00:00 AM"

     // Convert the 8-bit signed integer to its equivalent 16-bit
     // unsigned integer.
     SByte sbyReorderLevel = 33;
     UInt16 u16ReorderLevel = 0;
03   u16ReorderLevel = Convert.ToUInt16(sbyReorderLevel);
     // u16ReorderLevel = 33

     // Convert the single-precision (32-bit) floating-point number to its
     // equivalent double-precision (64-bit) floating-point number.
     Single sinAmount = 7.1234f;
     Double dblAmount = 0;
04   dblAmount = Convert.ToDouble(sinAmount);
     // dblAmount = 7.1234002113342285

     // Convert the 32-bit signed integer to its equivalent Boolean
     // value (true or false).
     Int32 i32Flag = 1;
     Boolean booFlag = false;
05   booFlag = Convert.ToBoolean(i32Flag);
     // booFlag = true

     // Convert the immutable, fixed-length string of Unicode characters
     // to its equivalent 8-bit unsigned integer.
     String strAge = "3";
     Byte bytAge = 0;
```

Figure 7-3. *Examples of converting one type to another type*

```
06   bytAge = Convert.ToByte(strAge);
     // bytAge = 3

     // Convert the immutable, fixed-length string of Unicode characters
     // to its equivalent DateTime structure.
     String strDateTime = "7/20/2017";
     DateTime datDateTime = new DateTime();
07   datDateTime = Convert.ToDateTime(strDateTime);
     // datDateTime = {7/20/2017 12:00:00 AM}

     // Convert the 16-bit unsigned integer to its equivalent 8-bit
     // signed integer.
     UInt16 u16NumberOnOrder = 100;
     SByte sbyNumberOnOrder = 0;
08   sbyNumberOnOrder = Convert.ToSByte(u16NumberOnOrder);
     // sbyNumberOnOrder = 100

     // Convert the double-precision (64-bit) floating-point number to
     // its equivalent single-precision (32-bit) floating-point number.
     Double dblRefund = -123.45;
     Single sinRefund = 0;
09   sinRefund = Convert.ToSingle(dblRefund);
     // sinRefund = -123.45

     // Convert the decimal (128-bit) value to its equivalent 16-bit
     // signed integer.
     Decimal decNumberInStock = 122.5m;
     Int16 i16NumberInStock = 0;
10   i16NumberInStock = Convert.ToInt16(decNumberInStock);
     // i16NumberInStock = 122
```

Figure 7-3. *(continued)*

Having the end user enter a value into a TextBox control and then converting that input (which is stored in the Text property of the control as a String type) to another type is a *very* common operation in ASP.NET Web applications. This is because we must often use that input in a non-string operation (e.g., a numeric computation) in the code behind. Figure 7-4 shows some examples of converting the Text property of a TextBox control to another type.

Notice at 01 and 02 that a single step is required for the conversion.

Notice at 03–06, however, that two steps are required for the conversion. In these examples, notice the significant potential for exception throwing due to the possibility of bad data being entered by the end user. This underscores the importance of the data validation techniques discussed in Chapter 5, titled "Data Validation Controls," and the exception handling techniques discussed in Chapter 6, titled "Assignment Operations."

CODE BEHIND

```
      // Convert the text box value to its equivalent
      // decimal (128-bit) value.
      txtInput.Text = "12.34"; // Entered by the end user.
      Decimal decPrice = 0;
01    decPrice = Convert.ToDecimal(txtInput.Text);
      // decPrice = 12.34

      // Convert the text box value to its equivalent
      // DateTime structure.
      txtInput.Text = "7/20/2017"; // Entered by the end user.
      DateTime datDateTime = new DateTime();
02    datDateTime = Convert.ToDateTime(txtInput.Text);
      // datDateTime = {7/20/2017 12:00:00 AM}

      // Convert the text box value to its equivalent
      // Boolean value (true or false).
      txtInput.Text = "1"; // Entered by the end user.
      Boolean booFlag = false;
03    Byte bytFlag = Convert.ToByte(txtInput.Text);
04    booFlag = Convert.ToBoolean(bytFlag);
      // booFlag = true

      // Convert the text box value to its equivalent
      // Unicode (16-bit) character.
      txtInput.Text = "65"; // Entered by the end user.
      Char[] chaUnicodeCharacter = new Char[1];
05    UInt16 u16Number = Convert.ToUInt16(txtInput.Text);
06    chaUnicodeCharacter[0] = Convert.ToChar(u16Number);
      // chaUnicodeCharacter[0] = "A"
```

Figure 7-4. *Examples of converting the Text property of a TextBox control to another type*

CHAPTER 8

Control Operations

8.1 Introduction

Control operations fall into two general categories—*decision operations* (a.k.a., selection operations, condition operations) and *iterative operations* (a.k.a., repeating operations, looping operations). Decision operations alter the path of a program's execution based on the truth or falseness of a relational, equality, and/or logical operation when multiple paths through a program are required. Iterative operations, on the other hand, execute a block of code repeatedly while or until a certain condition (i.e., a relational, equality, and/or logical condition) is true. Decision operations and iterative operations are so fundamental to computer programming that every procedural/imperative programming language requires such operations—regardless of their syntax.

In this chapter, we will begin by looking at the four relational operators. These are the less than operator, the greater than operator, the less than or equal to operator, and the greater than or equal to operator. Next, we will discuss the two equality operators—the equal to operator and the not equal to operator. After that, we will consider several logical operators, including the And operator, the Or operator, the Conditional And operator, the Conditional Or operator, and the Xor operator. We will then look at a number of decision structures, including the If structure, the If-Else structure, the If-Else-If structure, the Nested-If structure, the Switch structure, and the Switch-Through structure. Next, we will look at several iterative structures, including the While structure, the Do-While structure, the For structure, and the For-Each structure. And finally, we will consider two C# statements that permit us to alter the execution of the iterative structures discussed in the chapter—namely, the Break statement and the Continue statement.

© Robert E. Beasley 2020
R. E. Beasley, *Essential ASP.NET Web Forms Development*, https://doi.org/10.1007/978-1-4842-5784-5_8

8.2 Relational Operators

There are four fundamental relational operators. These are the *less than* operator (<), the *greater than* operator (>), the *less than or equal to* operator (<=), and the *greater than or equal to* operator (>=). A *relational operation* contains an operator and two operands. The general syntax of a relational operation in the C# programming language is

```
(Operand1 Operator Operand2);
```

The < operator returns *true* if Operand1 is less than Operand2. Otherwise, *false* is returned. The > operator returns *true* if Operand1 is greater than Operand2. Otherwise, *false* is returned. The <= operator returns *true* if Operand1 is less than or equal to Operand2. Otherwise, *false* is returned. And, the >= operator returns *true* if Operand1 is greater than or equal to Operand2. Otherwise, *false* is returned. As with any other operator in C#, there is an order of precedence in play when multiple operators are evaluated as a whole. This order of precedence defines the sequence in which the operations are evaluated. Table 8-1 shows the fundamental relational operators listed by their order of precedence.

Table 8-1. *Fundamental relational operators listed by their order of precedence*

Operator	Description	Comment
x < y	Less than	True if x is less than y. Otherwise, false.
x > y	Greater than	True if x is greater than y. Otherwise, false.
x <= y	Less than or equal to	True if x is less than or equal to y. Otherwise, false.
x >= y	Greater than or equal to	True if x is greater than or equal to y. Otherwise, false.

8.3 Equality Operators

There are two equality operators. These are the *equal to* operator (==) and the *not equal to* operator (!=). An equality operation contains an operator and two operands. The general syntax of an equality operation in the C# programming language is

```
(Operand1 Operator Operand2);
```

The == operator returns *true* if Operand1 is equal to Operand2. Otherwise, *false* is returned. The != operator returns *true* if Operand1 is *not* equal to Operand2. Otherwise, *false* is returned. As with any other operator in C#, there is an order of precedence in play when multiple operators are evaluated as a whole. This order of precedence defines the sequence in which the operations are evaluated. Table 8-2 shows some equality operators listed by their order of precedence.

Table 8-2. *Equality operators listed by their order of precedence*

Operator	Description	Comment
x == y	Equal to	True if x is equal to y. Otherwise, false.
x != y	Not equal to	True if x is not equal to y. Otherwise, false.

8.4 Logical Operators

Logical operators permit us to construct *compound* conditions. A compound condition is composed of two or more conditions that are evaluated as a whole. There are two fundamental logical operators. These are the *And* operator (&) and the *Or* operator (|). In addition to these, there is a *conditional And* operator (&&), a *conditional Or* operator (||), and an *Xor* operator (^). A logical operation contains an operator and two or more conditions, where the conditions are relational operations and/or equality operations. The general syntax of a logical operation in the C# programming language is

```
(Condition1 Operator Condition2 [Operator Condition3...]);
```

where Condition1 Operator Condition2 is required and [Operator Condition3...] is optional. The ellipse indicates that additional operators and conditions are permitted as well.

The & operator returns *true* if Condition1 *and* Condition2 are *both* true. Otherwise, *false* is returned. The | operator returns *true* if Condition1 *or* Condition2 is true. Otherwise, *false* is returned. The && operator returns *true* if Condition1 *and* Condition2 are *both* true. Otherwise, *false* is returned. However, Condition2 will *not* be evaluated if Condition1 is not true. Thus, this operator is referred to as the *shortcut And operator*. The || operator returns *true* if Condition1 *or* Condition2 is true. Otherwise, *false* is returned. However, Condition2 will *not* be evaluated if Condition1 is true. Thus, this operator is referred to as the *shortcut Or operator*. And finally, the ^ operator returns *true* if Condition1 *or* Condition2 is true, but both are not true. Otherwise, *false* is returned. As with any other operator in C#, there is an order of precedence in play when multiple operators are evaluated as a whole. This order of precedence defines the sequence in which the operations are evaluated. Table 8-3 shows some logical operators listed by their order of precedence.

Table 8-3. *Logical operators listed by their order of precedence*

Operator	Description	Comment
x & y	And	True if x *and* y are *both* true. Otherwise, false.
x | y	Or	True if x *or* y is true. Otherwise, false.
x && y	Conditional And	True if x *and* y are *both* true. Otherwise, false. Do *not* evaluate y if x is not true.
x || y	Conditional Or	True if x *or* y is true. Otherwise, false. Do *not* evaluate y if x is true.
x ^ y	Xor	True if x *or* y is true, but both are not true. Otherwise, false.

8.5 Decision Structures

Decision structures (a.k.a., selection structures, condition structures) alter the path of a program's execution based on the truth or falseness of a relational, equality, and/ or logical operation when multiple paths through a program are possible. When a given relational, equality, and/or logical operation evaluates to true, a block of code is executed. When it evaluates to false, either no block of code is executed or a different block of code is executed. In this section, we will look at the If structure, the If-Else structure, the If-Else-If structure, the Nested-If structure, the Switch structure, and the Switch-Through structure.

8.5.1 If Structure

An If structure (a.k.a., If statement) identifies the condition (or conditions) under which a single block of code (i.e., one or more imperative programming statements) will be executed. The general syntax of the If structure in the C# programming language is

```
if (Condition)
{
    Block of code
}
```

Notice that *one* alternative program path is possible when an If structure is employed. As can be seen, if the condition evaluates to true, the block of code will be executed. If the condition evaluates to false, the block of code will *not* be executed. In either case, program flow will continue at the point immediately after the last bracket of the If structure. Figure 8-1 shows an example of the If structure with a relational operator.

```
CODE BEHIND

    // Declare the variables.
    const Double dblDiscountRateSenior = 0.10;
    Double dblSubtotal = 100.00;
    Byte bytCustomerAge = 55;

    // If the customer is 55 or older, apply the senior discount.
    if (bytCustomerAge >= 55)
    {
        dblSubtotal = dblSubtotal * (1 - dblDiscountRateSenior);
    }
    // dblSubtotal = 90
```

Figure 8-1. *Example of the If structure with a relational operator*

Figure 8-2 shows an example of the If structure with an equality operator.

```
CODE BEHIND

    // Declare the variables.
    Int32 i32ProductID = 5;
    String strMessage = "";

    // If the Product ID is 2, put out a message.
    if (i32ProductID == 2)
    {
        strMessage = "Sorry. That product is currently on backorder.";
    }
    // strMessage = ""
```

Figure 8-2. *Example of the If structure with an equality operator*

Figure 8-3 shows an example of the If structure with an Or operator.

CODE BEHIND

```
// Declare the variables.
String strZipCode = "46131";
Boolean booDeliveryAvailable = false;

// If the zip code is 46131 or 46132, indicate that delivery service
// is available.
if (strZipCode == "46131" | strZipCode == "46132")
{
    booDeliveryAvailable = true;
}
// booDeliveryAvailable = true
```

Figure 8-3. *Example of the If structure with an Or operator*

Figure 8-4 shows an example of the If structure with a conditional And operator.

Notice at 01 that if the first condition evaluates to false, the second condition will not be evaluated, thus improving program efficiency.

CODE BEHIND

```
    // Declare the variables.
    Byte bytNumberInStock = 4;
    Byte bytNumberOnOrder = 0;
    Byte bytReorderLevel = 5;
    Boolean booReorderProduct = false;

    // If the number in stock is less than or equal to the reorder level,
    // and if there is nothing already on order, then set the number on order
    // to the reorder level and indicate that the product should be reordered.
01  if (bytNumberInStock <= bytReorderLevel && bytNumberOnOrder == 0)
    {
        bytNumberOnOrder = bytReorderLevel;
        booReorderProduct = true;
    }
    // bytNumberOnOrder = 5, booReorderProduct = true
```

Figure 8-4. *Example of the If structure with a conditional And operator*

8.5.2 If-Else Structure

An If-Else structure (a.k.a., If-Else statement) identifies the condition (or conditions) under which two distinct blocks of code (i.e., one or more imperative programming statements) will be executed. The general syntax of the If-Else structure in the C# programming language is

```
if (Condition)
{
    Block of code 1
}
else
{
    Block of code 2
}
```

Notice that *two* alternative program paths are possible when an If-Else structure is employed. As can be seen, if the condition evaluates to true, the first block of code will be executed. If the condition evaluates to false, the second block of code will be executed. In either case, program flow will continue at the point immediately after the last bracket of the If-Else structure. Figure 8-5 shows an example of the If-Else structure.

```
CODE BEHIND

// Declare the variables.
const Double dblSalesTaxRate = 0.7;
Double dblSubtotal = 100.00;
Double dblTotal = 0;
String strState = "OH";

// Only apply sales tax if the customer resides in Indiana.
if (strState == "IN")
{
    dblTotal = dblSubtotal + (dblSalesTaxRate * 10);
}
else
{
    dblTotal = dblSubtotal;
}
// dblTotal = 100
```

Figure 8-5. *Example of the If-Else structure*

8.5.3 If-Else-If Structure

An If-Else-If structure (a.k.a., If-Else-If statement) identifies the condition (or conditions) under which two or more distinct blocks of code (i.e., one or more imperative programming statements) will be executed. The general syntax of the If-Else-If structure in the C# programming language is

```
if (Condition 1)
{
    Block of code 1
}
else if (Condition 2)
{
    Block of code 2
}
else
{
    Block of code 3
}
```

Notice that *at least two* alternative program paths are possible when an If-Else-If structure is employed, since a matching Else may not be required for a given If condition. As can be seen, if the first condition evaluates to true, the first block of code will be executed. Otherwise, if the second condition evaluates to true, the second block of code will be executed. Otherwise, the third block of code will be executed. In all three cases, program flow will continue at the point immediately after the last bracket of the If-Else-If structure. Keep in mind that more than one *else if* condition can be included in a single If-Else-If structure. Figure 8-6 shows an example of the If-Else-If structure.

CODE BEHIND

```
// Declare the variables.
const Double dblDiscountRateStandard = 0.10;
const Double dblDiscountRateSelect = 0.20;
const Double dblDiscountRatePreferred = 0.30;
Double dblSubtotal = 100;
String strCustomerType = "Select";

// Apply the discount rate based on the type of customer.
if (strCustomerType == "Standard")
{
    dblSubtotal = dblSubtotal * (1 - dblDiscountRateStandard);
}
else if (strCustomerType == "Select")
{
    dblSubtotal = dblSubtotal * (1 - dblDiscountRateSelect);
}
else if (strCustomerType == "Preferred")
{
    dblSubtotal = dblSubtotal * (1 - dblDiscountRatePreferred);
}
else
{
    // Do not apply a discount.
}
// dblSubtotal = 80
```

Figure 8-6. *Example of the If-Else-If structure*

8.5.4 Nested-If Structure

A Nested-If structure (a.k.a., Nested-If statement) identifies the condition (or conditions) under which two or more distinct blocks of code (i.e., one or more imperative programming statements) will be executed. The general syntax of the Nested-If structure in the C# programming language is

```
if (Condition 1)
{
    Block of code 1
    if (Condition 2)
    {
        Block of code 2
    }
}
```

Notice that *two* alternative program paths are possible when a Nested-If structure is employed. As can be seen, if the first condition evaluates to true, the first block of code (which includes a second condition) will be executed. If the second condition evaluates to true, the second block of code will be executed. In either case, program flow will continue at the point immediately after the last bracket of the Nested-If structure. Keep in mind that *any* of the If structures discussed in this section (i.e., If, If-Else, and If-Else-If structures) can be nested. Figure 8-7 shows an example of the Nested-If structure. Notice in this particular example that the Nested-If structure nests two If-Else-If structures.

CODE BEHIND

```
// Declare the variables.
const Double dblDiscountRateSenior = 0.10;
const Double dblDiscountRateStandard = 0.10;
const Double dblDiscountRateSelect = 0.20;
const Double dblDiscountRatePreferred = 0.30;
Double dblSubtotal = 100;
Byte bytCustomerAge = 60;
String strCustomerType = "Preferred";

// If the customer is 55 or older, apply the senior discount.
if (bytCustomerAge >= 55)
{
    // Apply the discount rate based on the type of customer.
    if (strCustomerType == "Standard")
    {
        dblSubtotal = dblSubtotal * (1 - (dblDiscountRateStandard +
            dblDiscountRateSenior));
    }
    else if (strCustomerType == "Select")
    {
        dblSubtotal = dblSubtotal * (1 - (dblDiscountRateSelect +
            dblDiscountRateSenior));
    }
    else if (strCustomerType == "Preferred")
    {
        dblSubtotal = dblSubtotal * (1 - (dblDiscountRatePreferred +
            dblDiscountRateSenior));
    }
    else
    {
        // Do not apply a discount.
    }
}
```

Figure 8-7. *Example of the Nested-If structure*

```
    else
    {
        // Apply the discount rate based on the type of customer.
        if (strCustomerType == "Standard")
        {
            dblSubtotal = dblSubtotal * (1 - dblDiscountRateStandard);
        }
        else if (strCustomerType == "Select")
        {
            dblSubtotal = dblSubtotal * (1 - dblDiscountRateSelect);
        }
        else if (strCustomerType == "Preferred")
        {
            dblSubtotal = dblSubtotal * (1 - dblDiscountRatePreferred);
        }
        else
        {
            // Do not apply a discount.
        }
    }
    // dblSubtotal = 60
```

Figure 8-7. *(continued)*

8.5.5 Switch Structure

A Switch structure (a.k.a., Switch statement) identifies the condition (or conditions) under which one or more distinct blocks of code (i.e., one or more imperative programming statements) will be executed. The general syntax of the Switch structure in the C# programming language is

```
switch (Expression)
{
    case Matched Expression 1
        Block of code 1
    case Matched Expression 2 (optional)
        Block of code 2
    default (optional)
        Block of code 3
}
```

Notice that *at least* one alternative program path is possible when a Switch structure is employed, since neither a second case nor a default case may be required. As can be seen, if the first case matches the expression, the first block of code will be executed. Otherwise, if the second case matches the expression, the second block of code will be executed. Otherwise, the third block of code will be executed. In all cases, program flow will continue at the point immediately after the last bracket of the Switch structure.

There are several things to remember about the Switch structure. First, any number of cases can be included in a single Switch structure. Second, cases are always evaluated in order from top to bottom, except for the default case, which is always evaluated last. Third, only one case is executed. Fourth, the block of code that is executed within a case always ends with a break statement. And fifth, the Switch structure is often used as an alternative to the If-Else-If structure when a single expression is evaluated with two or more cases. This is because the Switch structure is easier to read and maintain than the If-Else-If structure—as we will see in a moment. Figure 8-8 shows an example of the Switch structure. Notice how much cleaner the Switch structure in the figure looks compared to the equivalent If-Else-If structure in Figure 8-6.

```
CODE BEHIND

    // Declare the variables.
    const Double dblDiscountRateStandard = 0.10;
    const Double dblDiscountRateSelect = 0.20;
    const Double dblDiscountRatePreferred = 0.30;
    Double dblSubtotal = 100;
    String strCustomerType = "Standard";

    // Apply the discount rate based on the type of customer.
    switch (strCustomerType)
    {
        case "Standard":
            dblSubtotal = dblSubtotal * (1 - dblDiscountRateStandard);
            break;
        case "Select":
            dblSubtotal = dblSubtotal * (1 - dblDiscountRateSelect);
            break;
        case "Preferred":
            dblSubtotal = dblSubtotal * (1 - dblDiscountRatePreferred);
            break;
        default:
            // Do not apply a discount.
            break;
    }
    // dblSubtotal = 90
```

Figure 8-8. *Example of the Switch structure*

8.5.6 Switch-Through Structure

The Switch-Through structure is not a different *type* of Switch structure. Instead, it is a *variation* of the Switch structure just discussed. In fact, the Switch-Through structure follows all the same rules of the Switch structure. The only difference is that the Switch-Through structure permits us to execute the *same* block of code in multiple cases, thus avoiding the need to write and maintain duplicate code. Figure 8-9 shows an example of the Switch-Through structure.

Notice at 01 that a discount will not be applied when a customer purchases 1 to 3 items.

Notice at 02, 03, and 04, however, that a 10%, 20%, or 30% discount will be applied when a customer purchases 4 to 6, 7 to 9, or 10 or more items, respectively.

```
CODE BEHIND

     // Declare the variables.
     Double dblSubtotal = 100;
     Double dblDiscountRate = 0;
     Byte bytNumberOfOrderLines = 5;

     // If the customer purchases 1-3 items, do not apply a discount.
     // If the customer purchases 4-6 items, apply a 10% discount.
     // If the customer purchases 7-9 items, apply a 20% discount.
     // If the customer purchases 10 or more items, apply a 30% discount.
     switch (bytNumberOfOrderLines)
     {
01       case 1:
         case 2:
         case 3:
             // Do not apply a discount.
             break;
02       case 4:
         case 5:
         case 6:
             dblDiscountRate = 0.10;
             break;
03       case 7:
         case 8:
         case 9:
             dblDiscountRate = 0.20;
             break;
04       default:
             dblDiscountRate = 0.30;
             break;
     }
     dblSubtotal = dblSubtotal * (1 - dblDiscountRate);
     // dblSubtotal = 90, dblDiscountRate = 0.1
```

Figure 8-9. *Example of the Switch-Through structure*

8.6 Iterative Structures

Iterative structures (a.k.a., repeating structures, looping structures) execute a block of code repeatedly while or until a certain condition (i.e., a relational, equality, and/or logical operation) is true. In this section, we will look at the While structure, the Do-While structure, the For structure, and the For-Each structure. In addition, we will look at two C# statements that permit us to alter the execution of the iterative structures discussed in this chapter—namely, the Break statement and the Continue statement.

8.6.1 While Structure

A While structure (a.k.a., While loop) identifies the condition (or conditions) under which a block of code (i.e., one or more imperative programming statements) will be executed repeatedly. The general syntax of the While structure in the C# programming language is

```
while (Condition)
{
    Block of code
}
```

As can be seen, the While loop is a *pretest* loop. When a While loop is employed, the block of code in the body of the loop will be executed as long as the condition remains true. Since the condition is tested at the *top* of the While loop (i.e., *before* the block of code is executed), the block of code can be executed zero or more times. If the condition evaluates to true, the block of code will be executed. If the condition evaluates to false, the block of code will *not* be executed, and program flow will continue at the point immediately after the last bracket of the While loop. Figure 8-10 shows an example of the While structure.

Notice at 01 the definition of an array that contains three customers.[1]

Notice at 02 the declaration and initialization of the variable used to control the execution of the loop (i.e., i16Index).

Notice at 03 the postfix increment of i16Index. Observe that this postfix increment may affect the truth or falseness of the loop condition, which is tested again at the top of the loop after the body of the loop is executed.

---

[1]See Chapter 12, titled "Array Operations," for an explanation of this array definition.

CODE BEHIND

```
    // Define an array of customers.
01  String[] strCustomerArray = new String[] {"Davis, Dan", "Jones, Jerry",
        "Smith, Sally"};
02  Int16 i16Index = 0;
    String strCustomerList = "";

    // Add customers to the customer list while i16Index is less than or equal
    // to 2.
    while (i16Index <= 2)
    {
        strCustomerList = strCustomerList + strCustomerArray[i16Index] + "; ";
03      i16Index++;
    }
    // strCustomerList = "Davis, Dan; Jones, Jerry; Smith, Sally; "
```

Figure 8-10. *Example of the While structure*

8.6.2 Do-While Structure

A Do-While structure (a.k.a., Do-While loop, Do-Until loop) identifies the condition (or conditions) under which a block of code (i.e., one or more imperative programming statements) will be executed repeatedly. The general syntax of the Do-While structure in the C# programming language is

```
do
{
    Block of code
} while (Condition)
```

As can be seen, the Do-While loop is a *posttest* loop. When a Do-While loop is employed, the block of code in the body of the loop will be executed *at least once* and then as long as the condition remains true. Since the condition is tested at the *bottom* of the Do-While loop (i.e., *after* the block of code is executed), the block of code is executed one or more times. If the condition evaluates to true, the block of code will be executed again. If the condition evaluates to false, the block of code will *not* be executed again, and program flow will continue at the point immediately after the last bracket of the Do-While loop. Figure 8-11 shows an example of the Do-While structure.

Notice at 01 the definition of an array that contains three customers.[2]

---

[2]See Chapter 12, titled "Array Operations," for an explanation of this array definition.

Notice at 02 the declaration and initialization of the variable used to control the execution of the loop (i.e., i16Index).

Notice at 03 the postfix increment of i16Index. Observe that this postfix increment may affect the truth or falseness of the loop condition, which is tested again at the bottom of the loop after the body of the loop is executed. And finally, notice that the first customer was added to the customer list, even though i16Index was initialized to 0.

CODE BEHIND

```
    // Define an array of customers.
01  String[] strCustomerArray = new String[] { "Davis, Dan", "Jones, Jerry",
        "Smith, Sally" };
02  Int16 i16Index = 0;
    String strCustomerList = "";

    // Add customers to the customer list until i16Index is less than or equal
    // to 0.
    do
    {
        strCustomerList = strCustomerList + strCustomerArray[i16Index] + "; ";
03      i16Index++;
    } while (i16Index <= 0);
    // strCustomerList = "Davis, Dan; "
```

Figure 8-11. *Example of the Do-While structure*

8.6.3 For Structure

A For structure (a.k.a., For loop) identifies the condition (or conditions) under which a block of code (i.e., one or more imperative programming statements) will be executed repeatedly. The general syntax of the For structure in the C# programming language is

```
for (Initializer; Condition; Iterator)
{
    Block of code
}
```

As can be seen, the For loop is a *pretest* loop. When a For loop is employed, the block of code in the body of the loop will be executed as long as the condition remains true. Since the condition is tested at the *top* of the For loop (i.e., *before* the block of code is executed), the block of code can be executed zero or more times. If the condition evaluates to true, the block of code will be executed. If the condition evaluates to false, the block of code will *not* be executed, and program flow will continue at the point immediately after the last bracket of the For loop.

The For loop is, essentially, a While loop with some special characteristics. Unlike the While loop, which only contains a condition at the top of the loop, the For loop contains an *initializer*, a condition, and an *iterator* at the top of the loop. The initializer initializes the variable used to control the loop. This variable is *local* to the loop, so it *cannot* be used outside the body of the loop. However, it *can* be used as desired inside the body of the loop. The initializer is executed before any other part of the loop, and it is executed only once—immediately before the condition is tested for the first time. The iterator, on the other hand, defines what is to happen *after* the block of code in the body of the loop is executed. Although other types of expressions can be used as iterators, they usually take the form of a postfix increment (i++) or a postfix decrement (i--). For loops are typically used when we know (or will know by the time the loop is encountered) the number of times the block of code in the body of the loop should be executed, such as when we need to iterate over all the elements of an array. Figure 8-12 shows an example of the For structure.

Notice at 01 the definition of an array that contains five suppliers.[3]

Notice at 02 the top of the For structure. There are three things to notice here. The first is the initialization of the variable used to control the execution of the loop (i.e., i = 0). As can be seen, we have suspended the variable naming standards established earlier in this book, since For structure indices have traditionally taken the form i, j, k, and so on. The second is the condition of the loop. Notice that the code within the loop will continue to execute while i is less than or equal to 4. And the third is the postfix increment of i. Observe that this postfix increment may affect the truth or falseness of the loop condition, which is tested again at the top of the loop after the body of the loop is executed.

---

[3]See Chapter 12, titled "Array Operations," for an explanation of this array definition.

CODE BEHIND

```
     // Define an array of suppliers.
01   String[] strSupplierArray = new String[] { "Adidas", "Babolat", "Head",
         "Nike", "Prince" };
     String strSupplierList = "";

     // Add suppliers to the supplier list while i is less than or equal to 4.
02   for (Int16 i = 0; i <= 4; i++)
     {
         strSupplierList = strSupplierList + strSupplierArray[i] + "; ";
     }
     // strSupplierList = "Adidas; Babolat; Head; Nike; Prince; "
```

Figure 8-12. *Example of the For structure*

8.6.4 For-Each Structure

A For-Each structure (a.k.a., For-Each loop) executes a block of code (i.e., one or more imperative programming statements) for every item encountered in a collection of items (e.g., an array, a queue, a linked list). The general syntax of the For-Each structure in the C# programming language is

```
foreach (Item in Collection)
{
    Block of code
}
```

As can be seen, the For-Each loop is a *pretest* loop. When a For-Each loop is employed, the block of code in the body of the loop will be executed as long as items are encountered in the collection as the collection is being traversed from beginning to end. Since the condition (i.e., there are still items to be processed) is tested at the *top* of the For-Each loop (i.e., *before* the block of code is executed), the block of code can be executed zero or more times. If the condition evaluates to true, the block of code will be executed. If the condition evaluates to false, the block of code will *not* be executed, and program flow will continue at the point immediately after the last bracket of the For-Each loop.

The For-Each loop is similar to the For loop, except that the For-Each loop has no *explicit* initializer (e.g., i = 0) or iterator (e.g., i++). Instead, the For-Each loop is initialized and iterated *implicitly*. In other words, the For-Each loop always initializes to the first item in the collection and always iterates through every item in the collection until no more items are left to be traversed (or the loop is terminated prematurely). For-Each loops are often used in place of For loops when there is a need to iterate over all the items of a collection, since the For-Each loop requires no explicit initializer or iterator and is, thus, easier to read and maintain. Figure 8-13 shows an example of the For-Each structure.

Notice at 01 the definition of an array that contains five suppliers.[4]

Notice at 02 the top of the For-Each structure. There are two things to notice here. The first is that no explicit initialization of a loop-controlling variable is being performed. This is because the loop will always begin with the first item in the collection. The second is that no explicit iteration of a loop-controlling variable is being performed. This is because the loop will automatically move to the next item in the collection and will terminate only after the last item in the collection is processed—unless the loop is terminated prematurely. Observe that attempting to move to the next item in the collection may affect the truth or falseness of the loop condition, which is tested again at the top of the loop after the body of the loop is executed.

CODE BEHIND

```
     // Define an array of suppliers.
01   String[] strSupplierArray = new String[] { "Adidas", "Babolat", "Head",
         "Nike", "Prince" };
     String strSupplierList = "";

     // Add suppliers to the supplier list while suppliers remain in the array.
02   foreach (String strSupplier in strSupplierArray)
     {
         strSupplierList = strSupplierList + strSupplier + "; ";
     }
     // strSupplierList = "Adidas; Babolat; Head; Nike; Prince; "
```

Figure 8-13. *Example of the For-Each structure*

---

[4]See Chapter 12, titled "Array Operations," for an explanation of this array definition.

8.6.5 Break Statement

The Break statement prematurely terminates a loop. Whenever such a statement is encountered in a loop, the loop is exited, and program flow continues at the point immediately after the last bracket of the loop. Any of the iterative structures described in this chapter can be prematurely terminated using the Break statement. Figure 8-14 shows an example of the Break statement. Notice 01 that a Break statement is being used to terminate a For loop if i is not less than or equal to 2.

```
CODE BEHIND

    // Define an array of suppliers.
    String[] strSupplierArray = new String[] { "Adidas", "Babolat", "Head",
        "Nike", "Prince" };
    String strSupplierList = "";

    // Add suppliers to the supplier list while i is less than or equal to 4
    // or until 3 suppliers have been added to the supplier list.
    for (Int16 i = 0; i <= 4; i++)
    {
        if (i <= 2)
        {
            strSupplierList = strSupplierList + strSupplierArray[i] + "; ";
        }
        else
        {
01          break;
        }
    }
    // strSupplierList = "Adidas; Babolat; Head; "
```

Figure 8-14. *Example of the Break statement*

8.6.6 Continue Statement

The Continue statement passes control to the next iteration of a loop. Whenever such a statement is encountered in a loop, program flow is transferred directly back to the condition of the loop, where it is evaluated again for truth or falseness. Any of the iterative structures described in this chapter can pass control to the next iteration of a loop using the Continue statement. Figure 8-15 shows an example of the Continue statement.

Notice at 01 that a Continue statement is being used to pass control to the next iteration of a For loop if i is not evenly divisible by 2.

CODE BEHIND

```
     // Define an array of suppliers.
     String[] strSupplierArray = new String[] { "Adidas", "Babolat", "Head",
         "Nike", "Prince" };
     String strSupplierList = "";

     // Add every other supplier to the supplier list while i is less than or
     // equal to 4.
     for (Int16 i = 0; i <= 4; i++)
     {
         if (i % 2 == 0)
         {
             strSupplierList = strSupplierList + strSupplierArray[i] + "; ";
         }
         else
         {
01           continue;
         }
     }
     // strSupplierList = "Adidas; Head; Prince; "
```

Figure 8-15. *Example of the Continue statement*

CHAPTER 9

String Operations

9.1 Introduction

A string operation is a process that is performed on a String *object*. A String object is a String type that has been instantiated from the String class—usually when a string literal is assigned to it. As an example, consider the following String object declaration:

```
String strLastName = "Jones";
```

In this example, the newly instantiated String object is strLastName. Once this String object is instantiated, we can use its methods to manipulate the string.

In this chapter, we will begin by looking at concatenations. Concatenations join two or more separate items (including strings) so that they can be treated as a single item. Next, we will discuss escape sequences, which permit us to include formatting information or special characters in a string. After that, we will look at verbatim literals. Verbatim literals allow us to add new lines, tabs, backslashes, and other formatting commands and special characters to a string without using escape sequences. And finally, we will discuss the String class, which permits us to perform many useful string manipulations.

9.2 Concatenations

The word *concatenate* comes from the Latin word *concatenare*, which means to link together or join. Thus, to concatenate means to take two or more distinct items and place them next to each other so that they can be treated as a single item. In computer programming, the concatenation operation is often used to link two or more strings together so that they can be utilized as a single string. Other types (e.g., Byte, Decimal, Int32) can be concatenated with strings as well. Figure 9-1 shows some examples of string concatenations. Notice in the figure that the plus sign (+) concatenates Strings types and other types together.

© Robert E. Beasley 2020
R. E. Beasley, *Essential ASP.NET Web Forms Development*, https://doi.org/10.1007/978-1-4842-5784-5_9

CODE BEHIND

```csharp
        // Concatenate three strings.
        String strLastName = "Billingsley";
        String strFirstName = "Beth";
        String strMiddleInitial = "B";
        String strFullName = strFirstName + " " + strMiddleInitial + " " +
            strLastName;
        // strFullName = "Beth B Billingsley"

        // Append seven strings using the += operator.
        String strAddress = "6785 Barker Rd.";
        String strCity = "Bickman";
        String strState = "MS";
        String strZipCode = "68321";
        String strFullAddress = "";
        strFullAddress += strAddress;
        strFullAddress += " ";
        strFullAddress += strCity;
        strFullAddress += ", ";
        strFullAddress += strState;
        strFullAddress += " ";
        strFullAddress += strZipCode;
        // strFullAddress = "6785 Barker Rd. Bickman, MS 68321"

        // Concatenate a string and a number.
        Decimal decPrice = 199.00m;
        String strPrice = "Price: " + decPrice;
        // strPrice = "Price: 199.00"
```

Figure 9-1. *Examples of string concatenations*

9.3 Escape Sequences

An *escape character* is a character that changes the meaning of the character (or characters) that follow it within a string. Thus, an escape character is treated as a command in a string—not as data. In C#, the escape character is the backslash (\). An *escape sequence*, on the other hand, is a series of characters that begins with the escape character and ends with a character (or characters) that has a predefined meaning. Such a sequence includes either *formatting information* or *special characters*. Common escape sequences include

- \n to include a new line in a string

- \t to include a tab in a string

- \\ to include a backslash in a string

- \" to include a quote in a string

Figure 9-2 shows some examples of escape sequences. Notice in these examples that we are concatenating a number of strings and that some of them contain escape sequences.

CODE BEHIND

```
// Use the new line escape sequence (\n).
String strAddress = "6785 Barker Rd.";
String strCity = "Bickman";
String strState = "MS";
String strZipCode = "68321";
String strFullAddress = "";
strFullAddress = strAddress + "\n" + strCity + ", " + strState + " " +
    strZipCode;
// strFullAddress = "6785 Barker Rd.
//                   Bickman, MS 68321"

// Use the tab escape sequence (\t).
String strLastName1 = "Jones";
String strFirstName1 = "Joe";
String strLastName2 = "Smith";
String strFirstName2 = "Sally";
String strNameList = strLastName1 + "\t" + strFirstName1 + "\n" +
    strLastName2 + "\t" + strFirstName2;
// strNameList = "Jones   Joe
//                Smith   Sally"

// Use the backslash escape sequence (\\).
String strFilePath = "c:\\myfolder\\myfile.txt";
// strFilePath = "c:\myfolder\myfile.txt"

// Use the quote escape sequence (\").
String strMessage = "Please click \"Submit\" to complete your order.";
// strMessage = "Please click "Submit" to complete your order."
```

Figure 9-2. *Examples of escape sequences*

9.4 Verbatim Literals

The word *verbatim* comes from the Latin word *verbātim*, which means "word for word" or "in exactly the same form as the original." Many programming languages permit the declaration and use of *verbatim literals*. Verbatim literals allow us to add to new lines, tabs, backslashes, and other formatting commands and special characters to a string without using escape sequences. In C#, a verbatim literal always begins with an at sign (@) and a double quote (") and always ends with another double quote ("). Inside these double quotes, we can format a string that will be treated (e.g., displayed) verbatim. That is, we can format a string that will be treated exactly as it appears in the string. The only exception to this is when we want to display a double quote itself. In this case, we must enter two double quotes. Thus, the only special character in a verbatim literal is the double quote character. Figure 9-3 shows some examples of verbatim literals.

```
CODE BEHIND

    // Use a verbatim literal.
    String strFilePath = @"c:\myfolder\myfile.txt";
    // strFilePath = "c:\myfolder\myfile.txt"

    // Use a verbatim literal.
    String strMessage = @"Please click ""Submit"" to complete your order.";
    // strMessage = "Please click "Submit" to complete your order."
```

Figure 9-3. *Examples of verbatim literals*

9.5 String Class

The String class permits us to manipulate the string contained in a String object. The string in a String object is zero based. Thus, the *first* character in the string is at position *zero*, the *second* character in the string is at position *one*, and so on. Table 9-1 shows some of the properties, methods, and events of the String class. Notice the number of methods available to us via this class. Although there are many others, the methods shown in the figure are used relatively frequently. Also notice that the methods of the class return one of four things—a new string, a value indicating whether or not something was found in the string, a zero-based index identifying the location of something in the string, or an array of strings. In addition, notice that some of the methods of the class require one or more parameters of type Int32. These parameters must be nonnegative integers. Keep in mind that if we attempt to invoke the methods of a String object that has been set to null, a NullReferenceException will be thrown. To test for a String object that may have been set to null, we can use the static IsNullOrEmpty method of the String class.

Table 9-1. *Some of the properties, methods, and events of the String class*

Class String	
Namespace System[1]	
Properties	
Length	Gets the number of characters in the current String object.
Methods	
Concat(String, String)	Concatenates two specified instances of String.
Contains(String)	Returns a value indicating whether a specified substring occurs within this string.
EndsWith(String)	Determines whether the end of this string instance matches the specified string.
IndexOf(String)	Reports the zero-based index of the first occurrence of the specified string in this instance.
Insert(Int32, String)	Returns a new string in which a specified string is inserted at a specified index position in this instance.
IsNullOrEmpty(String)	Indicates whether the specified string is null or an Empty string.
LastIndexOf(String)	Reports the zero-based index position of the last occurrence of a specified string within this instance.
PadLeft(Int32)	Returns a new string that right aligns the characters in this instance by padding them with spaces on the left, for a specified total length.

(continued)

---

[1]All property, method, and event descriptions were taken directly from Microsoft's official documentation. The event handler methods used to handle the events of this class were omitted to conserve space. See the reference for all of the methods of this class.

Table 9-1. *(continued)*

PadRight(Int32)	Returns a new string that left aligns the characters in this string by padding them with spaces on the right, for a specified total length.
Remove(Int32)	Returns a new string in which all the characters in the current instance, beginning at a specified position and continuing through the last position, have been deleted.
Replace(String, String)	Returns a new string in which all occurrences of a specified string in the current instance are replaced with another specified string.
Split(String[], StringSplitOptions)	Splits a string into substrings based on the strings in an array. You can specify whether the substrings include empty array elements.
StartsWith(String)	Determines whether the beginning of this string instance matches the specified string.
Substring(Int32, Int32)	Retrieves a substring from this instance. The substring starts at a specified character position and has a specified length.
ToLower()	Returns a copy of this string converted to lowercase.
ToUpper()	Returns a copy of this string converted to uppercase.
Trim()	Removes all leading and trailing white-space characters from the current String object.
Trim(Char[])	Removes all leading and trailing occurrences of a set of characters specified in an array from the current String object.

Events

(See reference.)

Reference

https://msdn.microsoft.com/en-us/library/system.string(v=vs.110).aspx

Figure 9-4 shows some examples of the String class.

CODE BEHIND

```
// Get the number of characters in the string.
String strAddress = "123 Main Street";
Int32 i32LengthOfString = strAddress.Length;
// i32LengthOfString = 15

// Concatenate three strings.
String strLastName = "Billingsley";
String strFirstName = "Beth";
String strMiddleInitial = "B";
String strFullName = String.Concat(strFirstName, " ", strMiddleInitial,
    " ", strLastName);
// strFullName = "Beth B Billingsley"

// Check to see if the word "unhappy" exists in the string.
String strNotes = "Mr. Richards was unhappy with his order.";
Boolean booUnhappy = strNotes.Contains("unhappy");
// booUnhappy = true

// Check to see if the string ends with ".jpg".
String strImage = "NMSFA7S.jpg";
Boolean booCorrectFileType = strImage.EndsWith(".jpg");
// booCorrectFileType = true

// Get the position of "gmail" in the string.
String strEmailAddress = "mmyers@gmail.com";
Int32 i32DomainLocation = strEmailAddress.IndexOf("gmail");
// i32DomainLocation = 7

// Insert dashes into the string.
String strPhoneOld = "1234567890";
String strPhoneNew = "";
strPhoneNew = strPhoneOld.Insert(3, "-");
strPhoneNew = strPhoneNew.Insert(7, "-");
// strPhoneNew = "123-456-7890"
```

Figure 9-4. *Examples of the String class*

```
// Determine whether or not the string is null.
String strAddress1 = null;
String strAddress2 = "";
String strAddress3 = "123 Main Street";
Boolean booIsNull;
booIsNull = String.IsNullOrEmpty(strAddress1);
// booIsNull = true
booIsNull = String.IsNullOrEmpty(strAddress2);
// booIsNull = true
booIsNull = String.IsNullOrEmpty(strAddress3);
// booIsNull = false

// Find the position of the last "." in the string.
strEmailAddress = "Cecil.C.Cook@yahoo.com";
Int32 i32LastPeriod = strEmailAddress.LastIndexOf(".");
// i32LastPeriod = 18

// Right-align the characters in a 15 character string by
// padding them with spaces on the left.
String strLastNameOld = "Fredericks";
String strLastNameNew = strLastNameOld.PadLeft(15);
// strLastNameNew = "     Fredericks"

// Left-align the characters in a 15 character string by
// padding them with spaces on the right.
strLastNameOld = "Fredericks";
strLastNameNew = strLastNameOld.PadRight(15);
// strLastNameNew = "Fredericks     "

// Remove all the characters in the string beginning
// with the 10th character.
String strZipCodeOld = "12345-0000";
String strZipCodeNew = strZipCodeOld.Remove(5);
// strZipCodeNew = "12345"

// Replace all of the "-" in the string with "/".
String strDateOld = "20xx-07-10";
String strDateNew = strDateOld.Replace("-", "/");
// strDateNew = "20xx/07/10"
```

Figure 9-4. *(continued)*

```csharp
// Split the string up by " ", ",", and "." and
// place each word in an array.
Char[] chaSeparator = new Char[] {' ', ',', '.'};
String[] strMessageArray = new String[5];
String strMessage = "For today's special, see below.";
strMessageArray = strMessage.Split(chaSeparator,
    StringSplitOptions.RemoveEmptyEntries);
// strMessageArray[0] = "For"
// strMessageArray[1] = "today's"
// strMessageArray[2] = "special"
// strMessageArray[3] = "see"
// strMessageArray[4] = "below"

// Check to see if the string begins with "Nike".
String strProduct = "Nike Flare Women's Shoe";
Boolean booNike = strProduct.StartsWith("Nike");
// booNike = true

// Extract characters from the string beginning at position
// 5 for a length of 2.
String strDate = "20xx-07-10";
String strMonth = strDate.Substring(5, 2);
// strMonth = "07"

// Force all of the characters in the string to lower case.
String strPasswordOld = "ABC123";
String strPasswordNew = strPasswordOld.ToLower();
// strPasswordNew = "abc123"

// Format the number as a string.
Decimal decPrice = 199.00m;
String strPrice = decPrice.ToString();
// strPrice = "199.00"

// Format the number as currency with the specified
// number of decimal places.
decPrice = 199.00m;
strPrice = decPrice.ToString("c2");
// strPrice = "$199.00"

// Format the number with the specified number of decimal places.
decPrice = 10.99m;
strPrice = decPrice.ToString("f4");
// strPrice = "10.9900"
```

Figure 9-4. *(continued)*

```
// Format the number with thousands separators with the specified
// number of decimal places.
decPrice = 1099m;
strPrice = decPrice.ToString("n2");
// strPrice = "1,099.00"

// Format the number as a percentage with the specified
// number of decimal places. Note: decNumberInStock and
// decReorderLevel cannot be defined as integers or
// integer division will take place, which will not
// yield the correct result.
Decimal decNumberInStock = 9m;
Decimal decReorderLevel = 2m;
Decimal decSafetyLevel = 1 - (decReorderLevel / decNumberInStock);
String strSafetyLevel = decSafetyLevel.ToString("p0");
// strSafetyLevel = "78%"

// Force all of the characters in the string to upper case.
strPasswordOld = "abc123";
strPasswordNew = strPasswordOld.ToUpper();
// strPasswordNew = "ABC123"

// Remove from the string all leading and trailing blanks.
strLastNameOld = "   Everest   ";
strLastNameNew = strLastNameOld.Trim();
// strLastNameNew = "Everest"

// Remove from the string all leading and trailing characters
// that are in the array of characters to be removed.
Char[] chaCharactersToRemove = new Char[] {'*', '#'};
strLastNameOld = "*#*Everest#*#";
strLastNameNew = strLastNameOld.Trim(chaCharactersToRemove);
// strLastNameNew = "Everest"
```

Figure 9-4.   *(continued)*

CHAPTER 10

Arithmetic Operations

10.1 Introduction

An arithmetic operation is a process that takes one or more input values (i.e., operands), performs some kind of mathematical function with those values, and then assigns the result to an output. The most basic arithmetic operations are addition, subtraction, multiplication, and division. However, there are many more arithmetic operations, including comparison operations (e.g., minimum, maximum), exponential operations (e.g., k^n), logarithmic operations (e.g., $\log_2 n$, $\ln n$), magnitude operations (e.g., absolute value), power operations (e.g., n^k), radical operations (e.g., square root, cube root), rounding operations (e.g., round, floor, ceiling, truncate), and trigonometric operations (e.g., sine, cosine, tangent).

In this chapter, we will begin by looking at several arithmetic operators, including the addition, subtraction, multiplication, division, modulo, postfix increment, postfix decrement, prefix increment, and prefix decrement operators. Next, we will look at the concept of order of precedence, which defines the sequence in which multiple arithmetic operations are performed in a single mathematical expression. We will also discuss the concept of associativity, which defines the sequence in which multiple arithmetic operations are performed in a single mathematical expression—when two or more arithmetic operators have the same order of precedence. After that, we will consider parentheses. Parentheses make the intent of a multiple-operator mathematical expression easier to understand, and they override the default order of precedence or associativity. And finally, we will look at the Math class, which is a powerful static class that permits us to perform comparison operations, exponential operations, logarithmic operations, magnitude operations, power operations, radical operations, rounding operations, trigonometric operations, and many other common mathematical operations very easily.

© Robert E. Beasley 2020
R. E. Beasley, *Essential ASP.NET Web Forms Development*, https://doi.org/10.1007/978-1-4842-5784-5_10

10.2 Arithmetic Operators

An arithmetic operator invokes a mathematical operation. All imperative programming languages contain at least a minimal set of arithmetic operators, including addition, subtraction, multiplication, and division. The C# programming language also includes the modulo operator as one of its basic operators. The addition operator (+) computes the *sum* of two operands (i.e., one addend plus another addend). The subtraction operator (-) is the opposite of the addition operator. The subtraction operator computes the *difference* between two operands (i.e., the minuend minus the subtrahend). The multiplication operator (∗) computes the *product* of two operands (i.e., the multiplicand times the multiplier). The division (/) operator is the opposite of the multiplication operator. The division operator computes the *quotient* of two operands (i.e., the dividend split into equal quantities by the divisor). And finally, the modulo operator (%) computes the *remainder* (a.k.a., modulus) after the division of one operand by another operand.

In addition to the addition, subtraction, multiplication, division, and modulo operators, the C# programming language includes the postfix increment and decrement operators and the prefix increment and decrement operators. The postfix increment operator (operand++) increments an operand *after* its associated assignment operation is performed. Thus, after the statement is executed, the value of the assigned variable will be *different than* the value of the operand. The postfix decrement operator (operand--) decrements an operand *after* its associated assignment operation is performed. Again, after the statement is executed, the value of the assigned variable will be *different than* the value of the operand. The prefix increment operator (++operand) increments an operand *before* its associated assignment operation is performed. Thus, after the statement is executed, the value of the assigned variable will be *the same as* the value of the operand. And finally, the prefix decrement operator (--operand) decrements an operand *before* its associated assignment operation is performed. Again, after the statement is executed, the value of the assigned variable will be *the same as* the value of the operand. As can be seen, there is a subtle difference between the postfix operators and the prefix operators. This is why we must carefully test any code that contains these operators to make sure they are behaving as expected.

Table 10-1 summarizes the common C# arithmetic operators and their respective descriptions. Notice that there are no arithmetic operators in C# for exponentiation and roots. This is because the Math class, which we will discuss later, contains methods for performing these operations.

Table 10-1. *Common C# arithmetic operators and their respective descriptions*

Operator	Description
z = x + y	Addition (i.e., compute the *sum* of x and y)
z = x − y	Subtraction (i.e., compute the *difference* between x and y)
z = x * y	Multiplication (i.e., compute the *product* of x and y)
z = x / y	Division (i.e., compute the *quotient* of x and y)
z = x % y	Modulo (i.e., compute the *remainder* after the division of x and y)
z = x++	Postfix increment (i.e., increment x *after* the assignment operation)
z = x--	Postfix decrement (i.e., decrement x *after* the assignment operation)
z = ++x	Prefix increment (i.e., increment x *before* the assignment operations)
z = --x	Prefix decrement (i.e., decrement x *before* the assignment operation)

Figure 10-1 shows some examples of the common arithmetic operators.

CODE BEHIND

```
    // Declare the variables.
    Int16 i16Number1 = 0;
    Double dblNumber1 = 0;
    Double dblNumber2 = 0;
    Double dblResult;

    // Add the numbers.
    dblNumber1 = 40;
    dblNumber2 = 8;
    dblResult = dblNumber1 + dblNumber2;
    // dblResult = 48

    // Subtract the numbers.
    dblNumber1 = 70;
    dblNumber2 = 10;
    dblResult = dblNumber1 - dblNumber2;
    // dblResult = 60

    // Multiply the numbers.
    dblNumber1 = 3;
    dblNumber2 = 2;
    dblResult = dblNumber1 * dblNumber2;
    // dblResult = 6

    // Divide the numbers.
    dblNumber1 = 7;
    dblNumber2 = 4;
    dblResult = dblNumber1 / dblNumber2;
    // dblResult = 1.75

    // Divide the first number by the second number giving the remainder.
    dblNumber1 = 12;
    dblNumber2 = 7;
    dblResult = dblNumber1 % dblNumber2;
    // dblResult = 5

    // Increment the number after the assignment.
    i16Number1 = 3;
    dblResult = i16Number1++;
    // dblResult = 3, i16Number1 = 4
```

Figure 10-1. *Examples of the common arithmetic operators*

```
// Decrement the number after the assignment.
i16Number1 = 7;
dblResult = i16Number1--;
// dblResult = 7, i16Number1 = 6

// Increment the number before the assignment.
i16Number1 = 12;
dblResult = ++i16Number1;
// dblResult = 13, i16Number1 = 13

// Decrement the number before the assignment.
i16Number1 = 40;
dblResult = --i16Number1;
// dblResult = 39, i16Number1 = 39
```

Figure 10-1. *(continued)*

10.3 Order of Precedence and Associativity

Arithmetic operations are performed according to an *order of precedence*. Order of precedence (i.e., operator precedence) defines the sequence in which arithmetic operations are performed in a multiple-operator mathematical expression. Associativity, on the other hand, defines the sequence in which arithmetic operations are performed in a multiple-operator mathematical expression *when two or more arithmetic operators have the same order of precedence. Left-associative operators* are evaluated from left to right, whereas *right-associative operators* are evaluated from right to left. When coding in any programming language, it is important to have a clear understanding of the order of precedence and associativity that that programming language applies when evaluating multiple-operator mathematical expressions. A lack of such an understanding can lead to unexpected results.

Table 10-2 shows the common C# arithmetic operators and their respective orders of precedence and associativities. Notice that the arithmetic operators in the figure are arranged in their order of precedence from high (1) to low (5) indicating the sequence in which the arithmetic operations are performed in a multiple-operator mathematical expression.

Table 10-2. *Common C# arithmetic operators and their respective orders of precedence and associativities*

Operator	Order of Precedence	Associativity
Operand++, Operand--	1	Left to right
++Operand, --Operand	2	Right to left
*, /, %	3	Left to right
+, -	4	Left to right
=	5	Right to left

Figure 10-2 shows some examples of order of precedence and associativity. Notice in the figure that all of the examples of order of precedence and associativity have equivalent examples. The parentheses in these equivalent examples demonstrate how order of precedence and associativity are actually carried out. The arithmetic operations in the innermost parentheses are carried out first, the arithmetic operations in the next most innermost parentheses are carried out next, and so on.

```
CODE BEHIND

    // Declare the variables.
    Byte bytValue;
    Double dblNumber1 = 2;
    Double dblNumber2 = 3;
    Double dblNumber3 = 4;
    Double dblResult;

    // This is an example of order of precedence.
    bytValue = 1;
    dblResult = dblNumber1 * dblNumber2 * ++bytValue;
    // dblResult = 12

    // This is the equivalent.
    bytValue = 1;
    dblResult = dblNumber1 * dblNumber2 * (++bytValue);
    // dblResult = 12

    // This is an example of order of precedence.
    dblResult = dblNumber1 + dblNumber2 * dblNumber3;
    // dblResult = 14

    // This is the equivalent.
    dblResult = dblNumber1 + (dblNumber2 * dblNumber3);
    // dblResult = 14

    // This is an example of left associativity.
    dblResult = dblNumber1 * dblNumber2 % dblNumber3;
    // dblResult = 2

    // This is the equivalent.
    dblResult = (dblNumber1 * dblNumber2) % dblNumber3;
    // dblResult = 2

    // This is an example of right associativity.
    dblResult = dblNumber1 = dblNumber2 = dblNumber3;
    // dblResult = 4

    // This is the equivalent.
    dblResult = (dblNumber1 = (dblNumber2 = dblNumber3));
    // dblResult = 4
```

Figure 10-2. *Examples of order of precedence and associativity*

10.4 Parentheses

Parentheses are used for two reasons when coding arithmetic operations. First, they *clarify* the order in which the operations in a multiple-operator mathematical expression are evaluated. That is, they make the intent of the expression easier to understand. This practice was applied in the previous section to demonstrate how order of precedence and associativity are actually carried out and is recommended when coding all but the simplest of multiple-operator expressions. Second, parentheses *override* the default order in which the operations in a multiple-operator mathematical expression are evaluated. In other words, they override the default order of precedence or associativity. Figure 10-3 shows some examples of using parentheses to override order of precedence and associativity. Again, the arithmetic operations in the innermost parentheses are carried out first, the arithmetic operations in the next most innermost parentheses are carried out next, and so on.

```
CODE BEHIND

        // Declare the variables.
        Double dblNumber1 = 2;
        Double dblNumber2 = 3;
        Double dblNumber3 = 4;
        Double dblResult;

        // This is an example of order of precedence.
        dblResult = dblNumber1 + dblNumber2 * dblNumber3;
        // dblResult = 14

        // This is the equivalent.
        dblResult = dblNumber1 + (dblNumber2 * dblNumber3);
        // dblResult = 14

        // This is overriding the order of precedence using parentheses.
        dblResult = (dblNumber1 + dblNumber2) * dblNumber3;
        // dblResult = 20

        // This is an example of left associativity.
        dblResult = dblNumber1 * dblNumber2 % dblNumber3;
        // dblResult = 2

        // This is the equivalent.
        dblResult = (dblNumber1 * dblNumber2) % dblNumber3;
        // dblResult = 2

        // This is overriding the left associativity using parentheses.
        dblResult = dblNumber1 * (dblNumber2 % dblNumber3);
        // dblResult = 6
```

Figure 10-3. *Examples of using parentheses to override order of precedence and associativity*

10.5 Math Class

In addition to the basic arithmetic operations of addition, subtraction, multiplication, division, modulo, postfix increment, postfix decrement, prefix increment, and prefix decrement, C# provides a number of more sophisticated operations via the methods of the Math class. The Math class is a static class whose methods include comparison operations, exponential operations, logarithmic operations, magnitude operations, power operations, radical operations, rounding operations, trigonometric operations, and other common arithmetic operations.

Table 10-3 shows some of the properties, methods, and events of the Math class. Note that all of the methods shown in the table operate on the Double type. However, many of them can operate on other numeric types as well. See the reference for more information.

Table 10-3. *Some of the properties, methods, and events of the Math class*

Class Math[1]

Namespace System

Properties

(See reference.)

Methods

Abs(Double)	Returns the absolute value of a double number.
Ceiling(Double)	Returns the smallest integral value that is greater than or equal to the specified double number.
Floor(Double)	Returns the largest integer less than or equal to the specified double number.
Max(Double, Double)	Returns the larger of two double numbers.
Min(Double, Double)	Returns the smaller of two double numbers.
Pow(Double, Double)	Returns a specified number raised to the specified power.

(continued)

---

[1]All property, method, and event descriptions were taken directly from Microsoft's official documentation. The event handler methods used to handle the events of this class were omitted to conserve space. See the reference for all of the methods of this class.

Table 10-3. (*continued*)

Round(Double, Int32, MidpointRounding)	Rounds a double value to a specified number of fractional digits. A parameter specifies how to round the value if it is midway between two numbers.
Sign(Double)	Returns an integer that indicates the sign of a double number.
Sqrt(Double)	Returns the square root of a specified number.
Truncate(Double)	Calculates the integral part of a specified double number.

Events

(See reference.)

Reference

```
https://msdn.microsoft.com/en-us/library/system.math(v=vs.110).aspx
```

Figure 10-4 shows some examples of the Math class. The results returned from the methods in the figure are described in Table 10-3. However, there is one method that requires some additional explanation.

Notice at 01–04 that the Round method of the Math class is being employed. In some programming languages, decimal values that end in 5 are, by default, rounded *up* to the nearest value during the rounding process. For example, the numbers 1.5 and 2.5 would be rounded *up* to 2 and 3, respectively, thus following the standard *mathematical rounding* convention. However, in C#, decimal values that end in 5 are, by default, rounded *up or down* to the nearest *even* value during the rounding process *depending on the number being rounded.* For example, the numbers 1.5 and 3.5 would be rounded *up* to 2 and 4, respectively, whereas the numbers 2.5 and 4.5 would be rounded *down* to 2 and 4, respectively. Thus, rounding to an odd value would never occur. This approach follows the standard *banker's rounding* convention. The reason given for using this particular method of rounding is that it avoids roundup bias when rounding a large set of numbers. So, if our intention is to perform standard mathematical rounding, we *must* use the MidpointRounding.AwayFromZero parameter in the Math.Round method.

CODE BEHIND

```
// Declare the variables.
Double dblNumber1 = 0;
Double dblNumber2 = 0;
Double dblResult;

// Compute the absolute value.
dblNumber1 = -3.21;
dblResult = Math.Abs(dblNumber1);
// dblResult = 3.21

// Compute the ceiling.
dblNumber1 = 3.21;
dblResult = Math.Ceiling(dblNumber1);
// dblResult = 4

// Compute the ceiling.
dblNumber1 = -3.21;
dblResult = Math.Ceiling(dblNumber1);
// dblResult = -3

// Compute the ceiling.
dblNumber1 = 0.21;
dblResult = Math.Ceiling(dblNumber1);
// dblResult = 1

// Compute the ceiling.
dblNumber1 = -0.21;
dblResult = Math.Ceiling(dblNumber1);
// dblResult = 0

// Compute the floor.
dblNumber1 = 3.21;
dblResult = Math.Floor(dblNumber1);
// dblResult = 3

// Compute the floor.
dblNumber1 = -3.21;
dblResult = Math.Floor(dblNumber1);
// dblResult = -4

// Compute the floor.
dblNumber1 = 0.21;
dblResult = Math.Floor(dblNumber1);
// dblResult = 0
```

Figure 10-4. *Examples of the Math class*

```
    // Compute the floor.
    dblNumber1 = -0.21;
    dblResult = Math.Floor(dblNumber1);
    // dblResult = -1

    // Get the larger of the two numbers.
    dblNumber1 = 3.5;
    dblNumber2 = 7.5;
    dblResult = Math.Max(dblNumber1, dblNumber2);
    // dblResult = 7.5

    // Get the smaller of the two numbers.
    dblNumber1 = 3.5;
    dblNumber2 = 7.5;
    dblResult = Math.Min(dblNumber1, dblNumber2);
    // dblResult = 3.5

    // Raise the number to the 3rd power.
    dblNumber1 = 3;
    dblResult = Math.Pow(dblNumber1, 3);
    // dblResult = 27

    // Round the number up or down to the nearest even value.
    // This is banker's rounding, which is the default.
    dblNumber1 = 1.5;
01  dblResult = Math.Round(dblNumber1, 0, MidpointRounding.ToEven);
    // dblResult = 2 (Rounded up.)

    // Round the number up or down to the nearest even value.
    // This is banker's rounding, which is the default.
    dblNumber1 = 2.5;
02  dblResult = Math.Round(dblNumber1, 0, MidpointRounding.ToEven);
    // dblResult = 2 (Rounded down.)

    // Round the number up or down to the nearest value.
    // This is standard rounding, which is not the default.
    dblNumber1 = 1.5;
03  dblResult = Math.Round(dblNumber1, 0, MidpointRounding.AwayFromZero);
    // dblResult = 2 (Rounded up.)

    // Round the number up or down to the nearest value.
    // This is standard rounding, which is not the default.
    dblNumber1 = 2.5;
```

Figure 10-4. *(continued)*

```
04  dblResult = Math.Round(dblNumber1, 0, MidpointRounding.AwayFromZero);
    // dblResult = 3 (Rounded up.)

    // Get the sign of the number.
    dblNumber1 = 12;
    dblResult = Math.Sign(dblNumber1);
    // dblResult = 1

    // Get the sign of the number.
    dblNumber1 = -12;
    dblResult = Math.Sign(dblNumber1);
    // dblResult = -1

    // Compute the square root of the number.
    dblNumber1 = 16;
    dblResult = Math.Sqrt(dblNumber1);
    // dblResult = 4

    // Truncate the number.
    dblNumber1 = 3.712;
    dblResult = Math.Truncate(dblNumber1);
    // dblResult = 3
```

Figure 10-4. *(continued)*

CHAPTER 11

Date and Time Operations

11.1 Introduction

Date and time operations manipulate temporal values (i.e., values related to time). Common date and time operations include retrieving the current date and time from the operating system, extracting the components of a date (e.g., year, month, day) or time (e.g., hour, minute, second), adding to or subtracting from the components of a date or time, comparing one date or time with another date or time, determining whether or not daylight saving time is in effect, determining whether or not it is a leap year, determining the interval between two dates or times, formatting a date or time, and parsing a date and time.

In this chapter, we will begin by looking at the DateTime structure, which permits us to create and work with dates and times. Next, we will discuss the date-related properties of the DateTime structure that permit us to retrieve the date from the operating system and extract the components of a date. Then, we will look at the date-related methods that permit us to add to or subtract from the components of a date, compare one date with another, determine whether or not daylight saving time is in effect, determine whether or not it is a leap year, and determine the time interval between two dates. After that, we will discuss the date-related methods that permit us to format a date to look the way we want it to. We will also look at the date-related method that permits us to parse a date (and time). After considering the date-related properties and methods of the DateTime structure, we will discuss the time-related properties and methods of the DateTime structure. First, we will consider the time-related properties of the DateTime structure that permit us to retrieve the time from the operating system and extract the components of a time. After that, we will look at the time-related methods that permit us to add to or subtract from the components of a time, compare one time with another, and determine the interval between two times. And finally, we will discuss the time-related methods that permit us to format a time to look the way we want it to.

© Robert E. Beasley 2020
R. E. Beasley, *Essential ASP.NET Web Forms Development*, https://doi.org/10.1007/978-1-4842-5784-5_11

11.2 DateTime Structure

The DateTime structure permits us to create and work with dates and times. This structure is capable of representing dates and times between 00:00:00 AM on January 1, 1 A.D., and 11:59:59 PM on December 31, 9999 A.D. In C#, time is measured in *ticks*, where 1 tick is equal to 100 nanoseconds (i.e., 1 billionth of a second). Thus, a given date and time is equal to the number of ticks that have occurred since 00:00:00 AM on January 1, 1 A.D. DateTime values are stated in terms of a calendar. The default calendar in .NET is the *Gregorian calendar* (a.k.a., the Western calendar or the Christian calendar), but other calendars can be used as well. The Gregorian calendar is the most widely used calendar in the world today and is based on a 365-day year that is divided into 12 months of irregular length. While most of the months in the Gregorian calendar have 30 or 31 days, one month (i.e., February) has 28 days—plus one day during a leap year, which makes the Gregorian leap year 366 days long.

Notice that the DateTime structure is referred to as a *structure*—not a *class*. This is because the DateTime structure is a *value* type, which holds a date and time *value* that has a set memory allocation size (i.e., 64 bits or 8 bytes). A class, on the other hand, is a *reference* type, which holds a *pointer* to another memory address that does *not* have a set memory allocation size. However, as we will soon see, the DateTime structure looks and behaves much like a class.

Table 11-1 shows some of the properties, methods, and events of the DateTime structure. Notice in the table that there are no methods shown for *subtracting* years, months, days, hours, minutes, seconds, and so on. This is because we can perform these operations by passing *negative* values to the associated Add methods. Notice as well the reference to *local time* in the description of the Now property. Local time is associated with a particular time zone—the time zone in which the server resides. US time zones include Hawaii, Alaska, Pacific, Mountain, Central, and Eastern. Depending on the how the date is configured on a particular server, the local time zone may automatically adjust to daylight saving time at 2:00 AM on the second Sunday in March and then revert back to standard time at 2:00 AM on the first Sunday in November—at least for most of the United States. If it were desirable for the local time of the *client* to be displayed in the Web browser, we would need to use JavaScript (discussed later in this book) to retrieve the local time from the client's operating system.

Table 11-1. *Some of the properties, methods, and events of the DateTime structure*

Structure DateTime[1]

Namespace System

Properties

Day	Gets the day of the month represented by this instance.
DayOfWeek	Gets the day of the week represented by this instance.
DayOfYear	Gets the day of the year represented by this instance.
Hour	Gets the hour component of the date represented by this instance.
Minute	Gets the minute component of the date represented by this instance.
Month	Gets the month component of the date represented by this instance.
Now	Gets a DateTime structure that is set to the current date and time on this computer, expressed as the local time.
Second	Gets the seconds component of the date represented by this instance.
TimeOfDay	Gets the time of day for this instance.
Today	Gets the current date.
Year	Gets the year component of the date represented by this instance.

Methods

AddDays(Double)	Returns a new DateTime that adds the specified number of days to the value of this instance.
AddHours(Double)	Returns a new DateTime that adds the specified number of hours to the value of this instance.
AddMinutes(Double)	Returns a new DateTime that adds the specified number of minutes to the value of this instance.
AddMonths(Int32)	Returns a new DateTime that adds the specified number of months to the value of this instance.

(continued)

---

[1]All property, method, and event descriptions were taken directly from Microsoft's official documentation. The event handler methods used to handle the events of this class were omitted to conserve space. See the reference for all of the methods of this class.

Table 11-1. (continued)

AddSeconds(Double)	Returns a new DateTime that adds the specified number of seconds to the value of this instance.
AddYears(Int32)	Returns a new DateTime that adds the specified number of years to the value of this instance.
CompareTo(DateTime)	Compares the value of this instance to a specified DateTime value and returns an integer that indicates whether this instance is earlier than, the same as, or later than the specified DateTime value.
IsDaylightSavingTime()	Indicates whether this instance of DateTime is within the daylight saving time range for the current time zone.
IsLeapYear(Int32)	Returns an indication whether the specified year is a leap year.
Subtract(DateTime)	Subtracts the specified date and time from this instance.
ToLongDateString()	Converts the value of the current DateTime structure to its equivalent long date string representation.
ToLongTimeString()	Converts the value of the current DateTime structure to its equivalent long time string representation.
ToShortDateString()	Converts the value of the current DateTime structure to its equivalent short date string representation.
ToShortTimeString()	Converts the value of the current DateTime structure to its equivalent short time string representation.
ToString()	Converts the value of the current DateTime structure to its equivalent string representation using the formatting conventions of the current culture.
ToString(String)	Converts the value of the current DateTime structure to its equivalent string representation using the specified format and the formatting conventions of the current culture.
TryParse(String, DateTime)	Converts the specified string representation of a date and time to its DateTime equivalent and returns a value that indicates whether the conversion succeeded.

(continued)

Table 11-1. (*continued*)

Events

(See reference.)

Reference

https://msdn.microsoft.com/en-us/library/system.datetime(v=vs.110).aspx

11.3 Date-Related Properties

The date-related properties described in this section permit us to retrieve the date from the operating system and extract the components of a date. Figure 11-1 shows some examples of date-related properties.

Notice at 01 that we are getting today's date from the operating system using the Today property. As can be seen, when we use this property to get the current date, the time part of the date is set to 12:00:00 AM. This is because we are only asking for the date.

```
CODE BEHIND

    // Get today's date.
01  String strDate = DateTime.Today.ToString();
    // strDate = "7/18/2017 12:00:00 AM"

    // Get the year.
    Int32 i32Year = DateTime.Today.Year;
    // i32Year = 2017

    // Get the month.
    Int32 i32Month = DateTime.Today.Month;
    // i32Month = 7

    // Get the day.
    Int32 i32Day = DateTime.Today.Day;
    // i32Day = 18

    // Get the day of the week.
    String strDayOfWeek = DateTime.Today.DayOfWeek.ToString();
    // strDayOfWeek = "Tuesday"

    // Get the day of the year.
    Int32 i32DayOfYear = DateTime.Today.DayOfYear;
    // i32DayOfYear = 199
```

Figure 11-1. *Examples of date-related properties*

11.4 Date-Related Methods

The date-related methods described in this section permit us to add to or subtract from the components of a date, compare one date with another, determine whether or not daylight saving time is in effect, determine whether or not it is a leap year, and determine the time interval between two dates. Figure 11-2 shows some examples of date-related methods.

```
CODE BEHIND

          // Create a new DateTime structure.
          DateTime datDateCurrent = new DateTime();
          datDateCurrent = DateTime.Today;
          // datDateCurrent = {7/18/2017 12:00:00 AM}
          String strDateNew = "";
          // strDateNew = ""

          // Add 1 year to the current date.
          strDateNew = datDateCurrent.AddYears(1).ToString();
          // strDateNew = "7/18/2018 12:00:00 AM"

          // Add 3 months to the current date.
          strDateNew = datDateCurrent.AddMonths(3).ToString();
          // strDateNew = "10/18/2017 12:00:00 AM"

          // Add 5 days to the current date.
          strDateNew = datDateCurrent.AddDays(5).ToString();
          // strDateNew = "7/23/2017 12:00:00 AM"

          // Compare the current date to the first-of-year date.
          // Less than zero = The current date is earlier than the first-of-year
          // date.
          // Zero = The current date is the same as the first-of-year date.
          // Greater than zero = The current date is later than the first-of-year
          // date.
          DateTime datDateFirstOfYear = new DateTime(2017, 01, 01);
          Int32 i32Result = datDateCurrent.CompareTo(datDateFirstOfYear);
          // i32Result = 1

          // Check to see if daylight saving time is in effect.
          Boolean booDaylightSavingTime = datDateCurrent.IsDaylightSavingTime();
          // booDaylightSavingTime = true

          // Check to see if this is a leap year.
          Boolean booLeapYear = DateTime.IsLeapYear(datDateCurrent.Year);
          // booLeapYear = false

          // Determine how many days have elapsed since the first-of-year date
          // using a TimeSpan structure.
          TimeSpan timTimeSpan = datDateCurrent.Subtract(datDateFirstOfYear);
          Int32 i32DifferenceDays = timTimeSpan.Days;
          // i32DifferenceDays = 198
```

Figure 11-2. *Examples of date-related methods*

11.5 Date Formatting

The date-related methods described in this section permit us to format a date to look the way we want it to. Since dates must often be displayed differently depending on cultural norms, international standards, application requirements, personal preference, and so on, the DateTime structure permits us to format dates via special formatting methods (e.g., the ToLongDateString method, the ToShortDateString method) and via the ToString method *overloaded* with *format specifiers*. Essentially, the ToString method is overloaded when we pass format specifiers to it as a parameter. Table 11-2 shows some of the custom date format specifiers.

Table 11-2. *Some of the custom date format specifiers*

Format Specifier	Description
"d"	The day of the month, from 1 through 31.
"dd"	The day of the month, from 01 through 31.
"ddd"	The abbreviated name of the day of the week.
"dddd"	The full name of the day of the week.
"g"	The period or era.
"M"	The month, from 1 through 12.
"MM"	The month, from 01 through 12.
"MMM"	The abbreviated name of the month.
"MMMM"	The full name of the month.
"y"	The year, from 0 to 99.
"yy"	The year, from 00 to 99.
"yyyy"	The year as a four-digit number.

Reference

https://docs.microsoft.com/en-us/dotnet/standard/base-types/custom-date-and-time-format-strings

Figure 11-3 shows some examples of date formatting.

```
CODE BEHIND

    // Declare the date string.
    String strDateNew = "";

    // Format the date as a long date.
    strDateNew = DateTime.Today.ToLongDateString();
    // strDateNew = "Tuesday, July 18, 2017"

    // Format the date as a short date.
    strDateNew = DateTime.Today.ToShortDateString();
    // strDateNew = "7/18/2017"

    // Customize the date using format specifiers.
    strDateNew = DateTime.Today.ToString("yyyy.MM.dd");
    // strDateNew = "2017.07.18"

    // Customize the date using format specifiers.
    strDateNew = DateTime.Today.ToString("dddd, MMMM dd, yyyy g");
    // strDateNew = "Tuesday, July 18, 2017 A.D."
```

Figure 11-3. *Examples of date formatting*

11.6 Date Parsing

The date-related method described in this section permits us to *parse* a date.[2] To parse a date means to take a date that is in the form of a string, break it down into its component parts, and convert it to a valid DateTime structure. To parse a date in the C# programming language, we can use the TryParse method of the DateTime structure. Figure 11-4 shows some examples of date parsing.

Notice at 01 that the TryParse method contains two parameters. The first is the method's *input* parameter. This parameter requires a date in the form of a String type. The second is the method's *output* parameter. This parameter returns a date in the form of a DateTime type. As can be seen in this example, since the parse was successful, the parsed date was placed in the output DateTime structure, and the method returned a true.

---

[2]A time can be parsed as well.

Notice at 01–03 that we are attempting to parse a date that contains dashes, a date that contains slashes, and a date that is written out. As can be seen, the parse was successful in all three cases. This demonstrates the flexibility of the TryParse method.

Notice at 04 that we are attempting to parse an invalid date. As can be seen in this example, since the parse was *not* successful, 1/1/0001 12:00:00 AM was placed in the output DateTime structure, and the method returned a false. This parse was unsuccessful because 02-29-2017 is not a valid date during a non-leap year.

```
CODE BEHIND

      // Declare the date structure and variables.
      DateTime datDate = new DateTime();
      String strDate = "";
      Boolean booSuccessful = false;

      // Attempt to parse a valid date (with dashes) from a string.
      // Check to make sure the parse was successful.
      strDate = "02-28-2017";
01    booSuccessful = DateTime.TryParse(strDate, out datDate);
      // datDate = {2/28/2017 12:00:00 AM}, booSuccessful = true

      // Attempt to parse a valid date (with slashes) from a string.
      // Check to make sure the parse was successful.
      strDate = "02/28/2017";
02    booSuccessful = DateTime.TryParse(strDate, out datDate);
      // datDate = {2/28/2017 12:00:00 AM}, booSuccessful = true

      // Attempt to parse a valid date (written out) from a string.
      // Check to make sure the parse was successful.
      strDate = "February 28, 2017";
03    booSuccessful = DateTime.TryParse(strDate, out datDate);
      // datDate = {2/28/2017 12:00:00 AM}, booSuccessful = true

      // Attempt to parse an invalid date from a string. Check to make
      // sure the parse was successful.
      strDate = "02-29-2017";
04    booSuccessful = DateTime.TryParse(strDate, out datDate);
      // datDate = {1/1/0001 12:00:00 AM}, booSuccessful = false
```

Figure 11-4. *Examples of date parsing*

11.7 Time-Related Properties

The time-related properties described in this section permit us to retrieve the time from the operating system and extract the components of a time. Figure 11-5 shows some examples of time-related properties.

Notice at 01 that we are getting the current date *and* time from the operating system using the Now property.

```
CODE BEHIND

    // Get today's date and time.
01  String strDateTime = DateTime.Now.ToString();
    // strDateTime = "7/18/2017 10:09:08 AM"

    // Hardcode the date and time for the following examples.
    DateTime datTimeCurrent = new DateTime(2017, 7, 18, 15, 30, 25);
    // datTimeCurrent = {7/18/2017 3:30:25 PM}

    // Get the time of day.
    String strTimeOfDay = datTimeCurrent.TimeOfDay.ToString();
    // strTimeOfDay = "15:30:25"

    // Get the hour.
    Int32 i32Hour = datTimeCurrent.Hour;
    // i32Hour = 15

    // Get the minute.
    Int32 i32Minute = datTimeCurrent.Minute;
    // i32Minute = 30

    // Get the second.
    Int32 i32Second = datTimeCurrent.Second;
    // i32Second = 25
```

Figure 11-5. *Examples of time-related properties*

11.8 Time-Related Methods

The time-related methods described in this section permit us to add to or subtract from the components of a time, compare one time with another, and determine the interval between two times. Figure 11-6 shows some examples of time-related methods.

CODE BEHIND

```
// Hardcode the date and time for the following examples.
DateTime datTimeCurrent = new DateTime(2017, 7, 18, 15, 30, 25);
// datTimeCurrent = {7/18/2017 3:30:25 PM}
String strTimeNew = "";
// strTimeNew = ""

// Add 2 hours to the current time.
strTimeNew = datTimeCurrent.AddHours(2).ToString();
// strTimeNew = "7/18/2017 5:30:25 PM"

// Add 4 minutes to the current time.
strTimeNew = datTimeCurrent.AddMinutes(4).ToString();
// strTimeNew = "7/18/2017 3:34:25 PM"

// Add 6 seconds to the current time.
strTimeNew = datTimeCurrent.AddSeconds(6).ToString();
// strTimeNew = "7/18/2017 3:30:31 PM"

// Compare the first time to the second time.
// Less than zero = The first time is earlier than the second time.
// Zero = The first is the same as the second time.
// Greater than zero = The first time is later than the second time.
DateTime datTimeFirst = new DateTime(2017, 7, 18, 12, 25, 30);
DateTime datTimeSecond = new DateTime(2017, 7, 18, 11, 30, 25);
Int32 i32Result = datTimeFirst.CompareTo(datTimeSecond);
// i32Result = 1

// Determine how many hours, minutes, and seconds have elapsed
// since the first-of-year date using a TimeSpan structure.
DateTime datDateFirstOfYear = new DateTime(2017, 01, 01);
DateTime datDateCurrent = new DateTime();
datDateCurrent = DateTime.Today;
// datDateCurrent = {7/18/2017 12:00:00 AM}
TimeSpan timTimeSpan = datDateCurrent.Subtract(datDateFirstOfYear);
Double dblDifferenceHours = timTimeSpan.TotalHours;
// dblDifferenceHours = 4752
Double dblDifferenceMinutes = timTimeSpan.TotalMinutes;
// dblDifferenceMinutes = 285120
Double dblDifferenceSeconds = timTimeSpan.TotalSeconds;
// dblDifferenceSeconds = 17107200
```

Figure 11-6. *Examples of time-related methods*

11.9 Time Formatting

The time-related methods described in this section permit us to format a time to look the way we want it to. Since times must often be displayed differently depending on cultural norms, international standards, application requirements, personal preference, and so on, the DateTime structure permits us to format times via special formatting methods (e.g., the ToLongTimeString method, the ToShortTimeString method) and via the ToString method *overloaded* with *format specifiers*. As mentioned previously, the ToString method is overloaded when we pass format specifiers to it as a parameter. Table 11-3 shows some of the custom time format specifiers.

Table 11-3. *Some of the custom time format specifiers*

Format Specifier	Description
"f"	The tenths of a second in a date and time value.
"ff"	The hundredths of a second in a date and time value.
"h"	The hour, using a 12-hour clock from 1 to 12.
"hh"	The hour, using a 12-hour clock from 01 to 12.
"H"	The hour, using a 24-hour clock from 0 to 23.
"HH"	The hour, using a 24-hour clock from 00 to 23.
"m"	The minute, from 0 through 59.
"mm"	The minute, from 00 through 59.
"s"	The second, from 0 through 59.
"ss"	The second, from 00 through 59.
"t"	The first character of the AM/PM designator.
"tt"	The AM/PM designator.

Reference

https://docs.microsoft.com/en-us/dotnet/standard/base-types/custom-date-and-time-format-strings

Figure 11-7 shows some examples of time formatting. Recall from Chapter 9, titled "String Operations," that escape sequences include formatting information or special characters in a string.

Notice at 01 that there are no escape sequences present in the time formatting parameter passed to the ToString method. As can be seen, the result of the formatting operation is quite strange.

Notice at 02 the same time formatting parameter but with escape sequences added. The result of this formatting operation is much more meaningful.

Notice at 03 that there are again no escape sequences present in the time formatting parameter passed to the ToString method. As can be seen, this operation throws a Format exception.

Notice at 04 the same time formatting parameter but with escape sequences added. This formatting operation now works as expected.

CODE BEHIND

```
       // Hardcode the date and time for the following examples.
       DateTime datTimeCurrent = new DateTime(2017, 7, 18, 15, 30, 25);
       // datTimeCurrent = {7/18/2017 3:30:25 PM}
       String strTimeNew = "";
       // strTimeNew = ""

       // Format the time as a long time.
       strTimeNew = datTimeCurrent.ToLongTimeString();
       // strTimeNew = "3:30:25 PM"

       // Format the time as a short time.
       strTimeNew = datTimeCurrent.ToShortTimeString();
       // strTimeNew = "3:30 PM"

       // Customize the time format without escape sequences.
01     strTimeNew = datTimeCurrent.ToString("HH Hours mm Minutes ss Seconds");
       // strTimeNew = "15 15our25 30 7inuPe25 25 Secon1825"

       // Customize the time format with escape sequences.
02     strTimeNew = datTimeCurrent.ToString("HH \\Hour\\s mm \\Minu\\te\\s ss
           \\Secon\\d\\s");
       // strTimeNew = "15 Hours 30 Minutes 25 Seconds"

       // Customize the time format without escape sequences.
03     strTimeNew = datTimeCurrent.ToString("h:mm O'clock tt");
       // Format exception is thrown. Cannot find a matching quote character
       // for the character '''.

       // Customize the time format with escape sequences.
04     strTimeNew = datTimeCurrent.ToString("h:mm O\\'clock tt");
       // strTimeNew = "3:30 O'clock PM"
```

Figure 11-7. *Examples of time formatting*

CHAPTER 12

Array Operations

12.1 Introduction

An array is a container that holds data while it is being manipulated by a computer program. More specifically, it is a *data structure* that consists of a collection of *elements* of the *same* type, where each element contains its own value and is identified by one or more *indices* (a.k.a., subscripts). Arrays can be one-dimensional or multidimensional.[1] The elements of a one-dimensional array are referenced by a single index, the elements of a two-dimensional array are referenced by two indices, and so on. It is not uncommon to see arrays of three or more dimensions.[2] The total number of elements in an array is its *length*. Each dimension of an array has a *lower bound* (i.e., the index of the *first* element of the array) and an *upper bound* (i.e., the index of the *last* element of the array). Since arrays are *zero based* in C# by default, the index of the first element in a one-dimensional array is [0], the index of the second element is [1], and so on. The index of the first element in a two-dimensional array is [0, 0], the index of the second element is [0, 1], and so on.[3] An array is *statically allocated*. That is, its capacity cannot be altered once it is declared. An array is considered an *internal* data structure because it resides in RAM and only remains there until the program that utilizes it terminates. Thus, the data in an array is said to be *nonpersistent*. This is in contrast to a database table, which is considered an *external* data structure because it resides on a peripheral device (e.g., a magnetic disk) and remains there even after the program that utilizes it terminates. Thus, the data in a database table is said to be *persistent*.

---

[1]Arrays can even contain other arrays. These arrays are called *jagged* arrays. We will not consider jagged arrays in this book.

[2]In C#, multidimensional arrays of up to 32 dimensions can be declared.

[3]The Array class permits us to define different lower bounds if desired.

© Robert E. Beasley 2020
R. E. Beasley, *Essential ASP.NET Web Forms Development*, https://doi.org/10.1007/978-1-4842-5784-5_12

In this chapter, we will begin by looking at the Array class. The Array class provides methods (some of them static) that permit us to get information about arrays, populate them with data, retrieve data from them, sort them, search them, copy them, or manipulate them in some other way. Next, we will discuss the one-dimensional array. A one-dimensional array is the simplest array to declare and utilize since it only embodies a single dimension and only utilizes a single index for referencing its elements. And finally, we will consider the two-dimensional array. A two-dimensional array is also relatively simple to declare and utilize since it embodies just two dimensions and utilizes just two indices for referencing its elements.

12.2 Array Class

The Array class provides methods (some of them static) that permit us to get information about arrays, populate them with data, retrieve data from them, sort them, search them, copy them, or manipulate them in some other way. In .NET, the Array class is considered a *collection*, even though it is *not* part of the System.Collections namespace that defines the Stack class, the Queue class, the LinkedList class, and the SortedList class. We will discuss those collections in Chapter 13, titled "Collection Operations." Table 12-1 shows some of the properties, methods, and events of the Array class.

Table 12-1. *Some of the properties, methods, and events of the Array class*

Class Array[4]

Namespace System

Properties

Length	Gets the total number of elements in all the dimensions of the Array.

Methods

BinarySearch(Array, Object)	Searches an entire one-dimensional sorted array for a specific element.
Clear(Array, Int32, Int32)	Sets a range of elements in an array to the default value of each element type.
Copy(Array, Int32, Array, Int32, Int32)	Copies a range of elements from an Array starting at the specified source index and pastes them to another Array starting at the specified destination index. The length and the indexes are specified as 32-bit integers.
GetLength(Int32)	Gets a 32-bit integer that represents the number of elements in the specified dimension of the Array. The parameter is the zero-based dimension of the array.
GetLowerBound(Int32)	Gets the index of the first element of the specified dimension in the array. The parameter is the zero-based dimension of the array.
GetUpperBound(Int32)	Gets the index of the last element of the specified dimension in the array. The parameter is the zero-based dimension of the array.
GetValue(Int32)	Gets the value at the specified position in the one-dimensional Array. The index is specified as a 32-bit integer.
GetValue(Int32, Int32)	Gets the value at the specified position in the two-dimensional Array. The indexes are specified as 32-bit integers.
Reverse(Array)	Reverses the sequence of the elements in the entire one-dimensional Array.

(continued)

[4]All property, method, and event descriptions were taken directly from Microsoft's official documentation. The event handler methods used to handle the events of this class were omitted to conserve space. See the reference for all of the methods of this class.

Table 12-1. *(continued)*

SetValue(Object, Int32)	Sets a value to the element at the specified position in the one-dimensional Array. The index is specified as a 32-bit integer.
SetValue(Object, Int32, Int32)	Sets a value to the element at the specified position in the two-dimensional Array. The indexes are specified as 32-bit integers.
Sort(Array)	Sorts the elements in an entire one-dimensional Array.

Events

NA

Reference

https://msdn.microsoft.com/en-us/library/system.array(v=vs.110).aspx

12.3 One-Dimensional Arrays

A one-dimensional array is the simplest array to declare and utilize since it only embodies a single dimension and only utilizes a single index for referencing its elements. Conceptually, a one-dimensional array is like a chest of drawers with, say, undergarments in the top drawer, socks in the second drawer, shirts in the third drawer, shorts in the fourth drawer, and trousers in the fifth drawer. When we want to put away a pair of socks, we go *directly* to the second drawer and place the pair of socks in it. Conversely, when we want to retrieve a pair of socks, we go *directly* to the second drawer and take the pair of socks out. Thus, we have *direct* access to any of the drawers in the chest of drawers. A one-dimensional array operates in the same way. Figure 12-1 shows some examples of declaring a one-dimensional array.

Notice at 01 that we are declaring a three-element one-dimensional array of strings. In this example, the String[] indicates that we are defining a one-dimensional array (not a single-value variable), and the String[3] indicates that we are defining an array of three elements. As can be seen, the first element of the array is at index [0], and the last element of the array is at index [2]. Notice in this example that all of the elements in the array contain null values since nothing has been assigned to them yet.

Notice at 02 that we are declaring a five-element one-dimensional array of strings. In this example, the String[] indicates that we are defining a one-dimensional array (not a single-value variable), and the String[5] indicates that we are defining an array of five elements. As can be seen, the first element of the array is at index [0], and the last element of the array is at index [4]. Notice in this example that all of the elements in the array contain data. This data was assigned to the elements of the array via the comma-separated list within the array definition itself. Keep in mind that we can declare arrays of virtually any .NET type.

```
CODE BEHIND

    // Declare a 3-element one-dimensional array of strings.
01  String[] strShipperArray = new String[3];
    // strShipperArray[0] = null
    // strShipperArray[1] = null
    // strShipperArray[2] = null

    // Declare a 5-element one-dimensional array of strings.
    // Add items to the elements of the array upon initialization.
02  String[] strCategoryArray = new String[5]
    {
        "Footwear - Men's", "Clothing - Men's", "Racquets",
        "Footwear - Women's", "Clothing - Women's"
    };
    // strCategoryArray[0] = "Footwear - Men's"
    // strCategoryArray[1] = "Clothing - Men's"
    // strCategoryArray[2] = "Racquets"
    // strCategoryArray[3] = "Footwear - Women's"
    // strCategoryArray[4] = "Clothing - Women's"
```

Figure 12-1. *Examples of declaring a one-dimensional array*

In addition to declaring one-dimensional arrays, we must often get information about them, populate them with data, retrieve data from them, sort them, search them, copy them, or manipulate them in some other way. Figure 12-2 shows an example of getting the total number of elements in a one-dimensional array.

```
CODE BEHIND

    // Get the total number of elements in the array.
    Int32 i32Length = strCategoryArray.Length;
    // i32Length = 5
```

Figure 12-2. *Example of getting the total number of elements in a one-dimensional array*

Figure 12-3 shows an example of populating the elements of a one-dimensional array using indices.

CODE BEHIND

```
// Add values to the elements of the array.
strCategoryArray[0] = "Footwear - Men's";
strCategoryArray[1] = "Clothing - Men's";
strCategoryArray[2] = "Racquets";
strCategoryArray[3] = "Footwear - Women's";
strCategoryArray[4] = "Clothing - Women's";
// strCategoryArray[0] = "Footwear - Men's"
// strCategoryArray[1] = "Clothing - Men's"
// strCategoryArray[2] = "Racquets"
// strCategoryArray[3] = "Footwear - Women's"
// strCategoryArray[4] = "Clothing - Women's"
```

Figure 12-3. *Example of populating the elements of a one-dimensional array using indices*

Figure 12-4 shows an example of populating the elements of a one-dimensional array using the SetValue method. As can be seen in this example, using the SetValue method of the Array class produces the same results as using indices. However, using indices produces cleaner code. On the other hand, the SetValue method has some additional functionality that may be useful in some situations. The interested reader is encouraged to explore the SetValue method on his or her own.

CODE BEHIND

```
// Add values to the elements of the array.
strCategoryArray.SetValue("Footwear - Men's", 0);
strCategoryArray.SetValue("Clothing - Men's", 1);
strCategoryArray.SetValue("Racquets", 2);
strCategoryArray.SetValue("Footwear - Women's", 3);
strCategoryArray.SetValue("Clothing - Women's", 4);
// strCategoryArray[0] = "Footwear - Men's"
// strCategoryArray[1] = "Clothing - Men's"
// strCategoryArray[2] = "Racquets"
// strCategoryArray[3] = "Footwear - Women's"
// strCategoryArray[4] = "Clothing - Women's"
```

Figure 12-4. *Example of populating the elements of a one-dimensional array using the SetValue method*

Figure 12-5 shows some examples of retrieving the elements of a one-dimensional array using indices.

CODE BEHIND

```
// Declare the variables.
String strCategory = "";
String strCategoryList = "";

// Get the third element of the array.
strCategory = strCategoryArray[2];
// strCategory = "Racquets"

// Get all the elements of the array and add them to the list using
// a For structure.
for (int i = 0; i < strCategoryArray.Length; i++)
{
    strCategoryList = strCategoryList + strCategoryArray[i] + "; ";
}
// strCategoryList = "Footwear - Men's; Clothing - Men's; Racquets;
// Footwear - Women's; Clothing - Women's; "
```

Figure 12-5. *Examples of retrieving the elements of a one-dimensional array using indices*

Figure 12-6 shows some examples of retrieving the elements of a one-dimensional array using the GetValue method. As can be seen in this example, using the GetValue method of the Array class produces the same results as using indices. However, keep in mind that the GetValue method has some additional functionality that may be useful in some situations. The interested reader is encouraged to explore the GetValue method on his or her own.

CODE BEHIND

```
    // Declare the variables.
    String strCategory = "";
    String strCategoryList = "";

    // Get the third element of the array.
    strCategory = strCategoryArray.GetValue(2).ToString();
    // strCategory = "Racquets"

    // Get all the elements of the array and add them to the list using
    // a For structure.
    for (int i = 0; i < strCategoryArray.Length; i++)
    {
        strCategoryList = strCategoryList + strCategoryArray.GetValue(i) +
            "; ";
    }
    // strCategoryList = "Footwear - Men's; Clothing - Men's; Racquets;
    // Footwear - Women's; Clothing - Women's; "
```

Figure 12-6. *Examples of retrieving the elements of a one-dimensional array using the GetValue method*

Figure 12-7 shows an example of sorting the elements of a one-dimensional array. As can be seen, the Sort method is a static method of the Array class.

CODE BEHIND

```
    // Sort the array.
    Array.Sort(strCategoryArray);
    // strCategoryArray[0] = "Clothing - Men's"
    // strCategoryArray[1] = "Clothing - Women's"
    // strCategoryArray[2] = "Footwear - Men's"
    // strCategoryArray[3] = "Footwear - Women's"
    // strCategoryArray[4] = "Racquets"
```

Figure 12-7. *Example of sorting the elements of a one-dimensional array*

Figure 12-8 shows some examples of searching the elements of a one-dimensional array. Keep in mind that the array used in a sequential search need not be sorted to work. However, a sequential search can be made much more efficient if the array to be searched is sorted. An array used in a binary search *must* be sorted in ascending order to work. When performing a binary search, a positive value (i.e., the index of the item) is returned if the search item is found in the array. Otherwise, a negative value is returned. As can be seen, the BinarySearch method is a static method of the Array class.

CODE BEHIND

```
// Declare the variables.
Int32 i32Index = 0;
Boolean booFound = false;

// This is a sequential search.
for (int i = 0; i < strCategoryArray.Length; i++)
{
    if (strCategoryArray[i] == "Footwear - Women's")
    {
        i32Index = i;
        booFound = true;
        break;
    }
}
// i32Index = 3, booFound = true

// This is a binary search.
i32Index = Array.BinarySearch(strCategoryArray, "Footwear - Women's");
if (i32Index >= 0)
{
    booFound = true;
}
// i32Index = 3, booFound = true
```

Figure 12-8. *Examples of searching the elements of a one-dimensional array*

Figure 12-9 shows an example of copying the elements of a one-dimensional array to another one-dimensional array. As can be seen, the Copy method is a static method of the Array class. Note that this method not only copies the elements between arrays of the *same* type but also copies the elements between arrays of *different* types. Any necessary casting is done automatically.

CODE BEHIND

```
// Declare another 5-element one-dimensional array of strings.
String[] strCategoryArrayCopy = new String[5];
// Copy the elements from the original array to the element
// values of the new array beginning at element [0] in both arrays
// for the length of the original array.
Array.Copy(strCategoryArray, 0, strCategoryArrayCopy, 0,
    strCategoryArray.Length);
// strCategoryArrayCopy[0] = "Footwear - Men's"
// strCategoryArrayCopy[1] = "Clothing - Men's"
// strCategoryArrayCopy[2] = "Racquets"
// strCategoryArrayCopy[3] = "Footwear - Women's"
// strCategoryArrayCopy[4] = "Clothing - Women's"
```

Figure 12-9. *Example of copying the elements of a one-dimensional array to another one-dimensional array*

Figure 12-10 shows an example of reversing the elements of a one-dimensional array. As can be seen, the Reverse method is a static method of the Array class.

CODE BEHIND

```
// Reverse the array.
Array.Reverse(strCategoryArray);
// strCategoryArray[0] = "Racquets"
// strCategoryArray[1] = "Footwear - Women's"
// strCategoryArray[2] = "Footwear - Men's"
// strCategoryArray[3] = "Clothing - Women's"
// strCategoryArray[4] = "Clothing - Men's"
```

Figure 12-10. *Example of reversing the elements of a one-dimensional array*

Figure 12-11 shows an example of clearing the elements of a one-dimensional array. As can be seen, the Clear method is a static method of the Array class.

CODE BEHIND

```
// Clear elements 1 through 3.
Array.Clear(strCategoryArray, 1, 3);
// strCategoryArray[0] = "Racquets"
// strCategoryArray[1] = null
// strCategoryArray[2] = null
// strCategoryArray[3] = null
// strCategoryArray[4] = "Clothing - Men's"
```

Figure 12-11. *Example of clearing the elements of a one-dimensional array*

12.4 Two-Dimensional Arrays

A two-dimensional array (a.k.a., a rectangular array) is also relatively simple to declare and utilize since it embodies just two dimensions and utilizes just two indices for referencing its elements. Conceptually, a two-dimensional array is like theater seating with rows of seats extending from the front of the theater to the back of the theater and individual seats stretching from the right side of the theater to the left side of the theater. To locate a reserved seat, say row 10 seat 15, we would first locate row 10, and then we would locate seat 15. A two-dimensional array operates in the same way. In C#, the *first* index of a two-dimensional array refers to the *row* of the array, whereas the *second* index refers to the *column* of the array. Figure 12-12 shows some examples of declaring a two-dimensional array.

Notice at 01 that we are declaring a six-element two-dimensional array of decimals. In this example, the Decimal[,] indicates that we are defining a two-dimensional array (not a single-value variable), and the Decimal[3, 2] indicates that we are defining an array of 3 rows and 2 columns for a total of six elements. As can be seen, the first element of the array is at index [0, 0], and the last element of the array is at index [2, 1]. Notice in this example that all of the elements in the array contain 0 since nothing has been assigned to them yet.

Notice at 02 that we are declaring a 21-element two-dimensional array of decimals. In this example, the Decimal[,] indicates that we are defining a two-dimensional array (not a single-value variable), and the Decimal[3, 7] indicates that we are defining an array of 3 rows and 7 columns for a total of 21 elements. As can be seen, the first element of the array is at index [0, 0], and the last element of the array is at index [2, 6]. Notice in this example that all of the elements in the array contain data. This data was assigned to the elements of the array via the comma-separated list within the array definition itself. Again, keep in mind that we can declare arrays of virtually any .NET type.

CODE BEHIND

```
      // Declare a 3x2 6-element two-dimensional array of decimals.
      // There are three salespersons, and each salesperson has a
      // commission rate for non-equipment sales and equipment sales.
01    Decimal[,] decCommissionRateArray = new Decimal[3, 2];
      // decCommissionRateArray[0, 0] = 0
      // decCommissionRateArray[0, 1] = 0
      // decCommissionRateArray[1, 0] = 0
      // decCommissionRateArray[1, 1] = 0
      // decCommissionRateArray[2, 0] = 0
      // decCommissionRateArray[2, 1] = 0


      // Declare a 3x7 21-element two-dimensional array of decimals.
      // Add items to the elements of the array upon initialization.
      // There are three salespersons, and each salesperson has
      // equipment sales for each day of the week (Sunday through Saturday).
02    Decimal[,] decEquipmentSalesArray = new Decimal[3, 7]
      {
          { 0, 119.99m, 170.92m, 134.50m, 234.76m, 102.99m, 0 },
          { 145.78m, 200.12m, 409.11m, 102.99m, 189.99m, 209.34m, 379.99m },
          { 230.45m, 0, 0, 0, 0, 0, 172.65m },
      };
      // decEquipmentSalesArray[0, 0] = 0
      // decEquipmentSalesArray[0, 1] = 119.99
      // decEquipmentSalesArray[0, 2] = 170.92
      // ⋮
      // ⋮ (Data continues.)
      // ⋮
      // decEquipmentSalesArray[2, 4] = 0
      // decEquipmentSalesArray[2, 5] = 0
      // decEquipmentSalesArray[2, 6] = 172.65
```

Figure 12-12. *Examples of declaring a two-dimensional array*

In addition to declaring two-dimensional arrays, we must often get information about them, populate them with data, retrieve data from them, sort them, search them, copy them, or manipulate them in some other way.[5] Figure 12-13 shows an example of getting the total number of elements, rows, and columns in a two-dimensional array.

---

[5]Although sorting was mentioned in this list of array operations, the Array class does *not* contain a static Sort method for sorting two-dimensional arrays. If sorting such an array were required, we would have to write the code necessary to sort it.

CODE BEHIND

```
// Get the total number of elements in the array.
Int32 i32Length = decEquipmentSalesArray.Length;
// i32Length = 21

// Get the total number of rows in the array.
Int32 i32LengthRows = decEquipmentSalesArray.GetLength(0);
// i32LengthRows = 3

// Get the total number of columns in the array.
Int32 i32LengthColumns = decEquipmentSalesArray.GetLength(1);
// i32LengthColumns = 7
```

Figure 12-13. *Example of getting the total number of elements, rows, and columns in a two-dimensional array*

Figure 12-14 shows an example of populating the elements of a two-dimensional array using indices.

CODE BEHIND

```
// Add values to the elements of the array.
decEquipmentSalesArray[0, 0] = 0;
decEquipmentSalesArray[0, 1] = 119.99m;
decEquipmentSalesArray[0, 2] = 170.92m;
decEquipmentSalesArray[0, 3] = 134.50m;
decEquipmentSalesArray[0, 4] = 234.76m;
decEquipmentSalesArray[0, 5] = 102.99m;
decEquipmentSalesArray[0, 6] = 0;
decEquipmentSalesArray[1, 0] = 145.78m;
decEquipmentSalesArray[1, 1] = 200.12m;
decEquipmentSalesArray[1, 2] = 409.11m;
decEquipmentSalesArray[1, 3] = 102.99m;
decEquipmentSalesArray[1, 4] = 189.99m;
decEquipmentSalesArray[1, 5] = 209.34m;
decEquipmentSalesArray[1, 6] = 379.99m;
decEquipmentSalesArray[2, 0] = 230.45m;
decEquipmentSalesArray[2, 1] = 0;
decEquipmentSalesArray[2, 2] = 0;
decEquipmentSalesArray[2, 3] = 0;
decEquipmentSalesArray[2, 4] = 0;
decEquipmentSalesArray[2, 5] = 0;
decEquipmentSalesArray[2, 6] = 172.65m;
// decEquipmentSalesArray[0, 0] = 0
// decEquipmentSalesArray[0, 1] = 119.99
// decEquipmentSalesArray[0, 2] = 170.92
// :
// : (Data continues.)
// :
// decEquipmentSalesArray[2, 4] = 0
// decEquipmentSalesArray[2, 5] = 0
// decEquipmentSalesArray[2, 6] = 172.65
```

Figure 12-14. *Example of populating the elements of a two-dimensional array using indices*

Figure 12-15 shows an example of populating the elements of a two-dimensional array using the SetValue method. As can be seen in this example, using the SetValue method of the Array class produces the same results as using indices. However, using indices produces cleaner code. On the other hand, the SetValue method has some additional functionality that may be useful in some situations. The interested reader is encouraged to explore the SetValue method on his or her own.

CODE BEHIND

```
// Add values to the elements of the array.
decEquipmentSalesArray.SetValue(0m, 0, 0);
decEquipmentSalesArray.SetValue(119.99m, 0, 1);
decEquipmentSalesArray.SetValue(170.92m, 0, 2);
decEquipmentSalesArray.SetValue(134.50m, 0, 3);
decEquipmentSalesArray.SetValue(234.76m, 0, 4);
decEquipmentSalesArray.SetValue(102.99m, 0, 5);
decEquipmentSalesArray.SetValue(0m, 0, 6);
decEquipmentSalesArray.SetValue(145.78m, 1, 0);
decEquipmentSalesArray.SetValue(200.12m, 1, 1);
decEquipmentSalesArray.SetValue(409.11m, 1, 2);
decEquipmentSalesArray.SetValue(102.99m, 1, 3);
decEquipmentSalesArray.SetValue(189.99m, 1, 4);
decEquipmentSalesArray.SetValue(209.34m, 1, 5);
decEquipmentSalesArray.SetValue(379.99m, 1, 6);
decEquipmentSalesArray.SetValue(230.45m, 2, 0);
decEquipmentSalesArray.SetValue(0m, 2, 1);
decEquipmentSalesArray.SetValue(0m, 2, 2);
decEquipmentSalesArray.SetValue(0m, 2, 3);
decEquipmentSalesArray.SetValue(0m, 2, 4);
decEquipmentSalesArray.SetValue(0m, 2, 5);
decEquipmentSalesArray.SetValue(172.65m, 2, 6);
// decEquipmentSalesArray[0, 0] = 0
// decEquipmentSalesArray[0, 1] = 119.99
// decEquipmentSalesArray[0, 2] = 170.92
// ⋮
// ⋮ (Data continues.)
// ⋮
// decEquipmentSalesArray[2, 4] = 0
// decEquipmentSalesArray[2, 5] = 0
// decEquipmentSalesArray[2, 6] = 172.65
```

Figure 12-15. *Example of populating the elements of a two-dimensional array using the SetValue method*

Figure 12-16 shows an example of retrieving all the elements of a two-dimensional array using indices.

Notice at 01 the *outer loop* of the code. For this loop, i will be initialized to 0 and will continue to be incremented while it is less than the length of the *first* dimension of the array (i.e., 3).

Notice at 02 the *inner loop* of the code. For this loop, j will be initialized to 0 and will continue to be incremented while it is less than the length of the *second* dimension of the array (i.e., 7). Notice that i and j will be 0 and 0, respectively, the first time the code inside the inner loop is executed. This will retrieve the value of first element [0, 0] in the array.

Next, j will be incremented, and the code inside the inner loop will be executed again. This will retrieve the value of second element [0, 1] in the array. The code inside the inner loop will continue to execute while j is less than the length of the *second* dimension of the array. When j becomes *not* less than the length of the *second* dimension of the array, the inner loop will be exited, program control will be passed back to the outer loop, i will be incremented, program control will be passed to the inner loop, j will be *reinitialized* to 0, and the inner loop will be executed again. This process will continue until all of the elements in the array have been traversed.

CODE BEHIND

```
    // Declare the variables.
    Decimal decEquipmentSales = 0;
    Decimal decEquipmentSalesTotal = 0;

    // Get the second row (sales person 2) third column (Wednesday) element
    // of the array.
    decEquipmentSales = decEquipmentSalesArray[1, 3];
    // decEquipmentSales = 102.99

    // Get all the elements of the array and sum them using a For structure.
01  for (int i = 0; i < decEquipmentSalesArray.GetLength(0); i++)
    {
02      for (int j = 0; j < decEquipmentSalesArray.GetLength(1); j++)
        {
            decEquipmentSalesTotal = decEquipmentSalesTotal +
                decEquipmentSalesArray[i, j];
        }
    }
    // decEquipmentSalesTotal = 2803.58
```

Figure 12-16. *Example of retrieving all the elements of a two-dimensional array using indices*

Figure 12-17 shows an example of retrieving all the elements of a two-dimensional array using the GetValue method. As can be seen in this example, using the GetValue method of the Array class produces the same results as using indices. However, keep in mind that the GetValue method has some additional functionality that may be useful in some situations. The interested reader is encouraged to explore the GetValue method on his or her own.

Notice at 01 the *outer loop* of the code. For this loop, i will be initialized to 0 and will continue to be incremented while it is less than the length of the *first* dimension of the array (i.e., 3).

Notice at 02 the *inner loop* of the code. For this loop, j will be initialized to 0 and will continue to be incremented while it is less than the length of the *second* dimension of the array (i.e., 7). Notice that i and j will be 0 and 0, respectively, the first time the code inside the inner loop is executed. This will retrieve the value of first element [0, 0] in the array. Next, j will be incremented, and the code inside the inner loop will be executed again. This will retrieve the value of second element [0, 1] in the array. The code inside the inner loop will continue to execute while j is less than the length of the *second* dimension of the array. When j becomes *not* less than the length of the *second* dimension of the array, the inner loop will be exited, program control will be passed back to the outer loop, i will be incremented, program control will be passed to the inner loop, j will be *reinitialized* to 0, and the inner loop will be executed again. This process will continue until all of the elements in the array have been traversed.

CODE BEHIND

```
    // Declare the variables.
    Decimal decEquipmentSales = 0;
    Decimal decEquipmentSalesTotal = 0;

    // Get the second row (sales person 2) third column (Wednesday) element
    // of the array.
    decEquipmentSales = (Decimal)decEquipmentSalesArray.GetValue(1, 3);
    // decEquipmentSales = 102.99

    // Get all the elements of the array and sum them using a For structure.
01  for (int i = 0; i < decEquipmentSalesArray.GetLength(0); i++)
    {
02      for (int j = 0; j < decEquipmentSalesArray.GetLength(1); j++)
        {
            decEquipmentSalesTotal = decEquipmentSalesTotal +
                (Decimal)decEquipmentSalesArray.GetValue(i, j);
        }
    }
    // decEquipmentSalesTotal = 2803.58
```

Figure 12-17. *Example of retrieving all the elements of a two-dimensional array using the GetValue method*

Figure 12-18 shows an example of searching the elements of a two-dimensional array.

Notice at 01 the *outer loop* of the code. For this loop, i will be initialized to 0 and will continue to be incremented while it is less than the length of the *first* dimension of the array (i.e., 3).

Notice at 02 the *inner loop* of the code. For this loop, j will be initialized to 0 and will continue to be incremented while it is less than the length of the *second* dimension of the array (i.e., 7). Notice that i and j will be 0 and 0, respectively, the first time the code inside the inner loop is executed. Next, j will be incremented, and the code inside the inner loop will be executed again. The code inside the inner loop will continue to execute while j is less than the length of the *second* dimension of the array. When j becomes *not* less than the length of the *second* dimension of the array, the inner loop will be exited, program control will be passed back to the outer loop, i will be incremented, program control will be passed to the inner loop, j will be *reinitialized* to 0, and the inner loop will be executed again. This process will continue until all of the elements in the array have been traversed *or* until the condition inside the inner loop is *true*, which indicates that the search item was found in the array.

Keep in mind that the array used in a sequential search need not be sorted to work. However, a sequential search can be made much more efficient if the array to be searched is sorted. Also note that the Array class does not contain a static BinarySearch method that can search an array of more than one dimension.

CODE BEHIND

```
    // Declare the variables.
    Int32 i32IndexI = 0;
    Int32 i32IndexJ = 0;
    Boolean booFound = false;

    // This is a sequential search.
01  for (int i = 0; i < decEquipmentSalesArray.GetLength(0); i++)
    {
02      for (int j = 0; j < decEquipmentSalesArray.GetLength(1); j++)
        {
            if (decEquipmentSalesArray[i, j] == 409.11m)
            {
                i32IndexI = i;
                i32IndexJ = j;
                booFound = true;
                break;
            }
        }
        if(booFound)
        {
            break;
        }
    }
    // i32IndexI = 1, i32IndexJ = 2, booFound = true
```

Figure 12-18. *Example of searching the elements of a two-dimensional array*

Figure 12-19 shows an example of copying the elements of a two-dimensional array to another two-dimensional array. As can be seen, the Copy method is a static method of the Array class. Note that this method not only copies the elements between arrays of the *same* type but also copies the elements between arrays of *different* types. Any necessary casting is done automatically.

CODE BEHIND

```
// Declare another 3x7 21-element two-dimensional array of decimals.
Decimal[,] decEquipmentSalesArrayCopy = new Decimal[3, 7];
// Copy the elements from the original array to the element
// values of the new array beginning at element [0] in both arrays
// for the length of the original array.
Array.Copy(decEquipmentSalesArray, 0, decEquipmentSalesArrayCopy, 0,
    decEquipmentSalesArray.Length);
// decEquipmentSalesArrayCopy[0, 0] = 0
// decEquipmentSalesArrayCopy[0, 1] = 119.99
// decEquipmentSalesArrayCopy[0, 2] = 170.92
// ⋮
// ⋮ (Data continues.)
// ⋮
// decEquipmentSalesArrayCopy[2, 4] = 0
// decEquipmentSalesArrayCopy[2, 5] = 0
// decEquipmentSalesArrayCopy[2, 6] = 172.65
```

Figure 12-19. *Example of copying the elements of a two-dimensional array to another two-dimensional array*

CHAPTER 13

Collection Operations

13.1 Introduction

A collection is a container that holds data while it is being manipulated by a computer program. More specifically, it is a *data structure* that consists of zero or more *items*, where each item contains its own value or values. Examples of collections include stacks, queues, linked lists, and sorted lists. The total number of items in a collection is its *count*. Unlike an array, a collection is dynamically allocated in memory. That is, its capacity is automatically increased (through memory reallocation) as additional items are added to it. Like an array, a collection is considered an *internal* data structure because it resides in RAM and only remains there until the program that utilizes it terminates. Thus, the data in a collection is said to be *nonpersistent*. This is in contrast to a database table, which is considered an *external* data structure because it resides on a peripheral device (e.g., a magnetic disk) and remains there even after the program that utilizes it terminates. Thus, the data in a database table is said to be *persistent*.

In this chapter, we will begin by looking at the Stack class. The Stack class permits us to create and manipulate a one-dimensional *last-in-first-out* (LIFO) data structure analogous to a stack of books that we want to read in order of priority from top to bottom. Next, we will discuss the Queue class. The Queue class enables us to create and manipulate a one-dimensional *first-in-first-out* (FIFO) data structure analogous to a line of people waiting to be checked out at a grocery store. After that, we will consider the LinkedList class. The LinkedList class permits us to create and manipulate a one-dimensional *linear* data structure analogous to a group of alphabetized folders in a file cabinet. And finally, we will look at the SortedList class. The SortedList class enables us to create and manipulate a two-dimensional *key-based* data structure analogous to a dictionary of alphabetized terms and their respective definitions.

© Robert E. Beasley 2020
R. E. Beasley, *Essential ASP.NET Web Forms Development*, https://doi.org/10.1007/978-1-4842-5784-5_13

13.2 Stack Class

A stack is a one-dimensional *last-in-first-out* (LIFO) data structure that contains zero or more *objects*. The *first* object on a stack is at the *bottom* of the stack, whereas the *last* object on a stack is at the *top* of the stack. Operations on a stack can only occur at the top of the stack. Conceptually, a stack is like a stack of books that we want to read in order of priority from top to bottom. First, we place the book of least priority on a table. Then, we place the book of next least priority on top of that, and so on. Once we have a stack of books with the most important book on top, the process is complete. Now we can simply pull the books off the top of the stack one at a time and read them in order of importance.

In C#, objects are *pushed* onto a stack and *popped* off a stack. Retrieving an object that is not on top of the stack requires popping one or more objects off the stack. This is because direct access to the objects under the object on the top of the stack is not possible. Table 13-1 shows some of the properties, methods, and events of the Stack class.

Table 13-1. *Some of the properties, methods, and events of the Stack class*

Class Stack[1]

Namespace System.Collections

Properties

Count	Gets the number of elements contained in the Stack.

Methods

Clear( )	Removes all objects from the Stack.
Peek( )	Returns the object at the top of the Stack without removing it.
Pop( )	Removes and returns the object at the top of the Stack.
Push(Object)	Inserts an object at the top of the Stack.

Events

NA

Reference

`https://msdn.microsoft.com/en-us/library/system.collections.stack(v=vs.110).aspx`

---

[1]All property, method, and event descriptions were taken directly from Microsoft's official documentation. The event handler methods used to handle the events of this class were omitted to conserve space. See the reference for all of the methods of this class.

Figure 13-1 shows an example of the Stack class.

Notice at 01 that we are declaring a stack of String types. Keep in mind, however, that we can declare stacks of any type. Notice as well that we are *not* specifying the size of the stack in the declaration. This is because a stack is dynamically allocated in memory. That is, its capacity is automatically increased (through memory reallocation) as additional items are added to it.

CODE BEHIND

```
     // Declare the stack.
01   Stack<String> strProductStack = new Stack<String>();

     // Add items to the stack.
     strProductStack.Push("Nike Men's Summer Flex Ace 7 Inch Short");
     strProductStack.Push("Nike Men's Summer RF Premier Jacket");
     strProductStack.Push("Nike Zoom Vapor 9.5 Tour");
     strProductStack.Push("Babolat Pure Aero French Open");
     // strProductStack[0] = "Babolat Pure Aero French Open" (Top)
     // strProductStack[1] = "Nike Zoom Vapor 9.5 Tour"
     // strProductStack[2] = "Nike Men's Summer RF Premier Jacket"
     // strProductStack[3] = "Nike Men's Summer Flex Ace 7 Inch Short"
     // (Bottom)

     // Get the number of items in the stack.
     Int32 i32Count = strProductStack.Count;
     // i32Count = 4

     // See what the next item on the stack is without removing it.
     String strProduct = "";
     strProduct = strProductStack.Peek();
     // strProduct = "Babolat Pure Aero French Open"
     // strProductStack[0] = "Babolat Pure Aero French Open" (Top)
     // strProductStack[1] = "Nike Zoom Vapor 9.5 Tour"
     // strProductStack[2] = "Nike Men's Summer RF Premier Jacket"
     // strProductStack[3] = "Nike Men's Summer Flex Ace 7 Inch Short"
     // (Bottom)

     // Remove an item from the stack.
     strProduct = strProductStack.Pop();
     // strProduct = "Babolat Pure Aero French Open"
     // strProductStack[0] = "Nike Zoom Vapor 9.5 Tour" (Top)
     // strProductStack[1] = "Nike Men's Summer RF Premier Jacket"
     // strProductStack[2] = "Nike Men's Summer Flex Ace 7 Inch Short"
     // (Bottom)

     // Clear the stack.
     strProductStack.Clear();
     // strProductStack = empty
```

Figure 13-1. *Example of the Stack class*

13.3 Queue Class

A queue is a one-dimensional *first-in-first-out* (FIFO) data structure that contains zero or more *objects*. The *first* object in a queue is at the *beginning* of the queue, whereas the *last* object in a queue is at the *end* of the queue. Operations on a queue can only occur at the beginning of the queue. Conceptually, a queue is like a line of people waiting to be checked out at a grocery store. The person at the beginning of the line is checked out first, the people in the middle of the line are checked out next, and the person at the end of the line is checked out last.

In C#, objects are *enqueued* onto a queue and dequeued from a queue. Retrieving an object that is not at the beginning of the queue requires dequeueing one or more objects from the queue since direct access to the objects after the object at the beginning of the queue is not possible. Table 13-2 shows some of the properties, methods, and events of the Queue class.

Table 13-2. *Some of the properties, methods, and events of the Queue class*

Class Queue[2]

Namespace System.Collections

Properties

Count	Gets the number of elements contained in the Queue.

Methods

Clear( )	Removes all objects from the Queue.
Dequeue( )	Removes and returns the object at the beginning of the Queue.
Enqueue(Object)	Adds an object to the end of the Queue.
Peek( )	Returns the object at the beginning of the Queue without removing it.

Events

NA

Reference

https://msdn.microsoft.com/en-us/library/system.collections.queue(v=vs.110).aspx

---

[2]All property, method, and event descriptions were taken directly from Microsoft's official documentation. The event handler methods used to handle the events of this class were omitted to conserve space. See the reference for all of the methods of this class.

Figure 13-2 shows an example of the Queue class.

Notice at 01 that we are declaring a queue of String types. Keep in mind, however, that we can declare queues of any type. Notice as well that we are *not* specifying the size of the queue in the declaration. This is because a queue is dynamically allocated in memory. That is, its capacity is automatically increased (through memory reallocation) as additional items are added to it.

CODE BEHIND

```
    // Declare the queue.
01  Queue<String> strProductQueue = new Queue<String>();

    // Add items to the queue.
    strProductQueue.Enqueue("Nike Men's Summer Flex Ace 7 Inch Short");
    strProductQueue.Enqueue("Nike Men's Summer RF Premier Jacket");
    strProductQueue.Enqueue("Nike Zoom Vapor 9.5 Tour");
    strProductQueue.Enqueue("Babolat Pure Aero French Open");
    // strProductQueue[0] = "Nike Men's Summer Flex Ace 7 Inch Short" (Beg.)
    // strProductQueue[1] = "Nike Men's Summer RF Premier Jacket"
    // strProductQueue[2] = "Nike Zoom Vapor 9.5 Tour"
    // strProductQueue[3] = "Babolat Pure Aero French Open" (End)

    // Get the number of items in the queue.
    Int32 i32Count = strProductQueue.Count;
    // i32Count = 4

    // See what the next item in the queue is without removing it.
    String strProduct = "";
    strProduct = strProductQueue.Peek();
    // strProduct = "Nike Men's Summer Flex Ace 7 Inch Short"
    // strProductQueue[0] = "Nike Men's Summer Flex Ace 7 Inch Short" (Beg.)
    // strProductQueue[1] = "Nike Men's Summer RF Premier Jacket"
    // strProductQueue[2] = "Nike Zoom Vapor 9.5 Tour"
    // strProductQueue[3] = "Babolat Pure Aero French Open" (End)

    // Remove an item from the queue.
    strProduct = strProductQueue.Dequeue();
    // strProduct = "Nike Men's Summer Flex Ace 7 Inch Short"
    // strProductQueue[0] = "Nike Men's Summer RF Premier Jacket" (Beg.)
    // strProductQueue[1] = "Nike Zoom Vapor 9.5 Tour"
    // strProductQueue[2] = "Babolat Pure Aero French Open" (End)

    // Clear the queue.
    strProductQueue.Clear();
    // strProductQueue = empty
```

Figure 13-2. *Example of the Queue class*

13.4 LinkedList Class

A linked list is a one-dimensional *linear* data structure that contains zero or more *nodes*. The *first* node in a linked list is at the *start* of the linked list, whereas the *last* node in a linked list is at the *end* of the linked list. Operations on a linked list can occur anywhere in the linked list. Conceptually, a linked list is like a group of alphabetized folders in a file cabinet. When we want to add a new folder to the group of folders, we scan the set of ordered folders, locate the point at which the folder should be added, and then add the folder. Conversely, when we want to remove an existing folder from the group of folders, we scan the set of ordered folders, locate the folder that we wish to remove, and then remove the folder.

In C#, nodes are *added* to a linked list, *found* in a linked list, and *removed* from a linked list. A node can be added to the start of a linked list, added immediately before a specified node in the linked list, added immediately after a specified node in the linked list, and added to the end of the linked list. In addition, a linked list can be searched in an effort to find a given node and/or retrieve its associated data. And finally, a node can be removed from the start of the linked list, removed from anywhere in the middle of the linked list, and removed from the end of the linked list. Table 13-3 shows some of the properties, methods, and events of the LinkedList class.

Table 13-3. *Some of the properties, methods, and events of the LinkedList class*

Class LinkedList[3]	
Namespace System.Collections.Generic	
Properties	
Count	Gets the number of nodes actually contained in the LinkedList.
First	Gets the first node of the LinkedList.
Last	Gets the last node of the LinkedList.
Methods	
AddAfter(LinkedListNode<T>, T)	Adds a new node containing the specified value after the specified existing node in the LinkedList.
AddBefore(LinkedListNode<T>, T)	Adds a new node containing the specified value before the specified existing node in the LinkedList.
AddFirst(T)	Adds a new node containing the specified value at the start of the LinkedList.
AddLast(T)	Adds a new node containing the specified value at the end of the LinkedList.
Clear()	Removes all nodes from the LinkedList.
Contains(T)	Determines whether a value is in the LinkedList.
Find(T)	Finds the first node that contains the specified value.
Remove(T)	Removes the first occurrence of the specified value from the LinkedList.
RemoveFirst()	Removes the node at the start of the LinkedList.
RemoveLast()	Removes the node at the end of the LinkedList.
Events	
NA	
Reference	
https://msdn.microsoft.com/en-us/library/he2s3bh7(v=vs.110).aspx	

---

[3]All property, method, and event descriptions were taken directly from Microsoft's official documentation. The event handler methods used to handle the events of this class were omitted to conserve space. See the reference for all of the methods of this class.

Figure 13-3 shows an example of the LinkedList class.

Notice at 01 that we are declaring a linked list of String types. Keep in mind, however, that we can declare linked lists of any type. Notice as well that we are *not* specifying the size of the linked list in the declaration. This is because a linked list is dynamically allocated in memory. That is, its capacity is automatically increased (through memory reallocation) as additional items are added to it.

CODE BEHIND

```
    // Declare the linked list.
01  LinkedList<String> strSupplierLinkedList = new LinkedList<String>();

    // Add a node to the beginning of the linked list.
    strSupplierLinkedList.AddFirst("Adidas");
    // strSupplierLinkedList[0] = "Adidas" (Start and End)

    // Add a node after the first node in the linked list.
    LinkedListNode<String> llnCurrentNode;
    llnCurrentNode = strSupplierLinkedList.First;
    strSupplierLinkedList.AddAfter(llnCurrentNode, "Babolat");
    // strSupplierLinkedList[0] = "Adidas" (Start)
    // strSupplierLinkedList[1] = "Babolat" (End)

    // Add a node after the current node in the linked list.
    llnCurrentNode = strSupplierLinkedList.Find("Babolat");
    strSupplierLinkedList.AddAfter(llnCurrentNode, "Nike");
    // strSupplierLinkedList[0] = "Adidas" (Start)
    // strSupplierLinkedList[1] = "Babolat"
    // strSupplierLinkedList[2] = "Nike" (End)

    // Add a node before the specified node in the linked list.
    llnCurrentNode = strSupplierLinkedList.Find("Nike");
    strSupplierLinkedList.AddBefore(llnCurrentNode, "Head");
    // strSupplierLinkedList[0] = "Adidas" (Start)
    // strSupplierLinkedList[1] = "Babolat"
    // strSupplierLinkedList[2] = "Head"
    // strSupplierLinkedList[3] = "Nike" (End)

    // Add a node to the end of the linked list.
    strSupplierLinkedList.AddLast("Prince");
    // strSupplierLinkedList[0] = "Adidas" (Start)
    // strSupplierLinkedList[1] = "Babolat"
    // strSupplierLinkedList[2] = "Head"
    // strSupplierLinkedList[3] = "Nike"
    // strSupplierLinkedList[4] = "Prince" (End)
```

Figure 13-3. *Example of the LinkedList class*

```
// Get the number of nodes in the linked list.
Int32 i32Count = strSupplierLinkedList.Count;
// i32Count = 5
// Get the first node of the linked list.
String strSupplier = "";
strSupplier = strSupplierLinkedList.First.Value;
// strSupplier = "Adidas"

// Get the last node of the linked list.
strSupplier = strSupplierLinkedList.Last.Value;
// strSupplier = "Prince"

// Determine whether or not a value exists in the linked list.
Boolean booFound = false;
booFound = strSupplierLinkedList.Contains("Nike");
// booFound = true

// Find the first node in the linked list that contains the specified
// value.
String strCurrentNodeValue = "";
llnCurrentNode = strSupplierLinkedList.Find("Head");
strCurrentNodeValue = llnCurrentNode.Value;
// llnCurrentNode = [3], strCurrentNodeValue = "Head"

// Find the first node in the linked list that contains the specified
// value. The specified value is not in the list.
llnCurrentNode = strSupplierLinkedList.Find("xyz");
// llnCurrentNode = null

// Remove the node at the beginning of the linked list.
strSupplierLinkedList.RemoveFirst();
// strSupplierLinkedList[0] = "Babolat" (Start)
// strSupplierLinkedList[1] = "Head"
// strSupplierLinkedList[2] = "Nike"
// strSupplierLinkedList[3] = "Prince" (End)

// Remove the node at the end of the linked list.
strSupplierLinkedList.RemoveLast();
// strSupplierLinkedList[0] = "Babolat" (Start)
// strSupplierLinkedList[1] = "Head"
// strSupplierLinkedList[2] = "Nike" (End)
```

Figure 13-3. *(continued)*

```
// Remove the first occurrence of the specified value from the linked
// list.
strSupplierLinkedList.Remove("Head");
// strSupplierLinkedList[0] = "Babolat" (Start)
// strSupplierLinkedList[1] = "Nike" (End)

// Clear the linked list.
strSupplierLinkedList.Clear();
// strSupplierLinkedList = empty
```

Figure 13-3. *(continued)*

13.5 SortedList Class

A sorted list is a two-dimensional *key-based* data structure that contains zero or more *elements*, each of which contains a *key/value pair*.[4] The *first* element in a sorted list is at the *start* of the sorted list, whereas the *last* element in a sorted list is at the *end* of the sorted list. Operations on a sorted list can occur anywhere in the sorted list. Conceptually, a sorted list is like a dictionary of alphabetized terms and their respective definitions. When we want to add a new term (i.e., key) and definition (i.e., value) to the dictionary, we scan the set of ordered terms, locate the point at which the term and definition should be added, and then add the term and definition. Conversely, when we want to remove an existing term and definition from the dictionary, we scan the set of ordered terms, locate the term and definition that we wish to remove, and then remove the term and definition.

In C#, elements are *added* to a sorted list, *looked up* in a sorted list, and *removed* from sorted list. When an element is added to a sorted list, the sorted list is automatically adjusted so that its keys remain in the proper sort sequence. Duplicate keys are *not* permitted in a sorted list since a given key must uniquely identify an element in the sorted list. When an element is looked up in a sorted list, it is looked up by its key.[5] And when an element is removed from a sorted list, the sorted list is again automatically adjusted so that its keys remain in the proper sort sequence. Table 13-4 shows some of the properties, methods, and events of the SortedList class.

---

[4]The key is the first dimension of a sorted list, whereas the value is the second dimension of a sorted list.

[5]Elements in a sorted list can also be accessed by their index.

Table 13-4. *Some of the properties, methods, and events of the SortedList class*

Class SortedList[6]

Namespace System.Collections

Properties

Count	Gets the number of elements contained in a SortedList object.
Item[Object]	Gets and sets the value associated with a specific key in a SortedList object.

Methods

Add(Object, Object)	Adds an element with the specified key and value to a SortedList object.
Clear()	Removes all elements from a SortedList object.
ContainsKey(Object)	Determines whether a SortedList object contains a specific key.
ContainsValue(Object)	Determines whether a SortedList object contains a specific value.
Remove(Object)	Removes the element with the specified key from a SortedList object.

Events

NA

Reference

https://msdn.microsoft.com/en-us/library/system.collections.
sortedlist(v=vs.110).aspx

Figure 13-4 shows an example of the SortedList class.

Notice at 01 that we are declaring the *key* of the key/value pair as a String type and the *value* of the key/value pair as a String type. Keep in mind, however, that we can declare keys and values of any type. Notice as well that we are *not* specifying the size of the sorted list in the declaration. This is because a sorted list is dynamically allocated in memory. That is, its capacity is automatically increased (through memory reallocation) as additional items are added to it.

Notice at 02 that although the elements are not added to the sorted list in alphabetical order, they are placed in alphabetical order automatically as they are added. Notice as well that United States Postal Service is misspelled.

Notice at 03 that United States Postal Service is no longer misspelled.

---

[6]All property, method, and event descriptions were taken directly from Microsoft's official documentation. The event handler methods used to handle the events of this class were omitted to conserve space. See the reference for all of the methods of this class.

CODE BEHIND

```
// Declare the sorted list.
01  SortedList<String, String> strShipperSortedList = new SortedList<String,
        String>();

    // Add an element with the specified key and value to the sorted list.
02  strShipperSortedList.Add("FedEx", "Federal Express");
    strShipperSortedList.Add("DHL", "Dalsey, Hillblom, and Lynn");
    strShipperSortedList.Add("UPS", "United Parcel Service");
    strShipperSortedList.Add("USPS", "Un St Po Se");
    // strShipperSortedList[0] = {[DHL, Dalsey, Hillblom, and Lynn]} (Start)
    // strShipperSortedList[1] = {[FedEx, Federal Express]
    // strShipperSortedList[2] = {[UPS, United Parcel Service]}
    // strShipperSortedList[3] = {[USPS, Un St Po Se]} (End)

    // Get the number of elements in the sorted list.
    Int32 i32Count = strShipperSortedList.Count;
    // i32Count = 4

    // Set the value associated with a specific key in the sorted list.
03  strShipperSortedList["USPS"] = "United States Postal Service";
    // strShipperSortedList[0] = {[DHL, Dalsey, Hillblom, and Lynn]} (Start)
    // strShipperSortedList[1] = {[FedEx, Federal Express]
    // strShipperSortedList[2] = {[UPS, United Parcel Service]}
    // strShipperSortedList[3] = {[USPS, United States Postal Service]} (End)

    // Get the value associated with a specific key in the sorted list.
    String strShipper = "";
    strShipper = strShipperSortedList["FedEx"];
    // strShipper = "Federal Express"

    // Determine whether or not the sorted list contains a specific key.
    Boolean booFound = false;
    booFound = strShipperSortedList.ContainsKey("UPS");
    // booFound = true

    // Determine whether or not the sorted list contains a specific value.
    booFound = strShipperSortedList.ContainsValue("United Parcel Service");
    // booFound = true
    // Remove the element with the specified key from the sorted list.
    strShipperSortedList.Remove("DHL");
    // strShipperSortedList[0] = {[FedEx, Federal Express] (Start)
    // strShipperSortedList[1] = {[UPS, United Parcel Service]}
    // strShipperSortedList[2] = {[USPS, United States Postal Service]} (End)

    // Clear the sorted list.
    strShipperSortedList.Clear();
    // strShipperSortedList = empty
```

Figure 13-4. *Example of the SortedList class*

CHAPTER 14

File System Operations

14.1 Introduction

A file system defines how a computer's data is stored on and retrieved from a mass storage device. Without a file system, the information on a mass storage device would be an accumulation of unorganized and non-retrievable data. The files in a file system are typically arranged into a set of hierarchically organized directories (a.k.a., folders) and subdirectories (a.k.a., subfolders). Among other things, a file system permits a computer's operating system to

- Maintain its system of directories and subdirectories

- Create, copy, move, store, retrieve, and delete its files

- Track the areas of its mass storage device(s) that contain files

- Track the areas of its mass storage device(s) that are unused and available for allocation to files

- Track the properties (e.g., owners, created dates and times, modified dates and times, accessed dates and times) and attributes (e.g., compressed, encrypted, read-only, hidden) of its files

When developing Web applications, we often encounter the need to interact with the Web server's file system to perform such operations.

In this chapter, we will look at the File class. The File class permits us to do such things as create a new file, write to or read from a file, delete a file, check for the existence of a file, get or set the properties and attributes of a file, and copy or move a file from one location to another.

© Robert E. Beasley 2020
R. E. Beasley, *Essential ASP.NET Web Forms Development*, https://doi.org/10.1007/978-1-4842-5784-5_14

14.2 File Class

The File class provides static methods that permit us to create, write to, read from, delete, check for the existence of, get the properties and attributes of, set the properties and attributes of, copy, and move a single file. All the methods of the File class require a *path*. A path is a unique location within the hierarchy of a file system's directories and subdirectories. A path can be a directory, subdirectory, or file. The *full path* of a directory, subdirectory, or file includes the entire path leading from the file system's *root directory* (e.g., c:\). The *relative path* of a directory, subdirectory, or file only includes the path leading from the *current* directory or subdirectory (e.g., c:\myfiles\). When a file is first created, full read/write access is granted to all users by default. Table 14-1 shows some of the properties, methods, and events of the File class.

Table 14-1. *Some of the properties, methods, and events of the File class*

Class File[1]

Namespace System.IO

Properties

(See reference.)

Methods

AppendAllText(String, String)	Opens a file, appends the specified string to the file, and then closes the file. If the file does not exist, this method creates a file, writes the specified string to the file, then closes the file.
Copy(String, String, Boolean)	Copies an existing file to a new file. Overwriting a file of the same name is allowed.
Create(String)	Creates or overwrites a file in the specified path.
Delete(String)	Deletes the specified file.
Exists(String)	Determines whether the specified file exists.

(continued)

[1]All property, method, and event descriptions were taken directly from Microsoft's official documentation. The event handler methods used to handle the events of this class were omitted to conserve space. See the reference for all of the methods of this class.

Table 14-1. (*continued*)

Methods

GetAttributes(String)	Gets the FileAttributes of the file on the path.
GetCreationTime(String)	Returns the creation date and time of the specified file or directory.
GetLastAccessTime(String)	Returns the date and time the specified file or directory was last accessed.
GetLastWriteTime(String)	Returns the date and time the specified file or directory was last written to.
Move(String, String)	Moves a specified file to a new location, providing the option to specify a new file name.
ReadAllText(String)	Opens a text file, reads all lines of the file, and then closes the file.
SetAttributes(String, FileAttributes)	Sets the specified FileAttributes of the file on the specified path.
SetCreationTime(String, DateTime)	Sets the date and time the file was created.
SetLastAccessTime(String, DateTime)	Sets the date and time the specified file was last accessed.
SetLastWriteTime(String, DateTime)	Sets the date and time that the specified file was last written to.
WriteAllText(String, String)	Creates a new file, writes the specified string to the file, and then closes the file. If the target file already exists, it is overwritten.

Events

(See reference.)

Reference

https://msdn.microsoft.com/en-us/library/system.io.file(v=vs.110).aspx

Figure 14-1 shows an example of creating a file using the File class.

Notice at 01 that the System.IO namespace has been added to the list of using directives (which appears at the top of the code behind file) to obviate the need to specify the fully qualified name of the File class (i.e., System.IO.File) each time we want to use one of its methods.

Notice at 02 that we are constructing the *full* path of the file to be created using the physical path of the application on the server, the Contracts directory of the application, and the name of the file.

Notice at 03 that we are using the Exists method of the File class to see if the file to be created already exists. If it does exist, we *do not* create the file. However, if it doesn't exist, we *do* create the file.

Notice at 04 that we are using the Create method of the File class to create the new file.

The first screenshot in the Result section of the figure shows the Contracts directory *before* the file has been created. The second screenshot shows the Contracts directory *after* the file has been created.

CODE BEHIND

```
01  using System.IO;

    // Create the file.
    String strMessage = "";
    String strFileName = "Contract_Adidas.txt";
02  String strFilePath = Request.PhysicalApplicationPath + "Contracts\\" +
        strFileName;
03  if (File.Exists(strFilePath))
    {
        strMessage = "That file name already exists.";
    }
    else
    {
04      File.Create(strFilePath);
        strMessage = "Contract file successfully created.";
    }
    // strMessage = "Contract file successfully created."
```

RESULT

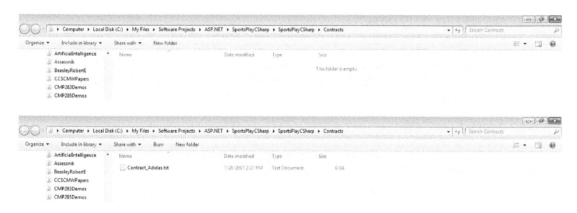

Figure 14-1. *Example of creating a file using the File class*

Figure 14-2 shows an example of writing to a file using the File class.

Notice at 01 that the System.IO namespace has been added to the list of using directives (which appears at the top of the code behind file) so we are not required to specify the fully qualified name of the File class (i.e., System.IO.File) each time we want to use one of its methods.

Notice at 02 that we are constructing the *full* path of the file to write to using the physical path of the application on the server, the Contracts directory of the application, and the name of the file.

Notice at 03 that we are using the AppendAllText method of the File class to write a newly constructed and formatted string to the file. Note that this method opens the file, appends the string to the file, and closes the file. If the file does not exist, the method will create the file first.

The screenshot in the Result section of the figure shows the contents of the file *after* it has been written to.

CODE BEHIND

```
01   using System.IO;

     // Write to the file.
     String strFileName = "Contract_Adidas.txt";
02   String strFilePath = Request.PhysicalApplicationPath + "Contracts\\" +
         strFileName;
     String strContract = "";
     strContract = "AGREEMENT BETWEEN SportsPlay AND Adidas" +
         Environment.NewLine + Environment.NewLine;
     strContract += "This Deed of Agreement is made and entered into on the
         4th day of July 20xx" +
         Environment.NewLine + Environment.NewLine;
     strContract += "BETWEEN" +
         Environment.NewLine + Environment.NewLine;
     strContract += "SportsPlay, Inc. (hereinafter referred to as the
         PURCHASER)" +
         Environment.NewLine + Environment.NewLine;
     strContract += "AND" +
         Environment.NewLine + Environment.NewLine;
     strContract += "Adidas, Inc. (hereinafter referred to as the SUPPLIER).";
03   File.AppendAllText(strFilePath, strContract);
```

RESULT

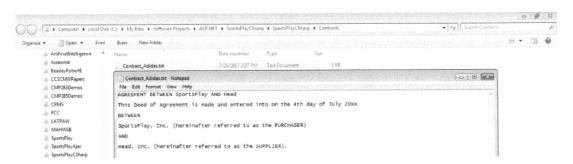

Figure 14-2. *Example of writing to a file using the File class*

Figure 14-3 shows an example of reading from a file using the File class.

Notice at 01 that the System.IO namespace has been added to the list of using directives (which appears at the top of the code behind file) to avoid the need to specify the fully qualified name of the File class (i.e., System.IO.File) each time we want to use one of its methods.

Notice at 02 that we are constructing the *full* path of the file to be read from using the physical path of the application on the server, the Contracts directory of the application, and the name of the file.

Notice at 03 that we are using the ReadAllText method of the File class to read from the file. Note that this method opens the file, reads the text from the file, and closes the file. As can be seen, the contents of the file have been read into a string variable.

```
CODE BEHIND

01  using System.IO;

    // Read from the file.
    String strFileName = "Contract_Adidas.txt";
02  String strFilePath = Request.PhysicalApplicationPath + "Contracts\\" +
        strFileName;
    String strContract = "";
03  strContract = File.ReadAllText(strFilePath);
    // strContract =
    // AGREEMENT BETWEEN SportsPlay AND Adidas
    //
    // This Deed of Agreement is made and entered into on the 4th day of July
    // 20xx
    //
    // BETWEEN
    //
    // SportsPlay, Inc. (hereinafter referred to as the PURCHASER)
    //
    // AND
    //
    // Adidas, Inc. (hereinafter referred to as the SUPPLIER).

RESULT

(See above.)
```

Figure 14-3. *Example of reading from a file using the File class*

Figure 14-4 shows an example of deleting a file using the File class.

Notice at 01 that the System.IO namespace has been added to the list of using directives (which appears at the top of the code behind file) so we are not required to specify the fully qualified name of the File class (i.e., System.IO.File) each time we want to use one of its methods.

Notice at 02 that we are constructing the *full* path of the file to be deleted using the physical path of the application on the server, the Contracts directory of the application, and the name of the file.

Notice at 03 that we are using the Exists method of the File class to see if the file to be deleted exists. If it does exist, we delete the file. If it doesn't exist, we *do not* attempt to delete the file.

Notice at 04 that we are using the Delete method of the File class to delete the existing file.

The screenshot in the Result section of the figure shows the Contracts directory *after* the file has been deleted.

CODE BEHIND

```
01  using System.IO;

    // Delete the file.
    String strMessage = "";
    String strFileName = "Contract_Adidas.txt";
02  String strFilePath = Request.PhysicalApplicationPath + "Contracts\\" +
        strFileName;
03  if (File.Exists(strFilePath))
    {
04      File.Delete(strFilePath);
        strMessage = "Contract file successfully deleted.";
    }
    else
    {
        strMessage = "Contract file NOT successfully deleted.";
    }
    // strMessage = "Contract file successfully deleted."
```

RESULT

***Figure 14-4.** Example of deleting a file using the File class*

Figure 14-5 shows some examples of getting and setting the properties and attributes of a file using the File class.

Notice at 01 that the System.IO namespace has been added to the list of using directives (which appears at the top of the code behind file) to avert the need to specify the fully qualified name of the File class (i.e., System.IO.File) each time we want to use one of its methods.

Notice at 02 that we are constructing the *full* path of the file whose properties and attributes are to be modified using the physical path of the application on the server, the Contracts directory of the application, and the name of the file.

The first screenshot in the Result section of the figure shows the properties (i.e., Created date and time, Modified date and time, and Accessed date and time) and attributes (i.e., Read-only and Hidden) of the file *before* they have been modified. The second screenshot shows the properties and attributes of the file *after* they have been modified. Note that the operating system has been configured to show hidden files for this example.

```
CODE BEHIND

01  using System.IO;

    // Get and set the attributes and properties of the file.
    String strFileName = "Contract_Adidas.txt";
02  String strFilePath = Request.PhysicalApplicationPath + "Contracts\\" +
        strFileName;

    // Get the date and time properties of the file.
    DateTime datCreated = File.GetCreationTime(strFilePath);
    // datCreated = {7/26/2017 2:27:00 PM}
    DateTime datModified = File.GetLastWriteTime(strFilePath);
    // datCreated = {7/26/2017 2:37:00 PM}
    DateTime datAccessed = File.GetLastAccessTime(strFilePath);
    // datCreated = {7/26/2017 2:37:00 PM}

    // Set the date and time properties of the file.
    File.SetCreationTime(strFilePath, DateTime.Now);
    File.SetLastWriteTime(strFilePath, DateTime.Now);
    File.SetLastAccessTime(strFilePath, DateTime.Now);
```

Figure 14-5. *Examples of getting and setting the properties and attributes of a file using the File class*

```
// Get the read-only and hidden attributes of the file.
FileAttributes fiaFileAttributes = File.GetAttributes(strFilePath);
Boolean booReadOnly = (fiaFileAttributes & FileAttributes.ReadOnly) ==
    FileAttributes.ReadOnly;
Boolean booHidden = (fiaFileAttributes & FileAttributes.Hidden) ==
    FileAttributes.Hidden;

// Toggle (i.e., make opposite) the read-only and hidden attributes of
// the file based on their current state.
if (booReadOnly && booHidden)
{
    // Make file not read-only and not hidden.
    File.SetAttributes(strFilePath, FileAttributes.Normal |
        FileAttributes.Normal);
}
else if (booReadOnly && !booHidden)
{
    // Make file not read-only and hidden.
    File.SetAttributes(strFilePath, FileAttributes.Normal |
        FileAttributes.Hidden);
}
else if (!booReadOnly && booHidden)
{
    // Make file read-only and not hidden.
    File.SetAttributes(strFilePath, FileAttributes.ReadOnly |
        FileAttributes.Normal);
}
else
{
    // Make file read-only and hidden.
    File.SetAttributes(strFilePath, FileAttributes.ReadOnly |
        FileAttributes.Hidden);
}
```

RESULT

Figure 14-5. (continued)

Figure 14-5. *(continued)*

Figure 14-6 shows an example of copying a file using the File class.

Notice at 01 that the System.IO namespace has been added to the list of using directives (which appears at the top of the code behind file) so we are not required to specify the fully qualified name of the File class (i.e., System.IO.File) each time we want to use one of its methods.

Notice at 02 that we are constructing the *full* path of the files to be used in the copy operation using the physical path of the application on the server and the Contracts directory of the application.

Notice at 03 that we are using the Copy method of the File class to copy the original file. As can be seen, the new file will be created in the same directory as the original file.

The screenshot in the Result section of the figure shows the Contracts directory *after* the original file has been copied.

CODE BEHIND

```
01  using System.IO;

    // Make a copy of the file.
    String strFileName = "Contract_Adidas.txt";
    String strFileNameCopy = "Contract_Adidas_Copy.txt";
02  String strFilePath = Request.PhysicalApplicationPath + "Contracts\\";
03  File.Copy(strFilePath + strFileName, strFilePath + strFileNameCopy);
```

RESULT

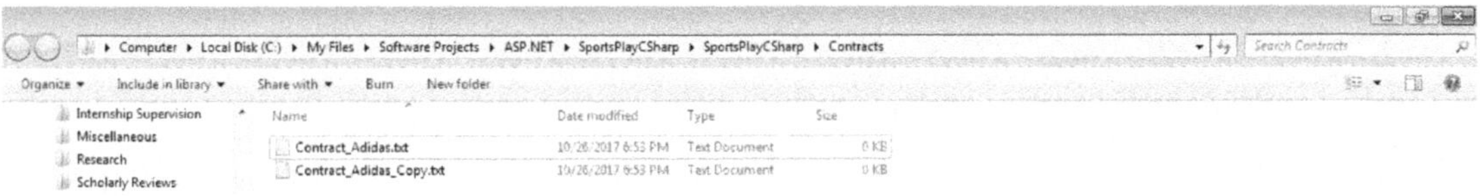

Figure 14-6. *Example of copying a file using the File class*

CHAPTER 15

Custom C# Classes

15.1 Introduction

Like the other C# classes we have discussed in this book, a custom C# class can contain properties, methods, and events. These classes are considered "custom" because the only properties, methods, and events they contain are the ones we define. Because of this, they do *exactly* what we want them to do—nothing more, nothing less. Custom C# classes are helpful when there are functions or procedures that we must perform in many places within a single Web application or across multiple Web applications. So, instead of writing a segment of code to perform a function or procedure and then copying that code to many places, we can write a single method within a custom C# class and then invoke that method as needed. This way, when a change to the logic of the code is required, we need only make the change in one place.

In C#, we can create both *non-static classes* and *static classes*. As a general rule, a non-static class contains non-static properties, non-static methods, and non-static events that we can utilize, but only *after* an object has been instantiated from the class.[1] We usually create non-static classes when their properties, methods, and events are intended to represent something in the real world, such as an employee or product. A static class, on the other hand, contains static properties, static methods, and static events that we can utilize *immediately*, without having to instantiate an object from the class. We usually create static classes when their properties, methods, and events are intended to perform a function or procedure, such as generating a password or constructing a login name.

---

[1]A *non-static* class can also contain *static* properties, *static* methods, and *static* events that we can utilize *immediately*, without having to instantiate an object from the class.

© Robert E. Beasley 2020
R. E. Beasley, *Essential ASP.NET Web Forms Development*, https://doi.org/10.1007/978-1-4842-5784-5_15

In this chapter, we will begin by looking at class design. Class design is the process of planning the properties, methods, and events of a class. As we will see, if we do a good job of class design, we can expect to develop custom classes that are reusable and methods that are *relatively* easy to read, understand, locate semantic errors in, debug, modify, and unit test. Next, we will discuss the C# class itself. The C# class permits us to create custom classes that contain our own properties, methods, and events. After that, we will add a folder to our project that will house our classes. We will then learn how to add a non-static C# class to our project, code it, and invoke it. And finally, we will learn how to add a static C# class to our project, code it, and invoke it. Note that, from this point forward, we will refer to *custom C# classes* as *C# classes* for convenience.

15.2 Class Design

Class design is the process of planning the properties, methods, and events of a class. One of the major goals of class design is *reuse*. When we are designing a class, and that class seems to have broad applicability (e.g., we expect that it might be usable across several applications in the future), we should design it with an eye toward reuse so that we don't spend time reinventing the wheel by writing the same code more than once. When a class is designed well, there is an increased probability that we will be able to reuse it when augmenting an existing application or developing a new one.

Another major goal of class design is the creation of methods that exhibit a *high* degree of *cohesion*. Cohesion is the degree to which a method's instructions are functionally related. In other words, it is the extent to which a method's programming statements work together to perform a *singular* task. The main problem with methods that do not perform a singular task is that they are relatively difficult to read, understand, locate semantic errors in, and modify.

A third major goal of class design is the creation of methods that exhibit a *low* degree of *coupling*. Coupling is the degree to which two or more methods are interdependent. Put another way, it is the extent to which two or more methods depend on one another for functionality or data. The main problem with methods that depend on one another for functionality or data is that changes in one method may require changes in other methods potentially creating a ripple effect of required changes. As can be imagined, this can lead to more difficult unit testing as well as the need to retest any related methods that have been modified.

15.3 C# Class

A C# class is a custom class that can contain any number of properties, methods, and/or events. Once a C# class is created, it can be used within a single application or across multiple applications. Again, this avoids the need to write the same code in more than one place. Table 15-1 shows the properties, methods, and events of a C# class. As can be seen, all the members of a C# class are custom. There are no predefined properties, methods, and events—only the ones we define. Notice that the name of the class in the table is MyClass. This indicates that we provide the name of the class when we create it. Notice as well that the namespace of the class is MyProject.MyFolder. This indicates that the class's definition resides in a folder that we have created inside a project that we have created. Although placing our C# classes in a folder is optional, doing so will help us keep them together in one place and will help us keep our Web applications well organized in general.

Table 15-1. *The properties, methods, and events of a C# class*

Class MyClass

Namespace MyProject.MyFolder

Properties

Custom

Methods

Custom

Events

Custom

Reference

https://docs.microsoft.com/en-us/dotnet/articles/csharp/programming-guide/
classes-and-structs/classes

15.4 Adding a Classes Folder

Before we add non-static and static C# classes to our project, we will add a folder called *Classes* to house them and any others we may need to create in the future. As mentioned earlier, adding a Classes folder to our project will help us keep our C# classes together in one place and will help us keep our Web application well organized in general. To add a *Classes* folder to a project

1. Open the Solution Explorer.

2. Right-click the project (not the solution).

3. Select *Add* ➤ *New Folder*.

4. Rename the folder *Classes*.

15.5 Adding a Non-static C# Class

In this section, we will create a new *non-static* C# class in our Classes folder. Recall from earlier that a non-static class contains non-static properties, non-static methods, and non-static events that we can utilize, but only *after* an object has been instantiated from the class.[2] We will call our new class *Employee*. This class will contain several properties and a single method called *GenerateEmailAddress* that will generate an employee email address for us whenever we need one. Keep in mind that we can add as many methods to a class as we want. To add a new non-static C# class to the Classes folder of the project

1. Open the Solution Explorer.

2. Right-click the Classes folder.

3. Select *Add* ➤ *New Item....*

When the *Add New Item* dialog appears

1. Select *Installed* ➤ *Visual C#* ➤ *Code* from the left pane of the dialog.

2. Select *Class* from the middle pane of the dialog.

3. Give the class a *Name* (Employee.cs) at the bottom of the dialog.

4. Click *Add.*

---

[2]A *non-static* class can also contain *static* properties, *static* methods, and *static* events that we can utilize *immediately*, without having to instantiate an object from the class.

Figure 15-1 shows an example of a non-static class. As can be seen, the class contains a number of properties and a method that generates an email address that is composed of an employee's first initial and last name and the domain of his or her company. Thus, if this method is invoked with the arguments *Billingsley* and *Beth*, respectively, the method will return bbillingsley@sportsplay.com.

Notice at 01 that our Employee class resides in the SportsPlayCSharp.Classes namespace, where SportsPlayCSharp is the name of the project and Classes is the name of the folder in which the class resides.

Notice at 02 the declaration of the Employee class. By default, this is a non-static class.

Notice at 03 the declarations of the class's properties. As can be seen, each of these has a *set* method that assigns a value to the property and a *get* method that retrieves a value from the property.

Notice at 04 the declaration of the GenerateEmailAddress method. Again, by default, this is a non-static method. There are a few other things to notice about the declaration of this method. First, the word *String* indicates that this method will return a value of type String to the method that invokes it. Second, the word *GenerateEmailAddress* indicates the name of the method itself. And third, the method has two input parameters—a last name of type String and a first name of type String. Thus, the invoking method is expected to pass this method two associated arguments.

Notice at 05 that once the logic of the method is executed, the value in the variable strEmailAddress will be returned to the invoking method.

CODE BEHIND

```
using System;
using System.Collections.Generic;
using System.Linq;
using System.Web;

01  namespace SportsPlayCSharp.Classes
    {
02      public class Employee
        {

            // Define the class's properties.
03          public String LastName { set; get; }
            public String FirstName { set; get; }
            public String MiddleInitial { set; get; }
            public String Address { set; get; }
            public String City { set; get; }
            public String State { set; get; }
            public String ZipCode { set; get; }
            public String Phone { set; get; }
            public String EmailAddress { set; get; }
            public String Password { set; get; }

04          public String GenerateEmailAddress(String strLastName,
                String strFirstName)
            {

                // Generate an email address.
                String strEmailAddress =
                    strFirstName.Substring(0, 1).ToLower() +
                    strLastName.ToLower() + "@sportsplay.com";
05              return strEmailAddress;

            }

        }

    }
```

Figure 15-1. *Example of a non-static class*

Figure 15-2 shows an example of creating an instance of a non-static class, setting and getting its properties, and invoking its method. Note that instances of this class can be created and used in *any* class in the Web application that requires its functionality. Thus, this class is reusable.

Notice at 01 that the SportsPlayCSharp.Classes namespace has been added to the list of using directives (which appears at the top of the code behind file) so that we don't have to specify the fully qualified name of the Employee class (i.e., SportsPlayCSharp. Classes.Employee) each time we want to use it.

Notice at 02 that we are assigning values to the variables we will be assigning to the properties of the soon-to-be-created Employee object. A close inspection of this list of assignment statements reveals that we have *not* assigned a value to the strEmailAddress variable. This is because we will be generating this email address automatically.

Notice at 03 that we are creating an instance of the Employee class. That is, we are creating an Employee *object* from the Employee class.

Notice at 04 that we are invoking the Employee object's GenerateEmailAddress method with two input parameters, and we are expecting an email address of type String to be returned.

Notice at 05 that we are setting the properties of the Employee object.

Notice at 06 that we are getting the properties of the Employee object.

CODE BEHIND

```
01   using SportsPlayCSharp.Classes;

     // Declare the variables.
02   String strLastName = "Billingsley";
     String strFirstName = "Beth";
     String strMiddleInitial = "B";
     String strAddress = "6785 Barker Rd.";
     String strCity = "Bickman";
     String strState = "MS";
     String strZipCode = "68321";
     String strPhone = "765-987-1432";
     String strEmailAddress = "";
     String strPassword = "abc";

     // Create an instance of the non-static Employee class.
03   Employee empEmployee = new Employee();

     // Generate an email address for the employee.
04   strEmailAddress = empEmployee.GenerateEmailAddress(strLastName,
         strFirstName);

     // Set the properties of the Employee object.
05   empEmployee.LastName = strLastName;
     empEmployee.FirstName = strFirstName;
     empEmployee.MiddleInitial = strMiddleInitial;
     empEmployee.Address = strAddress;
     empEmployee.City = strCity;
     empEmployee.State = strState;
     empEmployee.ZipCode = strZipCode;
     empEmployee.Phone = strPhone;
     empEmployee.EmailAddress = strEmailAddress;
     empEmployee.Password = strPassword;
```

Figure 15-2. *Example of creating an instance of a non-static class, setting and getting its properties, and invoking its method*

```
      // Get the properties of the Employee object.
06    String strLastName2 = empEmployee.LastName;
      // strLastName2 = "Billingsley"
      String strFirstName2 = empEmployee.FirstName;
      // strFirstName2 = "Beth"
      String strMiddleInitial2 = empEmployee.MiddleInitial;
      // strMiddleInitial2 = "B"
      String strAddress2 = empEmployee.Address;
      // strAddress2 = "6785 Barker Rd."
      String strCity2 = empEmployee.City;
      // strCity2 = "Bickman"
      String strState2 = empEmployee.State;
      // strState2 = "MS"
      String strZipCode2 = empEmployee.ZipCode;
      // strZipCode2 = "68321"
      String strPhone2 = empEmployee.Phone;
      // strPhone2 = "765-987-1432"
      String strEmailAddress2 = empEmployee.EmailAddress;
      // strEmailAddress2 = "bbillingsley@sportsplay.com"
      String strPassword2 = empEmployee.Password;
      // strPassword2 = "abc"
```

Figure 15-2. *(continued)*

15.6 Adding a Static C# Class

In this section, we will create a new *static* C# class in our Classes folder. Recall from earlier that a static class contains static properties, static methods, and static events that we can utilize *immediately*, without having to instantiate an object from the class. We will call our new class *Password*. This class will contain a single method called *Generate* that will generate a partially random password for us whenever we need one. Keep in mind that we can add as many methods to a class as we want. To add a new static C# class to the Classes folder of the project

1. Open the Solution Explorer.

2. Right-click the Classes folder.

3. Select *Add* ➤ *New Item....*

When the *Add New Item* dialog appears

1. Select *Installed* ➤ *Visual C#* ➤ *Code* from the left pane of the dialog.

2. Select *Class* from the middle pane of the dialog.

3. Give the class a *Name* (Password.cs) at the bottom of the dialog.

4. Click *Add*.

Figure 15-3 shows an example of a static class. As can be seen, the class contains a method that generates a password of a given length that is composed of the initials of a person's first name and last name followed by a group of randomly generated characters. Thus, if this method is invoked with the arguments *Jones*, *Jerry*, and *7*, respectively, the method will return something like *jj14$%5*.

Notice at 01 that our Password class resides in the SportsPlayCSharp.Classes namespace, where SportsPlayCSharp is the name of the project and Classes is the name of the folder in which the class resides.

Notice at 02 the declaration of the Password class. Note that we have added the word *static* immediately after the word *public* to indicate that this is a static class.

Notice at 03 the declaration of the Generate method. Again, we have added the word *static* immediately after the word *public* to indicate that this is a static method. There are a few other things to notice about the declaration of this method. First, the word *String* indicates that this method will return a value of type String to the method that invokes it. Second, the word *Generate* indicates the name of the method itself. And third, the method has three input parameters—a last name of type String, a first name of type String, and a length of type Byte. Thus, the invoking method is expected to pass this method three associated arguments.

Notice at 04 and 05, respectively, the instantiation of a new Random object from the Random class and the generation of a new random number between 1 and 10 (inclusive).

Notice at 06 that once the logic of the method is executed, the value in the variable strPassword will be returned to the invoking method.

CODE BEHIND

```csharp
using System;
using System.Collections.Generic;
using System.Linq;
using System.Web;

01  namespace SportsPlayCSharp.Classes
    {
02      public static class Password
        {

03          public static String Generate(String strLastName, String
                strFirstName, Byte bytLength)
            {

                // Generate a password. The first two characters of the
                // password are the initials of the person's first and
                // last names. The last bytLength-2 characters of the
                // password are randomly generated.
                String strFirstNameInitial = strFirstName.
                    Substring(0, 1).ToLower();
                String strLastNameInitial = strLastName.
                    Substring(0, 1).ToLower();
                String strPassword = strFirstNameInitial +
                    strLastNameInitial.ToString();
04              Random ranRandom = new Random();
                for (int i = 1; i <= bytLength - 2; i++)
                {
```

Figure 15-3. *Example of a static class*

```
05                        Int16 i16RandomNumber = (Int16)ranRandom.Next(1, 10);
                          switch (i16RandomNumber)
                          {
                              case 1:
                                  strPassword = strPassword + "1";
                                  break;
                              case 2:
                                  strPassword = strPassword + "2";
                                  break;
                              case 3:
                                  strPassword = strPassword + "3";
                                  break;
                              case 4:
                                  strPassword = strPassword + "4";
                                  break;
                              case 5:
                                  strPassword = strPassword + "5";
                                  break;
                              case 6:
                                  strPassword = strPassword + "!";
                                  break;
                              case 7:
                                  strPassword = strPassword + "#";
                                  break;
                              case 8:
                                  strPassword = strPassword + "$";
                                  break;
                              case 9:
                                  strPassword = strPassword + "%";
                                  break;
                              case 10:
                                  strPassword = strPassword + "*";
                                  break;
                          }
                      }
06                return strPassword;

                  }
              }
          }
```

Figure 15-3. *(continued)*

Figure 15-4 shows an example of invoking a static method in a static class. Note that this method can be invoked from *any* class in the Web application that requires its functionality. Thus, this class is reusable.

Notice at 01 that the SportsPlayCSharp.Classes namespace has been added to the list of using directives (which appears at the top of the code behind file) so that we don't have to specify the fully qualified name of the Password class (i.e., SportsPlayCSharp. Classes.Password) each time we want to use it.

Notice at 02 that we are invoking the Password class's Generate method with three input parameters, and we are expecting a password of type String to be returned.

```
CODE BEHIND

01   using SportsPlayCSharp.Classes;

     // Generate a password using the static Password class.
     String strLastName = "Jones";
     String strFirstName = "Jerry";
     Byte bytLength = 7;
02   String strPassword = Password.Generate(strLastName, strFirstName,
         bytLength);
     // strPassword = "jj14$%5"
```

Figure 15-4. *Example of invoking a static method in a static class*

PART IV

Multiple-Page Web Application Development

CHAPTER 16

State Maintenance

16.1 Introduction

State maintenance is the process of preserving the *state* of an end user's data as he or she navigates the pages of a Web application. This process is necessary because client-server Web applications are *stateless*, which means that once a server serves a page to a client, the server completely forgets about the client, the page it just served, and the state of any data associated with the page. In other words, once a page has been requested by the client via an HTTP request, and once the server has responded with the page via an HTTP response, any connection between the client and the server is lost. In fact, each new page request results in the creation and return of a brand new page, whether the end user is re-requesting the page he or she is currently on or is requesting a completely different page.

Because client-server Web applications are stateless, we need a way of preserving page data so that we can develop applications with multiple pages that work together as a coherent whole. When developing Web applications in ASP.NET, there are a number of methods we can use to preserve page data. However, the method (or methods) we choose depends mostly on how we would answer questions like

- How much data will need to be maintained between postbacks to the server?

- Will the data be sensitive?

- How long will the data need to persist?

- How many end users will be using the system at one time?

- How much RAM will the server have?

R. E. Beasley, *Essential ASP.NET Web Forms Development*, https://doi.org/10.1007/978-1-4842-5784-5_16

We have two fundamental options when it comes to maintaining state in a Web application. We can maintain state on the client, or we can maintain state on the server. We can maintain state using some combination of these as well.

In this chapter, we will begin by looking at client-based state maintenance. If we choose to maintain state on the client, we have a number of options. These include the use of view state, control state, hidden fields, cookies, and query strings. Next, we will discuss server-based state maintenance. If we decide to maintain state on the server, we also have some options. These include the use of session state, profile properties, database support, and application state. And finally, we will look at the process of maintaining the state of a data structure (e.g., an array, stack, queue, linked list, sorted list) so that it can be used across the pages of a Web application.

16.2 Client-Based State Maintenance

To maintain state on the client, we can utilize *view state*, *control state*, *hidden fields*, *cookies*, and/or *query strings*. In this section, we will limit our discussion to view state, cookies, and query strings as those methods seem to be the most commonly used methods of client-based state maintenance. Of course, control state and hidden fields are also useful methods of state maintenance, so the interested reader is encouraged to explore those methods as well.

16.2.1 View State

View state is a state-maintenance method that *automatically* preserves the values of the controls on a page (using a structure that resides in the page's source code) so that we can retrieve and use those values after a postback to the server that requests the *same* page. For example, when an end user selects an item from a drop-down list, enters a value into a text box, and then submits the page, the same drop-down list selection and the same text box value will be displayed on the page after the page completes its round trip from the client to the server and back to the client—all without the need to store the values of the controls on the page programmatically. View state data is hashed, compressed, encoded, and stored in a structure on the client in the page's source code. View state is turned on by default.

The advantages of using view state include

- Since view state data is stored in a page's source code, it does not require server memory.

- Since view state does not require any special programming, it is easy to implement.

- Since view state data is hashed, compressed, and encoded, it is relatively secure.

The disadvantages of using view state include

- Since view state data is stored in a page's source code, large amounts of page data can cause page requests and responses to be relatively slow.

- Since view state data is stored in a page's source code, large amounts of page data can overwhelm the memory of some mobile devices.

- Since view state data is stored in a page's source code, it can be accessed directly by viewing the page's source code and can thus be tampered with.

Figure 16-1 shows an example of page values before and after a postback to the server that requests the same page. As can be seen in the first screenshot of the figure, selections have been made from the two drop-down lists, and entries have been made in the seven text boxes. The second screenshot shows the result of clicking the *Save* button, which requested a postback to the server requesting the same page. Notice that both drop-down list selections and all of the text box entries have been preserved and that no code was required to preserve this data.

RESULT

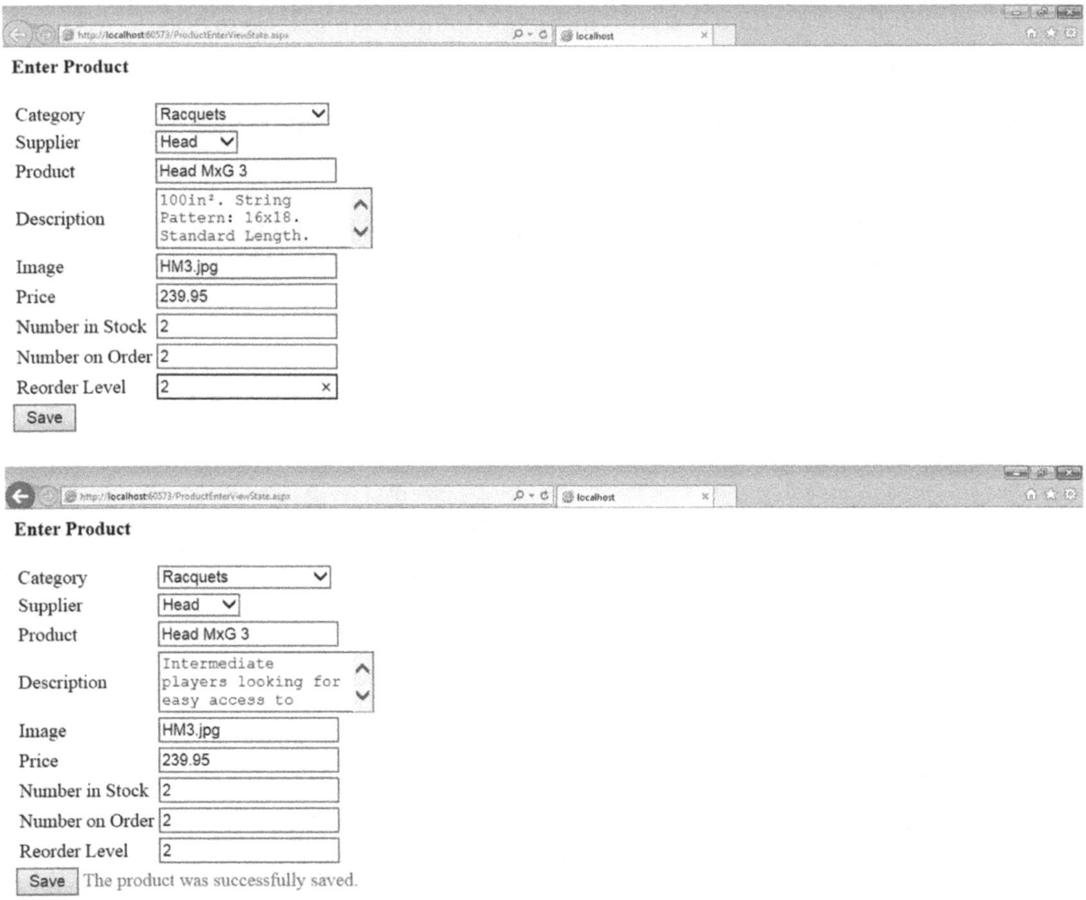

Figure 16-1. *Example of page values before and after a postback to the server that requests the same page*

16.2.2 Cookies

Cookies is a state-maintenance method that permits us to *programmatically* preserve the values of the controls on a page (using the client's memory or using a file that resides on the client's hard drive) so that we can retrieve and use those values on subsequent pages of the application. For example, when an end user selects an item from a drop-down list, enters a value into a text box, and then submits the page, the same drop-down list selection and the same text box value can be retrieved and used on the page that is displayed next.

There are two types of cookies—*nonpersistent cookies* and *persistent cookies*. A nonpersistent cookie (a.k.a., an in-memory cookie or a session cookie) is stored in the client's memory and expires (i.e., is automatically deleted) when its associated session terminates. Thus, a nonpersistent cookie is available to an application until the client's browser is closed. A persistent cookie, on the other hand, is stored in a browser file on the client's hard drive and does not expire (i.e., is not automatically deleted) when its associated session terminates. Thus, a persistent cookie is available to an application even after the client's browser is closed. In fact, a persistent cookie is available to an application until the date and time stored in the cookie's Expires property. Persistent cookies are often used to identify the language, theme, and menu preferences of end users who return to an application at some later time without requiring them to log into the application first. Whether nonpersistent or persistent, a cookie contains a simple text-based key-value pair (or set of simple text-based key-value pairs). Most browsers restrict the size of a cookie to between 4,096 and 8,192 bytes.

The advantages of using cookies include

- Since cookie data is stored in the client's memory or on the client's hard drive, it does not require server memory.

- Since a cookie contains a simple text-based key-value pair (or set of simple text-based key-value pairs), little processing overhead is required.

The disadvantages of using cookies include

- Since most browsers restrict the size of a cookie to between 4,096 and 8,192 bytes, there is a practical limit to how much data can be stored in a cookie.

- Since some end users configure their browsers so that they won't accept cookies, an application that relies on cookies for state maintenance will not always work properly.

- Since persistent cookie data is stored in a file on the client's hard drive, it can be accessed directly (by the end user or a hacker) by viewing the contents of the file and can thus be tampered with creating a potential security risk or causing an application malfunction.

Figure 16-2 shows an example of saving cookies on the client for use on another page.

Notice at 01 that we are saving the SelectedValue property of the first DropDownList control to the Value property of a cookie named *ddlCategory*.

Notice at 02 that we are saving the Text property of the first TextBox control, which is a string, to the Value property of a cookie named *strProduct*. Although such a naming standard is not technically required, we will adopt this standard as it will make keeping track of our cookies and their respective types much easier.

Notice at 03 that we are redirecting the current page to the next page (i.e., the confirmation page) *after* all of our cookies have been saved. By the way, if we want a cookie to persist on the client for, say, six months from now, we would modify its Expires property like this:

```
Response.Cookies["Cookie Name"].Expires = DateTime.Now.AddMonths(6);
```

where *Cookie Name* is the name of the cookie.

The screenshot in the Result section of the figure shows the current page after selections have been made from the two drop-down lists, and entries have been made in the seven text boxes.

CODE BEHIND

```
     protected void btnConfirm_Click(object sender, EventArgs e)
     {
         // Save the cookies.
01       Response.Cookies["ddlCategory"].Value = ddlCategory.SelectedValue;
         Response.Cookies["ddlSupplier"].Value = ddlSupplier.SelectedValue;
02       Response.Cookies["strProduct"].Value = txtProduct.Text;
         Response.Cookies["strDescription"].Value = txtDescription.Text;
         Response.Cookies["strImage"].Value = txtImage.Text;
         Response.Cookies["decPrice"].Value = txtPrice.Text;
         Response.Cookies["bytNumberInStock"].Value = txtNumberInStock.Text;
         Response.Cookies["bytNumberOnOrder"].Value = txtNumberOnOrder.Text;
         Response.Cookies["bytReorderLevel"].Value = txtReorderLevel.Text;
         // Go to the confirmation page.
03       Response.Redirect("ProductConfirmCookies.aspx");

     }
```

RESULT

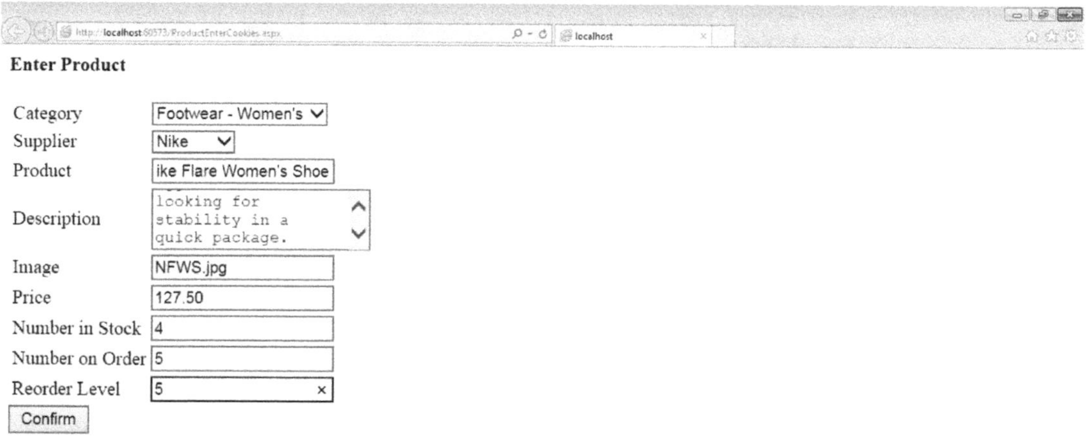

Figure 16-2. *Example of saving cookies on the client for use on another page*

Figure 16-3 shows an example of retrieving cookies from the client.

Notice at 01 that we are retrieving the cookies in the Page_Load event handler method of the next page (i.e., the confirmation page).

Notice at 02 that we are retrieving the SelectedValue property of the DropDownList control from the Value property of its associated cookie.

Notice at 03 that we are retrieving the Text property of the TextBox control, which is a string, from the Value property of its associated cookie.

Notice at 04 that we are converting the Value property of the cookie to a Decimal type. This is necessary because all cookie values are stored as strings and, thus, must be converted appropriately if we wish to use them in the form of a different type.

The screenshot in the Result section of the figure shows the next page (i.e., the confirmation page) after it has been rendered in the browser. Notice that both drop-down list selections and all text box entries have been preserved from the previous page.

CODE BEHIND

```
01   protected void Page_Load(object sender, EventArgs e)
     {
         // Retrieve the cookies.
02       ddlCategory.SelectedValue = Request.Cookies["ddlCategory"].Value;
         ddlSupplier.SelectedValue = Request.Cookies["ddlSupplier"].Value;
03       lblProduct.Text = Request.Cookies["strProduct"].Value;
         txtDescription.Text = Request.Cookies["strDescription"].Value;
         lblImage.Text = Request.Cookies["strImage"].Value;
04       Decimal decPrice =
             Convert.ToDecimal(Request.Cookies["decPrice"].Value);
         lblPrice.Text = decPrice.ToString("c");
         lblNumberInStock.Text = Request.Cookies["bytNumberInStock"].Value;
         lblNumberOnOrder.Text = Request.Cookies["bytNumberOnOrder"].Value;
         lblReorderLevel.Text = Request.Cookies["bytReorderLevel"].Value;
         // Compute and display the value in stock and the value on order.
         Byte bytNumberInStock =
             Convert.ToByte(Request.Cookies["bytNumberInStock"].Value);
         Byte bytNumberOnOrder =
             Convert.ToByte(Request.Cookies["bytNumberOnOrder"].Value);
         Decimal decValueInStock = decPrice * bytNumberInStock;
         Decimal decValueOnOrder = decPrice * bytNumberOnOrder;
         lblValueInStock.Text = decValueInStock.ToString("c");
         lblValueOnOrder.Text = decValueOnOrder.ToString("c");

     }
```

RESULT

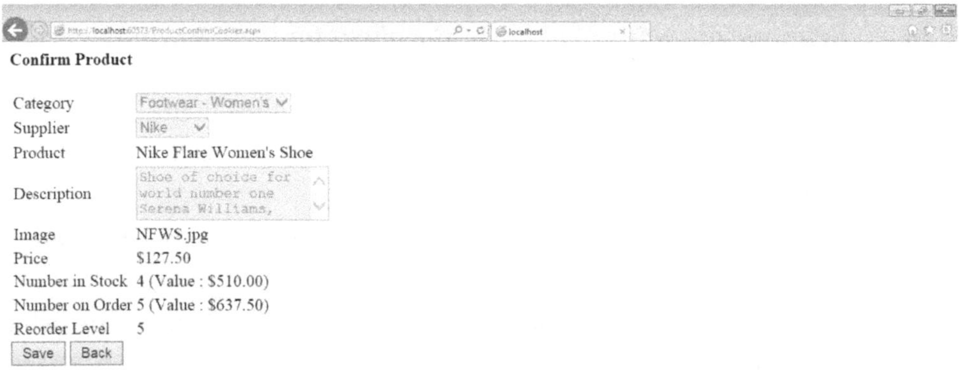

Figure 16-3. *Example of retrieving cookies from the client*

16.2.3 Query Strings

Query string is a state-maintenance method that permits us to *programmatically* preserve the values of the controls on a page (using a string that is appended to the page's URL) so that we can retrieve and use those values on subsequent pages of the application. For example, when an end user selects an item from a drop-down list, enters a value into a text box, and then submits the page, the same drop-down list selection and the same text box value can be retrieved and used on the page that is displayed next.

A query string can be used, for example, to pass a selected product number from one page to another or to pass an email address to a login page so that the end user need not manually enter it to login (à la Facebook). Query string data is passed from one page to another via the page's URL. A query string contains a set of simple text-based key-value parameter pairs. Most browsers restrict the size of an *encoded URL* (i.e., a URL that contains a query string) to between 2,000 and 6,000 characters.

The advantages of using query strings include

- Since query string data is passed from one page to another via the page's URL, it does not require server memory.

- Since a query string contains a set of simple text-based key-value pairs, little processing overhead is required.

- Since virtually all browsers support the use of query strings, they can be used with relative confidence.

The disadvantages of using query strings include

- Since query string data is passed from one page to another via the page's URL, it can be seen by the end user and can thus be tampered with creating a potential security risk or causing an application malfunction.

- Since query string data is passed from one page to another via the page's URL, it can be bookmarked or sent to another person, thus creating a potential security risk.

- Since some browsers restrict the size of an encoded URL, a URL with too much query string data will cause a page malfunction.

Figure 16-4 shows an example of passing a query string via an encoded URL for use on another page.

Notice at 01 that we are redirecting the current page to the next page (i.e., the confirmation page). As can be seen, the query string, which follows the name of the .aspx file, begins with a question mark (?), and all query string key-value parameter pairs are separated by ampersands (&). Also notice that we are attaching the SelectedValue property of the first DropDownList control to a query string parameter named *ddlCategory*. Notice as well that we are attaching the Text property of the first TextBox control, which is a string, to its associated query string parameter named *strProduct*. Although such a naming standard is not technically required, we will adopt this standard as it will make keeping track of our query string parameters and their respective types much easier.

The screenshot in the Result section of the figure shows the current page after selections have been made from the two drop-down lists, and entries have been made in the seven text boxes.

CODE BEHIND

```
protected void btnConfirm_Click(object sender, EventArgs e)
{

    // Go to the confirmation page with the encoded URL.
01  Response.Redirect
        (
        "ProductConfirmQueryStrings.aspx" +
        "?ddlCategory=" + ddlCategory.SelectedValue +
        "&ddlSupplier=" + ddlSupplier.SelectedValue +
        "&strProduct=" + txtProduct.Text +
        "&strDescription=" + txtDescription.Text +
        "&strImage=" + txtImage.Text +
        "&decPrice=" + txtPrice.Text +
        "&bytNumberInStock=" + txtNumberInStock.Text +
        "&bytNumberOnOrder=" + txtNumberOnOrder.Text +
        "&bytReorderLevel=" + txtReorderLevel.Text
        );

}
```

RESULT

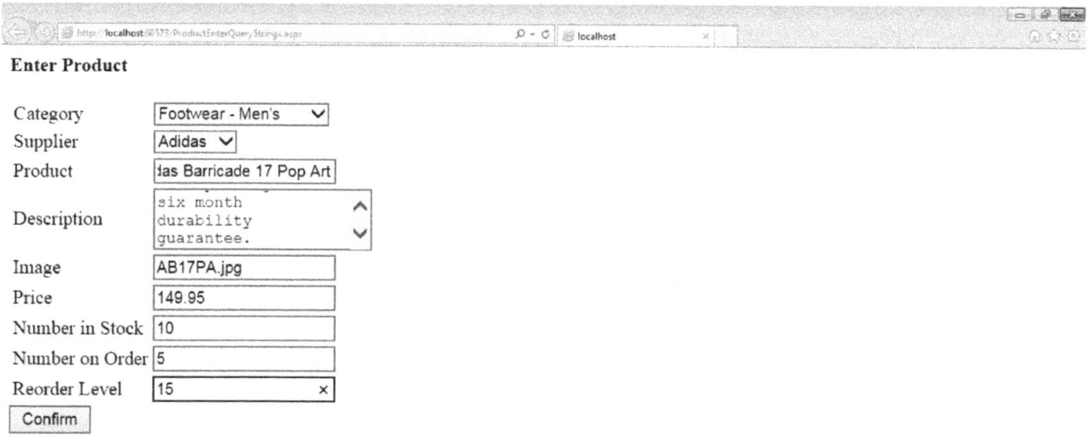

Figure 16-4. *Example of passing a query string via an encoded URL for use on another page*

Figure 16-5 shows an example of retrieving a query string's parameters from an encoded URL.

Notice at 01 that we are retrieving the query string's parameters in the Page_Load event handler method of the next page (i.e., the confirmation page).

Notice at 02 that we are retrieving the SelectedValue property of the DropDownList control from its associated query string parameter.

Notice at 03 that we are retrieving the Text property of the TextBox control, which is a string, from its associated query string parameter.

Notice at 04 that we are converting the value of the query string parameter to a Decimal type. This is necessary because all query string parameter values are passed as strings and, thus, must be converted appropriately if we wish to use them in the form of a different type.

The screenshot in the Result section of the figure shows the next page (i.e., the confirmation page) after it has been rendered in the browser. Notice that both drop-down list selections and all of the text box entries have been preserved from the previous page.

CODE BEHIND

```
01  protected void Page_Load(object sender, EventArgs e)
    {
        // Retrieve the query string's parameters from the encoded URL.
02      ddlCategory.SelectedValue = Request.QueryString["ddlCategory"];
        ddlSupplier.SelectedValue = Request.QueryString["ddlSupplier"];
03      lblProduct.Text = Request.QueryString["strProduct"];
        txtDescription.Text = Request.QueryString["strDescription"];
        lblImage.Text = Request.QueryString["strImage"];
04      Decimal decPrice =
            Convert.ToDecimal(Request.QueryString["decPrice"]);
        lblPrice.Text = decPrice.ToString("c");
        lblNumberInStock.Text = Request.QueryString["bytNumberInStock"];
        lblNumberOnOrder.Text = Request.QueryString["bytNumberOnOrder"];
        lblReorderLevel.Text = Request.QueryString["bytReorderLevel"];
        // Compute and display the value in stock and the value on order.
        Byte bytNumberInStock =
            Convert.ToByte(Request.QueryString["bytNumberInStock"]);
        Byte bytNumberOnOrder =
            Convert.ToByte(Request.QueryString["bytNumberOnOrder"]);
        Decimal decValueInStock = decPrice * bytNumberInStock;
        Decimal decValueOnOrder = decPrice * bytNumberOnOrder;
        lblValueInStock.Text = decValueInStock.ToString("c");
        lblValueOnOrder.Text = decValueOnOrder.ToString("c");

    }
```

RESULT

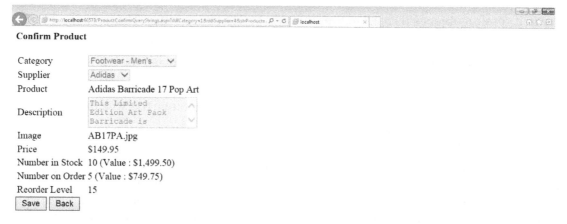

Figure 16-5. *Example of retrieving a query string's parameters from an encoded URL*

16.3 Server-Based State Maintenance

To maintain state on the server, we can utilize *session state*, *profile properties*, *database support*, and/or *application state*.[1] In this section, we will limit our discussion to session state as that method seems to be the most commonly used method of server-based state maintenance, and learning about it will be more than enough to get us started. Of course, profile properties, database support, and application state are all useful methods of state maintenance. The interested reader is encouraged to explore those methods as well.

16.3.1 Session State

Session state is a state-maintenance method that permits us to *programmatically* preserve the values of the controls on a page (using an object that resides in memory on the server) so that we can retrieve and use those values on subsequent pages of the application. For example, when an end user selects an item from a drop-down list, enters a value into a text box, and then submits the page, the same drop-down list selection and the same text box value can be retrieved and used on the page that is displayed next.

Session-state data is stored in the properties of a *session object* in RAM on the server—although it can also be stored in a database on the server or in a custom data source on the server. When a client contacts the server for the first time via an HTTP request, the server creates a session object and then passes the page *and* the newly created session object's ID back to the client via an HTTP response. The session object's ID (i.e., the *session ID*) is the *unique* identifier of the session object. It is this ID that enables the server to identify the unique *sessions* that exist between itself and all of the clients it serves. The session ID is (by default) stored as a cookie on the client and is passed to the server each time the client requests a page.[2] Since the session ID that

---

[1]Application state maintains state across multiple end-user sessions instead of within a single end-user session. Thus, the scope of an application variable includes all of the pages of an application for all of the end-user sessions of the application. In essence, an application variable is a global variable that any end-user session has access to. For this reason, application variables should be used with caution. Unlike session state that remains active until the end user closes his or her browser, application state remains active until the application is stopped.

[2]If a browser doesn't accept cookies, ASP.NET will attempt to pass the session ID between the client and the server via an encoded URL (i.e., a URL with the session ID in a query string) or via some other method.

is passed by the client is known to the server, the server can retrieve the data from the associated session object as required to instantiate any control values on the requested page before the page is sent back to the client for rendering.

By default, an *unreferenced* session object persists on the server for 20 minutes. If the session object is not accessed within that 20-minute time period, a *session timeout* will occur. When a session times out, the session object is deleted from the server's memory, and the session is *terminated*. This means that the session that once existed between the client and the server no longer exists. Fortunately, the 20-minute time period restarts each time the session object is referenced by a page request from the associated client. This way, sessions can last much longer than 20 minutes.

By the way, if an application requires it for some reason, we can allow more time between page requests. For example, if we have a situation where we need to permit the end user to remain on a page for up to 60 minutes before they submit the page for processing, we can modify the session object's Timeout property in the <system.web> section of the Web.config file. Figure 16-6 shows an example of extending the duration of an application's session state. Keep in mind that we may also need to configure IIS to allow for a session timeout greater than the default.

```
WEB.CONFIG CODE

<system.web>
  <sessionState timeout="60" />
</system.web>
```

Figure 16-6. *Example of extending the duration of an application's session state*

The advantages of using session state include

- Since session state is class based, it is familiar to .NET developers and is thus easy to use.

- Since session state is class based, session events can be raised and handled during a session.

- Since session-state data is preserved during an Internet Information Services (IIS) restart, session state is very reliable.

- Since session-state data can be preserved in multiple processes and/or on multiple servers, session state can be utilized in Web garden and Web farm environments, thus enhancing an application's scalability and reliability.

- Since a session ID can be passed via a query string in an encoded URL, session state can work with browsers that do not accept cookies.

The disadvantages of using session state include

- When a session ID is passed to the server via a query string in an encoded URL, it can be seen by the end user and can thus be tampered with creating a potential security risk or causing an application malfunction.

- When a session ID is passed to the server via a query string in an encoded URL, the URL can be bookmarked or sent to another person, thus creating a potential security risk.

- Since session-state data is stored and maintained in RAM on the server, server performance can degrade as more and more sessions require tracking.

16.3.2 HttpSessionState Class

The HttpSessionState class permits us to manage client-server sessions using session state. Table 16-1 shows some of the properties, methods, and events of the HttpSessionState class. Although most of the properties, methods, and events of this class will not be demonstrated in this chapter, they are displayed for reference, since they are so commonly used. For example, notice the Abandon method of the class. This method is often used when, for some reason, we want to permit the end user to terminate his or her session before they close their browser, such as when we provide them with a *Logout* or *Sign out* button.

Table 16-1. *Some of the properties, methods, and events of the HttpSessionState class*

Class HttpSessionState[3]	
Namespace System.Web.SessionState	
Properties	
Contents	Gets a reference to the current session-state object.
CookieMode	Gets a value that indicates whether the application is configured for cookieless sessions.
Count	Gets the number of items in the session-state collection.
IsCookieless	Gets a value indicating whether the session ID is embedded in the URL or stored in an HTTP cookie.
SessionID	Gets the unique identifier for the session.
Timeout	Gets and sets the amount of time, in minutes, allowed between requests before the session-state provider terminates the session.
Methods	
Abandon( )	Cancels the current session.
Add(String, Object)	Adds a new item to the session-state collection.
Clear( )	Removes all keys and values from the session-state collection.
Remove(String)	Deletes an item from the session-state collection.
RemoveAll( )	Removes all keys and values from the session-state collection.
Events	
(See reference.)	
Reference	
`https://msdn.microsoft.com/en-us/library/system.web.sessionstate.` `httpsessionstate(v=vs.110).aspx`	

---

[3]All property, method, and event descriptions were taken directly from Microsoft's official documentation. The event handler methods used to handle the events of this class were omitted to conserve space. See the reference for all of the methods of this class.

Figure 16-7 shows an example of saving session variables on the server for use on another page.

Notice at 01 that we are saving the SelectedValue property of the first DropDownList control to a session variable named *ddlCategory*.[4]

Notice at 02 that we are saving the Text property of the first TextBox control, which is a string, to a session variable named *strProduct*. Although such a naming standard is not technically required, we will adopt this standard as it will make keeping track of our session variables and their respective types much easier.

Notice at 03 that we are redirecting the current page to the next page (i.e., the confirmation page) *after* all of our session variables have been saved.

The screenshot in the Result section of the figure shows the current page after selections have been made from the two drop-down lists, and entries have been made in the seven text boxes.

---

[4]We could have saved this session variable using the Add method of the Session class like this: Session.Add("ddlCategory", ddlCategory.SelectedValue). However, we prefer the shortcut method shown in the example as it is more similar to the way we retrieve session variables.

CODE BEHIND

```
    protected void btnConfirm_Click(object sender, EventArgs e)
    {
        // Save the session variables.
01      Session["ddlCategory"] = ddlCategory.SelectedValue;
        Session["ddlSupplier"] = ddlSupplier.SelectedValue;
02      Session["strProduct"] = txtProduct.Text;
        Session["strDescription"] = txtDescription.Text;
        Session["strImage"] = txtImage.Text;
        Session["decPrice"] = txtPrice.Text;
        Session["bytNumberInStock"] = txtNumberInStock.Text;
        Session["bytNumberOnOrder"] = txtNumberOnOrder.Text;
        Session["bytReorderLevel"] = txtReorderLevel.Text;
        // Go to the confirmation page.
03      Response.Redirect("ProductConfirmSessionVariables.aspx");

    }
```

RESULT

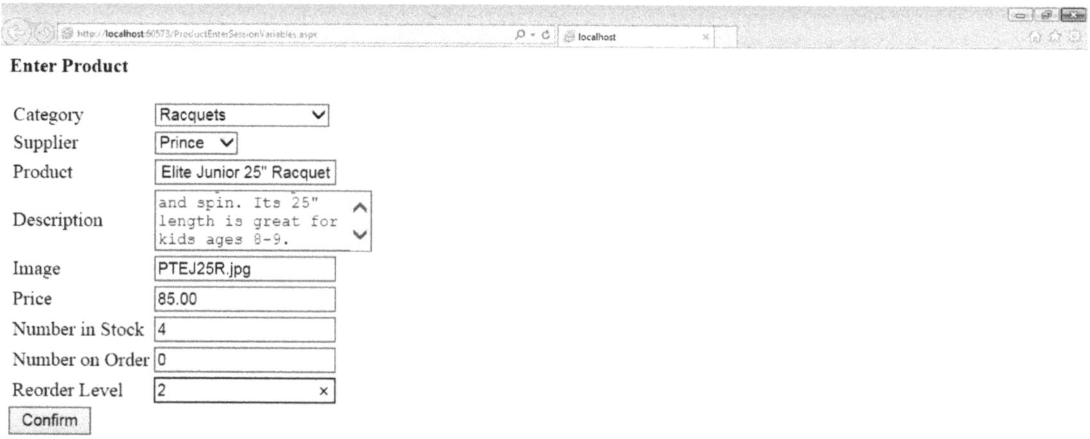

Figure 16-7. *Example of saving session variables on the server for use on another page*

Figure 16-8 shows an example of retrieving session variables from the server.

Notice at 01 that we are retrieving the session variables in the Page_Load event handler method of the next page (i.e., the confirmation page).

Notice at 02 that we are retrieving the SelectedValue property of the DropDownList control from its associated session variable.

Notice at 03 that we are retrieving the Text property of the TextBox control, which is a string, from its associated session variable.

Notice at 04 that we are converting the session variable to a Decimal type. This is necessary because all session variables are stored as objects and, thus, must be converted appropriately if we wish to use them in the form of a different type.

The screenshot in the Result section of the figure shows the next page (i.e., the confirmation page) after it has been rendered in the browser. Notice that both drop-down list selections and all of the text box entries have been preserved from the previous page.

CODE BEHIND

```
01   protected void Page_Load(object sender, EventArgs e)
     {

         // Retrieve the session variables.
02       ddlCategory.SelectedValue = Session["ddlCategory"].ToString();
         ddlSupplier.SelectedValue = Session["ddlSupplier"].ToString();
03       lblProduct.Text = Session["strProduct"].ToString();
         txtDescription.Text = Session["strDescription"].ToString();
         lblImage.Text = Session["strImage"].ToString();
04       Decimal decPrice =
             Convert.ToDecimal(Session["decPrice"]);
         lblPrice.Text = decPrice.ToString("c");
         lblNumberInStock.Text = Session["bytNumberInStock"].ToString();
         lblNumberOnOrder.Text = Session["bytNumberOnOrder"].ToString();
         lblReorderLevel.Text = Session["bytReorderLevel"].ToString();
         // Compute and display the value in stock and the value on order.
         Byte bytNumberInStock =
             Convert.ToByte(Session["bytNumberInStock"]);
         Byte bytNumberOnOrder =
             Convert.ToByte(Session["bytNumberOnOrder"]);
         Decimal decValueInStock = decPrice * bytNumberInStock;
         Decimal decValueOnOrder = decPrice * bytNumberOnOrder;
         lblValueInStock.Text = decValueInStock.ToString("c");
         lblValueOnOrder.Text = decValueOnOrder.ToString("c");

     }
```

RESULT

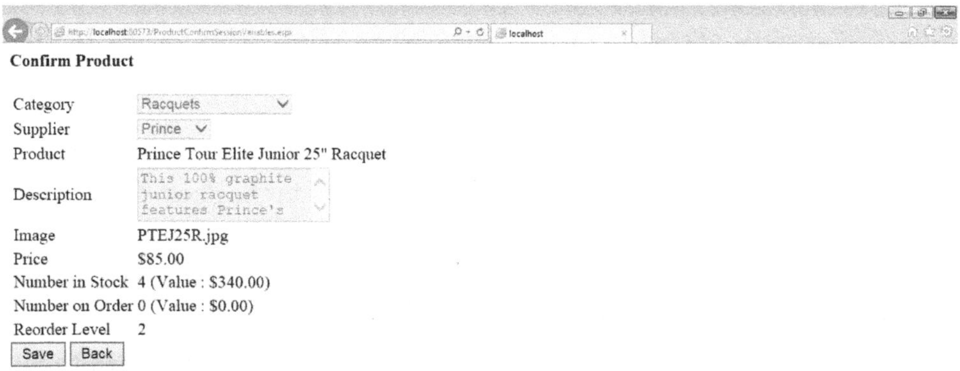

Figure 16-8. Example of retrieving session variables from the server

16.4 Maintaining the State of a Data Structure

When using a data structure (e.g., an array, stack, queue, linked list, sorted list) in a Web application, it is often necessary to maintain the state of that data structure so that it can be used in the same page (i.e., after a postback to the server that requests the same page) or in another page of the application. One way to do this is to save the data structure to a session variable. Figure 16-9 shows an example of saving a one-dimensional array to a session variable for use on another page.

CODE BEHIND

```
      protected void btnCreateArray_Click(object sender, EventArgs e)
      {

          // Declare and load the array.
01        String[] strCategoryArray = new String[5];
          strCategoryArray[0] = "Footwear - Men's";
          strCategoryArray[1] = "Clothing - Men's";
          strCategoryArray[2] = "Racquets";
          strCategoryArray[3] = "Footwear - Women's";
          strCategoryArray[4] = "Clothing - Women's";
          // Save the array in a session variable for future use.
02        Session["strCategoryArray"] = strCategoryArray;
          // Go to the next page.
03        Response.Redirect("CategoryUseArraySessionVariables.aspx");

      }
```

RESULT

Figure 16-9. *Example of saving a one-dimensional array to a session variable for use on another page*

Notice at 01 that we are declaring and loading a one-dimensional array that contains five elements.

Notice at 02 that we are saving the array to a session variable.

Notice at 03 that we are redirecting the current page to the next page.

Figure 16-10 shows an example of retrieving a one-dimensional array from a session variable.

Notice at 01 that we are looking at the btnLookup_Click event handler method of the next page.

Notice at 02 that we are declaring a new one-dimensional array with five elements.

Notice at 03 that we are retrieving the existing one-dimensional array from the session variable.

Notice at 04 that we are using the array as normal.

The screenshot in the Result section of the figure shows the result of entering an array index into the text box and clicking *Lookup*. This result clearly demonstrates that the state of the array was maintained from the previous page to the current page. Keep in mind that this approach to maintaining the state of a data structure will work for *any* type of data structure—not just one-dimensional arrays.

CODE BEHIND

```
01   protected void btnLookup_Click(object sender, EventArgs e)
     {
         // Declare a new array.
02       String[] strCategoryArray = new String[5];
         // Get the array from the session variable.
03       strCategoryArray = Session["strCategoryArray"] as String[];
         // Use the array as normal.
         Int32 i32Index = Convert.ToInt32(txtIndex.Text);
04       lblCategory.Text = strCategoryArray[i32Index];

     }
```

RESULT

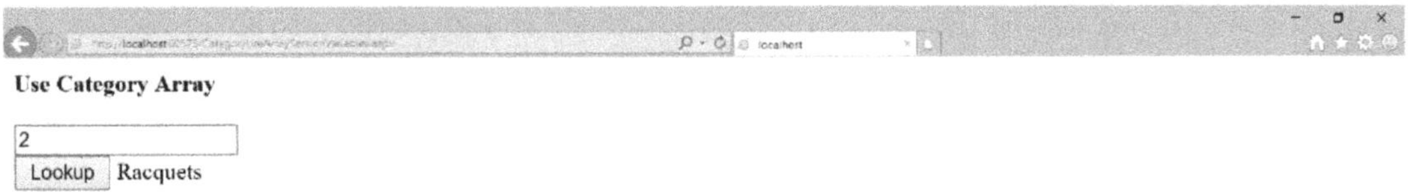

Figure 16-10. *Example of retrieving a one-dimensional array from a session variable*

CHAPTER 17

Master Pages

17.1 Introduction

A master page is a template that contains page elements (e.g., text, HTML, ASP.NET server controls) and a *content placeholder* that reserves space for its associated *content pages*. Every page element that is placed in a master page (outside of the content placeholder) is displayed on *every* content page associated with the master page. Thus, when a master page is employed, the master page itself remains consistent from one content page to the next. The only thing that changes is what is displayed in the content pages.

Master pages are useful because they permit us to display *common* page elements *consistently* across *many* pages of a Web application. For example, a well-designed Web application will consistently display in its master page elements like an organizational logo, a place to display the name of the application, a place to display the end user's name, a place to display the name of the current page, and a place to display messages. When such elements are included in an application's master page, their locations remain consistent from one content page to the next, which results in an application that is easier to use and more professional looking.

In this chapter, we will begin by looking at the MasterPage class. We will use this class to display a consistent structure, look, and feel across all of the content Page classes of our Web application. Next, we will learn how to add a master page to an ASP.NET Web Application project using Visual Studio. And finally, we will learn how to add a content Page class that is associated with the MasterPage class.

17.2 MasterPage Class

The MasterPage class serves as a container for the content pages of a .NET Web application. As such, it permits us to display a consistent structure, look, and feel across all of the content Page classes of an application. Although most Web applications have a single master page that is applied to *all* of the content pages of the application,

© Robert E. Beasley 2020
R. E. Beasley, *Essential ASP.NET Web Forms Development*, https://doi.org/10.1007/978-1-4842-5784-5_17

some Web applications have multiple master pages that are applied to *groups* of content pages within the application. In ASP.NET, a master page can be *statically* associated with a content page at *design time* (i.e., we can hard code the association in the Aspx code of the content page), or it can be *programmatically* associated with a content page at *runtime* (i.e., we can establish the association in the code behind of the content page). In this chapter, we will associate our master page with our content pages *statically*.

Before going much further, it would be a good idea to discuss the basics of how master pages work in ASP.NET. When a client requests a content page from the server, the server merges the content page and its associated master page into a single page with the same name as the content page. This results in a combination of the master page, which is the same for all of its associated content pages, and the content page, which is different from all of the other content pages. Although a content page and its associated master page are merged into a single page, it is very important to know that they are treated as separate objects from a coding perspective. In effect, the master page is treated as a control on the content page. Thus, if we wish to gain access to (i.e., get or set) the properties of the page elements in the master page, we must "expose" those properties to the content page. We will see an example of this later. Also, since the MasterPage class and the Page class raise some of the same events (e.g., the Load event), it is a good idea to look at the order in which these events are raised. For reference purposes, this order is

- Content page's PreInit event

- Master page controls' Init events

- Content page controls' Init events

- Master page's Init event

- Content page's Init event

- Content page's Load event

- Master page's Load event

- Master page controls' Load events

- Content page controls' Load events

- Content page's PreRender event

- Master page's PreRender event

- Master page controls' PreRender events

- Content page controls' PreRender events

- Master page controls' Unload events

- Content page controls' Unload events

- Master page's Unload event

- Content page's Unload event

Table 17-1 shows some of the properties, methods, and events of the MasterPage class.

Table 17-1. *Some of the properties, methods, and events of the MasterPage class*

Class MasterPage[1]

Namespace System.Web.UI

Properties

MasterPageFile   Gets or sets the name of the master page that contains the current content.

Methods

(See reference.)

Events

(See reference.)

Reference

https://msdn.microsoft.com/en-us/library/system.web.ui.masterpage(v=vs.110).aspx

17.3 Adding a MasterPage Class

When beginning a new Web application, it is *almost always* a good idea to add a MasterPage class to the project *before* adding *any* content Page classes to the project. This is because it is *much* easier to associate a content Page class with an existing

---

[1]All property, method, and event descriptions were taken directly from Microsoft's official documentation. The event handler methods used to handle the events of this class were omitted to conserve space. See the reference for all of the methods of this class.

MasterPage class when the content Page class is created than it is to convert a content Page class that *is not* associated with a MasterPage class to a content Page class that *is* associated with a MasterPage class. Thus, as a general rule, a master page should be one of the very first things we create when starting a new project. To add a MasterPage class to an ASP.NET Web Application project

1. Open the Solution Explorer.

2. Right-click the project (not the solution).

3. Select *Add* ➤ *New Item....*

When the *Add New Item* dialog appears

1. Select *Installed* ➤ *Visual C#* ➤ *Web* ➤ *Web Forms* from the left pane of the dialog.

2. Select *Web Forms Master Page* from the middle pane of the dialog.

3. Give the master page (i.e., MasterPage class) a *Name* at the bottom of the dialog.

4. Click *Add.*

Figure 17-1 shows the Aspx file of the newly added MasterPage class. Notice in the Solution Explorer that the MasterPage class has been added to the project. Whenever we want to access the code of this MasterPage class in the future, we will simply double-click it in the Solution Explorer. Next, notice the tab between the Visual Studio menu and the top of the code. This tab displays the name of the MasterPage class file (i.e., MasterPage.Master). It is in this file that we will design the master page of our application. Now look at the code itself. Notice the *master page directive* at the very top of the code. This master page directive indicates, among other things, that C# is used as the programming language for the class and that the name of the code behind file (i.e., where we will write our server-side ASP.NET and C# code) is MasterPage.Master.cs. And finally, notice that the remainder of this file contains a number of basic HTML tags, such as <head>, <title>, <body>, and <div>, and two ASP.NET server control tag pairs (i.e., <asp:ContentPlaceHolder> and </asp:ContentPlaceHolder>). We will concentrate on the *second* pair of content placeholder tags in this chapter.

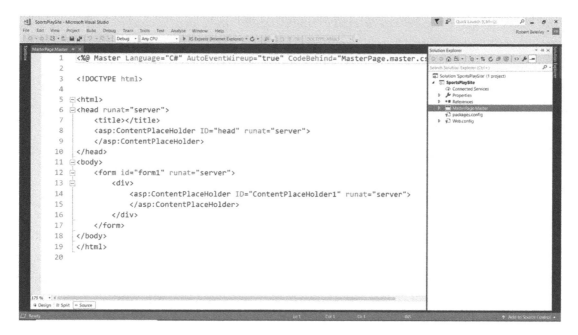

Figure 17-1. *Aspx file of the newly added MasterPage class*

Like the Page class, the MasterPage class has two main (and separate) parts—the user interface part and the code behind part. The *.Master* file contains the *user interface* part of the class. This part of the class is coded using HTML tags, ASP tags, or a combination of both. The *Master.cs* file, on the other hand, contains the *code behind* part of the class. This part of the class is coded using ASP.NET and C#. The beauty of this *separation of concerns* is that we can make changes to a master page's user interface without affecting its functionality, and we can make changes to a master page's functionality without affecting its user interface.

To write ASP.NET and C# code, we need to open the code behind file of the class. To access the code behind file

1. Expand the MasterPage class by clicking the *triangle* icon next to the MasterPage.Master file in the Solution Explorer.

2. Double-click the associated MasterPage.Master.cs file.

Figure 17-2 shows the code behind file of the newly added MasterPage class. Notice the tab between the Visual Studio menu and the top of the code. This tab displays the name of the code behind file of MasterPage class (i.e., MasterPage.Master.cs). It is in this file that we will write the ASP.NET and C# code of our master page. Now look at the code itself. Notice, at the very top of the code, a number of C# directives that begin with the word *using*. These *code behind directives* refer to the *namespaces* included in the class. Namespaces can contain other *classes* that provide the MasterPage class with additional functionality, or they can contain *types* (e.g., interface types, array types, value types, reference types, enumeration types) that are required by other namespaces. Now look at the line of code that starts with the word *namespace*. This indicates that our MasterPage class is in the SportsPlaySite namespace. If for some reason we need to refer to the properties and/or methods of this MasterPage class from some other class in the future, we will need to include the SportsPlaySite namespace in that class. Next, take a look at the line of code that starts with the phrase *public partial class*. The word *partial* here indicates that this file (i.e., MasterPage.Master.cs) contains one *part* of the MasterPage class. The other files (i.e., MasterPage.Master and MasterPage.Master.designer.cs) contain the other *parts* of the MasterPage class. And finally, look at the line of code that starts with the phrase *protected void*. This is the Page_Load event handler method of the class, which is generated automatically when the MasterPage class is added to the project. If there is any ASP.NET and/or C# code that needs to be executed when the master page loads (i.e., when the master page's Load event is raised), we will code it here.

Figure 17-2. *Code behind file of the newly added MasterPage class*

17.4 Adding a Page Class with a MasterPage

Now that we have added a MasterPage class to our project, we can begin adding any associated content Page classes. To add a Page class with a MasterPage to an ASP.NET Web Application project

1. Open the Solution Explorer.

2. Right-click the project (not the solution).

3. Select *Add* ➤ *New Item....*

When the *Add New Item* dialog appears

1. Select *Installed* ➤ *Visual C#* ➤ *Web* ➤ *Web Forms* from the left pane of the dialog.

2. Select *Web Form with Master Page* from the middle pane of the dialog.

3. Give the Web page (i.e., Page class) a *Name* at the bottom of the dialog.

4. Click *Add.*

When the *Select a Master Page* dialog appears

1. Select the master page from the right pane of the dialog.

2. Click *OK.*

Figure 17-3 shows the Aspx file of the newly added content Page class. Notice in the Solution Explorer that the content Page class has been added to the project. Whenever we want to access the code of this content Page class in the future, we will simply double-click it in the Solution Explorer. Next, notice the tab between the Visual Studio menu and the top of the code. This tab displays the name of the content Page class file (i.e., Home.aspx). Now look at the code itself. Notice the page directive at the very top of the code. This page directive indicates, among other things, that C# is used as the programming language for the class, that the associated master page file is MasterPage.Master, and that the name of the code behind file (i.e., where we will write our server-side ASP.NET and C# code) is Home.aspx.cs. And finally, notice that this file contains no HTML tags. It only contains two ASP.NET server control tag pairs (i.e., <asp:Content> and </asp:Content>). It is between the *second* pair of content tags that we will design the user interface for this content page.

Figure 17-3. *Aspx file of the newly added content Page class*

Like the MasterPage class, the content Page class has two main (and separate) parts—the user interface part and the code behind part. The *.aspx* file contains the *user interface* part of the class. This part of the class is coded using HTML tags, ASP tags, or a combination of both. The *.aspx.cs* file, on the other hand, contains the *code behind* part of the class. This part of the class is coded using ASP.NET and C#. The beauty of this *separation of concerns* is that we can make changes to a content page's user interface without affecting its functionality, and we can make changes to a content page's functionality without affecting its user interface.

To write ASP.NET and C# code, we need to open the code behind file of the class. To access the code behind file

1. Expand the content Page class by clicking the *triangle* icon next to the .aspx file in the Solution Explorer.

2. Double-click the associated .aspx.cs file.

Figure 17-4 shows the code behind file of the newly added content Page class. Notice the tab between the Visual Studio menu and the top of the code. This tab displays the name of the code behind file of content Page class (i.e., Home.aspx.cs). It is in this file that we will write the ASP.NET and C# code of our content page. Now look at the code itself. At the very top of the code, notice a number of C# directives that begin with the word *using*.

These *code behind directives* refer to the *namespaces* included in the class. Namespaces can contain other *classes* that provide the content Page class with additional functionality, or they can contain *types* (e.g., interface types, array types, value types, reference types, enumeration types) that are required by other namespaces. Now look at the line of code that starts with the word *namespace*. This indicates that the Home class is in the SportsPlaySite namespace. If for some reason we need to refer to the properties and/or methods of the Home class from some other class in the future, we will need to include the SportsPlaySite namespace in that class. Next, take a look at the line of code that starts with the phrase *public partial class*. The word *partial* here indicates that this file (i.e., Home.aspx.cs) contains one *part* of the Home class. The other files (i.e., Home.aspx and Home.aspx.designer.cs) contain the other *parts* of the Home class. And finally, look at the line of code that starts with the phrase *protected void*. This is the Page_Load event handler method of the class, which is generated automatically when the content Page class is added to the project. If there is any ASP.NET and/or C# code that needs to be executed when the page loads (i.e., when the page's Load event is raised), we will code it here.

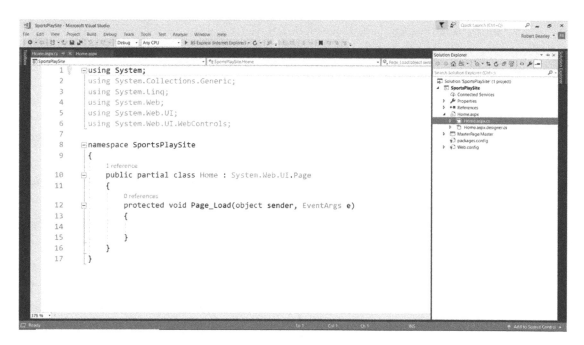

Figure 17-4. *Code behind file of the newly added content Page class*

Figure 17-5 shows an example of the MasterPage class.

Notice at 01 the master page directive. This directive indicates, among other things, that C# is used as the programming language for the class and that the name of the code behind file (i.e., where we will write our server-side ASP.NET and C# code) is MasterPage.Master.cs.

Notice at 02 the table that lays out the controls in the *header* of the master page. We know that this table is displayed in the header of the master page because it is located *above* the (second) content placeholder, which can be seen at 04.

Notice at 03 the Label control that will be used to display all of the messages in the application. Since this label exists in the master page, we will need to expose its properties in the code behind of the class.

Notice at 04 the (second) content placeholder. When the master page and an associated content page are merged during compilation, the controls on the content page will be placed in this location.

Notice at 05 the table that lays out the controls in the *footer* of the master page. We know that this table is displayed in the footer of the master page because it is located *below* the (second) content placeholder.

Now look at the code behind of the master page. Toward the top of this file, we have written the code necessary to expose some of the properties of four of the controls in the header of the master page (i.e., lblUser, lblPageTitle, lblMessage, and lblLog). By doing this, the content pages of the application have access to these controls and can manipulate them as desired.

Notice at 06 that we have defined a public MessageForeColor property for the MasterPage class. The System.Drawing.Color part of the declaration indicates the type of the property. In this case, the property is a color. The statement inside the curly brackets of the declaration indicates that the ForeColor property of the lblMessage control will be set to whatever color is indicated when the property is set from the code behind of an associated content page.

Notice at 07 that we have defined a public Message property for the MasterPage class. The String part of the declaration indicates the type of the property. In this case, the property is a string. The statement inside the curly brackets of the declaration indicates that the Text property of the lblMessage control will be set to whatever string is indicated when the property is set from the code behind of an associated content page. Notice that both of these public properties (i.e., MessageForeColor and Message) refer to the lblMessage control defined at 03.

Notice at 08 the Page_Load event handler method where we are setting the properties of several of the Label controls (i.e., lblServerName, lblVersion, lblDate, and lblContact) in the footer part of the master page's Aspx code. Thus, these properties are set every time the master page and its associated content page load.

ASPX CODE

```
01    <%@ Master Language="C#" AutoEventWireup="true"
          CodeBehind="MasterPage.Master.cs"
          Inherits="SportsPlaySite.MasterPage" %>

      <!DOCTYPE html>

      <html xmlns="http://www.w3.org/1999/xhtml">
      <head runat="server">
          <title></title>
          <asp:ContentPlaceHolder ID="head" runat="server">
          </asp:ContentPlaceHolder>
      </head>
      <body>
          <form id="form1" runat="server">
          <div>

02            <asp:Table runat="server">
                  <asp:TableRow>
                      <asp:TableCell>
                          <asp:Table runat="server">
                              <asp:TableRow>
                                  <asp:TableCell HorizontalAlign="Center">
                                      <%--Image from: www.freepik.com
                                      /free-vector/collection-of-people-
                                      doing-sport-silhouette_875950.htm--%>
                                      <asp:Image runat="server"
                                          ImageUrl="~/Images/SportsPlay.png" />
                                      <br />
                                  </asp:TableCell>
                              </asp:TableRow>
                          </asp:Table>
                      </asp:TableCell>
                      <asp:TableCell VerticalAlign="Top">
                          <asp:Table runat="server">
                              <asp:TableRow>
                                  <asp:TableCell>
                                      <asp:Label runat="server"
                                          Font-Bold="true" Text="SportsPlay" />
                                  </asp:TableCell>
                              </asp:TableRow>
                              <asp:TableRow>
                                  <asp:TableCell>
                                      <asp:Label runat="server" ID="lblUser"
                                          Text="User" />
                                  </asp:TableCell>
                              </asp:TableRow>
```

Figure 17-5. *Example of the MasterPage class*

313

```
                                   <asp:TableRow>
                                       <asp:TableCell>
                                           <asp:Label runat="server"
                                               ID="lblPageTitle" Text="Home" />
                                       </asp:TableCell>
                                   </asp:TableRow>
                                   <asp:TableRow>
                                       <asp:TableCell>
03                                         <asp:Label runat="server" ID="lblMessage"
                                               ForeColor="Green" Text="Please login."/>
                                       </asp:TableCell>
                                   </asp:TableRow>
                                   <asp:TableRow>
                                       <asp:TableCell>
                                           <asp:LinkButton runat="server" ID="btnLog"
                                               CausesValidation="false"
                                               PostBackUrl="~/Login.aspx"
                                               Text="[Login]" />
                                       </asp:TableCell>
                                   </asp:TableRow>
                               </asp:Table>
                           </asp:TableCell>
                       </asp:TableRow>
                   </asp:Table>

04          <asp:ContentPlaceHolder ID="ContentPlaceHolder1" runat="server">
            </asp:ContentPlaceHolder>

05          <asp:Table runat="server">
               <asp:TableRow>
                   <asp:TableCell>
                       <asp:Label runat="server" Font-Bold="true"
                           Text="Server " />
                       <asp:Label runat="server" ID="lblServerName" />
                       <asp:Label runat="server" Font-Bold="true"
                           Text=" Version " />
                       <asp:Label runat="server" ID="lblVersion" />
                       <asp:Label runat="server" Font-Bold="true"
                           Text=" Date " />
                       <asp:Label runat="server" ID="lblDate" />
                       <asp:Label runat="server" Font-Bold="true"
                           Text=" Contact " />
                       <asp:Label runat="server" ID="lblContact" />
                   </asp:TableCell>
               </asp:TableRow>
           </asp:Table>

        </div>
        </form>
    </body>
    </html>
```

Figure 17-5. *(continued)*

CODE BEHIND

```
using System;
using System.Collections.Generic;
using System.Linq;
using System.Web;
using System.Web.UI;
using System.Web.UI.WebControls;

namespace SportsPlaySite
{
    public partial class MasterPage : System.Web.UI.MasterPage
    {

        public String User
        {
            set { lblUser.Text = value; }
        }

        public String PageTitle
        {
            set { lblPageTitle.Text = value; }
        }

        public System.Drawing.Color MessageForeColor
        {
            set { lblMessage.ForeColor = value; }
        }

        public String Message
        {
            set { lblMessage.Text = value; }
        }

        public String LogText
        {
            set { btnLog.Text = value; }
        }
```

06 (marker next to `public System.Drawing.Color MessageForeColor`)

07 (marker next to `public String Message`)

Figure 17-5. (continued)

```
08              protected void Page_Load(object sender, EventArgs e)
                {
                    // Set the server name.
                    lblServerName.Text = Request.ServerVariables["Server_Name"];

                    // Set the version number.
                    lblVersion.Text = "1.00";

                    // Set the date.
                    lblDate.Text = DateTime.Today.ToShortDateString();

                    // Set the contact.
                    lblContact.Text = "If you have questions or experience
                        problems with this website, please contact....";

                }

            }

        }
```

Figure 17-5. *(continued)*

Figure 17-6 shows an example of a home page with a master page.

Notice at 01 the page directive at the very top of the code. This page directive indicates, among other things, that the associated master page file is MasterPage.Master.

Notice at 02 the *master type directive*. This directive provides access to the properties of the master page that we have exposed. If we do not provide access to these properties by including this directive, we will *not* be able to manipulate the properties of the master page in the code behind of the content page.

Notice at 03 the content placeholder tag. Every page element that we place between this tag and its associated end tag will be displayed between the header and the footer of the master page.

Notice at 04 the Page_Load event handler method of the content page. As can be seen, it is in this event handler method that we are setting several of the exposed properties of the MasterPage class.

Notice at 05 that we are setting the MessageForeColor property of the MasterPage class to *green* to indicate to the end user that all is well.

Notice at 06 that we are setting the Message property of the MasterPage class to *Please click [Login] to login to the system.*

The screenshot in the Result section of the figure shows the content page (i.e., Home.aspx) and its associated master page after the two have been merged, executed, and displayed in the browser.

ASPX CODE

```
01  <%@ Page Title="" Language="C#" MasterPageFile="~/MasterPage.Master"
        AutoEventWireup="true" CodeBehind=Home.aspx.cs
        Inherits="SportsPlaySite.Home" %>
02  <%@ MasterType VirtualPath="~/MasterPage.Master" %>
    <asp:Content ID="Content1" ContentPlaceHolderID="head" runat="server">
    </asp:Content>
03  <asp:Content ID="Content2" ContentPlaceHolderID="ContentPlaceHolder1"
        runat="server">

        <br />
        <asp:Label runat="server" Text="Welcome to SportsPlay!" />
        <br /><br />

    </asp:Content>
```

CODE BEHIND

```
04  protected void Page_Load(object sender, EventArgs e)
    {

        // Populate the master page fields.
        this.Master.User = "*";
        this.Master.PageTitle = "Home";
05      this.Master.MessageForeColor = System.Drawing.Color.Green;
06      this.Master.Message = "Please click [Login] to login to the system.";
        this.Master.LogText = "[Login]";

    }
```

RESULT

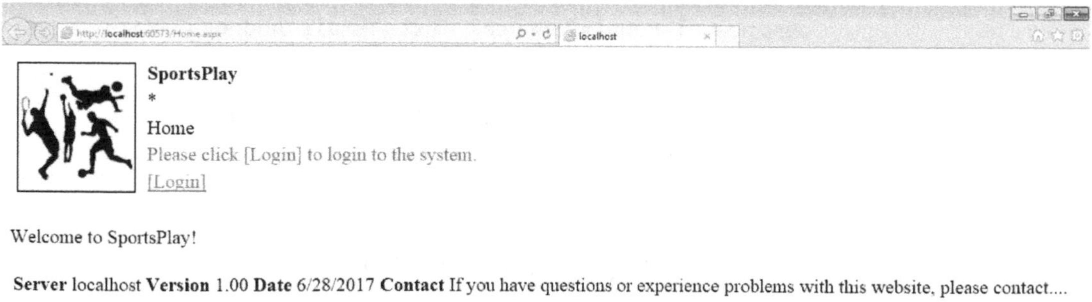

Figure 17-6. *Example of a home page with a master page*

Figure 17-7 shows an example of a login page with a master page.

Notice at 01, 02, and 03 the page directive, the master type directive, and the content placeholder tag, respectively. These were discussed previously. As can be seen, the code between the content placeholder tag and its associated end tag is different from that in the Home.aspx file.

Notice at 04 the Page_Load event handler method of the content page. Again, it is in this event handler method that we are setting several of the exposed properties of the MasterPage class.

Notice at 05 that we are setting the MessageForeColor property of the MasterPage class to *green* to indicate to the end user that all is well.

Notice at 06 that we are setting the Message property of the MasterPage class to *Please enter your email address and password and click Login.*

The screenshot in the Result section of the figure shows the content page (i.e., Login.aspx) and its associated master page after the two have been merged, executed, and displayed in the browser, and the end user has typed in his or her email address and password.

ASPX CODE

```
01  <%@ Page Title="" Language="C#" MasterPageFile="~/MasterPage.Master"
        AutoEventWireup="true" CodeBehind="Login.aspx.cs"
        Inherits="SportsPlaySite.Login" %>
02  <%@ MasterType VirtualPath="~/MasterPage.Master" %>
    <asp:Content ID="Content1" ContentPlaceHolderID="head" runat="server">
    </asp:Content>
03  <asp:Content ID="Content2" ContentPlaceHolderID="ContentPlaceHolder1"
        runat="server">

        <br />
        <asp:Table runat="server">
            <asp:TableRow>
                <asp:TableCell>
                    <asp:Label runat="server" Text="Email Address" />
                </asp:TableCell>
                <asp:TableCell>
                    <asp:TextBox runat="server" ID="txtEmailAddress"
                        MaxLength="50" Width="240px" />
                </asp:TableCell>
            </asp:TableRow>
```

Figure 17-7. *Example of a login page with a master page*

```
    <asp:TableRow>
        <asp:TableCell>
            <asp:Label runat="server" Text="Password" />
        </asp:TableCell>
        <asp:TableCell>
            <asp:TextBox runat="server" ID="txtPassword"
                MaxLength="10" TextMode="Password" Width="240px" />
        </asp:TableCell>
    </asp:TableRow>
    <asp:TableRow>
        <asp:TableCell>
            <asp:Button runat="server" ID="btnLogin"
                OnClick="btnLogin_Click" Text="Login" />
        </asp:TableCell>
    </asp:TableRow>
</asp:Table>
<br />

</asp:Content>
```

CODE BEHIND

```
04  protected void Page_Load(object sender, EventArgs e)
    {

        // Populate the master page fields.
        this.Master.User = "*";
        this.Master.PageTitle = "Login";
05      this.Master.MessageForeColor = System.Drawing.Color.Green;
06      this.Master.Message = "Please enter your email address and password
            and click Login.";
        this.Master.LogText = "";
        // Set the focus of the page.
        txtEmailAddress.Focus();

    }
```

RESULT

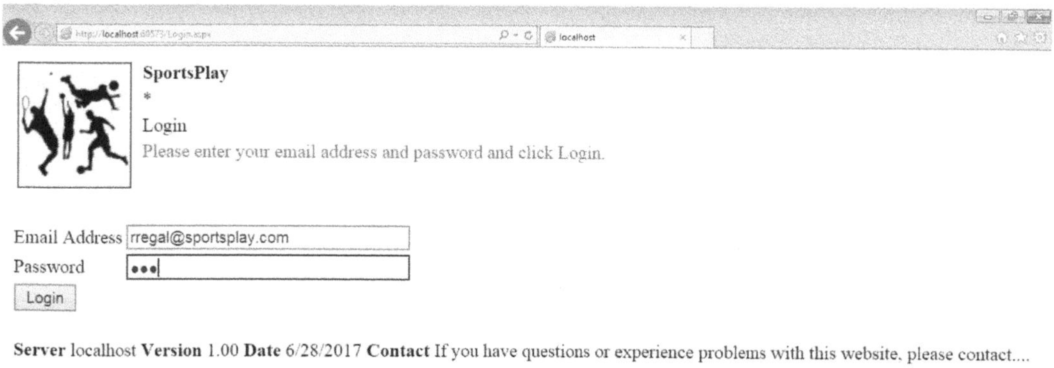

Figure 17-7. *(continued)*

Figure 17-8 shows an example of an options page with a master page.

Notice at 01, 02, and 03 the page directive, the master type directive, and the content placeholder tag, respectively. These were discussed previously. Notice that the code between the content placeholder tag and its associated end tag is different from that in the Home.aspx file and the Login.aspx file.

Notice at 04 the Page_Load event handler method of the content page. Once again, it is in this event handler method that we are setting several of the exposed properties of the MasterPage class.

Notice at 05 that we are setting the User property of the MasterPage class to the name of the end user that logged in. We can assume that this name was saved to the session variable when the end user successfully logged in.

Notice at 06 that we are setting the MessageForeColor property of the MasterPage class to *green* to indicate to the end user that all is well.

Notice at 07 that we are setting the Message property of the MasterPage class to *Please choose from the options below.*

The screenshot in the Result section of the figure shows the content page (i.e., Options.aspx) and its associated master page after the two have been merged, executed, and displayed in the browser. Notice that the end user's name is displayed on the page.

ASPX CODE

```
01   <%@ Page Title="" Language="C#" MasterPageFile="~/MasterPage.Master"
         AutoEventWireup="true" CodeBehind="Options.aspx.cs"
         Inherits="SportsPlaySite.Options" %>
02   <%@ MasterType VirtualPath="~/MasterPage.Master" %>
     <asp:Content ID="Content1" ContentPlaceHolderID="head" runat="server">
     </asp:Content>
03   <asp:Content ID="Content2" ContentPlaceHolderID="ContentPlaceHolder1"
         runat="server">

         <br />
         <asp:Label runat="server" Text="This is the options page." />
         <br /><br />

     </asp:Content>
```

CODE BEHIND

```
04   protected void Page_Load(object sender, EventArgs e)
     {

         // Populate the master page fields.
05       this.Master.User = Session["strFullName"].ToString();
         this.Master.PageTitle = "Options";
06       this.Master.MessageForeColor = System.Drawing.Color.Green;
07       this.Master.Message = "Please choose from the options below.";
         this.Master.LogText = "[Logout]";

     }
```

RESULT

Figure 17-8. *Example of an options page with a master page*

CHAPTER 18

Themes

18.1 Introduction

A theme allows us to define, in one place, the default display characteristics of a Web application's page controls so that they have a consistent appearance within a single page and across multiple pages. In an ASP.NET Web application, themes are defined in a special directory called App_Themes. A single theme, which is itself a directory within the App_Themes directory, contains zero or more *skin* files and zero or more *cascading style sheet (css)* files.

In this chapter, we will begin by adding a theme to a project. As we will see, adding a theme to a project early (i.e., before coding *any* of the display properties of the application's page controls) will save us a lot of time and effort when we want to change the display characteristics of the ASP.NET server controls and HTML elements across the pages of an application. Next, we will look at skin files. A skin file is where we define the display characteristics (i.e., skins) of an application's *ASP.NET server controls*. We will then add a skin file to our theme so that it can be applied to the ASP.NET server controls of our application. Then, we will discuss cascading style sheet files. A cascading style sheet file is where we define the display characteristics (i.e., styles) of an application's *HTML elements*. We will then add a cascading style sheet to our theme and apply it to the HTML elements of our application.

18.2 Adding a Theme

When beginning a new Web application, it is almost always a good idea to add a theme (and its associated skin and css files) to the project and then use that theme to format the application's ASP.NET server controls and HTML elements. If we fail to do this, we will be inclined to set the formatting properties of these items individually throughout the entire application as we develop it. We will then need to go back at a later time

© Robert E. Beasley 2020
R. E. Beasley, *Essential ASP.NET Web Forms Development*, https://doi.org/10.1007/978-1-4842-5784-5_18

(after we have finally made the wise decision to employ a theme) and remove these individual formatting properties—a tedious task indeed. So, as a general rule, creating a theme should be one of the very first things we do when starting a new project. To add a theme to an ASP.NET Web Application project

1. Open the Solution Explorer.

2. Right-click the project (not the solution).

3. Select *Add* ➤ *Add ASP.NET Folder* ➤ *Theme.*

Figure 18-1 shows the newly added theme. Notice in the Solution Explorer that Theme1 (the name given to the theme by default) has been added to the project. We can rename this theme if we want to, but we will keep the name for the examples in this chapter.

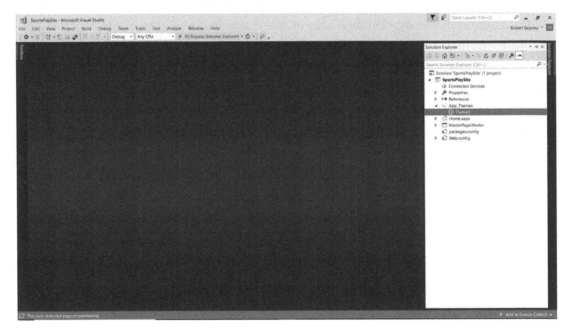

Figure 18-1. *Newly added theme*

Once we have added a theme to our project, we can apply it to the individual pages of an application by setting the *Theme* property of each page's Page directive, or we can apply it to all of the pages of the application by setting the *theme* property of the <pages> element in the Web.config file of the application. Although most applications utilize a single theme, we can add and utilize multiple themes if we so desire. For example, we may want to modify the BackColor and Font-Names properties of all our application's

TextBox controls depending on the season of the year or the type of end user that is logged in—just to give the pages a different look. Keep in mind that themes can only be used to define the properties of ASP.NET server controls and HTML elements that deal with *appearance* or *static content*. They cannot be used to define the properties of ASP. NET server controls and HTML elements that deal with *behavior*.

18.3 Skin Files

A skin file has a .skin file extension and is where we define the display characteristics (i.e., skins) of an application's *ASP.NET server controls*, such as its Button controls, Label controls, and TextBox controls. There are two types of skins—*default skins* and *named skins*. A default skin does *not* have a SkinID and is applied to *all* of the controls of a given type (e.g., all Button controls, all Label controls, all TextBox controls). For example, if we wish to format *all* of the ASP.NET Button controls in an application so that they display with a double border style and an Arial font, we would define the default skin like this in our skin file:

```
<asp:Button runat="server" BorderStyle="Double" Font-Names="Arial" />
```

A named skin, on the other hand, has a SkinID and is only applied to those controls of a given type that have the *same* SkinID. Named skins permit us to apply different formatting to different controls of the same type. For example, if we wish to format *only* those ASP.NET Button controls in an application with a SkinID of *skiButton* so that they display with a double border style and an Arial font, we would define the named skin like this in our skin file:

```
<asp:Button runat="server" SkinID="skiButton" BorderStyle="Double"
    Font-Names="Arial" />
```

18.4 Adding a Skin File

To add a skin file to an ASP.NET Web Application project

1. Open the Solution Explorer.

2. Expand the App_Themes folder by clicking the *triangle* icon next to it.

3. Right-click the Theme.

4. Select *Add* ➤ *New Item....*

When the *Add New Item* dialog appears

1. Select *Installed* ➤ *Visual C#* ➤ *Web* ➤ *Web Forms* from the left pane of the dialog.

2. Select *Web Form Skin File* from the middle pane of the dialog.

3. Give the skin file a *Name* at the bottom of the dialog.

4. Click *Add*.

Figure 18-2 shows the code of the newly added skin file. Notice in the Solution Explorer that the skin file has been added to the theme. We can rename this skin file if we want to, but we will keep the name for the examples in this chapter. Now take a look at the contents of the skin file. As can be seen, a couple of skin examples have been automatically generated for us and commented out. We will remove these and write our own skin code.

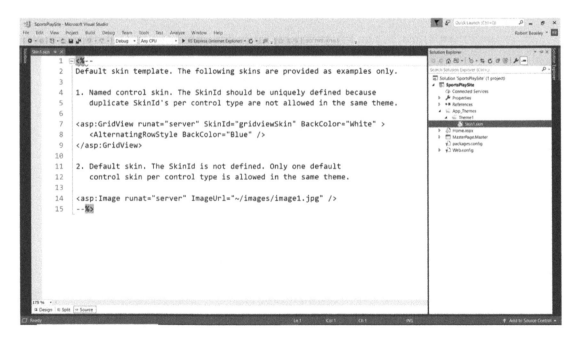

Figure 18-2. *Code of the newly added skin file*

Figure 18-3 shows an example of a skin file's contents and its associated Web. config file entry. The first thing to notice in the figure is that the skins for the individual ASP.NET server controls are listed in alphabetical order. Although placing the skins in order may seem like a trivial detail from what can be seen in the figure, it becomes an important detail when we have dozens of skins in the file. When this is the case, having the skins in order will permit us to locate individual skins quickly and will help us avoid duplicate skins as such duplicates will be easy to see. The second thing to notice in the figure is that the formatting properties of the individual skins are placed on separate lines and are listed in alphabetical order. Since a single skin can contain dozens of formatting properties, it is a good idea to place them on separate lines and order them alphabetically for the same reasons just mentioned. The third thing to notice in the figure is that all of the SkinID properties begin with the three-letter prefix *ski* and end with the *type of control* of the skin (possibly followed by a qualifier of some kind to further identify the skin—like at 03 and 06, where we have added *PageTitle* and *MultiLine*, respectively, to further identify the skins). This is not a requirement of the language, but it will be the naming standard we use in this chapter.

Notice at 01 that the Button skin does not have a SkinID. Thus, this skin is a *default skin* that will be applied to *all* of the Button controls in the application, except for those that have their SkinID property set to a skin or those that have their EnableTheming property set to *false*. Setting the EnableTheming property of a given control to *false* keeps the control from taking on the formatting characteristics defined in its skin.

Notice at 02–06 that all of the skins have a SkinID. Thus, these skins are all *named skins* that will be applied to *all* of the controls (of the same type) in the application that have their SkinID property set to the name of a skin (of the same type) and that don't have their EnableTheming property set to *false*.

Notice at 07 that we have added to our Web.config file a <system.web> section that includes a <pages> tag with its *theme* property set to the name of the theme we created earlier. This configuration setting identifies the theme we want to apply to our application and can be changed manually or programmatically.

SKIN CODE

```
01   <asp:Button runat="server"
         BorderStyle="Double"
         Font-Names="Arial"
     />

02   <asp:DropDownList runat="server" SkinID="skiDropDownList"
         BackColor="Wheat"
         Font-Names="Arial"
         Width="200px"
     />

03   <asp:Label runat="server" SkinID="skiLabelPageTitle"
         Font-Bold="true"
         Font-Size="20pt"
     />

04   <asp:TableCell runat="server" SkinID="skiTableCell"
         BackColor="LightGray"
     />

05   <asp:TextBox runat="server" SkinID="skiTextBox"
         Font-Names="Arial"
         Width="196px"
     />

06   <asp:TextBox runat="server" SkinID="skiTextBoxMultiLine"
         Font-Names="Arial"
         Width="194px"
     />
```

WEB.CONFIG CODE

```
07   <system.web>
       <pages theme="Theme1" />
     </system.web>
```

Figure 18-3. *Example of a skin file's contents and its associated Web.config file entry*

Figure 18-4 shows an example of skins applied in a page.

Notice at 01–04 that the SkinID properties of the controls have been set. Thus, the formatting that will be applied to these controls is defined in the associated *named skins* in the skin file.

Notice at 05 that *no* SkinID property has been set for the Button control. Thus, the formatting that will be applied to this control is defined in the associated *default skin* in the skin file.

The screenshot in the Result section of the figure shows the *Enter Product* page of the application with the Theme1 skin file applied to it. Notice the larger font of the page title, the shaded back color of the table cells that contain labels, the shaded back color of the drop-down lists, the consistent widths of the drop-down lists and text boxes, the different fonts used to display the data in the drop-down lists and text boxes, and the modified font and border style of the button.

ASPX CODE

```
       ⋮
       ⋮ (Code continues.)
       ⋮
01     <asp:Label runat="server" SkinID="skiLabelPageTitle"
           Text="Enter Product" /><br /><br />

       <asp:Table runat="server">
           ⋮
           ⋮ (Code continues.)
           ⋮
           <asp:TableRow>
02             <asp:TableCell SkinID="skiTableCell">
                   <asp:Label runat="server" Text="Product" />
               </asp:TableCell>
               <asp:TableCell>
03                 <asp:TextBox runat="server" ID="txtProduct"
                       SkinID="skiTextBox" />
               </asp:TableCell>
           </asp:TableRow>
           <asp:TableRow>
               <asp:TableCell SkinID="skiTableCell">
                   <asp:Label runat="server" Text="Description" />
               </asp:TableCell>
               <asp:TableCell>
04                 <asp:TextBox runat="server" ID="txtDescription" Rows="3"
                       SkinID="skiTextBoxMultiLine" TextMode="MultiLine" />
               </asp:TableCell>
           </asp:TableRow>
           ⋮
           ⋮ (Code continues.)
           ⋮
       </asp:Table>

05     <asp:Button runat="server" ID="btnSave" OnClick="btnSave_Click"
           Text="Save" />
```

Figure 18-4. *Example of skins applied in a page*

RESULT

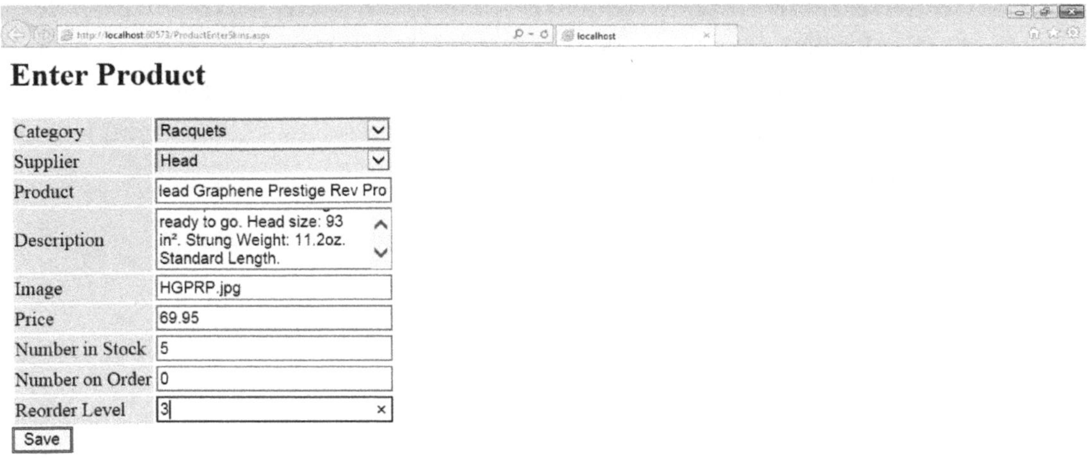

Enter Product

Category	Racquets ▾
Supplier	Head ▾
Product	lead Graphene Prestige Rev Pro
Description	ready to go. Head size: 93 in². Strung Weight: 11.2oz. Standard Length.
Image	HGPRP.jpg
Price	69.95
Number in Stock	5
Number on Order	0
Reorder Level	3

Save

Figure 18-4. *(continued)*

Figure 18-5 shows an example of skins applied in another page.

Notice at 01–04 that the SkinID properties of the controls have been set. Thus, the formatting that will be applied to these controls is defined in the associated *named skins* in the skin file.

Notice at 05 and 06 that *no* SkinID property has been set for these Button controls. Thus, the formatting that will be applied to these controls is defined in the associated *default skin* in the skin file.

The screenshot in the Result section of the figure shows the *Enter Order* page of the application with the Theme1 skin file applied to it. Notice the larger font of the page title, the shaded back color of the table cells that contain labels, the shaded back color of the drop-down lists, the consistent widths of the drop-down lists and text boxes, the different fonts used to display the data in the drop-down lists and text boxes, and the modified font and border styles of the buttons. As can be seen, the display properties of this page are exactly the same as those displayed in Figure 18-4.

ASPX CODE

```
⋮
⋮ (Code continues.)
⋮
01  <asp:Label runat="server" SkinID="skiLabelPageTitle"
        Text="Enter Order" /><br /><br />

    <asp:Table runat="server">
        ⋮
        ⋮ (Code continues.)
        ⋮
        <asp:TableRow>
02          <asp:TableCell SkinID="skiTableCell">
                <asp:Label runat="server" Text="Date" />
            </asp:TableCell>
            <asp:TableCell>
03              <asp:TextBox runat="server" ID="txtDate"
                    SkinID="skiTextBox" />
            </asp:TableCell>
        </asp:TableRow>
        ⋮
        ⋮ (Code continues.)
        ⋮
        <asp:TableRow>
            <asp:TableCell SkinID="skiTableCell">
                <asp:Label runat="server" Text="State" />
            </asp:TableCell>
            <asp:TableCell>
04              <asp:DropDownList runat="server" ID="ddlState"
                    SkinID="skiDropDownList">
                    <asp:ListItem Value="IL" Text="Illinois" />
                    <asp:ListItem Value="IN" Text="Indiana" Selected="True" />
                    <asp:ListItem Value="KY" Text="Kentucky" />
                    <asp:ListItem Value="OH" Text="Ohio" />
                    <asp:ListItem Value="MI" Text="Michigan" />
                </asp:DropDownList>
            </asp:TableCell>
        </asp:TableRow>
        ⋮
        ⋮ (Code continues.)
        ⋮
    </asp:Table>
05  <asp:Button runat="server" ID="btnSave" OnClick="btnSave_Click"
        Text="Save" />
06  <asp:Button runat="server" ID="btnAddOrderLine"
        OnClick="btnAddOrderLine_Click" Text="Add Order Line" />
```

Figure 18-5. *Example of skins applied in another page*

RESULT

Figure 18-5. *(continued)*

The main takeaway here is that if we use a skin file and we want to change the display characteristics of the server controls across *all* the pages of an ASP.NET Web application, we need only modify those display characteristics in *one* place—the skin file.

18.5 Cascading Style Sheet Files

A cascading style sheet file has a .css file extension and is where we define the display characteristics (i.e., styles) of an application's *HTML elements*, such as its input elements, label elements, and table row elements. A cascading style sheet file contains one or more *css selectors*. There are many types of css selectors, including *element selectors* and *class selectors*. An element selector has an HTML element type followed by its related css formatting declarations. This type of selector is applied to *all* of the HTML elements of that type (e.g., all h1 elements, all input elements, all label elements). For example, if we wish to format *all* of the HTML label elements in an application so that they display with a 20-pixel font size and a bold font weight, we would define the element selector like this in our css file:

```
label {font-size: 20px; font-weight: bold;}
```

A class selector, on the other hand, has a period followed by a class name followed by its related css formatting declarations. This type of selector is only applied to those HTML elements that have their *class* property set to the name of a class selector. Class selectors permit us to apply different formatting to different HTML elements of the same type. For example, if we wish to format *only* those HTML label elements in an application with a class property of *.LabelPageTitle* so that they display with a 20-pixel font size and a bold font weight, we would define the class selector like this in our css file:

```
.LabelPageTitle {font-size: 20px; font-weight: bold;}
```

18.6 Adding a Cascading Style Sheet File

To add a cascading style sheet file to an ASP.NET Web Application project

1. Open the Solution Explorer.

2. Right-click the Theme.

3. Select *Add ➤ New Item....*

When the *Add New Item* dialog appears

1. Select *Installed ➤ Visual C# ➤ Web ➤ Markup* from the left pane of the dialog.

2. Select *Style Sheet* from the middle pane of the dialog.

3. Give the cascading style sheet file a *Name* at the bottom of the dialog.

4. Click *Add*.

Figure 18-6 shows the code of the newly added cascading style sheet file. Notice in the Solution Explorer that the css file has been added to the theme. We can rename this css file if we want to, but we will keep the name for the examples in this chapter. Now take a look at the contents of the css file. As can be seen, a css <body> element selector has been automatically generated for us. We will remove this and write our own css code.

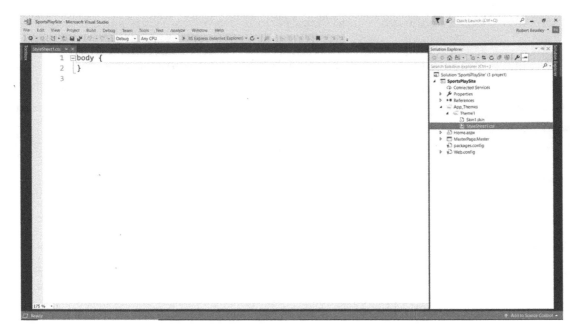

Figure 18-6. *Code of the newly added cascading style sheet file*

Figure 18-7 shows an example of a cascading style sheet's contents and its associated Web.config entry. The first thing to notice in this figure is that there is a one-to-one relationship between the *default* and *named skins* shown in Figure 18-3 and the *element* and *class selectors* shown in this figure. This was done to help illustrate the fact that ASP. NET server controls and HTML elements can be formatted identically. The second thing to notice in the figure is that the element selectors and the class selectors are separated and listed in alphabetical order. Although separating the element selectors from the class selectors and listing them in order may seem like a minor issue from what can be seen in the figure, it becomes an important issue when we have dozens of selectors in the file. When this is the case, having the selectors in order will permit us to locate the individual selectors quickly and will help us avoid duplicate selectors as such duplicates will be easy to see. The third thing to notice in the figure is that the formatting properties of the individual selectors are placed on separate lines and are listed in alphabetical order. Since a single selector can contain dozens of formatting properties, it is a good idea to place them on separate lines and order them alphabetically for the same reasons just mentioned. The fourth thing to notice in the figure is that all of the class selectors begin with a *period* (.) and end with the *type of control* of the selector (possibly followed by a qualifier of some kind to further identify the selector—like at 03 and 07, where we have added *PageTitle* and *MultiLine*, respectively, to further identify the selectors). Again, this is not a requirement of the language, but it will be the naming standard we use in this chapter.

Notice at 01 that the input button selector is an element selector. Thus, this selector will be applied to *all* of the input button controls in the application, except for those that have their *class* property set to a class selector.

Notice at 02–07 that all of the selectors are class selectors. Thus, these selectors will be applied to all of the controls (of the same type) in the application that have their *class* property set to the name of the class selector.

Notice at 04 the special MenuCursor class selector. This selector makes the end user's mouse pointer look like a mouse pointer, instead of an I-beam, as it hovers over an ASP.NET Menu control.

Notice at 08 that we have added to our Web.config file a <system.web> section that includes a <pages> tag with its theme property set to the name of the theme we created earlier. This configuration setting identifies the theme we want to apply to our application and can be changed manually or programmatically.

CSS CODE

```
    /* Element selectors go here. They are used when the formatting /*
    /* is to be applied to an HTML element universally. */

01  input[type=button] {
        border-style: double;
        font-family: Arial;
    }

    /* Class selectors go here. They are used when the formatting /*
    /* is not to be applied to an HTML element universally. */

02  .DropDownList {
        background-color: wheat;
        font-family: Arial;
        width: 200px;
    }

03  .LabelPageTitle {
        font-size: 20px;
        font-weight: bold;
    }

04  .MenuCursor { /* This is used so that a proper mouse pointer is
        displayed when hovering over a menu. */
        cursor: pointer !important;
    }

05  .TableCell {
        background-color: lightgray;
    }

06  .TextBox {
        font-family: Arial;
        width: 196px;
    }

07  .TextBoxMultiLine {
        font-family: Arial;
        width: 194px;
    }
```

WEB.CONFIG CODE

```
    <system.web>
08    <pages theme="Theme1" />
    </system.web>
```

Figure 18-7. *Example of a cascading style sheet's contents and its associated Web.config entry*

Figure 18-8 shows an example of css selectors applied in a page. The first thing to notice in the figure is that the page is marked up using HTML elements instead of ASP. NET server controls. This was done to illustrate the use of css selectors. However, as a general rule, we will use skins in this book instead of css selectors to perform control formatting.

Notice at 01–04 that class properties have been set for the controls. Thus, the formatting that will be applied to these controls is defined in the associated *class selectors* in the css file.

Notice at 05 that no class property has been set for the input button control. Thus, the formatting that will be applied to this control is defined in the associated *element selector* in the css file.

The screenshot in the Result section of the figure shows the *Enter Product* page of the application with the Theme1 css file applied to it. Notice the larger font of the page title, the shaded back color of the table cells that contain labels, the shaded back color of the drop-down lists, the consistent widths of the drop-down lists and text boxes, the different fonts used to display the data in the drop-down lists and text boxes, and the modified font and border style of the button. As can be seen, this page appears identical to the page shown in Figure 18-4.

ASPX CODE

```
     ⋮
     ⋮ (Code continues.)
     ⋮
01   <label class="LabelPageTitle">Enter Product</label><br /><br />

     <table>
         ⋮
         ⋮ (Code continues.)
         ⋮
         <tr>
02           <td class="TableCell">
                 Product
             </td>
             <td>
03               <input runat="server" id="txtProduct"
                     class="TextBox" type="text" />
             </td>
         </tr>
         <tr>
             <td class="TableCell">
                 Description
             </td>
             <td>
04               <textarea runat="server" id="txtDescription"
                     class="TextBoxMultiLine" rows="3"></textarea>
             </td>
         </tr>
         ⋮
         ⋮ (Code continues.)
         ⋮
     </table>

05   <input runat="server" onserverclick="btnSave_Click" type="button"
         value="Save" />
```

***Figure 18-8.** Example of css selectors applied in a page*

RESULT

Figure 18-8. *(continued)*

Figure 18-9 shows an example of css selectors applied in another page.

Notice at 01–03 that class properties have been set for the controls. Thus, the formatting that will be applied to these controls is defined in the associated *class selectors* in the css file.

Notice at 04 and 05 that no class property has been set for the input button controls. Thus, the formatting that will be applied to these controls is defined in the associated *element selector* in the css file.

The screenshot in the Result section of the figure shows the *Enter Order* page of the application with the Theme1 css file applied to it. Notice the larger font of the page title, the shaded back color of the table cells that contain labels, the shaded back color of the drop-down lists, the consistent widths of the drop-down lists and text boxes, the different fonts used to display the data in the drop-down lists and text boxes, and the modified font and border styles of the buttons. As can be seen, the display properties of this page are exactly the same as those displayed in Figure 18-5.

ASPX CODE

```
    ⋮
    ⋮ (Code continues.)
    ⋮
01  <label class="LabelPageTitle">Enter Order</label><br /><br />

    <table>
        ⋮
        ⋮ (Code continues.)
        ⋮
        <tr>
02          <td class="TableCell">
                Date
            </td>
            <td>
03              <input runat="server" id="txtDate" class="TextBox"
                    type="text" />
            </td>
        </tr>
        ⋮
        ⋮ (Code continues.)
        ⋮
    </table>

04  <input runat="server" onserverclick="btnSave_Click"
        type="button" value="Save" />
05  <input runat="server" onserverclick="btnAddOrderLine_Click"
        type="button" value="Add Order Line" />
```

RESULT

Figure 18-9. *Example of css selectors applied in another page*

The main thing to remember is that if we use a css file and we want to change the display characteristics of the HTML elements across *all* the pages of an ASP.NET Web application, we need only modify those display characteristics in *one* place—the css file.

And finally, it is important to understand one more technical detail. If a change is made to a css file, and that change does not appear when a page is requested, the browser's cache probably needs to be cleared. This is because cascading style sheet information is, by default, cached once by a browser and then reused by subsequent pages of the application as needed. Because of this, it may be a good idea to configure the development browser to delete its browsing history upon exiting *while its HTML elements are being formatted using CSS selectors.*

CHAPTER 19

Navigation

19.1 Introduction

ASP.NET provides a number of classes that can be used to help the end user navigate the pages of a Web application. These classes not only make it easy for the end user to jump directly to a desired page within the application, but they also make it easy for us to manage how the pages of the application are organized. There are four main site navigation classes in ASP.NET. These are the SiteMap class, the Menu class, the TreeView class, and the SiteMapPath class.

In this chapter, we will begin by looking at the SiteMap class. The SiteMap class stores a hierarchically organized list of SiteMapNode objects, each of which contains a menu option and/or a page URL. Using a SiteMap class permits us to define a Web application's structure and store its page links in a single location. Next, we will learn to add a SiteMap class to a project. After that, we will discuss the Menu class, which displays a list of options and sub-options that the end user can use to navigate the pages of an application. And finally, we will consider the TreeView class. The TreeView class displays an expandable tree structure that the end user can use to navigate the pages of an application.

We won't be discussing the SiteMapPath class in this chapter, except to say that it displays the path the end user has taken from the home page of an application to the page he or she is currently viewing. Thus, a SiteMapPath control is sometimes referred to as a *breadcrumb*, which is an allusion to the story of Hansel and Gretel, where Hansel leaves a trail of breadcrumbs to help him and his sister find their way back home as they walk through the trees. The interested reader is encouraged to explore the SiteMapPath class on his or her own.

© Robert E. Beasley 2020
R. E. Beasley, *Essential ASP.NET Web Forms Development*, https://doi.org/10.1007/978-1-4842-5784-5_19

19.2 SiteMap Class

The SiteMap class stores a hierarchically organized list of SiteMapNode objects, each of which contains a menu option and/or a page URL. As we will soon see, the layout and link options of a Menu control and a TreeView control typically correspond to the hierarchical organization of the SiteMapNode objects in the SiteMap class. Using a SiteMap class permits us to define a Web application's structure and store its page links in a single location, which makes it much easier for us to manage the organization of the application's pages as we add new pages to the application or modify the application's structure. The SiteMap class in an application has a .sitemap file extension. Table 19-1 shows some of the properties, methods, and events of the SiteMap class.

Table 19-1. *Some of the properties, methods, and events of the SiteMap class*

Class SiteMap[1]	
Namespace System.Web	
Properties	
Providers	Gets a read-only collection of named SiteMapProvider objects that are available to the SiteMap class.
Methods	
(See reference.)	
Events	
(See reference.)	
Reference	
`https://msdn.microsoft.com/en-us/library/system.web.sitemap(v=vs.110).aspx`	

---

[1]All property, method, and event descriptions were taken directly from Microsoft's official documentation. The event handler methods used to handle the events of this class were omitted to conserve space. See the reference for all of the methods of this class.

19.3 Adding a SiteMap Class

To add a SiteMap class to an ASP.NET Web Application project

1. Open the Solution Explorer.

2. Right-click the project (not the solution).

3. Select *Add ➤ New Item....*

When the *Add New Item* dialog appears

1. Select *Installed ➤ Visual C# ➤ Web ➤ General* from the left pane
    of the dialog.

2. Select *Site Map* from the middle pane of the dialog.

3. Give the sitemap (i.e., SiteMap class) a *Name* at the bottom of the
    dialog.

4. Click *Add.*

Figure 19-1 shows the code of the newly added SiteMap class. Notice in the Solution
Explorer that the SiteMap class has been added to the project. Also notice the tab
between the Visual Studio menu and the top of the code. This tab displays the name
of the SiteMap class file (i.e., Web.sitemap). It is in this file that we will lay out the
hierarchical organization of our application. Now look at the code itself. Notice all of the
SiteMapNode objects. The URL property of a SiteMapNode object indicates the page
address of the page to be displayed when the end user clicks the associated menu or
tree view option. The Title property indicates the text to be displayed in the associated
menu or tree view option. And the Description property indicates the tooltip text to
be displayed when the end user hovers over the associated menu or tree view option.
In addition, notice that some of the SiteMapNode objects are nested within other
SiteMapNode objects. As we will see, nesting the SiteMapNode objects in a SiteMap class
is what creates the hierarchical organization of a Web application.

Figure 19-1. *Code of the newly added SiteMap class*

Figure 19-2 shows an example of a complete SiteMap class and its associated Web.config entry. The first thing to notice in the figure is that there are a number of SiteMapNode objects that are nested within other SiteMapNode objects. Again, the nesting of these objects will give our Menu and TreeView controls their hierarchical organization.

Notice at 01 that the highest-level SiteMapNode points to the application's Home page (i.e., Home.aspx) and that this item will display the word "Home" in the associated menu or tree view.

Notice at 02 and 03 the *Database* option and the *Maintain Products* sub-option, respectively. As can be seen, the *Database* option doesn't have a URL—just a title. Thus, clicking this option won't take the end user to a page. It will simply reveal its sub-options (e.g., *Maintain Categories, Maintain Customers, Maintain Employees*). In addition, notice the tooltip text (i.e., "Add/modify/delete products.") that will be displayed when the end user hovers over the *Maintain Products* option with his or her mouse pointer.

Notice at 04–08 the progression of the menu options from *Products* to *Clothing* to *Women's* to *Adidas* and *Nike*.

Notice at 09 that we have added a sitemap provider in the <system.web> <sitemap> <providers> section of the Web.config file. As can be seen, we have given the provider a name (i.e., SiteMap). We will use this name when we are ready to connect our sitemap to a Menu or TreeView control via a SiteMapDataSource. We have also specified the sitemap file (i.e., Web.sitemap), which points to the file in the project that contains our sitemap code. Once we have coded the structure and link options of our sitemap file, we can use it as the source of a Menu control and/or TreeView control.

Note that a misspelled URL in the url property of a SiteMapNode object (including the omission of the .aspx file extension) will result in a *404 error*. A 404 error is a standard HTTP response code that is sent from the server to the browser when the requested page on the server cannot be found. A misspelled URL in the argument of a Response. Redirect() method will also result in a 404 error.

WEB.SITEMAP CODE

```
     <?xml version="1.0" encoding="utf-8" ?>
     <siteMap xmlns="http://schemas.microsoft.com/AspNet/SiteMap-File-1.0" >
01     <siteMapNode url="Home.aspx" title="Home" description="">
02       <siteMapNode url="" title="Database" description="">
           <siteMapNode url="CategoryMaintain.aspx" title="Maintain Categories"
               description="Add/modify/delete categories." />
           <siteMapNode url="CustomerMaintain.aspx" title="Maintain Customers"
               description="Add/modify/delete customers." />
           <siteMapNode url="EmployeeMaintain.aspx" title="Maintain Employees"
               description="Add/modify/delete employees." />
           <siteMapNode url="OrderMaintain.aspx" title="Maintain Orders"
               description="Add/modify/delete orders." />
03         <siteMapNode url="ProductMaintain.aspx" title="Maintain Products"
               description="Add/modify/delete products." />
           <siteMapNode url="ShipperMaintain.aspx" title="Maintain Shippers"
               description="Add/modify/delete shippers." />
           <siteMapNode url="SupplierMaintain.aspx" title="Maintain Suppliers"
               description="Add/modify/delete suppliers." />
         </siteMapNode>
04       <siteMapNode url="" title="Products" description="">
           <siteMapNode url="" title="Racquets" description="">
             <siteMapNode url="RacquetDisplayBabolat.aspx" title="Babolat"
                 description="" />
             <siteMapNode url="RacquetDisplayHead.aspx" title="Head"
                 description="" />
             <siteMapNode url="RacquetDisplayPrince.aspx" title="Prince"
                 description="" />
           </siteMapNode>
```

Figure 19-2. *Example of a complete SiteMap class and its associated Web.config entry*

```
            <siteMapNode url="" title="Footwear" description="">
              <siteMapNode url="" title="Men's" description="">
                <siteMapNode url="FootwearMensAdidas.aspx" title="Adidas"
                    description="" />
                <siteMapNode url="FootwearMensNike.aspx" title="Nike"
                    description="" />
              </siteMapNode>
              <siteMapNode url="" title="Women's" description="">
                <siteMapNode url="FootwearWomensAdidas.aspx" title="Adidas"
                    description="" />
                <siteMapNode url="FootwearWomensNike.aspx" title="Nike"
                    description="" />
              </siteMapNode>
            </siteMapNode>
05          <siteMapNode url="" title="Clothing" description="">
              <siteMapNode url="" title="Men's" description="">
                <siteMapNode url="ClothingMensAdidas.aspx" title="Adidas"
                    description="" />
                <siteMapNode url="ClothingMensNike.aspx" title="Nike"
                    description="" />
              </siteMapNode>
06            <siteMapNode url="" title="Women's" description="">
07              <siteMapNode url="ClothingWomensAdidas.aspx" title="Adidas"
                    description="" />
08              <siteMapNode url="ClothingWomensNike.aspx" title="Nike"
                    description="" />
              </siteMapNode>
            </siteMapNode>
          </siteMapNode>
          <siteMapNode url="ContactUs.aspx" title="Contact Us" description="" />
          <siteMapNode url="SiteMap.aspx" title="Site Map" description="" />
          <siteMapNode url="About.aspx" title="About" description="" />
        </siteMapNode>
    </siteMap>
```

WEB.CONFIG CODE

```
    <system.web>
      <siteMap>
        <providers>
09        <add name="SiteMap" type="System.Web.XmlSiteMapProvider"
              siteMapFile="~/Web.sitemap" />
        </providers>
      </siteMap>
    </system.web>
```

Figure 19-2. *(continued)*

19.4 Menu Class

The Menu class displays a list of options and sub-options that the end user can use to navigate the pages of a Web application. A menu item that contains subitems is automatically expanded when the end user hovers over the item with his or her mouse pointer. Although most Menu controls are populated statically from the SiteMapNode objects in the SiteMap class, a Menu control can also be populated programmatically from other hierarchically organized data sources. In addition, a Menu control can be customized via a skin.

A Menu control actually contains two menus—a *static menu* and a *dynamic menu*. The static menu is always displayed. By default, all of the items at the root level of the menu (i.e., level 0) are displayed in the static menu. Additional levels of the static menu can be displayed by setting the StaticDisplayLevels property of the Menu control. Any items with a higher level than that specified in the StaticDisplayLevels property are displayed in the dynamic menu. The dynamic menu is only displayed when the end user uses his or her mouse pointer to hover over an item that contains a dynamic submenu. A dynamic submenu automatically disappears when the end user clicks outside of the submenu. The number of levels to display in the dynamic menu can be controlled by setting the MaximumDynamicDisplayLevels property of the Menu control. Any items with a higher level than the level specified in the MaximumDynamicDisplayLevels property of the Menu control are not displayed. Table 19-2 shows some of the properties, methods, and events of the Menu class.

Table 19-2. *Some of the properties, methods, and events of the Menu class*

Class Menu[2]

Namespace System.Web.UI.WebControls

Properties

DataSourceID	Gets or sets the ID of the control from which the data-bound control retrieves its list of data items.
DynamicHoverStyle	Gets a reference to the Style object that allows you to set the appearance of a dynamic menu item when the mouse pointer is positioned over it.
DynamicMenuItemStyle	Gets a reference to the MenuItemStyle object that allows you to set the appearance of the menu items within a dynamic menu.
MaximumDynamic DisplayLevels	Gets or sets the number of menu levels to render for a dynamic menu.
Orientation	Gets or sets the direction in which to render the Menu control.
StaticDisplayLevels	Gets or sets the number of menu levels to display in a static menu.
StaticHoverStyle	Gets a reference to the Style object that allows you to set the appearance of a static menu item when the mouse pointer is positioned over it.
StaticMenuItemStyle	Gets a reference to the MenuItemStyle object that allows you to set the appearance of the menu items in a static menu.

Methods

(See reference.)

Events

(See reference.)

Reference

```
https://msdn.microsoft.com/en-us/library/system.web.ui.webcontrols.
menu(v=vs.110).aspx
```

---

[2]All property, method, and event descriptions were taken directly from Microsoft's official documentation. The event handler methods used to handle the events of this class were omitted to conserve space. See the reference for all of the methods of this class.

Figure 19-3 shows an example of the Menu class.

Notice at 01 the SiteMapDataSource control. As can be seen, the SiteMapProvider property of this control is set to *SiteMap*, which is the name of the sitemap provider we added to the <system.web> <sitemap> <providers> section of the Web.config file (see Figure 19-2).

Notice at 02 that the DataSourceID property of the Menu control is set to *smdSiteMap*, which is the same as the ID property of the SiteMapDataSource control at 01. This connects the Menu control to the SiteMapDataSource control. Also notice that the DynamicMenuItemStyle-CssClass property and the StaticMenuItemStyle-CssClass property are both set to *MenuCursor*. This will make the end user's mouse pointer look like a mouse pointer, instead of an I-beam, as it hovers over the Menu control (see the .MenuCursor class selector in Figure 18-7). Notice as well that the Orientation property is set to *Horizontal*, which will display the menu from side to side instead of from top to bottom. In addition, notice that the StaticDisplayLevels property is set to *2*. This means that the number of menu levels to display in the static menu is two, where the *Home* option is at level one and the *Database, Products, Contact Us, Site Map*, and *About* options are at level two. And finally, notice that the formatting properties of the Menu control are listed on separate lines and in alphabetical order. Although listing the properties like this may seem like a trivial detail from what can be seen in the figure, it becomes an important detail when we are setting and maintaining dozens of Menu control properties. When this is the case, having the properties listed in alphabetical order will permit us to locate the individual properties quickly.

The first screenshot in the Result section of the figure shows the menu after the end user has hovered over the *Database* and *Maintain Products* options. Notice the tooltip text that is displayed as the end user hovers over the *Maintain Products* option. The second screenshot shows the menu after the end user has hovered over the *Products, Clothing*, and *Women's* options. Selecting the *Adidas* option or the *Nike* option will take the end user directly to the associated page. By the way, in this example, the SiteMapDataSource control and the Menu control are defined in the project's master page. By placing these controls in the master page, we are able to display the menu on *all* of the application's pages.

ASPX CODE

```
01  <asp:SiteMapDataSource runat="server" ID="smdSiteMap"
        SiteMapProvider="SiteMap" />
02  <asp:Menu runat="server" DataSourceID="smdSiteMap"
        DynamicHoverStyle-BackColor="LightGray"
        DynamicMenuItemStyle-BackColor="Silver"
        DynamicMenuItemStyle-CssClass="MenuCursor"
        DynamicMenuItemStyle-ForeColor="Black"
        Font-Bold="True"
        Font-Size="12pt"
        Orientation="Horizontal"
        StaticDisplayLevels="2"
        StaticHoverStyle-BackColor="LightGray"
        StaticMenuItemStyle-BackColor="Silver"
        StaticMenuItemStyle-CssClass="MenuCursor"
        StaticMenuItemStyle-ForeColor="Black"
        StaticMenuItemStyle-HorizontalPadding="10"
    />
```

RESULT

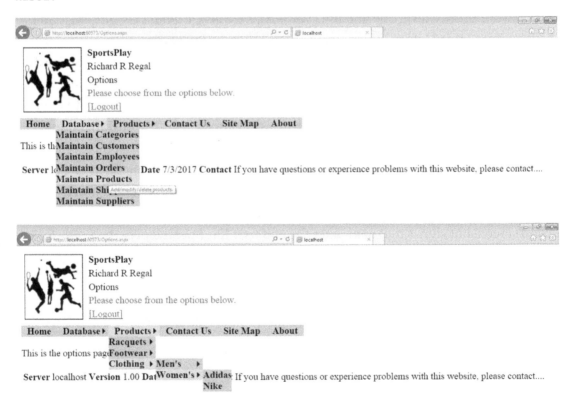

Figure 19-3. *Example of the Menu class*

19.5 TreeView Class

The TreeView class displays an expandable tree structure that the end user can use to navigate the pages of a Web application. A tree view item that contains subitems can be expanded or collapsed when the end user clicks it with his or her mouse pointer. Although most TreeView controls are populated statically from the SiteMapNode objects in the SiteMap class, a TreeView control can also be populated programmatically from other hierarchically organized data sources. In addition, a TreeView control can be customized via a skin.

A TreeView control contains a set of *nodes*, each of which is represented by a TreeNode object. This type of control contains a *root node*, one or more *parent nodes*, one or more *child nodes*, and one or more *leaf nodes*. The root node of a TreeView control has no parent node and is the ancestor of all the other nodes in the control, whereas a parent node has one or more child nodes, a child node has a parent node, and a leaf node has no child nodes. The ExpandDepth property of a TreeView control indicates the number of levels that should be displayed when the control is displayed for the first time. The ShowExpandCollapse property indicates whether or not the control should be expandable and collapsible. The nodes of a TreeView control can be displayed in text form or in hyperlink form, and they can have a checkbox displayed next to them for selection purposes. Table 19-3 shows some of the properties, methods, and events of the TreeView class.

Table 19-3. *Some of the properties, methods, and events of the TreeView class*

Class TreeView[3]

Namespace System.Web.UI.WebControls

Properties

ExpandDepth	Gets or sets the number of levels that are expanded when a TreeView control is displayed for the first time.
NodeIndent	Gets or sets the indentation amount (in pixels) for the child nodes of the TreeView control.
NodeStyle	Gets a reference to the TreeNodeStyle object that allows you to set the default appearance of the nodes in the TreeView control.
ShowExpandCollapse	Gets or sets a value indicating whether expansion node indicators are displayed.
ShowLines	Gets or sets a value indicating whether lines connecting child nodes to parent nodes are displayed.

Methods

(See reference.)

Events

(See reference.)

Reference

```
https://msdn.microsoft.com/en-us/library/system.web.ui.webcontrols.
treeview(v=vs.110).aspx
```

Figure 19-4 shows an example of the TreeView class.

Notice at 01 the SiteMapDataSource control. As can be seen, the SiteMapProvider property of this control is set to *SiteMap*, which is the name of the sitemap provider we added to the <system.web> <sitemap> <providers> section of the Web.config file (see Figure 19-2).

---

[3]All property, method, and event descriptions were taken directly from Microsoft's official documentation. The event handler methods used to handle the events of this class were omitted to conserve space. See the reference for all of the methods of this class.

Notice at 02 that the DataSourceID property of the TreeView control is set to *smdSiteMap*, which is the same as the ID property of the SiteMapDataSource control at 01. This connects the TreeView control to the SiteMapDataSource control. Also notice that the ExpandDepth property is set to *1*. This means that the level one node (i.e., the *Home* node) will be expanded when the tree view is initially displayed, thus exposing the *Database, Products, Contact Us, Site Map,* and *About* nodes. Notice as well that the NodeIndent property is set to *15*, which will indent all child nodes by 15 pixels to enhance the readability of the tree view. In addition, notice that the ShowExpandCollapse property is set to *true*. Because of this, the end user will be able to expand and collapse the nodes of the tree view. Notice too that the ShowLines property is set to *true*, which will display lines connecting any parent nodes to their child nodes, which will, once again, enhance the readability of the tree view. And finally, notice that the formatting properties of the TreeView control are listed on separate lines and in alphabetical order. Although listing the properties like this may seem like a trivial detail from what can be seen in the figure, it becomes an important detail when we are setting and maintaining dozens of TreeView control properties. When this is the case, having the properties listed in alphabetical order will permit us to locate the individual properties quickly.

The first screenshot in the Result section of the figure shows the tree view upon its initial display. Notice that the level one node (i.e., the *Home* node) is expanded, all child nodes are indented by 15 pixels, all parent nodes are expandable and collapsible, and all parent nodes are connected to their child nodes via lines. The second screenshot shows the tree view after the end user has expanded the *Products* node.

ASPX CODE

```
01  <asp:SiteMapDataSource runat="server" ID="smdSiteMap"
        SiteMapProvider="SiteMap" />
02  <asp:TreeView runat="server" DataSourceID="smdSiteMap"
        ExpandDepth="1"
        NodeIndent="15"
        NodeStyle-ForeColor="Gray"
        ShowExpandCollapse="true"
        ShowLines="true"
    />
```

RESULT

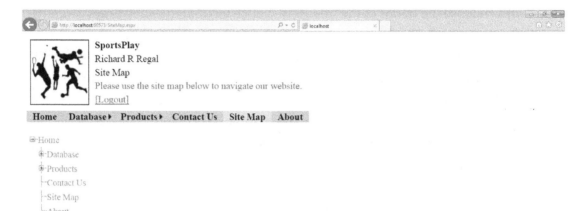

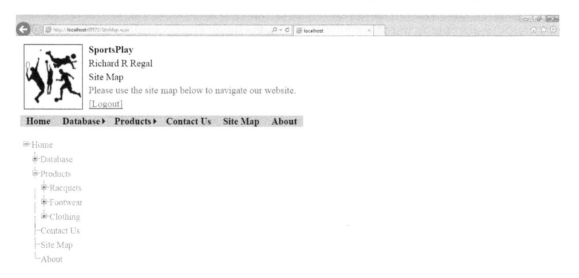

Figure 19-4. *Example of the TreeView class*

PART V

Database Connectivity

CHAPTER 20

Database Design, SQL, and Data Binding

20.1 Introduction

Many contemporary Web applications require the use of a *relational database*. Such a database is used to store the application's data and produce the application's information. For a database to be effective, we must *carefully* plan its details. This is usually done by constructing one or more *data models*. The importance of good database design cannot be understated. A database that is well designed will make the development of an application much easier and more efficient. What's more is the fact that good database design leads to good data, which leads to good information, which leads to good decision making, which leads to organizational stability (in a not-for-profit context) or competitive advantage (in a for-profit context).

Relational databases are created and maintained via a *relational database management system* (RDBMS), which we will call a *database management system* (DBMS) from this point forward. Examples of DBMSs include Access (Microsoft), DB2 (IBM), Informix (IBM), MySQL (Open Source), Oracle (Oracle Corporation), Postgres (Global Development Group), SQL Server (Microsoft), and Sybase (SAP). Since we will be developing database-driven Web applications in this part of the book, it would be a good idea at this point to install one of these DBMSs and become familiar with how to use it. The process of installing and using a DBMS is beyond the scope of this book; however, tutorials should be easy to find. Note that the examples in this book were created using *Microsoft SQL Server* and *Microsoft SQL Server Management Studio*, where SQL Server is the DBMS that will manage our database and SQL Server Management Studio is the user interface that will permit us to interact directly with SQL Server.

© Robert E. Beasley 2020
R. E. Beasley, *Essential ASP.NET Web Forms Development*, https://doi.org/10.1007/978-1-4842-5784-5_20

In this chapter, we will begin by looking at the concept of a database schema. A database schema is a data model that represents the structure of a database. Next, we will discuss the concepts of tables, attributes, and relationships, where a table is a two-dimensional data structure that stores the data of something of interest in an application, an attribute stores a specific characteristic of something of interest in an application, and a relationship indicates the logical association between two tables. After that, we will examine the Structured Query Language. The Structured Query Language is a fourth-generation programming language that retrieves (i.e., queries) and manages (i.e., inserts, updates, and deletes) the data in a relational database. We will then discuss the DataBoundControl class, which serves as the base class for all of the data-bound classes that display data in tabular or list form. And finally, we will look at the SqlDataSource class, which can be used in conjunction with a data-bound control to retrieve data from, insert data into, update data in, and delete data from a SQL Server database.

20.2 Database Schema

A database schema is a data model that represents the structure of a database in terms of its tables, attributes, and relationships. When designing and coding a Web application, it is important to keep a correct and up-to-date database schema handy as it is central to the correct design and implementation of the application. In fact, the database schema informs many of the other processes required to bring an application to fruition, including the modeling process, the input design process, the user interface design process, the output design process, the coding process, and the testing process.

Figure 20-1 shows the database schema of the SportsPlay database. This database is used by SportsPlay, Inc., a hypothetical online sporting goods store that specializes in men's and women's equipment, footwear, and clothing. We will make use of this database in many of the examples in this chapter and subsequent chapters. The database schema shown in the figure was implemented in SQL Server. The details of this schema are described next.

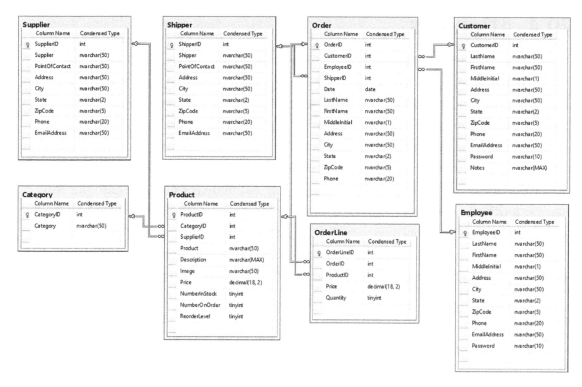

Figure 20-1. *Database schema of the SportsPlay database*

20.3 Tables

A database table is a two-dimensional data structure that contains one or more *rows*
(a.k.a., records, tuples) and one or more *columns* (a.k.a., attributes, fields). A table
stores the data of *something of interest* in an application. As can be seen in Figure 20-1,
there are eight tables in the SportsPlay database, each of which represents something
of interest to SportsPlay, Inc. These are the Category table, the Customer table, the
Employee table, the Order table, the OrderLine table, the Product table, the Shipper
table, and the Supplier table. Notice that these tables are named using a singular noun
(or singular noun phrase). Naming tables in this way will be our standard.

20.4 Attributes

As just mentioned, a database table contains one or more columns. In this book, we will refer to columns as *attributes* as this terminology is more consistent with the language associated with data modeling in general. An attribute stores a *characteristic of something of interest* in an application. As can be seen in Figure 20-1, there are nine attributes in the Supplier table, each of which represents a characteristic of a supplier. In addition, there are ten attributes in the Product table, each of which represents a characteristic of a product. Notice that these attributes are named using a singular noun (or singular noun phrase). Naming attributes in this way will be our standard. Also notice that the first attribute in each table has a key symbol next to it. This indicates that the attribute is the table's *primary key*, which we will define in the next section. And finally, notice that each attribute is of a specific *type* and *size*. Figure 20-2 shows some of the data in the Supplier table.

SupplierID	Supplier	PointOfContact	Address	City	State	ZipCode	Phone	EmailAddress
1	Nike	Nate Niko	123 Nike Way	New City	ND	12345	111-111-1111	nniko@nike.com
2	Prince	Phil Pelkin	098 Prince Road	Pingo	PA	87654	999-999-9999	ppelkin@prince.com
4	Adidas	Alan Alte	100 Adidas Lane	Altuna	AZ	67890	234-098-0897	aalte@adidas.com
5	Head	Hailey Hawkins	265 W. Head Avenue	Hankton	NH	45365	849-012-0873	hhawkins@head.com
6	Babolat	Bill Baker	9807 Bandy Street	Bakersfield	CA	90089	841-890-1274	bbaker@babolat.com
NULL	NULL	NULL	NULL	NULL	NULL	NULL	NULL	NULL

Figure 20-2. *Some of the data in the Supplier table*

Figure 20-3 shows some of the data in the Product table.

ProductID	CategoryID	SupplierID	Product	Description	Image	Price	NumberInStock	NumberOnOrder	ReorderLevel
1	3	2	Prince Tour Elit...	This 100% grap...	PTEJ25R.jpg	85.00	4	0	2
2	3	2	Prince Lightnin...	Perfect for begi...	PL110.jpg	75.00	12	0	4
3	3	2	Prince Textrem...	This fast and ve...	PTW100.jpg	199.00	15	0	5
4	3	6	Babolat Pure A...	Babolat celebra...	BPAFO.jpg	229.00	8	0	3
5	3	6	Babolat Pure A...	Dressed in hot ...	BPALP.jpg	195.00	4	2	4
6	3	5	Head MxG 3	Intermediate pl...	HM3.jpg	239.95	2	2	2
7	3	5	Head Graphene...	The Prestige Mi...	HGPRP.jpg	69.95	5	0	3
8	2	1	Nike Men's Su...	Sport a clean lo...	NMSFA7S.jpg	85.00	20	5	20
9	2	1	Nike Men's Su...	This Nike Premi...	NMSRFPJ.jpg	150.00	15	10	15
10	6	1	Nike Women's ...	Capture a new ...	NWSPPR.jpg	150.00	16	0	10
12	5	1	Nike Zoom Vap...	Designed with s...	NZV9.5TWS.jpg	105.00	20	0	5
14	5	1	Nike Flare Wo...	Shoe of choice ...	NFWS.jpg	127.50	4	5	5
15	1	1	Nike Zoom Vap...	Nike's most po...	NZV9.5T.jpg	105.00	30	0	10
16	1	4	Adidas Barricad...	This Limited Ed...	AB17PA.jpg	149.95	10	5	15
20	2	4	Adidas Men's R...	Celebrate tenni...	AMROTCT.jpg	25.00	0	10	5
NULL	NULL	NULL	NULL	NULL	NULL	NULL	NULL	NULL	NULL

Figure 20-3. *Some of the data in the Product table*

20.5 Relationships

A database *relationship* is the logical association between two database tables. This relationship is implemented via a *primary key* in one table and a *foreign key* in another table. A primary key is the attribute (or combination of attributes) in a table that uniquely identifies each row in the table. There are two rules associated with the creation of a primary key value. These are

1.   A primary key value must be unique.

2.   A primary key value must not be null.

These are the rules of *entity integrity*. There are no exceptions. A foreign key, on the other hand, is an attribute (or combination of attributes) in a table that corresponds to the primary key in a related table. There are two rules associated with the creation of a foreign key value. These are

1.   A foreign key value must exist as a primary key value in a related table.

2.   A foreign key value must be null.

These are the rules of *referential integrity*. There are no exceptions. As can be seen in Figure 20-1, there are seven relationships in the SportsPlay database, each of which is represented by a line that terminates as either a key symbol or an infinity symbol. The key symbol represents the *one side* of a relationship, whereas the infinity symbol represents the *many side* of a relationship. Thus, according to the database schema in the figure, the following relationships exist between the tables of the SportsPlay database:

- A supplier *supplies* one or more products, and a product *is supplied by* exactly one supplier.

- A category *is associated with* one or more products, and a product *is associated with* exactly one category.

- A product *appears on* one or more order lines, and an order line *contains* exactly one product.

- An order *contains* one or more order lines, and an order line *appears on* exactly one order.

- A shipper *ships* one or more orders, and an order *is shipped by* exactly one shipper.

- A customer *places* one or more orders, and an order *is placed by* exactly one customer.

- An employee *can take* one or more orders, and an order *can be taken by* exactly one employee.

Notice that the last bullet point is written in *can* language. This is because an employee can place an order for a customer *or* a customer can place an order online. In the latter scenario, the value in the EmployeeID attribute in the Order table, which is a foreign key, would be set to *null*. Notice as well that the relationships (shown in italics and read in both directions) are described using either an action verb (or action verb phrase) or a linking verb (or linking verb phrase). An action verb is a verb that expresses a physical or mental action, whereas a linking verb is a verb that expresses a state of being. Naming relationships in this way will be our standard.

By looking at the data in the Supplier table in Figure 20-2 and the data in the Product table in Figure 20-3, we can see how the relationship between suppliers and products is actually maintained. Notice that the primary key attribute in the Supplier table is SupplierID. As can be seen, the values in this attribute uniquely identify the rows in the table as they are all unique *and* not null. Notice as well that the associated foreign key attribute in the Product table is also SupplierID. The values in this attribute correspond to the values in the SupplierID attribute of the Supplier table. As can be seen, all of the values in the SupplierID attribute in the Product table exist as primary key values in the SupplierID attribute in the Supplier table. If a given product were not associated with a supplier for some reason, the value in that product's SupplierID attribute would be null.

20.6 Structured Query Language

The Structured Query Language (SQL) is a *fourth-generation programming language* that retrieves (i.e., queries) and manages (i.e., inserts, updates, and deletes) the data in a relational database. First-, second-, and third-generation programming languages are *imperative programming languages*. These programming languages require the software developer to write code that instructs the computer *how* to do something.

Thus, loops, conditionals, and other imperative statements are required. Fourth-generation programming languages, on the other hand, are *declarative programming languages*. These programming languages require the software developer to write code that instructs the computer *what* to do. Thus, loops, conditionals, and other imperative statements are *not* required. As we will see, SQL does not require us to describe *how* to query, insert, update, or delete a database's data. Instead, it only requires us to describe *what* database data to query, insert, update, or delete.[1] The required imperative code is generated for us in the background.

SQL is, by far, the most widely used relational database language. The language is standardized by the American National Standards Institute (ANSI) and the International Organization for Standardization (ISO), so most SQL code is portable from one DBMS to another—often with no (or just a few) tweaks to its syntax. The programming statements of the Structured Query Language are divided into four categories—*data definition language* (DDL) statements (e.g., statements for creating, altering, and dropping tables, attributes, and relationships), *data control language* (DCL) statements (e.g., statements for granting, revoking, and denying end user and application access privileges), *data query language* (DQL) statements (e.g., statements for selecting and displaying table data), and *data manipulation language* (DML) statements (e.g., statements for inserting, updating, and deleting table data). The first two categories of SQL statements are related to *database administration*, whereas the last two categories of SQL statements are related to *database usage*. Thus, we will focus mostly on the last two categories of SQL statements as they are the most germane to our discussion.

Before we look at specific SQL statements, we should say something about the standards we will apply when formatting SQL statements. First, although it is not necessary to capitalize the *reserved words* of a SQL statement, we will *always* do so as this will enhance the readability of the SQL statement. And second, although it is not necessary to write a SQL statement on *multiple lines*, we will *always* do so as this will make the SQL statement *much* easier to write, read, and maintain. These standards become especially important as the SQL statements we write become more complex.

---

[1]SQL does include some procedural statements.

20.6.1 Select Statement

The Select statement *queries* a database. More specifically, it retrieves one or more rows from one or more tables in a database and then displays the result. Again, since SQL is a declarative programming language, we need not specify *how* to retrieve and display the data. We need only specify *what* data we want to retrieve and display. How to retrieve and display the data from a database is done by the DBMS, which translates the SQL query we write into a *query plan*. This query plan is then optimized by the DBMS's *query optimizer*, which determines the best possible *execution plan* for the query. The Select statement has two *required* clauses. These are

- *Select clause* – Specifies the attributes that should be returned from a query

- *From clause* – Specifies the table or tables from which the data should be retrieved

The order in which these clauses are included in a Select statement is very important. If they are not included in the correct order, a syntax error will occur. Figure 20-4 shows an example of the Select statement.

Notice at 01 the asterisk (*) after the Select clause of the statement. This asterisk means that *all* of the attributes in the table (i.e., SupplierID, Supplier, PointOfContact, Address, City, State, ZipCode, Phone, and EmailAddress) should be displayed in the result of the SQL call.

Notice at 02 the name of the table after the From clause of the statement. This indicates the name of the table (i.e., Supplier) from which the data should be retrieved.

The screenshot in the Result section of the figure shows the result of the query.

SQL CODE

```
01   SELECT *
02      FROM Supplier
```

RESULT

SupplierID	Supplier	PointOfContact	Address	City	State	ZipCode	Phone	EmailAddress
1	Nike	Nate Niko	123 Nike Way	New City	ND	12345	111-111-1111	nniko@nike.com
2	Prince	Phil Pelkin	098 Prince Road	Pingo	PA	87654	999-999-9999	ppelkin@prince.com
4	Adidas	Alan Alte	100 Adidas Lane	Altuna	AZ	67890	234-098-0897	aalte@adidas.com
5	Head	Hailey Hawkins	265 W. Head Avenue	Hankton	NH	45365	849-012-0873	hhawkins@head.com
6	Babolat	Bill Baker	9807 Bandy Street	Bakersfield	CA	90089	841-890-1274	bbaker@Babolat.com

***Figure 20-4.** Example of the Select statement*

Figure 20-5 shows an example of the Select statement with specific attributes displayed.

Notice at 01 that specific attributes have been listed after the Select clause of the statement. This means that *only* those attributes in the table (i.e., Supplier, PointOfContact, Phone, and EmailAddress) should be displayed in the result of the SQL call.

The screenshot in the Result section of the figure shows the result of the query.

```
SQL CODE

01   SELECT Supplier,
            PointOfContact,
            Phone,
            EmailAddress
        FROM Supplier

RESULT
```

Supplier	PointOfContact	Phone	EmailAddress
Nike	Nate Niko	111-111-1111	nniko@nike.com
Prince	Phil Pelkin	999-999-9999	ppelkin@prince.com
Adidas	Alan Alte	234-098-0897	aalte@adidas.com
Head	Hailey Hawkins	849-012-0873	hhawkins@head.com
Babolat	Bill Baker	841-890-1274	bbaker@Babolat.com

Figure 20-5. *Example of the Select statement with specific attributes displayed*

The Select statement has several *optional* clauses that we can use to qualify (i.e., fine-tune) the results we want a query to return. These are

- *Order By clause* – Specifies the order (i.e., ascending or descending) in which the rows should be returned

- *Where clause* – Specifies the subset of rows that should be returned

- *Group By clause* – Specifies the rows that should be treated as a group when an aggregate function (e.g., Count, Avg, Sum) is applied

- *Having clause* – Specifies the subset of rows that should be returned when a Group By clause is used

- *As clause* – Specifies the alias (e.g., an abbreviated name, a different name) that should be used when referring to a table or attribute

Again, the order in which these clauses are included in a Select statement is very important. If they are not included in the correct order, a syntax error will occur. Figure 20-6 shows an example of the Select statement with an Order By clause.

Notice at 01 that the result of the SQL call should be sorted in ascending order (the default) by Supplier.

The screenshot in the Result section of the figure shows the result of the query.

```
SQL CODE

    SELECT Supplier,
           PointOfContact,
           Phone,
           EmailAddress
      FROM Supplier
01    ORDER BY Supplier

RESULT
```

Supplier	PointOfContact	Phone	EmailAddress
Adidas	Alan Alte	234-098-0897	aalte@adidas.com
Babolat	Bill Baker	841-890-1274	bbaker@babolat.com
Head	Hailey Hawkins	849-012-0873	hhawkins@head.com
Nike	Nate Niko	111-111-1111	nniko@nike.com
Prince	Phil Pelkin	999-999-9999	ppelkin@prince.com

Figure 20-6. *Example of the Select statement with an Order By clause*

Figure 20-7 shows an example of the Select statement with a Where clause (equality).

Notice at 01 that only those products with a SupplierID equal to 6 should be returned.

The screenshot in the Result section of the figure shows the result of the query.

SQL CODE

```
    SELECT SupplierID,
           Product,
           Description,
           Price
      FROM Product
01    WHERE SupplierID = 6
      ORDER BY Product
```

RESULT

SupplierID	Product	Description	Price
6	Babolat Pure Aero French Open	Babolat celebrates the sacred dirt of Roland Gar...	229.00
6	Babolat Pure Aero Lite Pink	Dressed in hot pink, this light and explosive racq...	195.00

Figure 20-7. *Example of the Select statement with a Where clause (equality)*

Figure 20-8 shows an example of the Select statement with a Where clause (relational).

Notice at 01 that only those products with a price less than or equal to 100 should be returned.

Notice at 02 that the result of the SQL call should be sorted in descending order by Price.

The screenshot in the Result section of the figure shows the result of the query.

SQL CODE

```
    SELECT Product,
           Description,
           Price
      FROM Product
01    WHERE Price <= 100
02    ORDER BY Price DESC
```

RESULT

Product	Description	Price
Prince Tour Elite Junior 25" Racquet	This 100% graphite junior racquet features Princ...	85.00
Nike Men's Summer Flex Ace 7 Inch Short	Sport a clean look the next time you head out to...	85.00
Prince Lightning 110	Perfect for beginner and intermediate level playe...	75.00
Head Graphene Prestige Rev Pro	The Prestige Mid gets lighter and faster. Anyone...	69.95
Adidas Men's Reign on the Court T-Shirt	Celebrate tennis in London with this tongue in c...	25.00

Figure 20-8. *Example of the Select statement with a Where clause (relational)*

Figure 20-9 shows an example of the Select statement with a Where clause (And compound condition).

Notice at 01 that only those products with a CategoryID equal to 2 *and* where the number in stock is less than or equal to the reorder level should be returned.

The screenshot in the Result section of the figure shows the result of the query.

SQL CODE

```
    SELECT CategoryID,
           Product,
           NumberInStock,
           ReorderLevel
      FROM Product
01    WHERE CategoryID = 2
        AND NumberInStock <= ReorderLevel
```

RESULT

CategoryID	Product	NumberInStock	ReorderLevel
2	Adidas Men's Reign on the Court T-Shirt	0	5
2	Nike Men's Summer RF Premier Jacket	15	15
2	Nike Men's Summer Flex Ace 7 Inch Short	20	20

Figure 20-9. *Example of the Select statement with a Where clause (And compound condition)*

Figure 20-10 shows an example of the Select statement with a Where clause (Or compound condition).

Notice at 01 that only those products with a CategoryID equal to 2 *or* a CategoryID equal to 3 should be returned.

Notice at 02 that the result of the SQL call should be sorted in ascending order (the default) by CategoryID, then by SupplierID (within CategoryID), then by Product (within SupplierID).

The screenshot in the Result section of the figure shows the result of the query.

SQL CODE

```
      SELECT CategoryID,
             SupplierID,
             Product,
             Description,
             Price
        FROM Product
01     WHERE CategoryID = 2
          OR CategoryID = 3
02     ORDER BY CategoryID, SupplierID, Product
```

RESULT

CategoryID	SupplierID	Product	Description	Price
2	1	Nike Men's Summer Flex Ace 7 Inch Short	Sport a clean look the next time you head out to pl...	85.00
2	1	Nike Men's Summer RF Premier Jacket	This Nike Premier RF N98 Jacket will keep you war...	150.00
2	4	Adidas Men's Reign on the Court T-Shirt	Celebrate tennis in London with this tongue in chee...	25.00
3	2	Prince Lightning 110	Perfect for beginner and intermediate level players i...	75.00
3	2	Prince Textreme Warrior 100	This fast and very spin friendly racquet offers amazi...	199.00
3	2	Prince Tour Elite Junior 25" Racquet	This 100% graphite junior racquet features Prince's ...	85.00
3	5	Head Graphene Prestige Rev Pro	The Prestige Mid gets lighter and faster. Anyone lo...	69.95
3	5	Head MxG 3	Intermediate players looking for easy access to po...	239.95
3	6	Babolat Pure Aero French Open	Babolat celebrates the sacred dirt of Roland Garros...	229.00
3	6	Babolat Pure Aero Lite Pink	Dressed in hot pink, this light and explosive racquet...	195.00

Figure 20-10. *Example of the Select statement with a Where clause (Or compound condition)*

Although the ability to query the data of a single database table is a powerful feature of the Structured Query Language, its ability to query the data of two or more related tables is where the real power of the language lies. Querying the data of two or more related tables is accomplished via a *join operation*. Although there are many types of join operations (e.g., cross joins, natural joins, inner joins, outer joins, left joins, right joins), we will discuss the most basic and most frequently used one—the inner join. From this point forward, we will use the term join to refer to an inner join. Figure 20-11 shows an example of a two-table join operation.

Notice at 01 that we are qualifying the SupplierID attribute by coding the name of a table (i.e., Supplier) followed by a period (.) followed by the name of the attribute itself (i.e., SupplierID). This is necessary because the SupplierID attribute is found in *both* the Supplier table and the Product table—the two tables we are joining. Thus, we must specify which SupplierID we want to display. Note that since the other attributes in the Select clause are *not* found in *both* the Supplier table *and* the Product table, we need not qualify them with a table name.

Notice at 02 that the From clause indicates the two tables we are joining—the Supplier table and the Product table.

Notice at 03 that we have set the SupplierID of the Supplier table equal to the SupplierID of the Product table. It is this condition that joins the two tables together. This part of the Where clause is telling the DBMS to return a row of data wherever a SupplierID in the Supplier table matches a SupplierID in the Product table. As can be seen, there are the other qualifiers in the Where clause as well. These qualifiers ensure that only the products with a SupplierID of 2, 5, or 6 are displayed.

The screenshot in the Result section of the figure shows the result of the query.

```
SQL CODE

01   SELECT Supplier.SupplierID,
            Supplier,
            Product,
            Description,
            Price
02     FROM Supplier, Product
03    WHERE Supplier.SupplierID = Product.SupplierID
        AND (
            Supplier.SupplierID = 2
         OR Supplier.SupplierID = 5
         OR Supplier.SupplierID = 6
            )
     ORDER BY Supplier, Product
```

RESULT

SupplierID	Supplier	Product	Description	Price
6	Babolat	Babolat Pure Aero French Open	Babolat celebrates the sacred dirt of Roland Gar...	229.00
6	Babolat	Babolat Pure Aero Lite Pink	Dressed in hot pink, this light and explosive racq...	195.00
5	Head	Head Graphene Prestige Rev Pro	The Prestige Mid gets lighter and faster. Anyone...	69.95
5	Head	Head MxG 3	Intermediate players looking for easy access to ...	239.95
2	Prince	Prince Lightning 110	Perfect for beginner and intermediate level playe...	75.00
2	Prince	Prince Textreme Warrior 100	This fast and very spin friendly racquet offers am...	199.00
2	Prince	Prince Tour Elite Junior 25" Racquet	This 100% graphite junior racquet features Princ...	85.00

Figure 20-11. *Example of a two-table join operation*

Figure 20-12 shows an example of a six-table join operation.

Notice at 01 that we have enclosed the word *Order* in square brackets ([ ]). This was done because Order is a SQL reserved word that is associated with the Order By clause. By placing square brackets around Order, we are indicating to the DBMS that Order is the name of a table and not part of an Order By clause. Notice as well that we have specified the table from which the OrderID should be retrieved. This is necessary since this attribute is found in two of the tables being joined—Order and OrderLine. Likewise, we have specified the tables from which the LastName and FirstName should be retrieved. This is necessary since these attributes are found in three of the tables being joined—Customer, Employee, and Order. In addition, notice that we are concatenating each customer's last name with a comma, a space, and a first name and then displaying that as the single attribute called CustomerName. The EmployeeName attribute is constructed in the same way.

Notice at 02 that the From clause indicates the six tables we are joining—the Customer table, the Employee table, the Order table, the OrderLine table, the Product table, and the Shipper table.

Notice at 03 that we have set the CustomerID of the Order table equal to the CustomerID of the Customer table, we have set the EmployeeID of the Order table equal to the EmployeeID of the Employee table, we have set the ShipperID of the Order table equal to the ShipperID of the Shipper table, and so on. It is these conditions that join the six tables together. This part of the Where clause is telling the DBMS to return a row of data wherever a CustomerID in the Order table matches a CustomerID in the Customer table, an EmployeeID in the Order table matches an EmployeeID in the Employee table, a ShipperID in the Order table matches a ShipperID in the Shipper table, and so on. As can be seen, the only order that should be returned is OrderID 2.

The screenshot in the Result section of the figure shows the result of the query.

SQL CODE

```
01   SELECT [Order].OrderID,
             Customer.LastName + ', ' + Customer.FirstName AS CustomerName,
             Date,
             Product,
             OrderLine.Price,
             Employee.LastName + ', ' + Employee.FirstName AS EmployeeName,
             Shipper
02     FROM Customer, Employee, [Order], OrderLine, Product, Shipper
03     WHERE [Order].OrderID = 2
         AND [Order].CustomerID = Customer.CustomerID
         AND [Order].EmployeeID = Employee.EmployeeID
         AND [Order].ShipperID = Shipper.ShipperID
         AND [Order].OrderID = OrderLine.OrderID
         AND OrderLine.ProductID = Product.ProductID
       ORDER BY Product
```

RESULT

OrderID	CustomerName	Date	Product	Price	EmployeeName	Shipper
2	Jones, Jacob	2017-05-25	Prince Lightning 110	75.00	Regal, Richard	UPS
2	Jones, Jacob	2017-05-25	Prince Tour Elite Junior 25" Racquet	85.00	Regal, Richard	UPS

Figure 20-12. *Example of a six-table join operation*

20.6.2 Insert Statement

The Insert statement adds one or more rows to a database table. When inserting a row, the values to be inserted into the table must satisfy all of the applicable table constraints (i.e., entity integrity constraints, referential integrity constraints, and not null constraints). Otherwise, the DBMS will not insert the row into the table and will return an error message. Figure 20-13 shows an example of the Insert statement.

Notice at 01 that we will be inserting a row of data into the Product table. As can be seen, we have articulated all of the attributes that will be inserted into the table—except for the ProductID, which is the primary key of the table. We won't be inserting a primary key value because, when we created the table, we instructed the DBMS to automatically generate a primary key value (i.e., an automatically incremented integer) for a newly inserted row. Keep in mind that we need only list the attributes we wish to add to an inserted row. For any attribute values we don't list, the DBMS will automatically insert the default values we specified when we created the table. However, our standard will be to list *all* of the attributes in an Insert statement—except for any automatically generated primary keys.

Notice at 02 that the list and sequence of the attribute values in the Values clause correspond directly to the list and sequence of the attribute names at 01. If these do not match exactly, the Insert statement will not work as expected. It is important to note that when an Insert statement is part of an application, we almost never hard code the attribute values like they are hard coded in the figure. Instead, we typically code variables in the Values clause of the Insert statement and then programmatically instantiate those variables with values before the Insert statement is executed.

The screenshot in the Result section of the figure shows the result of the insert. Notice the newly inserted row that appears at the very bottom of the table. Also notice the automatically generated ProductID value.

SQL CODE

```
        INSERT
01      INTO Product
                (
                CategoryID,
                SupplierID,
                Product,
                Description,
                Image,
                Price,
                NumberInStock,
                NumberOnOrder,
                ReorderLevel
                )
02      VALUES
                (
                3,
                6,
                'Babolat PLAY Pure Aero',
                'Babolat adds PLAY Technology to the Pure Aero! This stick....,
                'BPPA.jpg',
                249.00,
                2,
                0,
                1
                )
```

RESULT

ProductID	CategoryID	SupplierID	Product	Description	Image	Price	NumberInStock	NumberOnOrder	ReorderLevel
1	3	2	Prince Tour Elite Junior 25" Racquet	This 100% grap...	PTEJ25R.jpg	85.00	4	0	2
2	3	2	Prince Lightning 110	Perfect for begi...	PL110.jpg	75.00	12	0	4
3	3	2	Prince Textreme Warrior 100	This fast and ve...	PTW100.jpg	199.00	15	0	5
4	3	6	Babolat Pure Aero French Open	Babolat celebra...	BPAFO.jpg	229.00	8	0	3
5	3	6	Babolat Pure Aero Lite Pink	Dressed in hot ...	BPALP.jpg	195.00	4	2	4
6	3	5	Head MxG 3	Intermediate pl...	HM3.jpg	239.95	2	2	2
7	3	5	Head Graphene Prestige Rev Pro	The Prestige Mi...	HGPRP.jpg	69.95	5	0	3
8	2	1	Nike Men's Summer Flex Ace 7 Inch Short	Sport a clean lo...	NMSFA7S.jpg	85.00	20	5	20
9	2	1	Nike Men's Summer RF Premier Jacket	This Nike Premi...	NMSRFPJ.jpg	150.00	15	10	15
10	6	1	Nike Women's Summer Power Premier Romper	Capture a new ...	NWSPPR.jpg	150.00	16	0	10
12	5	1	Nike Zoom Vapor 9.5 Tour Women's	Designed with s...	NZV9.5TWS.jpg	105.00	20	0	5
14	5	1	Nike Flare Women's Shoe	Shoe of choice ...	NFWS.jpg	127.50	4	5	5
15	1	1	Nike Zoom Vapor 9.5 Tour	Nike's most po...	NZV9.5T.jpg	105.00	30	0	10
16	1	4	Adidas Barricade 17 Pop Art	This Limited Ed...	AB17PA.jpg	149.95	10	5	15
20	2	4	Adidas Men's Reign on the Court T-Shirt	Celebrate tenni...	AMROTCT.jpg	25.00	0	10	5
23	3	6	Babolat PLAY Pure Aero	Babolat adds P...	BPPA.jpg	249.00	2	0	1
NULL	NULL	NULL	NULL	NULL	NULL	NULL	NULL	NULL	NULL

Figure 20-13. *Example of the Insert statement*

20.6.3 Update Statement

The Update statement modifies one or more rows in a database table. When updating a row, the values to be updated in the table must satisfy all of the applicable table constraints (i.e., entity integrity constraints, referential integrity constraints, and not null constraints). Otherwise, the DBMS will not update the row in the table and will return an error message. When updating a specific row in a table, we must be *very* careful to include a Where clause that identifies the primary key value of the row to be updated. If we include a nonexistent primary key value in the Where clause, no row will be updated. If we include an incorrect primary key value in the Where clause, the wrong row will be updated. And if we neglect to include a Where clause altogether, all of the rows in the table will be updated. Figure 20-14 shows an example of the Update statement.

Notice at 01 that we will be updating the Product table.

Notice at 02 that we will be updating the Price and NumberInStock attribute values. It is important to note that when an Update statement is part of an application, we almost never hard code the attribute values like they are hard coded in the figure. Instead, we typically code variables in the Set clause of the Update statement and then programmatically instantiate those variables with values before the Update statement is executed.

Notice at 03 that we will be updating the row whose primary key is 23.

The screenshot in the Result section of the figure shows the result of the update. Notice the newly updated row that appears at the very bottom of the table. Also notice the new Price and NumberInStock values.

SQL CODE

```
01   UPDATE Product
02      SET Price = 349.00,
            NumberInStock = 3
03   WHERE ProductID = 23
```

RESULT

ProductID	CategoryID	SupplierID	Product	Description	Image	Price	NumberInStock	NumberOnOrder	ReorderLevel
1	3	2	Prince Tour Elite Junior 25" Racquet	This 100% grap...	PTEJ25R.jpg	85.00	4	0	2
2	3	2	Prince Lightning 110	Perfect for begi...	PL110.jpg	75.00	12	0	4
3	3	2	Prince Textreme Warrior 100	This fast and ve...	PTW100.jpg	199.00	15	0	5
4	3	6	Babolat Pure Aero French Open	Babolat celebra...	BPAFO.jpg	229.00	8	0	3
5	3	6	Babolat Pure Aero Lite Pink	Dressed in hot ...	BPALP.jpg	195.00	4	2	4
6	3	5	Head MxG 3	Intermediate pl...	HM3.jpg	239.95	2	2	2
7	3	5	Head Graphene Prestige Rev Pro	The Prestige Mi...	HGPRP.jpg	69.95	5	0	3
8	2	1	Nike Men's Summer Flex Ace 7 Inch Short	Sport a clean lo...	NMSFA7S.jpg	85.00	20	5	20
9	2	1	Nike Men's Summer RF Premier Jacket	This Nike Premi...	NMSRFPJ.jpg	150.00	15	10	15
10	6	1	Nike Women's Summer Power Premier Romper	Capture a new ...	NWSPPR.jpg	150.00	16	0	10
12	5	1	Nike Zoom Vapor 9.5 Tour Women's	Designed with s...	NZV9.5TWS.jpg	105.00	20	0	5
14	5	1	Nike Flare Women's Shoe	Shoe of choice ...	NFWS.jpg	127.50	4	5	5
15	1	1	Nike Zoom Vapor 9.5 Tour	Nike's most po...	NZV9.5T.jpg	105.00	30	0	10
16	1	4	Adidas Barricade 17 Pop Art	This Limited Ed...	AB17PA.jpg	149.95	10	5	15
20	2	4	Adidas Men's Reign on the Court T-Shirt	Celebrate tenni...	AMROTCT.jpg	25.00	0	10	5
23	3	6	Babolat PLAY Pure Aero	Babolat adds P...	BPPA.jpg	349.00	3	0	1
NULL	NULL	NULL	NULL	NULL	NULL	NULL	NULL	NULL	NULL

Figure 20-14.   *Example of the Update statement*

20.6.4 Delete Statement

The Delete statement removes one or more rows from a database table. When deleting a row, all referential integrity constraints must remain satisfied. Otherwise, the DBMS will not delete the row from the table and will return an error message. When deleting a specific row from a table, we must be *very* careful to include a Where clause that identifies the primary key value of the row to be deleted. If we include a nonexistent primary key value in the Where clause, no row will be deleted. If we include an incorrect primary key value in the Where clause, the wrong row will be deleted. And if we neglect to include a Where clause altogether, all of the rows in the table will be deleted. Figure 20-15 shows an example of the Delete statement.

Notice at 01 that we will be deleting a row from the Product table.

Notice at 02 that we will be deleting the row whose primary key is 23.

The screenshot in the Result section of the figure shows the result of the delete. Notice that the row with the primary key of 23 has been removed from the table.

SQL CODE

```
    DELETE
01    FROM Product
02    WHERE ProductID = 23
```

RESULT

ProductID	CategoryID	SupplierID	Product	Description	Image	Price	NumberInStock	NumberOnOrder	ReorderLevel
1	3	2	Prince Tour Elite Junior 25" Racquet	This 100% grap...	PTEJ25R.jpg	85.00	4	0	2
2	3	2	Prince Lightning 110	Perfect for begi...	PL110.jpg	75.00	12	0	4
3	3	2	Prince Textreme Warrior 100	This fast and ve...	PTW100.jpg	199.00	15	0	5
4	3	6	Babolat Pure Aero French Open	Babolat celebra...	BPAFO.jpg	229.00	8	0	3
5	3	6	Babolat Pure Aero Lite Pink	Dressed in hot ...	BPALP.jpg	195.00	4	2	4
6	3	5	Head MxG 3	Intermediate pl...	HM3.jpg	239.95	2	2	2
7	3	5	Head Graphene Prestige Rev Pro	The Prestige Mi...	HGPRP.jpg	69.95	5	0	3
8	2	1	Nike Men's Summer Flex Ace 7 Inch Short	Sport a clean lo...	NMSFA7S.jpg	85.00	20	5	20
9	2	1	Nike Men's Summer RF Premier Jacket	This Nike Premi...	NMSRFPJ.jpg	150.00	15	10	15
10	6	1	Nike Women's Summer Power Premier Romper	Capture a new ...	NWSPPR.jpg	150.00	16	0	10
12	5	1	Nike Zoom Vapor 9.5 Tour Women's	Designed with s...	NZV9.5TWS.jpg	105.00	20	0	5
14	5	1	Nike Flare Women's Shoe	Shoe of choice ...	NFWS.jpg	127.50	4	5	5
15	1	1	Nike Zoom Vapor 9.5 Tour	Nike's most po...	NZV9.5T.jpg	105.00	30	0	10
16	1	4	Adidas Barricade 17 Pop Art	This Limited Ed...	AB17PA.jpg	149.95	10	5	15
20	2	4	Adidas Men's Reign on the Court T-Shirt	Celebrate tenni...	AMROTCT.jpg	25.00	0	10	5
NULL	NULL	NULL	NULL	NULL	NULL	NULL	NULL	NULL	NULL

Figure 20-15.   *Example of the Delete statement*

20.7 DataBoundControl Class

The DataBoundControl class serves as the base class for all of the data-bound classes that display data in tabular or list form. As such, all data-bound classes inherit properties, methods, and events from this class. The data-bound classes include the AdRotator class, the BulletedList class, the CheckBoxList class, the DetailsView class, the DropDownList class, the FormView class, the GridView class, the ListBox class, the ListView class, the Menu class, the RadioButtonList class, the Repeater class, and the TreeView class. We have already seen some of these classes in action (e.g., the DropDownList class, the ListBox class, the Menu class, the TreeView class), and we will see others in the chapters that follow (e.g., the FormView class, the ListView class). Table 20-1 shows some of the properties, methods, and events of the DataBoundControl class.

Table 20-1. *Some of the properties, methods, and events of the DataBoundControl class*

Class DataBoundControl[2]

Namespace System.Web.UI.WebControls

Properties

DataSourceID   Gets or sets the ID of the control from which the data-bound control
                            retrieves its list of data items.

Methods

(See reference.)

Events

(See reference.)

Reference

```
https://msdn.microsoft.com/en-us/library/system.web.ui.webcontrols.
databoundcontrol(v=vs.110).aspx
```

20.8 SqlDataSource Class

The SqlDataSource class accesses an application's underlying SQL Server database. A SqlDataSource control can be used in conjunction with a data-bound control to retrieve data from, insert data into, update data in, and delete data from a SQL Server database. The data-bound controls that can be used with a SqlDataSource control to perform such operations are listed in the previous section.

Table 20-2 shows some of the properties, methods, and events of the SqlDataSource class. The ConnectionString property of the SqlDataSource class indicates the connection string associated with an underlying SQL Server database. The SelectCommand property indicates the SQL call used to *retrieve* data from a SQL Server database, and the SelectParameters property contains the collection of parameters used by the SQL call defined in the SelectCommand property. The InsertCommand property indicates the SQL call used to *insert* data into a SQL Server table, and the

---

[2]All property, method, and event descriptions were taken directly from Microsoft's official documentation. The event handler methods used to handle the events of this class were omitted to conserve space. See the reference for all of the methods of this class.

InsertParameters property contains the collection of parameters used by the SQL call defined in the InsertCommand property. The Inserting method is invoked *before* an insert operation occurs, whereas the Inserted method is invoked *after* an insert operation occurs. The UpdateCommand property indicates the SQL call used to *update* data in a SQL Server table, and the UpdateParameters property contains the collection of parameters used by the SQL call defined in the UpdateCommand property. The Updating method is invoked *before* an update operation occurs, whereas the Updated method is invoked *after* an update operation occurs. The DeleteCommand property indicates the SQL call used to *delete* data from a SQL Server table, and the DeleteParameters property contains the collection of parameters used by the SQL call defined in the DeleteCommand property. The Deleting method is invoked *before* a delete operation occurs, whereas the Deleted method is invoked *after* a delete operation occurs.

Keep in mind that the value of the SelectCommand, InsertCommand, UpdateCommand, and DeleteCommand property can be a SQL call in string form, or it can be the name of a stored procedure. Furthermore, the SelectParameters, InsertParameters, UpdateParameters, and DeleteParameters property collections can contain *control parameters* (which bind to server control properties), *cookie parameters* (which bind to cookies), *form parameters* (which bind to form fields), *profile parameters* (which bind to profile fields), *query string parameters* (which bind to query string parameters), *route parameters* (which bind to route URL parameters), and *session parameters* (which bind to session variables). As we will soon see, these types of parameters are used in *parameterized queries*.

Table 20-2. *Some of the properties, methods, and events of the SqlDataSource class*

Class SqlDataSource[3]

Namespace System.Web.UI.WebControls

Properties

ConnectionString	Gets or sets the ADO.NET provider–specific connection string that the SqlDataSource control uses to connect to an underlying database.
DeleteCommand	Gets or sets the SQL string that the SqlDataSource control uses to delete data from the underlying database.
DeleteParameters	Gets the parameters collection that contains the parameters that are used by the DeleteCommand property from the SqlDataSourceView object that is associated with the SqlDataSource control.
InsertCommand	Gets or sets the SQL string that the SqlDataSource control uses to insert data into the underlying database.
InsertParameters	Gets the parameters collection that contains the parameters that are used by the InsertCommand property from the SqlDataSourceView object that is associated with the SqlDataSource control.
OldValuesParameterFormatString	Gets or sets a format string to apply to the names of any parameters that are passed to the Delete or Update method.
SelectCommand	Gets or sets the SQL string that the SqlDataSource control uses to retrieve data from the underlying database.
SelectParameters	Gets the parameters collection that contains the parameters that are used by the SelectCommand property from the SqlDataSourceView object that is associated with the SqlDataSource control.
UpdateCommand	Gets or sets the SQL string that the SqlDataSource control uses to update data in the underlying database.

(continued)

---

[3]All property, method, and event descriptions were taken directly from Microsoft's official documentation. The event handler methods used to handle the events of this class were omitted to conserve space. See the reference for all of the methods of this class.

Table 20-2. (*continued*)

UpdateParameters	Gets the parameters collection that contains the parameters that are used by the UpdateCommand property from the SqlDataSourceView control that is associated with the SqlDataSource control.
Methods	
DataBind()	Binds a data source to the invoked server control and all its child controls. (Inherited from Control.)
Events	
Deleted	Occurs when a delete operation has completed.
Deleting	Occurs before a delete operation.
Inserted	Occurs when an insert operation has completed.
Inserting	Occurs before an insert operation.
Updated	Occurs when an update operation has completed.
Updating	Occurs before an update operation.
Reference	

https://msdn.microsoft.com/en-us/library/system.web.ui.webcontrols.
sqldatasource(v=vs.110).aspx

20.8.1 Connection Strings

A connection string provides an application with the details of its underlying SQL Server database. Figure 20-16 shows the connection string associated with the SportsPlay database. As can be seen, this connection string is defined in the <connectionStrings> section of the application's Web.config file. Notice that the name of the computer on which SQL Server resides is *MATRBeasley-18*, the name of the SQL Server instance[4] is *SQLEXPRESS*, the name of the initial catalog (i.e., the database) is *SportsPlay*, and the type of integrated security is *SSPI* (Security Support Provider Interface). SSPI (the preferred type of integrated security) permits our application (as a Windows server user) to connect to the database without having to provide additional SQL Server username and password credentials. We place the connection

---

[4]A SQL Server instance is a complete SQL Server *service* with its own databases, credentials, and so forth. A computer can have more than one SQL Server instance installed and running at one time.

string in the Web.config file so that it can be modified in *one* place yet can be *referred to* in *many* places in the application. Thus, if we need to install the database on a different computer, add the database to a different SQL Server instance, and/or change the name of the database, we need only change the connection string in the Web.config file. The references to the connection string throughout the application need not be modified.

```
WEB.CONFIG CODE

<connectionStrings>
  <add name="SportsPlay"
      connectionString="Data Source=MATRBeasley-18\SQLEXPRESS;
      Initial Catalog=SportsPlay; Integrated Security=SSPI" />
</connectionStrings>
```

Figure 20-16. *Connection string associated with the SportsPlay database*

In the sections that follow, we will employ a ListBox data-bound control to illustrate the use of the SqlDataSource class and its SelectCommand property. In Chapter 21, titled "Single-Row Database Table Maintenance," and Chapter 22, titled "Multiple-Row Database Table Maintenance," we will employ the InsertCommand, UpdateCommand, and DeleteCommand properties of the SqlDataSource class as well.

20.8.2 Data-Bound Control Population

We often need to populate a data-bound control with data from a SQL Server database. For example, we may need to provide the end user with a list box for selecting products. Figure 20-17 shows an example of populating a ListBox control with a SqlDataSource control. In this example, we will be populating the list box with *all* of the products from the Product table. No row filtering will be done.

Notice at 01 the SqlDataSource control. This data source will be used to populate the list box at 02. As can be seen, the ConnectionString property of the SqlDataSource control is set to *<%$ConnectionStrings:SportsPlay%>* to indicate the connection string (i.e., SportsPlay) associated with the application's underlying SQL Server database. Notice in the SelectCommand property of the control that we will be returning the ProductID and the Product from the Product table and that the result will be sorted in ascending order by Product. This way, the end user will be able to easily locate products in the list box.

Notice at 02 the ListBox control used to display the products in the Product table. Observe that the DataSourceID of this control is set to the ID of the SqlDataSource control at 01 to identify the data source associated with the list box. Also notice that the DataTextField property is set to *Product* to indicate that the Product attribute is to be displayed in the list box. Notice as well that the DataValueField property is set to *ProductID* to indicate that the ProductID attribute (i.e., the primary key of the Product table) is to be placed in the SelectedValue property of the list box when the end user selects a product.

Notice at 03 that we have added a <connectionStrings> section to our Web.config file as well as a connection string called *SportsPlay*.

The screenshot in the Result section of the figure shows the list box populated with *all* of the products in the Product table.

ASPX CODE

```
01  <asp:SqlDataSource runat="server" ID="sdsListBoxProduct"
        ConnectionString="<%$ConnectionStrings:SportsPlay%>"
        SelectCommand="SELECT ProductID, Product
                        FROM Product
                        ORDER BY Product;">
    </asp:SqlDataSource>

    <asp:Label runat="server" Text="Product" /><br />
02  <asp:ListBox runat="server" ID="libProduct"
        DataSourceID="sdsListBoxProduct" DataTextField="Product"
        DataValueField="ProductID" Rows="7" />
```

WEB.CONFIG CODE

```
03  <connectionStrings>
      <add name="SportsPlay"
          connectionString="Data Source=MATRBeasley-18\SQLEXPRESS;
          Initial Catalog=SportsPlay; Integrated Security=SSPI" />
    </connectionStrings>
```

RESULT

Figure 20-17. *Example of populating a ListBox control with a SqlDataSource control*

20.8.3 Data-Bound Control Filtering

Sometimes populating a data-bound control with data from a database (like we did in the previous section) would return so many rows of data that the page would take an unacceptable amount of time to load, or the control would contain so many items that it would be inefficient for the end user to use (e.g., selecting a product from a ListBox control that contains ten thousand products). In this situation, we need a way of limiting the number of rows of data returned from the database. To do this, we need to apply one or more *filters* to our database call. Filtering is accomplished by adding a Where clause to the Select statement of the database call that includes one or more parameters that limit the number of rows of data returned. In the sections that follow, we will discuss two of the more common types of parameters used to filter the data of a data-bound control— *control parameters* and *session parameters*.

20.8.3.1 Filtering with Control Parameters

One way to filter the rows returned from a database is to employ one or more control parameters. A control parameter is associated with an ASP.NET server control. Such a control can contain a *naturally occurring subsetting criterion* (e.g., a product category), or it can contain a *custom subsetting criterion* (e.g., an end user–supplied string). Figure 20-18 shows an example of filtering a ListBox control with a DropDownList control. As we learned earlier in this chapter, a category *is associated with* one or more products, and a product *is associated with* exactly one category. Since category is a naturally occurring subsetting criterion for products in the SportsPlay database, we are populating the list box with only those products associated with the category selected from the drop-down list.

Notice at 01 the SqlDataSource control for the drop-down list of *categories*. This data source will be used to populate the category drop-down list at 05. Notice in the SelectCommand property of the control that we will be returning the CategoryID and the Category from the Category table and that the result will be sorted in ascending order by Category. Such a sort order will permit the end user to easily locate categories in the drop-down list.

Notice at 02 the SqlDataSource control for list box of *products*. This data source will be used to populate the product list box at 06. Notice in the SelectCommand property of the control that we will be returning the ProductID and the Product from the Product table and that the result will be sorted in ascending order by Product. Such a sort order will permit the end user to easily locate products in the list box. Notice as well that we have included a Where clause in the Select statement. This Where clause will be used to limit the products returned from the Product table to those that have a CategoryID equal to @CategoryID. Here, @CategoryID is a *control parameter* that is defined within the collection of *select parameters*.

Notice at 03 the data source's <SelectParameters> tag, which identifies the beginning of the data source's select parameters collection. This collection contains any parameters required by the Select command. In this case, the Select command requires the @CategoryID parameter.

Notice at 04 that we have added a control parameter to the select parameters collection. The first thing to notice about this control parameter is that its Name property is set to *CategoryID*. This associates the control parameter with the @CategoryID parameter in the Where clause of the Select command at 02. The next thing to notice is that the ControlID property is set to *ddlCategory* (which is the ID of the category drop-down list at 05), and the PropertyName property is set to *SelectedValue*. This indicates that the @CategoryID parameter of the Where clause comes from the SelectedValue property of the category DropDownList control. Also notice that the Direction property is set to *Input* to indicate that this is an input parameter, and the Type property is set to *Int32* to indicate that the data type of the control parameter is a 32-bit integer.

Notice at 06 the ListBox control used to display the products in the Product table. Observe that the DataSourceID of this control is set to the ID of the SqlDataSource control at 02 to identify the data source associated with the list box. Also notice that the DataTextField property is set to *Product* to indicate that the Product attribute is to be displayed in the list box. Notice as well that the DataValueField property is set to *ProductID* to indicate that the ProductID attribute (i.e., the primary key of the Product table) is to be placed in the SelectedValue property of the list box when the end user selects a product.

Notice at 07 that we have added a <connectionStrings> section to our Web.config file as well as a connection string called *SportsPlay*.

The first screenshot in the Result section of the figure shows the list box populated with only those products associated with women's footwear. The second screenshot shows the list box populated with only those products associated with racquets.

ASPX CODE

```
01   <asp:SqlDataSource runat="server" ID="sdsDropDownListCategory"
         ConnectionString="<%$ConnectionStrings:SportsPlay%>"
         SelectCommand="SELECT CategoryID, Category
                          FROM Category
                          ORDER BY Category;">
     </asp:SqlDataSource>

02   <asp:SqlDataSource runat="server" ID="sdsListBoxProduct"
         ConnectionString="<%$ConnectionStrings:SportsPlay%>"
         SelectCommand="SELECT ProductID, Product
                          FROM Product
                          WHERE CategoryID = @CategoryID
                          ORDER BY Product;">
03       <SelectParameters>
04           <asp:ControlParameter ControlID="ddlCategory" Direction="Input"
                 Name="CategoryID" PropertyName="SelectedValue"
                 Type="Int32" />
         </SelectParameters>
     </asp:SqlDataSource>

     <asp:Label runat="server" Text="Category" /><br />
05   <asp:DropDownList runat="server" ID="ddlCategory" AutoPostBack="true"
         DataSourceID="sdsDropDownListCategory" DataTextField="Category"
         DataValueField="CategoryID" /><br />
     <asp:Label runat="server" Text="Product" /><br />
06   <asp:ListBox runat="server" ID="libProduct"
         DataSourceID="sdsListBoxProduct" DataTextField="Product"
         DataValueField="ProductID" Rows="7" />
```

WEB.CONFIG CODE

```
07   <connectionStrings>
       <add name="SportsPlay"
           connectionString="Data Source=MATRBeasley-18\SQLEXPRESS;
           Initial Catalog=SportsPlay; Integrated Security=SSPI" />
     </connectionStrings>
```

Figure 20-18. *Example of filtering a ListBox control with a DropDownList control*

RESULT

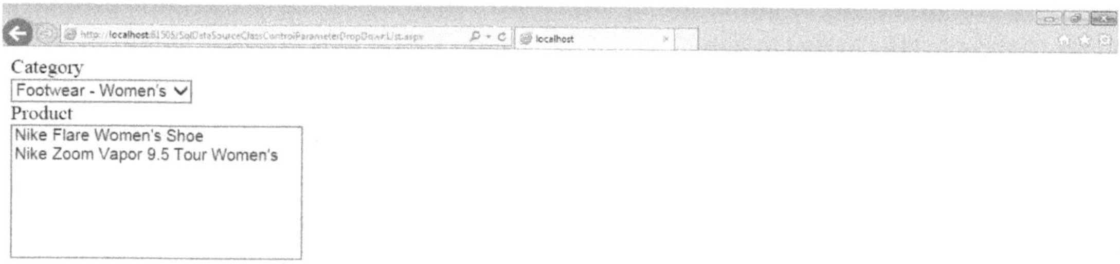

Figure 20-18. *(continued)*

Figure 20-19 shows an example of filtering a ListBox control with a TextBox control. In this example, we are populating the list box with only those products that contain the string entered into the associated text box.

Notice at 01 the SqlDataSource control for the list box of products. This data source will be used to populate the product list box at 06. Notice in the SelectCommand property of the control that we will be returning the ProductID and the Product from the Product table and that the result will be sorted in ascending order by Product. Such a sort order will permit the end user to easily locate products in the list box. Notice as well that we have included a Where clause in the Select statement. This Where clause will be used to limit the products returned from the Product table to those that contain @Product *anywhere* in the Product attribute. This is accomplished by including the key word LIKE in the Where clause with percent signs (%), which are wildcard characters in SQL, on *both* sides of the @Product parameter. Here, @Product is a *control parameter* that is defined within the collection of *select parameters*.

Notice at 02 the data source's <SelectParameters> tag, which identifies the beginning of the data source's select parameters collection. This collection contains any parameters required by the Select command. In this case, the Select command requires the @Product parameter.

Notice at 03 that we have added a control parameter to the select parameters collection. The first thing to notice about this control parameter is that its Name property is set to *Product*. This associates the control parameter with the @Product parameter in the Where clause of the Select command at 01. The next thing to notice is that the ControlID property is set to *txtProduct* (which is the ID of the product text box at 04), and the PropertyName property is set to *Text*. This indicates that the @Product parameter of the Where clause comes from the Text property of the product TextBox control. Also notice that the Direction property is set to *Input* to indicate that this is an input parameter and the Type property is set to *String* to indicate that the data type of the control parameter is a string.

Notice at 05 the Button control used to filter the items displayed in the product list box. When this button is clicked, the page will post back to the server, where the filter will be applied to the list of products returned from the database.

Notice at 06 the ListBox control used to display the products in the Product table. Observe that the DataSourceID of this control is set to the ID of the SqlDataSource control at 01 to identify the data source associated with the list box. Also notice that the DataTextField property is set to *Product* to indicate that the Product attribute is to be displayed in the list box. Notice as well that the DataValueField property is set to *ProductID* to indicate that the ProductID attribute (i.e., the primary key of the Product table) is to be placed in the SelectedValue property of the list box when the end user selects a product.

Notice at 07 that we have added a <connectionStrings> section to our Web.config file as well as a connection string called *SportsPlay*.

The first screenshot in the Result section of the figure shows the list box populated with only those products that contain the word *women* somewhere in the product. The second screenshot shows the list box populated with only those products that contain the characters *prin* somewhere in the product.

ASPX CODE

```
01  <asp:SqlDataSource runat="server" ID="sdsListBoxProduct"
        ConnectionString="<%$ConnectionStrings:SportsPlay%>"
        SelectCommand="SELECT ProductID, Product
                          FROM Product
                          WHERE Product LIKE '%' + @Product + '%'
                          ORDER BY Product;">
02      <SelectParameters>
03          <asp:ControlParameter ControlID="txtProduct" Direction="Input"
                Name="Product" PropertyName="Text" Type="String" />
        </SelectParameters>
    </asp:SqlDataSource>

    <asp:Label runat="server" Text="Product" /><br />
04  <asp:TextBox runat="server" ID="txtProduct" />
05  <asp:Button runat="server" ID="btnFilter" Text="Filter" /><br />
06  <asp:ListBox runat="server" ID="libProduct"
        DataSourceID="sdsListBoxProduct" DataTextField="Product"
        DataValueField="ProductID" Rows="7" />
```

WEB.CONFIG CODE

```
07  <connectionStrings>
      <add name="SportsPlay"
          connectionString="Data Source=MATRBeasley-18\SQLEXPRESS;
          Initial Catalog=SportsPlay; Integrated Security=SSPI" />
    </connectionStrings>
```

RESULT

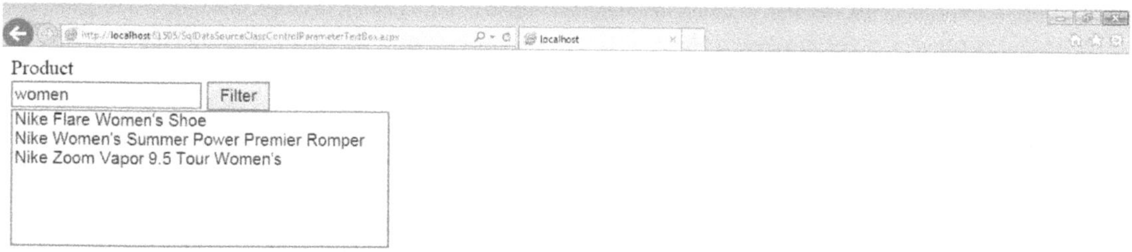

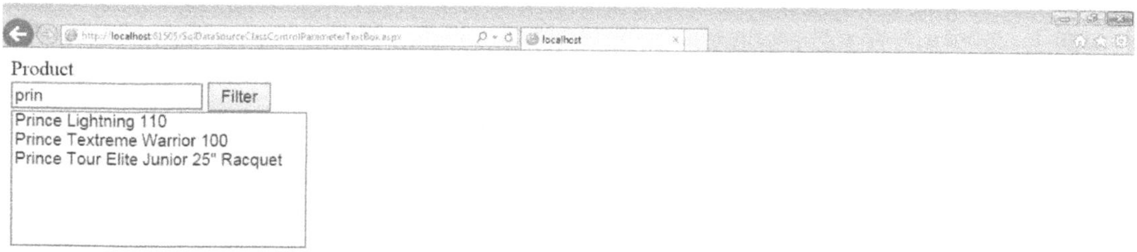

Figure 20-19. *Example of filtering a ListBox control with a TextBox control*

20.8.3.2 Filtering with Session Parameters

Another way to filter the rows returned from a database is to employ one or more session parameters. A session parameter is associated with a session variable that has already been set (perhaps on a previous page of the application) and thus resides in RAM on the server. Such a variable can contain a *naturally occurring subsetting criterion* (e.g., a product category), or it can contain a *custom subsetting criterion* (e.g., an end user–supplied string). Figure 20-20 shows an example of filtering a ListBox control with a session variable. As we learned earlier in this chapter, a category *is associated with* one or more products, and a product *is associated with* exactly one category. Since category is a naturally occurring subsetting criterion for products in the SportsPlay database, we are populating the list box with only those products associated with the category selected from, say, a drop-down list that exists *on a previous page of the application.*

Notice at 01 the SqlDataSource control for the list box of products. This data source will be used to populate the product list box at 04. Notice in the SelectCommand property of the control that we will be returning the ProductID and the Product from the Product table and that the result will be sorted in ascending order by Product. Such a sort order will permit the end user to easily locate products in the list box. Notice as well that we have included a Where clause in the Select statement. This Where clause will be used to limit the products returned from the Product table to those that have a CategoryID equal to @CategoryID. Here, @CategoryID is a *session parameter* that is defined within the collection of *select parameters.*

Notice at 02 the data source's <SelectParameters> tag, which identifies the beginning of the data source's select parameters collection. This collection contains any parameters required by the Select command. In this case, the Select command requires the @CategoryID parameter.

Notice at 03 that we have added a session parameter to the select parameters collection. The first thing to notice about this session parameter is that its Name property is set to *CategoryID*. This associates the session parameter with the @CategoryID parameter in the Where clause of the Select command at 01. The next thing to notice is that the SessionField property is set to *intCategoryID*. This is the session variable that contains the ID of the category selected from a drop-down list that exists on a previous page of the application. Also notice that the Direction property of the session parameter is set to *Input* to indicate that this is an input parameter and the Type property of the session parameter is set to *Int32* to indicate that the data type of the session parameter is a 32-bit integer.

Notice at 04 the ListBox control used to display the products in the Product table. Observe that the DataSourceID of this control is set to the ID of the SqlDataSource control at 01 to identify the data source associated with the list box. Also notice that the DataTextField property is set to *Product* to indicate that the Product attribute is to be displayed in the list box. Notice as well that the DataValueField property is set to *ProductID* to indicate that the ProductID attribute (i.e., the primary key of the Product table) is to be placed in the SelectedValue property of the list box when the end user selects a product.

Notice at 05 that we have added a <connectionStrings> section to our Web.config file as well as a connection string called *SportsPlay*.

The first screenshot in the Result section of the figure shows the list box populated with only those products associated with racquets. The second screenshot shows the list box populated with only those products associated with men's clothing. In both cases, it is assumed that the category was selected from a drop-down list that exists on a previous page of the application and that the CategoryID associated with the selection was saved in a session variable.

ASPX CODE

```
01  <asp:SqlDataSource runat="server" ID="sdsListBoxProduct"
        ConnectionString="<%$ConnectionStrings:SportsPlay%>"
        SelectCommand="SELECT ProductID, Product
                           FROM Product
                       WHERE CategoryID = @CategoryID
                       ORDER BY Product;">
02      <SelectParameters>
03          <asp:SessionParameter Direction="Input" Name="CategoryID"
                SessionField="intCategoryID" Type="Int32" />
        </SelectParameters>
    </asp:SqlDataSource>

    <asp:Label runat="server" Text="Product" /><br />
04  <asp:ListBox runat="server" ID="libProduct"
        DataSourceID="sdsListBoxProduct" DataTextField="Product"
        DataValueField="ProductID" Rows="7" />
```

WEB.CONFIG CODE

```
05  <connectionStrings>
      <add name="SportsPlay"
          connectionString="Data Source=MATRBeasley-18\SQLEXPRESS;
          Initial Catalog=SportsPlay; Integrated Security=SSPI" />
    </connectionStrings>
```

RESULT

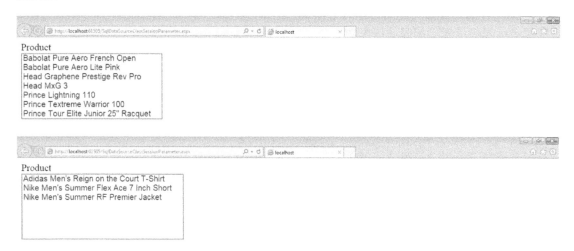

Figure 20-20. *Example of filtering a ListBox control with a session variable*

CHAPTER 21

Single-Row Database Table Maintenance

21.1 Introduction

Many modern Web applications require pages that *maintain* database table data. Such table maintenance implies the addition of new rows of table data and the modification and deletion of existing rows of table data. Although it is sometimes appropriate to display *several rows* of data simultaneously when maintaining table data, there are other times when it is better to display *a single row* of data. Displaying a single row of data on a page is most appropriate when the table being maintained contains so many *attributes* that those attributes cannot be displayed comfortably *across* the page (i.e., horizontally without the attributes disappearing off the page).

In this chapter, we will look at the FormView class. This class maintains the data in a database table (or other data sources) one row at a time. The FormView class has built-in insert, update, and delete functionality making table maintenance much easier than it would be if we were to code such functionality manually. A FormView control is bound to a *data source control*, and this data source control references an underlying data structure of some type. In the section that follows, we will bind a FormView control to a SqlDataSource control that will reference a SQL Server database table.

21.2 FormView Class

The FormView class displays a form that can be used by an end user to maintain the data in a database table (or other *data sources*) one row at a time. This class has built-in insert, update, delete, and paging functionality and can be customized using themes. To use a FormView control, we must define one or more *templates*. These templates correspond to the different *modes* that the control can be in and provide a great deal of flexibility

© Robert E. Beasley 2020
R. E. Beasley, *Essential ASP.NET Web Forms Development*, https://doi.org/10.1007/978-1-4842-5784-5_21

in terms of how the data in a table row is displayed. There are a number of FormView control templates. The ItemTemplate is the only template that is required. However, we must define a template for each mode that the control can be in. The seven FormView control templates are

- EditItemTemplate – Specifies the content and layout of the FormView control when it is in Edit mode. This template usually contains input controls and command buttons that the end user can use to modify an existing row of data in a table.

- EmptyDataTemplate – Specifies the content and layout of the FormView control when it does not contain any data. This template usually contains a message that alerts the end user to the fact that no data is available for display.

- FooterTemplate – Specifies the content and layout of the FormView control's footer row. This template usually contains any additional content that should be displayed in the footer row of the control.

- HeaderTemplate – Specifies the content and layout of the FormView control's header row. This template usually contains any additional content that should be displayed in the header row of the control.

- InsertItemTemplate – Specifies the content and layout of the FormView control when it is in Insert mode. This template usually contains input controls and command buttons that the end user can use to add a new row of data to a table.

- ItemTemplate – Specifies the content and layout of the FormView control when it is in Read-Only mode and is, thus, only being used to display data. This template is required and can contain command buttons that the end user can use to place the control into Insert or Edit mode. It can also contain a command button that the end user can use to delete an existing row of data from a table.

- PagerTemplate – Specifies the content and layout of the FormView control's pager row when the control's AllowPaging property is set to *true*. This template usually contains controls that the end user can use to move between the rows of data in a table.

A FormView control is bound to a *data source control*, and this data source control references an underlying data structure of some type. FormView controls can be bound to different kinds of data source controls, including SqlDataSource controls, ObjectDataSource controls, and AccessDataSource controls. They can also be bound to collections, like array lists. In this chapter, we will bind a FormView control to a SqlDataSource control that will reference a SQL Server database table. To bind a FormView control to a SqlDataSource control, we will set the DataSourceID property of the FormView control to the ID of the associated SqlDataSource control. By doing this, the FormView control will be able to exploit the insert, update, delete, and paging functionality of the SqlDataSource control.

A FormView control recognizes a number of special buttons. Each of these buttons behaves in a specific way, and each one invokes its own set of FormView control events. These buttons are

- Cancel button – Cancels an insert or update operation and discards any values entered by the end user. When this button is clicked, the FormView control is returned to the mode specified in the DefaultMode property.

- Delete button – Attempts to delete the displayed row from the data source. When this button is clicked, the ItemDeleting and ItemDeleted events are raised.

- Edit button – Puts the FormView control into Edit mode. When this button is clicked, the content specified in the EditItemTemplate property is displayed. The EditItemTemplate property is usually defined in such a way that the Edit button is replaced with Update and Cancel buttons when the end user clicks it.

- Insert button – Attempts to insert a new row into the data source using the values supplied by the end user. When this button is clicked, the ItemInserting and ItemInserted events are raised.

- New button – Puts the FormView control into Insert mode. When this button is clicked, the content specified in the InsertItemTemplate property is displayed. The InsertItemTemplate property is usually defined in such a way that the New button is replaced with Insert and Cancel buttons when the end user clicks it.

- Page button – Represents a button in the pager row of the
  FormView control. To specify a paging operation, we set the
  CommandArgument property of the button to *First*, *Prev*, *Next*, or
  Last or to the index of a specific page. When a page button is clicked,
  the PageIndexChanging and PageIndexChanged events are raised.

- Update – Attempts to update the displayed row in the data source
  using the values supplied by the end user. When this button is
  clicked, the ItemUpdating and ItemUpdated events are raised.

Table 21-1 shows some of the properties, methods, and events of the FormView class.

Table 21-1. *Some of the properties, methods, and events of the FormView class*

Class FormView[1]

Namespace System.Web.UI.WebControls

Properties

AllowPaging	Gets or sets a value indicating whether the paging feature is enabled.
DataKeyNames	Gets or sets an array that contains the names of the key fields for the data source.
DefaultMode	Gets or sets the data-entry mode to which the FormView control returns after an update, insert, or cancel operation.
DeleteMethod	Gets or sets the name of the method on the page that is called when the control performs a delete operation.
EditItemTemplate	Gets or sets the custom content for an item in edit mode.
EmptyDataTemplate	Gets or sets the user-defined content for the empty data row rendered when a FormView control is bound to a data source that does not contain any records.

(continued)

---

[1]All property, method, and event descriptions were taken directly from Microsoft's official documentation. The event handler methods used to handle the events of this class were omitted to conserve space. See the reference for all of the methods of this class.

Table 21-1. (*continued*)

EmptyDataText	Gets or sets the text to display in the empty data row rendered when a FormView control is bound to a data source that does not contain any records.
EnableModelValidation	Gets or sets a value that indicates whether a validator control will handle exceptions that occur during insert or update operations.
FooterTemplate	Gets or sets the user-defined content for the footer row in a FormView control.
FooterText	Gets or sets the text to display in the footer row of a FormView control.
GridLines	Gets or sets the gridline style for a FormView control.
HeaderTemplate	Gets or sets the user-defined content for the header row in a FormView control.
HeaderText	Gets or sets the text to display in the header row of a FormView control.
InsertItemTemplate	Gets or sets the custom content for an item in insert mode.
InsertMethod	Gets or sets the name of the method on the page that is called when the control performs an insert operation.
ItemTemplate	Defines the content for the data row when the FormView control is in read-only mode. This template usually contains content to display the values of an existing record.
PageCount	Gets the total number of pages required to display every record in the data source.
PageIndex	Gets or sets the index of the displayed page.
PagerTemplate	Defines the content for the pager row displayed when the paging feature is enabled (when the AllowPaging property is set to true). This template usually contains controls with which the user can navigate to another record.
SelectedValue	Gets the data-key value of the current record in a FormView control.
UpdateMethod	Gets or sets the name of the method on the page that is called when the control performs an update operation.

(*continued*)

Table 21-1. *(continued)*

Methods	
DeleteItem()	Deletes the current record in the FormView control from the data source.
InsertItem(Boolean)	Inserts the current record in the data source.
UpdateItem(Boolean)	Updates the current record in the data source.
Events	
ItemCommand	Occurs when a button within a FormView control is clicked.
ItemDeleted	Occurs when a Delete button within a FormView control is clicked, but after the delete operation.
ItemDeleting	Occurs when a Delete button within a FormView control is clicked, but before the delete operation.
ItemInserted	Occurs when an Insert button within a FormView control is clicked, but after the insert operation.
ItemInserting	Occurs when an Insert button within a FormView control is clicked, but before the insert operation.
ItemUpdated	Occurs when an Update button within a FormView control is clicked, but after the update operation.
ItemUpdating	Occurs when an Update button within a FormView control is clicked, but before the update operation.
ModeChanged	Occurs when the FormView control switches between edit, insert, and read-only mode, but after the mode has changed.
ModeChanging	Occurs when the FormView control switches between edit, insert, and read-only mode, but before the mode changes.
PageIndexChanged	Occurs when the value of the PageIndex property changes after a paging operation.
PageIndexChanging	Occurs when the value of the PageIndex property changes before a paging operation.

Reference

```
https://msdn.microsoft.com/en-us/library/system.web.ui.webcontrols.
formview(v=vs.110).aspx
```

Figure 21-1 shows an example of the FormView class.

Notice at 01 the SqlDataSource for the *product* DropDownList control. This data source will be used to populate the drop-down list at 06. As can be seen in the SelectCommand property, we will be returning the ProductID and the Product from the Product table, and the result will be sorted in ascending order by Product so that the end user can easily locate products in the drop-down list.

Notice at 02 the SqlDataSource for the *category* DropDownList control. This data source will be used to populate the drop-down list at 10, which is *inside* the FormView control. As can be seen in the SelectCommand property, we will be returning the CategoryID and the Category from the Category table, and the result will be sorted in ascending order by Category so that the end user can easily locate categories in the drop-down list.

Notice at 03 the SqlDataSource for the *product* FormView control. This data source will be used to insert new rows of data into the Product table and update and delete existing rows of data in the Product table—all via the form view, which begins at 07. As we look at this data source in detail, we will see a number of attributes that begin with an *at sign* (@). These attributes represent the data source's input and output parameters. Notice the OldValuesParameterFormatString property of the data source. As can be seen, this property is set to *original_{0}*. We will see the word *original* again in a moment. Now look at the OnInserted property of the data source. This property indicates the event handler method that will be executed immediately after a row is inserted into the Product table. This event handler method, which is defined at 22, will be used to get the primary key value of the newly inserted row so that we can position the product drop-down list and the form view on the newly inserted row. As can be seen in the SelectCommand property, we will be returning *all* of the attributes of the Product table since we will be displaying them for the end user—except when the form view is in Insert mode. Also, notice the Select statement at the end of the InsertCommand property. This statement will return the ProductID of the newly inserted product so that we can position the product drop-down list and the form view on the newly inserted row. And finally, notice in the Where clauses of the UpdateCommand and DeleteCommand properties that the ProductID is set to the *original* ProductID. The word *original* here corresponds directly with the word *original* in OldValuesParameterFormatString property we just mentioned. Setting the ProductID to the original ProductID in this fashion will ensure that the product being updated or deleted is the same product that is currently being displayed.

Notice at 04 the <SelectParameters> section of the data source. As the name implies, the parameters in this section correspond to the parameters in the Select statement of the SelectCommand property, which is defined at 03. As can be seen, we have a single select parameter. This parameter is a control parameter (i.e., its value comes from a control) and has the name ProductID, which corresponds directly to the @ProductID parameter in the Where clause of the Select statement. The value of this parameter comes from the SelectedValue property of the ddlProduct drop-down list and is a 32-bit integer.

Notice at 05 the <InsertParameters> section of the data source. As the name implies, the parameters in this section correspond to the parameters in the Insert statement of the InsertCommand property, which is defined at 03. As can be seen, we have a single insert parameter. This parameter has the name ProductID, which corresponds directly to the @ProductID parameter in the Select statement at the bottom of the InsertCommand property. Observe that this parameter is an output parameter that will hold the primary key value of the newly inserted row and that it is a 32-bit integer.

Notice at 06 the product DropDownList control. This drop-down list will be used to select the product that is displayed in the form view. There are several things to notice in this control. First, its DataSourceID property is set to *sdsDropDownListProduct*, which is the ID of the SqlDataSource defined at 01. Second, its DataTextField property is set to *Product*, which is the table attribute that will be displayed in the drop-down list. Third, its DataValueField property is set to *ProductID*, which is the primary key of the item that will be displayed in the drop-down list. And fourth, its AutoPostBack property is set to *true* so that whenever the end user selects a new product, the page will post back to the server and the newly selected product will be displayed in the form view.

Notice at 07 the product FormView control. This control will be used to insert new rows into the Product table, update existing rows in the Product table, and delete existing rows from the Product table. Notice that the DataKeyNames property of the control is set to *ProductID*. This indicates that the primary key of the data source (i.e., the Product table) is the ProductID. Notice as well the four event handler method properties. The OnItemInserted property indicates the event handler method that will be executed immediately after a row is inserted into the Product table. This event handler method, which is defined at 23, will be used to make sure that the insert was successful. The OnItemUpdated property indicates the event handler method that will be executed immediately after a row is updated in the Product table. This event handler method, which is defined at 24, will be used to make sure that the update was successful. The OnItemDeleted property indicates the event handler method that will be executed immediately after a row is deleted from the Product table. This event handler method, which is defined at 25, will be used to make sure that the delete was successful. The OnItemDeleting property indicates the event handler method that will be executed immediately *before* a row is deleted from the Product table. This event handler method, which is defined at 26, will be used to delete the product's image file from the hard drive. Since we need the name of the image file to be deleted *before* the product is deleted from the table (and removed from the form view), we must execute the code at 26 *before* the row is deleted from the Product table.[2] And finally, the OnModeChanging property indicates the event handler method that will be executed when the form view switches from Insert to Read-Only mode or from Edit to Read-Only mode. This event handler method, which is defined at 27, will be used to display a message for the end user indicating that the insert or update operation has been canceled.

Notice at 08 the beginning of the ItemTemplate, which specifies the content and layout of the FormView control when it is in Read-Only mode and is, thus, only being used to display data. As can be seen, three buttons will be displayed when the form view is initially rendered—Add, Modify, and Delete. When the Add button is clicked, the form view will go into Insert mode, since the CommandName property of the button is set to *New*. This mode will display the InsertItemTemplate at 13. When the Modify button is clicked, the form view will go into Edit mode, since the CommandName property of the button is set to *Edit*. This mode will display the EditItemTemplate at 16. And when the Delete button is clicked, the form view will go into Delete mode, since the CommandName property of the button is set to *Delete*. Note that this mode will continue to display the ItemTemplate since the end user will not be adding for modifying data. As can be seen, the OnClientClick property of the button is set to execute a JavaScript confirm function. If the end user clicks OK when the confirmation message is displayed, the delete command will be executed. However, if the end user clicks Cancel when the confirmation message is displayed, the delete command will *not* be executed.

Notice at 09 and 12 the *Copy Area Start* and *Copy Area End* comments, respectively. The technique we will use to ensure that the ItemTemplate, the InsertItemTemplate, and the EditItemTemplate are all identical (and thus look consistent from mode to mode) is to code and test the table rows between these two comments first and then copy and

---

[2]If the product's image file is deleted from the hard drive and the database table delete is unsuccessful, the product will still exist in the Product table, but the image file will no longer exist on the hard drive. Thus, a more sophisticated approach to keeping the two in sync may be necessary.

paste those table rows between the *Copy Area Start* and *Copy Area End* comments at 14 and 15 and between the *Copy Area Start* and *Copy Area End* comments at 17 and 18. If the code between *any* of the comments in the ItemTemplate, the InsertItemTemplate, or the EditItemTemplate is modified, that code should be copied and pasted between the comments in the other two templates. A failure to employ this technique (or something similar to it) will almost certainly result in more expensive modifications to the three templates down the road in an effort to keep the templates in sync.

Notice at 10 the category DropDownList control. There are several things to notice about this control. First, its DataSourceID property is set to *sdsDropDownListCategory*, which is the ID of the SqlDataSource defined at 02. Second, its DataTextField property is set to *Category*, which is the table attribute that will be displayed in the drop-down list. Third, its DataValueField property is set to *CategoryID*, which is the primary key of the item that will be displayed in the drop-down list. And fourth, its SelectedValue property is set to *<%# Bind("CategoryID") %>*, which binds the CategoryID of the currently selected category to the CategoryID of the currently displayed product. Thus, when a new row is inserted into the Product table or an existing row is updated in the Product table, the CategoryID attribute of the product will be set to the CategoryID attribute of the currently selected category.

Notice at 11 the product TextBox control. There are two things to notice about this control. First, its MaxLength property is set to *50* so that the end user cannot enter a product longer than 50 characters. If he or she were permitted to enter a product longer than 50 characters and did so, the insert or update would fail due to a *truncation* error. This is because the maximum size of the Product attribute in the Product table is 50 characters (see Figure 20-1). Keep in mind that, in a real-world application, we would *also* need to use the validation controls supplied by ASP.NET to help us avoid other types of insert and update failures (e.g., null errors, type errors) and to make sure we keep bad data out of the database in general. And second, its Text property is set to *<%# Bind("Product") %>*, which binds the Text property of the TextBox control to the Product attribute of the currently displayed product. Thus, when a new row is inserted into the Product table or an existing row is updated in the Product table, the Product attribute of the product will be set to the Text property of the TextBox control.

Notice at 13 the beginning of the InsertItemTemplate, which specifies the content and layout of the FormView control when it is in Insert mode. As can be seen, two buttons will be displayed when the form view is in Insert mode—Save and Cancel. When the Save button is clicked, the form view will attempt to insert a new product into the Product table, since the CommandName property of the button is set to *Insert*. When the Cancel button is clicked, the form view will cancel the insert operation, discard any values entered by the end user, return to Read-Only mode, and display the ItemTemplate at 08, since the CommandName property of the button is set to *Cancel*.

Notice at 16 the beginning of the EditItemTemplate, which specifies the content and layout of the FormView control when it is in Edit mode. As can be seen, two buttons will be displayed when the form view is in Edit mode—Save and Cancel. When the Save button is clicked, the form view will attempt to update the currently displayed product in the Product table, since the CommandName property of the button is set to *Update*. When the Cancel button is clicked, the form view will cancel the update operation, discard any values entered by the end user, return to Read-Only mode, and display the ItemTemplate at 08, since the CommandName property of the button is set to *Cancel*.

Notice at 19 that the System.Data.SqlClient namespace has been added to the list of using directives (which appears at the top of the code behind file). This was done to obviate the need to specify the fully qualified name of the SqlException class (i.e., System.Data.SqlClient.SqlException) each time we want to use one of its properties. We will need the SqlException class to check for foreign key constraint violations at 25.

Notice at 20 that the System.IO namespace has also been added to the list of using directives so we are not required to specify the fully qualified name of the File class (i.e., System.IO.File) each time we want to use one of its methods. We will need the File class to delete a file from the server's hard drive after we have checked for its existence. This code is shown at 26.

Notice at 21 that we have defined a variable that will store the primary key value of a newly inserted product.

Notice at 22 that we are getting the primary key value of a newly inserted product and assigning that value to the variable defined at 21. Note that the primary key value of a newly inserted row is retrieved from the database by the Select statement at the end of the InsertCommand property at 03. After the primary key value is saved, it will be used in the FormViewItemInserted method at 23 to position the product drop-down list and the form view itself on the newly inserted product.

Notice at 23 the ItemInserted event handler method of the product form view. This method is executed when the ItemInserted event of the form view is raised, which is immediately after an insert operation is attempted. Notice in the definition of the event handler method the FormViewInsertedEventArgs class—the alias of which is e. This class is passed to the event handler method so we can determine the status of our insert operations. As can be seen, if an exception is not returned from the database and exactly one row in the database is affected (i.e., inserted), we will display a message stating that the product was successfully added. In addition, we will rebind the Product table (with its new product) to the product drop-down list, set the SelectedValue property of the product drop-down list to the value of the newly inserted primary key, and rebind the Product table (with its new product) to the form view. This process is necessary if we want the newly inserted product to immediately display in the product drop-down list and form view. If an exception is not returned from the database, but something other than one row in the database is affected (i.e., inserted), we will display an appropriate error message and keep the form view in insert mode. And finally, if an exception *is* returned from the database, we will display an appropriate error message, keep the form view in insert mode, and indicate that we are handling the exception programmatically.

Notice at 24 the ItemUpdated event handler method of the product form view. This method is executed when the ItemUpdated event of the form view is raised, which is immediately after an update operation is attempted. Notice in the definition of the event handler method the FormViewUpdatedEventArgs class—the alias of which is e. This class is passed to the event handler method so we can determine the status of our update operations. As can be seen, if an exception is not returned from the database and exactly one row in the database is affected (i.e., updated), we will display a message stating that the product was successfully modified. In addition, we will rebind the Product table (with its updated product) to the product drop-down list and rebind the Product table (with its updated product) to the form view. This process is necessary if we want the newly updated product to immediately display in the product drop-down list and form view. If an exception is not returned from the database, but something other than one row in the database is affected (i.e., updated), we will display an appropriate error message and keep the form view in edit mode. And finally, if an exception *is* returned from the database, we will display an appropriate error message, keep the form view in edit mode, and indicate that we are handling the exception programmatically.

Notice at 25 the ItemDeleted event handler method of the product form view. This method is executed when the ItemDeleted event of the form view is raised, which is immediately after a delete operation is attempted. Notice in the definition of the event handler method the FormViewDeletedEventArgs class—the alias of which is e. This class is passed to the event handler method so we can determine the status of our delete operations. As can be seen, if an exception is not returned from the database, and exactly one row in the database is affected (i.e., deleted), we will display a message stating that the product was successfully deleted. In addition, we will rebind the Product table (without the deleted product) to the product drop-down list and rebind the Product table (without the deleted product) to the form view. This process is necessary if we no longer want the newly deleted product to display in the product drop-down list and form view. If an exception is not returned from the database, but something other than one row in the database is affected (i.e., deleted), we will display an appropriate error message. If an exception *is* returned from the database and the SqlException number is 547, which indicates that a foreign key constraint violation has occurred, we will display an appropriate error message and indicate that we are handling the exception programmatically. And finally, if some other exception is returned from the database, we will display an appropriate error message and indicate that we are handling the exception programmatically.

Notice at 26 the ItemDeleting event handler method of the product form view. This method is executed when the ItemDeleting event of the form view is raised, which is immediately *before* a delete operation is attempted. Notice in this method that we are deleting from the server's hard drive the image file associated with the product to be deleted from the Product table (if the file exists). Note that since the image TextBox control exists *within* the form view, it is *not* directly accessible in the code behind of the page like the other server controls are. Thus, we must first locate the TextBox control in the form view (via its ID property using the FindControl method of the Control class) and then get the Text property of the control as usual.

Notice at 27 the ModeChanging event handler method of the product form view. This method is executed when the ModeChanging event of the form view is raised, which is when the form view switches from Insert mode to Read-Only mode or from Edit mode to Read-Only mode. Notice in the definition of the event handler method the FormViewModeEventArgs class—the alias of which is e. This class is passed to the event handler method so that we can determine, among other things, whether or not the end user is canceling an insert or update operation. As can be seen, if the end user cancels such an operation, we will display a message indicating that the insert or update operation was canceled and that no data was affected.

Notice at 28 that we have added a <connectionStrings> section to our Web.config file as well as a connection string called *SportsPlay*. This connection string provides the details of the SQL Server database that will be used by the data sources at 01, 02, and 03. See Chapter 20, titled "Database Design, SQL, and Data Binding," for a detailed description of this connection string.

The first screenshot in the Result section of the figure shows the product form view in Read-Only mode. Thus, the ItemTemplate is being displayed. The second screenshot shows the product form view in Insert mode. Thus, the InsertItemTemplate is being displayed. The third screenshot shows the product form view in Edit mode. Thus, the

EditItemTemplate is being displayed. Notice that the product description is being modified. The fourth screenshot shows the product form view in Read-Only mode again—after the product description has been modified. Thus, the ItemTemplate is being displayed once again. And the fifth screenshot shows the product form view in Read-Only mode after the end user has clicked the Delete button.

```
ASPX CODE

01   <asp:SqlDataSource runat="server" ID="sdsDropDownListProduct"
         ConnectionString="<%$ConnectionStrings:SportsPlay%>"
         SelectCommand="SELECT ProductID, Product
                          FROM Product
                          ORDER BY Product;">
     </asp:SqlDataSource>

02   <asp:SqlDataSource runat="server" ID="sdsDropDownListCategory"
         ConnectionString="<%$ConnectionStrings:SportsPlay%>"
         SelectCommand="SELECT CategoryID, Category
                          FROM Category
                          ORDER BY Category;">
     </asp:SqlDataSource>

     ⋮
     ⋮ (Code continues.)
     ⋮

03   <asp:SqlDataSource runat="server" ID="sdsFormViewProduct"
         ConnectionString="<%$ConnectionStrings:SportsPlay%>"
         OldValuesParameterFormatString="original_{0}"
         OnInserted="sdsFormViewProduct_Inserted"
         SelectCommand="SELECT *
                          FROM Product
                          WHERE ProductID = @ProductID;"
         InsertCommand="INSERT
                          INTO Product
                              (
                              CategoryID,
                              SupplierID,
                              Product,
                              Description,
                              Image,
                              Price,
                              NumberInStock,
                              NumberOnOrder,
                              ReorderLevel
                              )
                      VALUES
```

Figure 21-1. *Example of the FormView class*

```
                                    (
                                    @CategoryID,
                                    @SupplierID,
                                    @Product,
                                    @Description,
                                    @Image,
                                    @Price,
                                    @NumberInStock,
                                    @NumberOnOrder,
                                    @ReorderLevel
                                    );
                        SELECT @ProductID = SCOPE_IDENTITY();"
         UpdateCommand="UPDATE Product
                           SET CategoryID = @CategoryID,
                               SupplierID = @SupplierID,
                               Product = @Product,
                               Description = @Description,
                               Image = @Image,
                               Price = @Price,
                               NumberInStock = @NumberInStock,
                               NumberOnOrder = @NumberOnOrder,
                               ReorderLevel = @ReorderLevel
                         WHERE ProductID = @original_ProductID;"
         DeleteCommand="DELETE
                          FROM Product
                         WHERE ProductID = @original_ProductID;">
04       <SelectParameters>
             <asp:ControlParameter ControlID="ddlProduct" Name="ProductID"
                 PropertyName="SelectedValue" Type="Int32" />
         </SelectParameters>
05       <InsertParameters>
             <asp:Parameter Direction="Output" Name="ProductID" Type="Int32" />
         </InsertParameters>
     </asp:SqlDataSource>

     <asp:Label runat="server" Font-Bold="true" Text="Maintain Products" />
     <br /><br />

     <asp:Label runat="server" Text="Message " />
     <asp:Label runat="server" ID="lblMessage" /><br /><br />

     <asp:Label runat="server" Text="Product" /><br />
06   <asp:DropDownList runat="server" ID="ddlProduct" AutoPostBack="true"
         DataSourceID="sdsDropDownListProduct" DataTextField="Product"
         DataValueField="ProductID" /><br /><br />
```

Figure 21-1. (continued)

```
07   <asp:FormView runat="server" ID="fovProduct"
         DataKeyNames="ProductID"
         DataSourceID="sdsFormViewProduct"
         EmptyDataText="No data to display"
         OnModeChanging="fovProduct_ModeChanging"
         OnItemDeleted="fovProduct_ItemDeleted"
         OnItemDeleting="fovProduct_ItemDeleting"
         OnItemInserted="fovProduct_ItemInserted"
         OnItemUpdated="fovProduct_ItemUpdated">
08       <ItemTemplate>
             <asp:Button runat="server" ID="btnAdd" CausesValidation="false"
                 CommandName="New" Text="Add" />
             <asp:Button runat="server" ID="btnModify" CausesValidation="false"
                 CommandName="Edit" Text="Modify" />
             <asp:Button runat="server" ID="btnDelete" CausesValidation="false"
                 CommandName="Delete" OnClientClick="return confirm('Are you
                 sure you want to delete this item? Click OK to delete it.
                 Click Cancel to keep it.');" Text="Delete" /><br /><br />
             <asp:Table runat="server" Enabled="false">
09               <%--Copy Area Start--%>
                 <asp:TableRow VerticalAlign="Top">
                     <asp:TableCell>
                         <asp:Table runat="server">
                             <asp:TableRow>
                                 <asp:TableCell>
                                     <asp:Label runat="server"
                                         Text="Category" />
                                 </asp:TableCell>
                                 <asp:TableCell>
10                                   <asp:DropDownList runat="server"
                                         ID="ddlCategory"
                                         DataSourceID="sdsDropDownListCategory"
                                         DataTextField="Category"
                                         DataValueField="CategoryID"
                                         SelectedValue='<%# Bind("CategoryID")
                                         %>' />
                                 </asp:TableCell>
                             </asp:TableRow>
                             ⋮
                             ⋮ (Code continues.)
                             ⋮
                             <asp:TableRow>
                                 <asp:TableCell>
                                     <asp:Label runat="server"
                                         Text="Product" />
                                 </asp:TableCell>
```

Figure 21-1. (continued)

```
                                <asp:TableCell>
11                                  <asp:TextBox runat="server"
                                        ID="txtProduct" MaxLength="50"
                                        Text='<%# Bind("Product") %>' />
                                </asp:TableCell>
                            </asp:TableRow>
                              ⋮
                              ⋮ (Code continues.)
                              ⋮
                        </asp:Table>
                    </asp:TableCell>
                </asp:TableRow>
12              <%--Copy Area End--%>
            </asp:Table>
        </ItemTemplate>
13      <InsertItemTemplate>
            <asp:Button runat="server" ID="btnAddSave"
                CausesValidation="true" CommandName="Insert"
                Text="Save" />
            <asp:Button runat="server" ID="btnAddCancel"
                CausesValidation="false" CommandName="Cancel"
                Text="Cancel" /><br /><br />
            <asp:Table runat="server" Enabled="true">
14              <%--Copy Area Start--%>
                  ⋮
                  ⋮ (Code continues.)
                  ⋮
15              <%--Copy Area End--%>
            </asp:Table>
        </InsertItemTemplate>
16      <EditItemTemplate>
            <asp:Button runat="server" ID="btnModifySave"
                CausesValidation="true" CommandName="Update"
                Text="Save" />
            <asp:Button runat="server" ID="btnModifyCancel"
                CausesValidation="false" CommandName="Cancel"
                Text="Cancel" /><br /><br />
            <asp:Table runat="server" Enabled="true">
17              <%--Copy Area Start--%>
                  ⋮
                  ⋮ (Code continues.)
                  ⋮
18              <%--Copy Area End--%>
            </asp:Table>
        </EditItemTemplate>
    </asp:FormView>
```

Figure 21-1. *(continued)*

CODE BEHIND

```
19   using System.Data.SqlClient;
20   using System.IO;

     // Define the variable used to store the newly inserted primary key.
21   Int32 i32NewlyInsertedPrimaryKey;

     protected void Page_Load(object sender, EventArgs e)
     {
     }

22   protected void sdsFormViewProduct_Inserted(object sender,
         SqlDataSourceStatusEventArgs e)
     {

         // Get the primary key of the newly inserted row. This is used
         // in the FormViewItemInserted method to position the associated
         // DropDownList and FormView on the newly inserted row.
         if (e.Exception == null)
         {
             i32NewlyInsertedPrimaryKey =
                 (Int32)e.Command.Parameters["@ProductID"].Value;
         }

     }

23   protected void fovProduct_ItemInserted(object sender,
         FormViewInsertedEventArgs e)
     {

         // Make sure the database call was successful.
         if (e.Exception == null)
         {
             if (e.AffectedRows == 1)
             {
                 lblMessage.ForeColor = System.Drawing.Color.Green;
                 lblMessage.Text = "Product successfully added.";
                 // Refresh the page data.
                 ddlProduct.DataBind();
                 ddlProduct.SelectedValue =
                     i32NewlyInsertedPrimaryKey.ToString();
                 fovProduct.DataBind();
             }
```

Figure 21-1. *(continued)*

```
            else
            {
                lblMessage.ForeColor = System.Drawing.Color.Red;
                lblMessage.Text = "Product NOT successfully added. Please
                    report this message to....: The number of products
                    added was not equal to 1.";
                e.KeepInInsertMode = true;
            }
        }
        else
        {
            // An exception has occurred.
            lblMessage.ForeColor = System.Drawing.Color.Red;
            lblMessage.Text = "Product NOT successfully added. Please report
                this message to....: " + e.Exception.Message;
            e.KeepInInsertMode = true;
            e.ExceptionHandled = true;
        }

    }

24  protected void fovProduct_ItemUpdated(object sender,
        FormViewUpdatedEventArgs e)
    {

        // Make sure the database call was successful.
        if (e.Exception == null)
        {
            if (e.AffectedRows == 1)
            {
                lblMessage.ForeColor = System.Drawing.Color.Green;
                lblMessage.Text = "Product successfully modified.";
                // Refresh the page data.
                String strSelectedValue;
                strSelectedValue = ddlProduct.SelectedValue;
                ddlProduct.DataBind();
                ddlProduct.SelectedValue = strSelectedValue.ToString();
                fovProduct.DataBind();
            }
            else
            {
                lblMessage.ForeColor = System.Drawing.Color.Red;
                lblMessage.Text = "Product NOT successfully modified.
                    Please report this message to....: The number of products
                    modified was not equal to 1.";
                e.KeepInEditMode = true;
            }
        }
```

Figure 21-1. *(continued)*

```
        else
        {
            // An exception has occurred.
            lblMessage.ForeColor = System.Drawing.Color.Red;
            lblMessage.Text = "Product NOT successfully modified.
                Please report this message to....: " +
                e.Exception.Message;
            e.KeepInEditMode = true;
            e.ExceptionHandled = true;
        }

    }
25  protected void fovProduct_ItemDeleted(object sender,
        FormViewDeletedEventArgs e)
    {

        // Make sure the database call was successful.
        if (e.Exception == null)
        {
            if (e.AffectedRows == 1)
            {
                lblMessage.ForeColor = System.Drawing.Color.Green;
                lblMessage.Text = "Product successfully deleted.";
                // Refresh the page data.
                ddlProduct.DataBind();
                fovProduct.DataBind();
            }
            else
            {
                lblMessage.ForeColor = System.Drawing.Color.Red;
                lblMessage.Text = "Product NOT successfully deleted.
                    Please report this message to....: The number of products
                    deleted was not equal to 1.";
            }
        }
        else
        {
            if (((SqlException)e.Exception).Number.Equals(547))
            {
                // A foreign key constraint violation has occurred.
                lblMessage.ForeColor = System.Drawing.Color.Red;
                lblMessage.Text = "Product NOT successfully deleted because it
                    is associated with at least one order line. To delete this
                    product, you must first delete all of its associated order
                    lines.";
                e.ExceptionHandled = true;
            }
```

Figure 21-1. *(continued)*

```
        else
        {
            // Some other exception has occurred.
            lblMessage.ForeColor = System.Drawing.Color.Red;
            lblMessage.Text = "Product NOT successfully deleted.
                Please report this message to....: " +
                e.Exception.Message;
            e.ExceptionHandled = true;
        }
    }

}

26 protected void fovProduct_ItemDeleting(object sender,
        FormViewDeleteEventArgs e)
    {

        // Get the filename of the image to be deleted.
        TextBox txtImage = (TextBox)fovProduct.FindControl("txtImage");
        String strImage = txtImage.Text;
        // Delete the associated file from the hard drive.
        String strFilePath = Request.PhysicalApplicationPath + "Images\\" +
            strImage;
        if (File.Exists(strFilePath))
        {
            File.Delete(strFilePath);
        }

    }

27  protected void fovProduct_ModeChanging(object sender,
        FormViewModeEventArgs e)
    {

        // Cancel the insert or update operation.
        if (e.CancelingEdit)
        {
            lblMessage.ForeColor = System.Drawing.Color.Red;
            lblMessage.Text = "Operation cancelled. No data was affected.";
        }

    }
```

Figure 21-1. (continued)

WEB.CONFIG CODE

```
28  <connectionStrings>
      <add name="SportsPlay"
          connectionString="Data Source=MATRBeasley-18\SQLEXPRESS;
          Initial Catalog=SportsPlay; Integrated Security=SSPI" />
    </connectionStrings>
```

RESULT

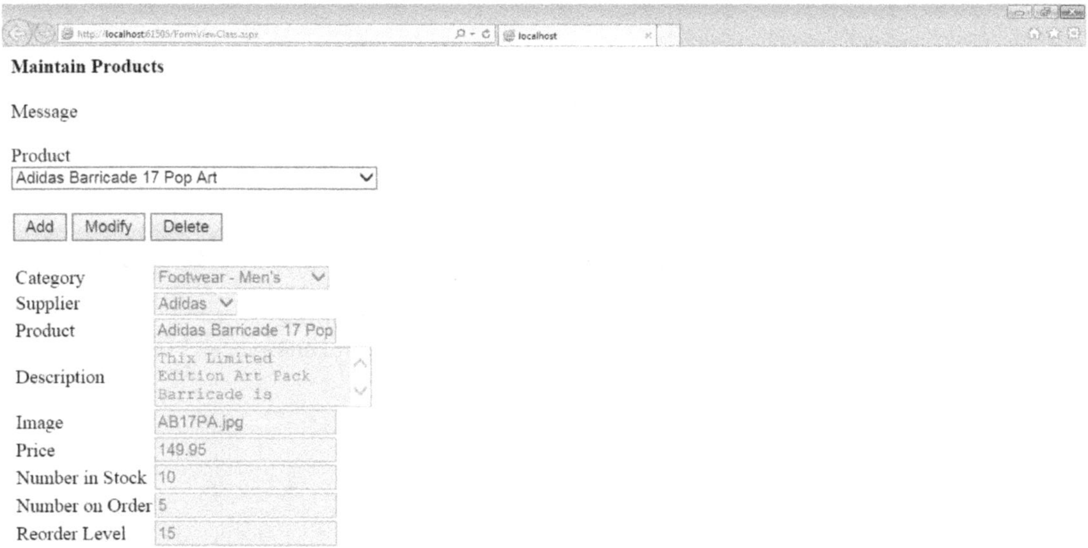

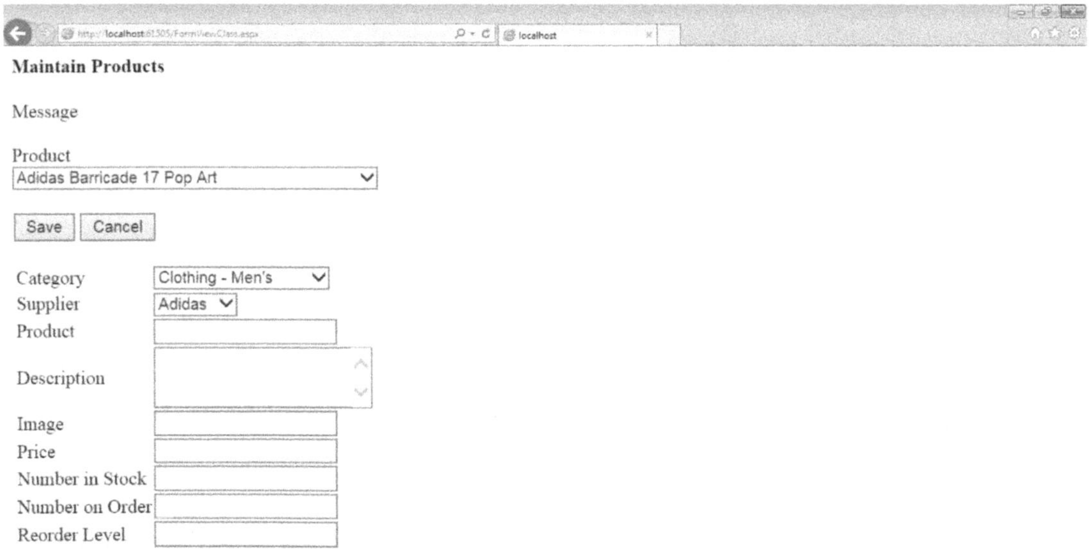

Figure 21-1. *(continued)*

Image	AB17PA.jpg
Price	149.95
Number in Stock	10
Number on Order	5
Reorder Level	15

Maintain Products

Message Product successfully modified.

| Product | |
| Adidas Barricade 17 Pop Art | ∨ |

| Add | Modify | Delete |

| Product | |
| Adidas Barricade 17 Pop | |

| Description | This Limited Edition Art Pack Barricade is |

Category	Footwear - Men's ∨
Supplier	Adidas ∨
Image	AB17PA.jpg
Price	149.95
Number in Stock	10
Number on Order	5
Reorder Level	15

Message from webpage

Are you sure you want to delete this item? Click OK to delete it. Click Cancel to keep it.

| OK | Cancel |

Figure 21-1. *(continued)*

417

CHAPTER 22

Multiple-Row Database Table Maintenance

22.1 Introduction

Many modern Web applications require pages that *maintain* database table data. Such table maintenance implies the addition of new rows of table data and the modification and deletion of existing rows of table data. Although it is sometimes appropriate to display a *single row* of data when maintaining table data, there are other times when it is better to display *several rows* of data simultaneously. Displaying several rows of data on a page is most appropriate when the table being maintained contains few enough *attributes* that those attributes can be displayed comfortably *across* the page (i.e., horizontally without the attributes disappearing off the page). When the table being maintained contains so many *rows* that those rows cannot be displayed comfortably *down* the page (i.e., too much scrolling is required to locate a given row), we can employ a row filter of some kind, or we can utilize data paging (discussed later).

In this chapter, we will begin by looking at the ListView class. This class maintains the data in a database table (or other data sources) several rows at a time. The ListView class has built-in insert, update, delete, sort, and item selection functionality making table maintenance much easier than it would be if we were to code such functionality manually. A ListView control is bound to a *data source control*, and this data source control references an underlying data structure of some type. We will bind a ListView control to a SqlDataSource control that will reference a SQL Server database table. After that, we will discuss the DataPager class, which displays paging controls that can be used by an end user to view the data pages of a ListView control. Next, we will consider the NextPreviousPagerField class. This class displays navigation controls in a DataPager control that can be used by an end user to jump to the *first* page of a ListView control,

© Robert E. Beasley 2020

R. E. Beasley, *Essential ASP.NET Web Forms Development*, https://doi.org/10.1007/978-1-4842-5784-5_22

move to the *previous* page of a ListView control, move to the *next* page of a ListView control, and/or jump to the *last* page of a ListView control. And finally, we will look at the NumericPagerField class, which displays navigation controls in a DataPager control that can be used by an end user to select a page in a ListView control by its page number.

22.2 ListView Class

The ListView class displays a list that can be used by an end user to maintain the data in a database table (or other *data sources*) several rows at a time. This class has built-in insert, update, delete, sort, and item selection functionality, can be used in conjunction with a DataPager control for paging functionality, and can be customized using themes. To use a ListView control, we must define one or more *templates*. These templates correspond to the different *modes* that the control can be in and provide a great deal of flexibility in terms of how the data in a table row is displayed. There are a number of ListView control templates. The ItemTemplate is the only template that is required. However, we must define a template for each mode that the control can be in. The eleven ListView control templates are

- AlternatingItemTemplate – Specifies alternating ItemTemplates so that it is easier to distinguish between consecutive items in the ListView control. (See the ItemTemplate below.)

- EditItemTemplate – Specifies the content and layout of an individual item in the ListView control when the control is in Edit mode. This template usually contains input controls and command buttons that the end user can use to modify an existing row of data in a table.

- EmptyDataTemplate – Specifies the content and layout of the ListView control when it does not contain any data. This template usually contains a message that alerts the end user to the fact that no data is available for display.

- EmptyItemTemplate – Specifies the content and layout of the individual items in the ListView control when there are no more items to display in the last row of the current data page.

- GroupSeparatorTemplate – Specifies the content and layout to display between the groups of items in the ListView control.

- GroupTemplate – Specifies a container control (e.g., table) that will hold the content defined in the ItemTemplate or EmptyItemTemplate.

- InsertItemTemplate – Specifies the content and layout of an individual item in the ListView control when the control is in Insert mode. This template usually contains input controls and command buttons that the end user can use to add a new row of data to a table. The InsertItemTemplate can be positioned at the top of the ListView control or at the bottom of the ListView control by specifying the desired location in the InsertItemPosition property of the ListView control. The InsertItemTemplate will only be displayed if the InsertItemPosition property of the ListView control is set to *FirstItem* or *LastItem*.

- ItemSeparatorTemplate – Specifies the content and layout to display between individual items.

- ItemTemplate – Specifies the content and layout of an individual item in the ListView control when the control is in Read-Only mode and is, thus, only being used to display data. This template is required and can contain command buttons that the end user can use to place the control into Edit mode. It can also contain a command button that the end user can use to delete an existing row of data from a table.

- LayoutTemplate – Specifies the content of the root container of a ListView control.

- SelectedItemTemplate – Specifies the content and layout of an individual item in the ListView control after the item has been selected so that it can be differentiated from the other items in the ListView control. This template can contain input controls and command buttons that the end user can use to modify an existing row of data in a table or delete an existing row of data from a table.

A ListView control is bound to a *data source control*, and this data source control references an underlying data structure of some type. ListView controls can be bound to different kinds of data source controls, including SqlDataSource controls, ObjectDataSource controls, and AccessDataSource controls. They can also be bound to collections, like array lists. In this chapter, we will bind a ListView control to a

SqlDataSource control that will reference a SQL Server database table. To bind a ListView control to a SqlDataSource control, we will set the DataSourceID property of the ListView control to the ID of the associated SqlDataSource control. By doing this, the ListView control will be able to exploit the insert, update, delete, and sorting functionality of the SqlDataSource control.

A ListView control recognizes a number of special buttons. Each of these buttons behaves in a specific way, and each one invokes its own set of ListView control events. These buttons are

- Cancel button – Cancels an insert or update operation and discards any values entered by the end user. When this button is clicked, the ItemCanceling event is raised.

- Delete button – Attempts to delete the selected row from the data source. When this button is clicked, the ItemDeleting and ItemDeleted events are raised.

- Edit button – Puts the selected item of the ListView control into Edit mode. When this button is clicked, the content specified in the EditItemTemplate property is displayed and the ItemEditing event is raised. The EditItemTemplate property is usually defined in such a way that the Edit button is replaced with Update and Cancel buttons when the end user clicks it.

- Insert button – Attempts to insert a new row into the data source using the values supplied by the end user. When this button is clicked, the ItemInserting and ItemInserted events are raised.

- Select button – Sets the SelectedIndex property of the ListView control to the DisplayIndex property value of the selected item. When this button is clicked, the SelectedIndexChanging and SelectedIndexChanged events are raised.

- Sort – Sorts the columns listed in the CommandArgument property of the button. When this button is clicked, the Sorting and Sorted events are raised.

- Update – Attempts to update the selected row in the data source using the values supplied by the end user. When this button is clicked, the ItemUpdating and ItemUpdated events are raised.

Table 22-1 shows some of the properties, methods, and events of the ListView class.

Table 22-1. *Some of the properties, methods, and events of the ListView class*

Class ListView[1]

Namespace System.Web.UI.WebControls

Properties

AlternatingItemTemplate	Gets or sets the custom content for the alternating data item in a ListView control.
DataKeyNames	Gets or sets an array that contains the names of the primary key fields for the items displayed in a ListView control.
DeleteMethod	Gets or sets the name of the method to call in order to delete data.
EditItemTemplate	Gets or sets the custom content for the item in edit mode.
EmptyDataTemplate	Gets or sets the user-defined content for the empty template that is rendered when a ListView control is bound to a data source that does not contain any records.
EmptyItemTemplate	Gets or sets the user-defined content for the empty item that is rendered in a ListView control when there are no more data items to display in the last row of the current data page.
GroupSeparatorTemplate	Gets or sets the user-defined content for the separator between groups in a ListView control.
GroupTemplate	Gets or sets the user-defined content for the group container in a ListView control.
InsertItemPosition	Gets or sets the location of the InsertItemTemplate template when it is rendered as part of the ListView control.
InsertItemTemplate	Gets or sets the custom content for an insert item in the ListView control.
InsertMethod	Gets or sets the name of the method to call in order to insert data.

(continued)

---

[1]All property, method, and event descriptions were taken directly from Microsoft's official documentation. The event handler methods used to handle the events of this class were omitted to conserve space. See the reference for all of the methods of this class.

Table 22-1. (*continued*)

Properties

ItemSeparatorTemplate	Gets or sets the custom content for the separator between the items in a ListView control.
ItemTemplate	Gets or sets the custom content for the data item in a ListView control.
LayoutTemplate	Gets or sets the custom content for the root container in a ListView control.
SelectedDataKey	Gets the data-key value for the selected item in a ListView control.
SelectedIndex	Gets or sets the index of the selected item in a ListView control.
SelectedItemTemplate	Gets or sets the custom content for the selected item in a ListView control.
SelectedValue	Gets the data-key value of the selected item in a ListView control.
SortDirection	Gets the sort direction of the field or fields that are being sorted.
SortExpression	Gets the sort expression that is associated with the field or fields that are being sorted.
UpdateMethod	Gets or sets the name of the method to call in order to update data.

Methods

DeleteItem(Int32)	Deletes the record at the specified index from the data source.
InsertNewItem(Boolean)	Inserts the current record in the data source.
UpdateItem(Int32, Boolean)	Updates the record at the specified index in the data source.

Events

ItemCanceling	Occurs when a cancel operation is requested, but before the ListView control cancels the insert or edit operation.
ItemCommand	Occurs when a button in a ListView control is clicked.
ItemDataBound	Occurs when a data item is bound to data in a ListView control.
ItemDeleted	Occurs when a delete operation is requested, after the ListView control deletes the item.

(*continued*)

Table 22-1. (*continued*)

Events

ItemDeleting	Occurs when a delete operation is requested, but before the ListView control deletes the item.
ItemEditing	Occurs when an edit operation is requested, but before the ListView item is put in edit mode.
ItemInserted	Occurs when an insert operation is requested, after the ListView control has inserted the item in the data source.
ItemInserting	Occurs when an insert operation is requested, but before the ListView control performs the insert.
ItemUpdated	Occurs when an update operation is requested, after the ListView control updates the item.
ItemUpdating	Occurs when an update operation is requested, but before the ListView control updates the item.
SelectedIndexChanged	Occurs when an item's Select button is clicked, after the ListView control handles the select operation.
SelectedIndexChanging	Occurs when an item's Select button is clicked, but before the ListView control handles the select operation.
Sorted	Occurs when a sort operation is requested, after the ListView control handles the sort operation.
Sorting	Occurs when a sort operation is requested, but before the ListView control handles the sort operation.

Reference

https://msdn.microsoft.com/en-us/library/system.web.ui.webcontrols.
listview(v=vs.110).aspx

Figure 22-1 shows an example of the ListView class.

Notice at 01 the SqlDataSource for the *category* DropDownList control. This data source will be used to populate the drop-down list at 09, which is *inside* the ListView control. As can be seen in the SelectCommand property, we will be returning the CategoryID and the Category from the Category table, and the result will be sorted in ascending order by Category so that the end user can easily locate categories in the drop-down list.

Notice at 02 the SqlDataSource for the *product* ListView control. This data source will be used to insert new rows of data into the Product table and update and delete existing rows of data in the Product table—all via the list view, which begins at 03. As we look at this data source in detail, we will see a number of attributes that begin with an *at sign* (@). These attributes represent the data source's input parameters. Notice the OldValuesParameterFormatString property of the data source. As can be seen, this property is set to *original_{0}*. We will see the word *original* again in a moment. Notice in the SelectCommand property that we will be joining the Category, Supplier, and Product tables and returning *all* of their respective attributes since we will be displaying most of them for the end user—except when the list view is in Insert mode. And finally, notice in the Where clauses of the UpdateCommand and DeleteCommand properties that the ProductID is set to the *original* ProductID. The word *original* here corresponds directly with the word *original* in OldValuesParameterFormatString property just mentioned. Setting the ProductID to the original ProductID in this fashion will ensure that the product being updated or deleted is the same product that is currently being displayed.

Notice at 03 the product ListView control. This control will be used to insert new rows into the Product table, update existing rows in the Product table, and delete existing rows from the Product table. Notice that the DataKeyNames property of the control is set to *ProductID*. This indicates that the primary key of the data source (i.e., the Product table) is the ProductID. Also notice that the InsertItemPosition property is set to *FirstItem*, which indicates that the InsertItemTemplate will be positioned at the top of the ListView control. Although we *can* position the InsertItemTemplate at the bottom of a ListView control, doing so can be quite inefficient from the end user's perspective— especially when many table rows will be displayed or when data paging will be used. Notice as well the five event handler method properties. The OnItemInserted property indicates the event handler method that will be executed immediately after a row is inserted into the Product table. This event handler method, which is defined at 20, will be used to make sure that the insert was successful. The OnItemUpdated property indicates the event handler method that will be executed immediately after a row is updated in the Product table. This event handler method, which is defined at 21, will be used to make sure that the update was successful. The OnItemDeleted property indicates the event handler method that will be executed immediately after a row is deleted from the Product table. This event handler method, which is defined at 22, will be used to make sure that the delete was successful. The OnItemDeleting property indicates the event handler method that will be executed immediately *before* a row is deleted from the Product table. This event handler method, which is defined at 23, will be used to delete the product's image file from the hard drive. Since we need the name of the image file to be deleted *before* the product is deleted from the table (and removed from the list view), we must execute the code at 23 *before* the row is deleted from the Product table.[2] And finally, the OnItemCanceling property indicates the event handler method that will be executed when a cancel operation is requested. This event handler method, which is defined at 24, will be used to display a message indicating that the insert or update operation has been canceled.

Notice at 04 the beginning of the LayoutTemplate, which specifies the content of the root container of the ListView control. In this case, the layout template consists of an HTML table of clickable column headings. We will see in a moment why we have defined this table using HTML tags and not ASP.NET server tags.

Notice at 05 that we have defined column headings for the HTML table. As can be seen, each of these headings is displayed as a LinkButton control. Notice that the first link button has its CommandArgument property set to *Category* and its CommandName property set to *Sort*. This combination indicates that the list view will be sorted by the Category attribute when the link button is clicked. The other column headings are defined and behave similarly.

Notice at 06 the HTML table row that has its ID property set to *itemPlaceholder*. This placeholder indicates where in the LayoutTemplate (i.e., the root container of the ListView control) to place the ItemTemplate when the list view is rendered on the page. It is the function of this placeholder that requires us to use HTML elements when defining the layout template of the list view. Although it is a clear deviation from our normal practice of using only ASP.NET server controls, using an <asp:TableRow> server control will not work in this particular scenario.

Notice at 07 the beginning of the ItemTemplate, which specifies the content and layout of an individual item in the ListView control when the control is in Read-Only mode and is, thus, only being used to display data. As can be seen, two buttons will be displayed when the list view is initially rendered—Modify and Delete. When the Modify button is clicked, the list view will go into Edit mode, since the CommandName property of the button is set to *Edit*. This mode will display the EditItemTemplate at 15.

---

[2]If the product's image file is deleted from the hard drive, and the database table delete is unsuccessful, the product will still exist in the Product table, but the image file will no longer exist on the hard drive. Thus, a more sophisticated approach to keeping the two in sync may be necessary.

When the Delete button is clicked, the list view will go into Delete mode, since the CommandName property of the button is set to *Delete*. Note that this mode will continue to display the ItemTemplate since the end user will not be adding for modifying data. As can be seen, the OnClientClick property of this button is set to execute a JavaScript Confirm function. If the end user clicks OK when the confirmation message is displayed, the delete command will be executed. However, if the end user clicks Cancel when the confirmation message is displayed, the delete command will *not* be executed.

Notice at 08 and 11 the *Copy Area Start* and *Copy Area End* comments, respectively. The technique we will use to ensure that the ItemTemplate, the InsertItemTemplate, and the EditItemTemplate are all identical (and thus look consistent from mode to mode) is to code and test the table columns between these two comments first and then copy and paste those table columns between the *Copy Area Start* and *Copy Area End* comments at 13 and 14 and between the *Copy Area Start* and *Copy Area End* comments at 16 and 17. Notice in each of these copy areas that the Enabled and ValidationGroup properties of the server controls should be set differently depending on the template they are in. Thus, if the code between *any* of the comments in the ItemTemplate, the InsertItemTemplate, or the EditItemTemplate is modified, that code should be copied and pasted between the comments in the other two templates, and the Enabled and ValidationGroup properties should be set appropriately. A failure to employ this technique (or something similar to it) will almost certainly result in more expensive modifications to the three templates down the road in an effort to keep the templates in sync.

Notice at 09 the category DropDownList control. There are several things to notice about this control. First, its DataSourceID property is set to *sdsDropDownListCategory*, which is the ID of the SqlDataSource defined at 01. Second, its DataTextField property is set to *Category*, which is the table attribute that will be displayed in the drop-down list. Third, its DataValueField property is set to *CategoryID*, which is the primary key of the item that will be displayed in the drop-down list. And fourth, its SelectedValue property is set to *<%# Bind("CategoryID") %>*, which binds the CategoryID of the *category* to the CategoryID of the *product*. Thus, when a new row is inserted into the Product table or an existing row is updated in the Product table, the CategoryID attribute of the *product* will be set to the CategoryID attribute of the currently selected *category*.

Notice at 10 the product TextBox control. There are two things to notice about this control. First, its MaxLength property is set to *50* so that the end user cannot enter a product longer than 50 characters. If he or she *were* permitted to enter a product longer than 50 characters and did so, the insert or update would fail due to a *truncation* error. This is because the maximum size of the Product attribute in the Product table is 50 characters (see Figure 20-1). Keep in mind that, in a real-world application, we would *also* need to use the validation controls supplied by ASP.NET to help us avoid other types of insert and update failures (e.g., null errors, type errors) and keep bad data out of the database in general. And second, its Text property is set to *<%# Bind("Product") %>*, which binds the Text property of the TextBox control to the Product attribute of the product. Thus, when a new row is inserted into the Product table or an existing row is updated in the Product table, the Product attribute of the product will be set to the Text property of the TextBox control.

Notice at 12 the beginning of the InsertItemTemplate, which specifies the content and layout of the ListView control when it is in Insert mode. As can be seen, two buttons will be displayed when the list view is in Insert mode—Save and Cancel. When the Save button is clicked, the list view will attempt to insert a new product into the Product table, since the CommandName property of the button is set to *Insert*. When the Cancel button is clicked, the list view will cancel the insert operation and discard any values entered by the end user, since the CommandName property of the button is set to *Cancel*.

Notice at 15 the beginning of the EditItemTemplate, which specifies the content and layout of the ListView control when it is in Edit mode. As can be seen, two buttons will be displayed when the list view is in Edit mode—Save and Cancel. When the Save button is clicked, the list view will attempt to update the currently selected product in the Product table, since the CommandName property of the button is set to *Update*. When the Cancel button is clicked, the list view will cancel the update operation and discard any values entered by the end user, since the CommandName property of the button is set to *Cancel*.

Notice at 18 that the System.Data.SqlClient namespace has been added to the list of using directives (which appears at the top of the code behind file). This was done to obviate the need to specify the fully qualified name of the SqlException class (i.e., System.Data.SqlClient.SqlException) each time we want to use one of its properties. We will need the SqlException class to check for foreign key constraint violations at 22.

Notice at 19 that the System.IO namespace has also been added to the list of using directives so we don't have to specify the fully qualified name of the File class (i.e., System.IO.File) each time we want to use one of its methods. We will need the File class to delete a file from the server's hard drive after we have checked for its existence. This code is shown at 23.

Notice at 20 the ItemInserted event handler method of the product list view. This method is executed when the ItemInserted event of the list view is raised, which is immediately after an insert operation is attempted. Notice in the definition of the event handler method the ListViewInsertedEventArgs class—the alias of which is e.

This class is passed to the event handler method so we can determine the status of our insert operations. As can be seen, if an exception is not returned from the database and exactly one row in the database is affected (i.e., inserted), we will display a message stating that the product was successfully added. If an exception is not returned from the database, but something other than one row in the database is affected (i.e., inserted), we will display an appropriate error message and keep the list view in insert mode. And finally, if an exception *is* returned from the database, we will display an appropriate error message, keep the list view in insert mode, and indicate that we are handling the exception programmatically.

Notice at 21 the ItemUpdated event handler method of the product list view. This method is executed when the ItemUpdated event of the list view is raised, which is immediately after an update operation is attempted. Notice in the definition of the event handler method the ListViewUpdatedEventArgs class—the alias of which is e. This class is passed to the event handler method so we can determine the status of our update operations. As can be seen, if an exception is not returned from the database and exactly one row in the database is affected (i.e., updated), we will display a message stating that the product was successfully modified. If an exception is not returned from the database, but something other than one row in the database is affected (i.e., updated), we will display an appropriate error message and keep the list view in edit mode. And finally, if an exception *is* returned from the database, we will display an appropriate error message, keep the list view in edit mode, and indicate that we are handling the exception programmatically.

Notice at 22 the ItemDeleted event handler method of the product list view. This method is executed when the ItemDeleted event of the list view is raised, which is immediately after a delete operation is attempted. Notice in the definition of the event handler method the ListViewDeletedEventArgs class—the alias of which is e. This class is passed to the event handler method so we can determine the status of our delete operations. As can be seen, if an exception is not returned from the database and exactly one row in the database is affected (i.e., deleted), we will display a message stating that the product was successfully deleted. If an exception is not returned from the database, but something other than one row in the database is affected (i.e., deleted), we will display an appropriate error message. If an exception *is* returned from the database and the SqlException number is 547, which indicates that a foreign key constraint violation has occurred, we will display an appropriate error message and indicate that we are handling the exception programmatically. And finally, if some other exception is returned from the database, we will display an appropriate error message and indicate that we are handling the exception programmatically.

Notice at 23 the ItemDeleting event handler method of the product list view. This method is executed when the ItemDeleting event of the list view is raised, which is immediately *before* a delete operation is attempted. Notice in this method that we are deleting from the server's hard drive the image file associated with the product to be deleted from the Product table (if the file exists). Note that since the image TextBox control exists *within* the list view, it is *not* directly accessible in the code behind of the page like the other server controls are. Thus, we must first locate the TextBox control in the list view (via its ID property using the FindControl method of the Control class) and then get the Text property of the control as usual.

Notice at 24 the ItemCanceling event handler method of the product list view. This method is executed when the ItemCanceling event of the list view is raised, which is when a cancel operation is requested. When this event handler method is executed, we will display a message indicating that the insert or update operation was canceled and that no data was affected.

Notice at 25 that we have added a <connectionStrings> section to our Web.config file as well as a connection string called *SportsPlay*. This connection string provides the details of the SQL Server database that will be used by the data sources at 01 and 02. See Chapter 20, titled "Database Design, SQL, and Data Binding," for a detailed description of this connection string.

The first screenshot in the Result section of the figure shows the product list view. Notice the clickable column headings that we defined in the LayoutTemplate of the list view. As mentioned earlier, clicking one of these column headings will sort the list view by its corresponding attribute. Notice as well that the InsertItemTemplate is located at the *top* of list view, since we set the InsertItemPosition property of the list view to *FirstItem*. To insert a new product into the Product table, the end user need only select the appropriate category and supplier, enter the required values into their respective text boxes, and click Save. The second screenshot shows the currently selected product row in Edit mode. Thus, the EditItemTemplate is being displayed. Notice that the product description is being modified. Once the product description is modified, the end user need only click Save to update the product in the Product table. The third screenshot shows the previously selected product row in Read-Only mode again—after the product description has been modified. Thus, the ItemTemplate is being displayed once again. And the fourth screenshot shows the currently selected product row in Read-Only mode after the end user has clicked the Delete button.

ASPX CODE

```
01  <asp:SqlDataSource runat="server" ID="sdsDropDownListCategory"
        ConnectionString="<%$ConnectionStrings:SportsPlay%>"
        SelectCommand="SELECT CategoryID, Category
                          FROM Category
                        ORDER BY Category;">
    </asp:SqlDataSource>

    ⋮
    ⋮ (Code continues.)
    ⋮

02  <asp:SqlDataSource runat="server" ID="sdsListViewProduct"
        ConnectionString="<%$ConnectionStrings:SportsPlay%>"
        OldValuesParameterFormatString="original_{0}"
        SelectCommand="SELECT *
                          FROM Category, Supplier, Product
                         WHERE Category.CategoryID = Product.CategoryID
                           AND Supplier.SupplierID = Product.SupplierID
                         ORDER BY Category, Supplier, Product;"
        InsertCommand="INSERT
                          INTO Product
                               (
                               CategoryID,
                               SupplierID,
                               Product,
                               Description,
                               Image,
                               Price,
                               NumberInStock,
                               NumberOnOrder,
                               ReorderLevel
                               )
                        VALUES
                               (
                               @CategoryID,
                               @SupplierID,
                               @Product,
                               @Description,
                               @Image,
                               @Price,
                               @NumberInStock,
                               @NumberOnOrder,
                               @ReorderLevel
                               );"
```

Figure 22-1. *Example of the ListView class*

```
        UpdateCommand="UPDATE Product
                    SET CategoryID = @CategoryID,
                        SupplierID = @SupplierID,
                        Product = @Product,
                        Description = @Description,
                        Image = @Image,
                        Price = @Price,
                        NumberInStock = @NumberInStock,
                        NumberOnOrder = @NumberOnOrder,
                        ReorderLevel = @ReorderLevel
                  WHERE ProductID = @original_ProductID;"
        DeleteCommand="DELETE
                    FROM Product
                  WHERE ProductID = @original_ProductID;">
    </asp:SqlDataSource>

    <asp:Label runat="server" Font-Bold="true" Text="Maintain Products" />
    <br /><br />

    <asp:Label runat="server" Text="Message " />
    <asp:Label runat="server" ID="lblMessage" /><br /><br />

03  <asp:ListView runat="server" ID="livProduct"
        DataKeyNames="ProductID"
        DataSourceID="sdsListViewProduct"
        EmptyDataText="No data to display"
        InsertItemPosition="FirstItem"
        OnItemCanceling="livProduct_ItemCanceling"
        OnItemDeleted="livProduct_ItemDeleted"
        OnItemDeleting="livProduct_ItemDeleting"
        OnItemInserted="livProduct_ItemInserted"
        OnItemUpdated="livProduct_ItemUpdated">
04      <LayoutTemplate>
            <asp:Table runat="server">
                <asp:TableRow>
                    <asp:TableCell>
                        <table>
                            <tr>
                                <th></th>
```

Figure 22-1. *(continued)*

```
05                                    <th style="text-align:left">
                                          <asp:LinkButton runat="server"
                                              CausesValidation="false"
                                              CommandArgument="Category"
                                              CommandName="Sort">
                                              Category
                                          </asp:LinkButton>
                                      </th>
                                      ⋮
                                      : (Code continues.)
                                      ⋮
                                      <th style="text-align:left">
                                          <asp:LinkButton runat="server"
                                              CausesValidation="false"
                                              CommandArgument="Product"
                                              CommandName="Sort">
                                              Product
                                          </asp:LinkButton>
                                      </th>
                                      ⋮
                                      : (Code continues.)
                                      ⋮
                                      <th style="text-align:right">
                                          <asp:LinkButton runat="server"
                                              CausesValidation="false"
                                              CommandArgument="ReorderLevel"
                                              CommandName="Sort">
                                              Reorder<br />Level
                                          </asp:LinkButton>
                                      </th>
                                  </tr>
06                                <tr runat="server" id="itemPlaceholder" />
                          </table>
                      </asp:TableCell>
                  </asp:TableRow>
              </asp:Table>
          </LayoutTemplate>
07        <ItemTemplate>
              <tr>
                  <td>
                      <asp:Button runat="server" ID="btnModify"
                          CausesValidation="false" CommandName="Edit"
                          Text="Modify" Width="60px" />
                      <asp:Button runat="server" ID="btnDelete"
                          CausesValidation="false" CommandName="Delete"
                          Text="Delete" Width="60px" OnClientClick="return
                          confirm('Are you sure you want to delete this item?
                          Click OK to delete it. Click Cancel to keep it.');" />
                  </td>
```

Figure 22-1. *(continued)*

```
08              <%--Copy Area Start (Set Enabled="false".)--%>
                <td>
09                  <asp:DropDownList runat="server" ID="ddlCategory"
                        DataSourceID="sdsDropDownListCategory"
                        DataTextField="Category" DataValueField="CategoryID"
                        Enabled="false"
                        SelectedValue='<%# Bind("CategoryID") %>' />
                </td>
                 ⋮
                 ⋮ (Code continues.)
                 ⋮
                <td>
10                  <asp:TextBox runat="server" ID="txtProduct"
                        Enabled="false" MaxLength="50"
                        Text='<%# Bind("Product") %>' />
                </td>
                 ⋮
                 ⋮ (Code continues.)
                 ⋮
11              <%--Copy Area End--%>
            </tr>
        </ItemTemplate>
12      <InsertItemTemplate>
            <tr>
                <td>
                    <asp:Button runat="server" ID="btnAddSave"
                        CausesValidation="true" CommandName="Insert"
                        Text="Save" ValidationGroup="AddSave" Width="60px" />
                    <asp:Button runat="server" ID="btnAddCancel"
                        CausesValidation="false" CommandName="Cancel"
                        Text="Cancel" Width="60px" />
                </td>
13              <%--Copy Area Start (Set Enabled="true". Set
                ValidationGroup="AddSave".)--%>
                 ⋮
                 ⋮ (Code continues.)
                 ⋮
14              <%--Copy Area End--%>
            </tr>
        </InsertItemTemplate>
```

Figure 22-1.   *(continued)*

435

```
15      <EditItemTemplate>
            <tr>
                <td>
                    <asp:Button runat="server" ID="btnModifySave"
                        CausesValidation="true" CommandName="Update"
                        Text="Save" ValidationGroup="ModifySave"
                        Width="60px" />
                    <asp:Button runat="server" ID="btnModifyCancel"
                        CausesValidation="false" CommandName="Cancel"
                        Text="Cancel" Width="60px" />
                </td>
16              <%--Copy Area Start (Set Enabled="true". Set
                ValidationGroup="ModifySave".)--%>
                    ⋮
                    ⋮ (Code continues.)
                    ⋮
17              <%--Copy Area End--%>
            </tr>
        </EditItemTemplate>
    </asp:ListView>


CODE BEHIND

18  using System.Data.SqlClient;
19  using System.IO;

    protected void Page_Load(object sender, EventArgs e)
    {
    }

20  protected void livProduct_ItemInserted(object sender,
        ListViewInsertedEventArgs e)
    {

        // Make sure the database call was successful.
        if (e.Exception == null)
        {
            if (e.AffectedRows == 1)
            {
                lblMessage.ForeColor = System.Drawing.Color.Green;
                lblMessage.Text = "Product successfully added.";
            }
```

Figure 22-1. *(continued)*

```
            else
            {
                lblMessage.ForeColor = System.Drawing.Color.Red;
                lblMessage.Text = "Product NOT successfully added.
                    Please report this message to....: The number of products
                    added was not equal to 1.";
                e.KeepInInsertMode = true;
            }
        }
        else
        {
            // An exception has occurred.
            lblMessage.ForeColor = System.Drawing.Color.Red;
            lblMessage.Text = "Product NOT successfully added.
                Please report this message to....: " +
                e.Exception.Message;
            e.KeepInInsertMode = true;
            e.ExceptionHandled = true;
        }

    }

21  protected void livProduct_ItemUpdated(object sender,
        ListViewUpdatedEventArgs e)
    {

        // Make sure the database call was successful.
        if (e.Exception == null)
        {
            if (e.AffectedRows == 1)
            {
                lblMessage.ForeColor = System.Drawing.Color.Green;
                lblMessage.Text = "Product successfully modified.";
            }
            else
            {
                lblMessage.ForeColor = System.Drawing.Color.Red;
                lblMessage.Text = "Product NOT successfully modified.
                    Please report this message to....: The number of products
                    modified was not equal to 1.";
                e.KeepInEditMode = true;
            }
        }
```

Figure 22-1. *(continued)*

```
        else
        {
            // An exception has occurred.
            lblMessage.ForeColor = System.Drawing.Color.Red;
            lblMessage.Text = "Product NOT successfully modified.
                Please report this message to....: " +
                e.Exception.Message;
            e.KeepInEditMode = true;
            e.ExceptionHandled = true;
        }

    }

22  protected void livProduct_ItemDeleted(object sender,
        ListViewDeletedEventArgs e)
    {

        // Make sure the database call was successful.
        if (e.Exception == null)
        {
            if (e.AffectedRows == 1)
            {
                lblMessage.ForeColor = System.Drawing.Color.Green;
                lblMessage.Text = "Product successfully deleted.";
            }
            else
            {
                lblMessage.ForeColor = System.Drawing.Color.Red;
                lblMessage.Text = "Product NOT successfully deleted.
                    Please report this message to....: The number of products
                    deleted was not equal to 1.";
            }
        }
        else
        {
            if (((SqlException)e.Exception).Number.Equals(547))
            {
                // A foreign key constraint violation has occurred.
                lblMessage.ForeColor = System.Drawing.Color.Red;
                lblMessage.Text = "Product NOT successfully deleted because it
                    is associated with at least one order line. To delete this
                product, you must first delete all of its associated order
                lines.";
                e.ExceptionHandled = true;
            }
```

Figure 22-1. *(continued)*

```
          else
          {
              // Some other exception has occurred.
              lblMessage.ForeColor = System.Drawing.Color.Red;
              lblMessage.Text = "Product NOT successfully deleted.
                  Please report this message to....: " +
                  e.Exception.Message;
              e.ExceptionHandled = true;
          }
      }

  }

23  protected void livProduct_ItemDeleting(object sender,
        ListViewDeleteEventArgs e)
    {

        // Get the filename of the image to be deleted.
        ListViewItem lviListViewItem = livProduct.Items[e.ItemIndex];
        TextBox txtImage = (TextBox)lviListViewItem.FindControl("txtImage");
        String strImage = txtImage.Text;
        // Delete the associated file from the hard drive.
        String strFilePath = Request.PhysicalApplicationPath + "Images\\" +
            strImage;
        if (File.Exists(strFilePath))
        {
            File.Delete(strFilePath);
        }

    }

24  protected void livProduct_ItemCanceling(object sender,
        ListViewCancelEventArgs e)
    {

        // Cancel the insert or update operation.
        lblMessage.ForeColor = System.Drawing.Color.Red;
        lblMessage.Text = "Operation cancelled. No data was affected.";

    }
```

WEB.CONFIG CODE

```
25  <connectionStrings>
      <add name="SportsPlay"
          connectionString="Data Source=MATRBeasley-18\SQLEXPRESS;
          Initial Catalog=SportsPlay; Integrated Security=SSPI" />
    </connectionStrings>
```

RESULT

Figure 22-1. *(continued)*

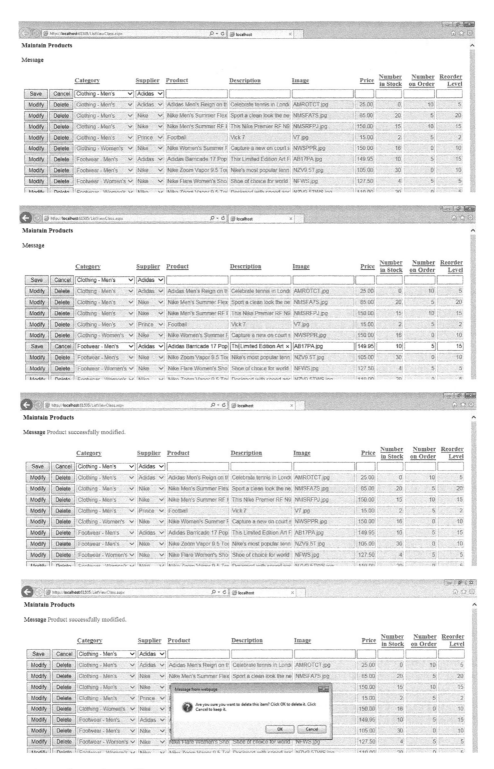

Figure 22-1. *(continued)*

22.3 DataPager Class

The DataPager class displays paging controls that can be used by an end user to view the *data pages* of a ListView control (or other pageable controls). To associate a DataPager control with a ListView control, we set the PagedControlID property of the DataPager control to the ID property of the ListView control. To set the number of ListView control items to be displayed in a single page of data, we set the PageSize property of the DataPager control. And to display navigation controls in a DataPager control, we add one or more *paging controls* to the Fields property of the DataPager control. These paging controls are the NextPreviousPagerField control, the NumericPagerField control, and the TemplatePagerField control. The first two paging controls will be discussed in more detail soon. The third paging control won't be discussed in this chapter. Suffice it to say that we can utilize the TemplatePagerField if we want to define our own paging controls. Table 22-2 shows some of the properties, methods, and events of the DataPager class.

Table 22-2. *Some of the properties, methods, and events of the DataPager class*

Class DataPager[3]

Namespace System.Web.UI.WebControls

Properties

Fields	Gets a collection of DataPagerField objects that represent the pager fields that are specified in a DataPager control.
PagedControlID	Gets or sets the ID of the control that contains the data that will be paged by the DataPager control.
PageSize	Gets or sets the number of records that are displayed for each page of data.

Methods

(See
reference.)

(continued)

---

[3]All property, method, and event descriptions were taken directly from Microsoft's official documentation. The event handler methods used to handle the events of this class were omitted to conserve space. See the reference for all of the methods of this class.

Table 22-2. (*continued*)

Events

(See
reference.)

Reference

https://msdn.microsoft.com/en-us/library/system.web.ui.webcontrols.
datapager(v=vs.110).aspx

22.4 NextPreviousPagerField Class

The NextPreviousPagerField class displays navigation controls in a DataPager control
that can be used by an end user to jump to the *first* page of a ListView control, move
to the *previous* page of a ListView control, move to the *next* page of a ListView control,
and/or jump to the *last* page of a ListView control. To indicate the type of button to
display, we set the ButtonType property of the control to *Button*, *Image*, or *Link*. To
specify the text to display in the buttons, we set the FirstPageText, PreviousPageText,
NextPageText, and LastPageText properties of the control. To hide the buttons, we
set the ShowFirstPageButton, ShowPreviousPageButton, ShowNextPageButton, and
ShowLastPageButton properties of the control to *false*. Table 22-3 shows some of the
properties, methods, and events of the NextPreviousPagerField class.

Table 22-3. *Some of the properties, methods, and events of the*
NextPreviousPagerField class

Class NextPreviousPagerField[4]

Namespace System.Web.UI.WebControls

Properties

ButtonType	Gets or sets the button type to display in the pager field.
FirstPageText	Gets or sets the text that is displayed for the first-page button.
LastPageText	Gets or sets the text that is displayed for the last-page button.
NextPageText	Gets or sets the text that is displayed for the next-page button.
PreviousPageText	Gets or sets the text that is displayed for the previous-page button.
ShowFirstPageButton	Gets or sets a value that indicates whether the first-page button is displayed in a NextPreviousPagerField object.
ShowLastPageButton	Gets or sets a value that indicates whether the last-page button is displayed in a NextPreviousPagerField object.
ShowNextPageButton	Gets or sets a value that indicates whether the next-page button is displayed in a NextPreviousPagerField object.
ShowPreviousPageButton	Gets or sets a value that indicates whether the previous-page button is displayed in a NextPreviousPagerField object.

Methods

(See reference.)

Events

(See reference.)

Reference

https://msdn.microsoft.com/en-us/library/system.web.ui.webcontrols.nextpre
viouspagerfield(v=vs.110).aspx

---

[4]All property, method, and event descriptions were taken directly from Microsoft's official
documentation. The event handler methods used to handle the events of this class were omitted
to conserve space. See the reference for all of the methods of this class.

Figure 22-2 shows an example of the DataPager and NextPreviousPagerField classes.

Notice at 01 that the PagedControlID property of the DataPager control is set to *livProduct*, which is the ID of the ListView control that begins at 03 in Figure 22-1. Notice as well that we will be displaying five list view items in each page of the list view.

Notice at 02 the Fields property of the control. As can be seen, this is a collection property that contains a single NextPreviousPagerField control.

Notice at 03 that *Next* will be displayed as the Next button, *Prev* will be displayed as the Previous button, and since all four of the "show" properties of the control are set to *true*, the NextPreviousPagerField control will permit the end user to jump to the *first* page of the list view, move to the *previous* page of the list view, move to the *next* page of the list view, and jump to the *last* page of the list view.

By the way, the left-to-right ordering of the paging options in the figure is very deliberate. This order corresponds to the way we typically navigate the pages of a book, so displaying the options in this way will avoid confusion in the end user.

The screenshot in the Result section of the figure shows the list view we created earlier being used in conjunction with our DataPager control and its associated NextPreviousPagerField control.

ASPX CODE

```
01   <asp:DataPager runat="server" PagedControlID="livProduct" PageSize="5">
02       <Fields>
03           <asp:NextPreviousPagerField NextPageText="Next"
                 PreviousPageText="Prev" ShowFirstPageButton="true"
                 ShowLastPageButton="true" ShowNextPageButton="true"
                 ShowPreviousPageButton="true" />
         </Fields>
     </asp:DataPager>
```

RESULT

Figure 22-2. *Example of the DataPager and NextPreviousPagerField classes*

22.5 NumericPagerField Class

The NumericPagerField class displays navigation controls in a DataPager control that can be used by an end user to select a page in a ListView control by its page number. To indicate the type of button to display, we set the ButtonType property of the control to *Button*, *Image*, or *Link*. To indicate the number of buttons to display, we set the ButtonCount property of the control. Table 22-4 shows some of the properties, methods, and events of the NumericPagerField class.

Table 22-4. *Some of the properties, methods, and events of the NumericPagerField class*

Class NumericPagerField[5]

Namespace System.Web.UI.WebControls

Properties

ButtonCount	Gets or sets the number of buttons to display in a NumericPagerField object.
ButtonType	Gets or sets the button type to display in the pager field.

Methods

(See reference.)

Events

(See reference.)

Reference

https://msdn.microsoft.com/en-us/library/system.web.ui.webcontrols.
numericpagerfield(v=vs.110).aspx

---

[5]All property, method, and event descriptions were taken directly from Microsoft's official documentation. The event handler methods used to handle the events of this class were omitted to conserve space. See the reference for all of the methods of this class.

Figure 22-3 shows an example of the DataPager and NumericPagerField classes.

Notice at 01 that the PagedControlID property of the DataPager control is set to *livProduct*, which is the ID of the ListView control that begins at 03 in Figure 22-1. Notice as well that we will be displaying five list view items in each page of the list view.

Notice at 02 the Fields property of the control. As can be seen, this is a collection property that contains a single NumericPagerField control between two NextPreviousPagerField controls. Notice that we will be hiding the *last*-page button and the *next*-page button of the *first* NextPreviousPagerField control. Notice as well that we will be hiding the *first*-page button and the *previous*-page button of the *second* NextPreviousPagerField control. Hiding the buttons in this manner is necessary so that the combination of the NextPreviousPagerField control and the NumericPagerField control makes sense.

Notice at 03 that we will be displaying three NumericPagerField buttons. When the ListView control contains more than three data pages, their presence will be indicated with an ellipse (…).

The screenshot in the Result section of the figure shows the list view we created earlier being used in conjunction with our DataPager control and its associated NextPreviousPagerField controls and NumericPagerField control.

ASPX CODE

```
01   <asp:DataPager runat="server" PagedControlID="livProduct" PageSize="5">
02       <Fields>
             <asp:NextPreviousPagerField NextPageText="Next"
                 PreviousPageText="Prev" ShowFirstPageButton="true"
                 ShowLastPageButton="false" ShowNextPageButton="false"
                 ShowPreviousPageButton="true" />
03           <asp:NumericPagerField ButtonCount="3" />
             <asp:NextPreviousPagerField NextPageText="Next"
                 PreviousPageText="Prev" ShowFirstPageButton="false"
                 ShowLastPageButton="true" ShowNextPageButton="true"
                 ShowPreviousPageButton="false" />
         </Fields>
     </asp:DataPager>
```

RESULT

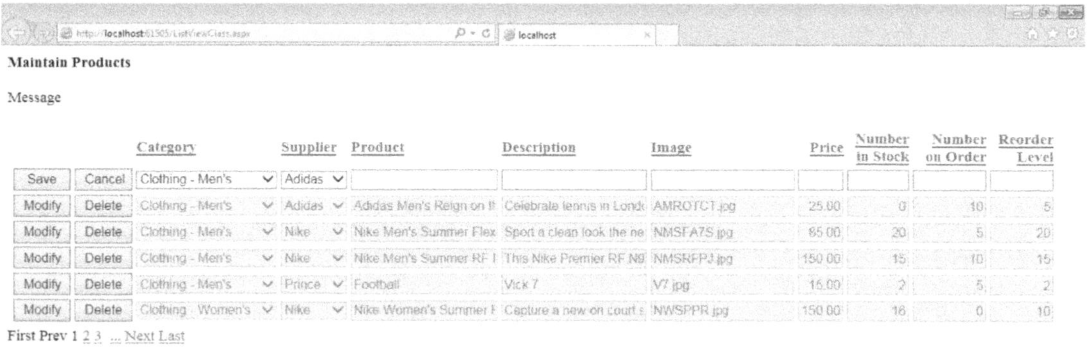

Figure 22-3. *Example of the DataPager and NumericPagerField classes*

CHAPTER 23

Code Behind Database Operations

23.1 Introduction

There are many times when it is necessary to establish a connection to a database and execute SQL commands against that database from the code behind of a page. For example, we may require the end user to click a Display button to display the contact information of his or her organization's customers in a non-data-bound control like a multiline text box. Or we may require the end user to enter his or her login credentials and click a Login button to gain access to their application's functionality. In both of these scenarios, we would need a page that interacts with a database from the button Click event handler method in the page's code behind.

In this chapter, we will begin by looking at the SqlConnection class. This class defines, opens, and closes a connection to a SQL Server database. Next, we will consider the WebConfigurationManager class, which provides access to the connection string we have defined in our Web.config file so that we can create a new SqlConnection object. After that, we will discuss the SqlCommand class. This class executes SQL commands (e.g., Select, Insert, Update, and Delete commands) against a SQL Server database. We will then consider the SqlDataReader class. This class creates a read-only, move-forward-only data structure that holds the data retrieved by a SqlCommand object so that we can read and process that data one row at a time. Next, we will contrast two types of SQL queries—non-parameterized queries and parameterized queries. And finally, we will discuss stored procedures, where a stored procedure is a group of one or more SQL statements stored in a database.

© Robert E. Beasley 2020
R. E. Beasley, *Essential ASP.NET Web Forms Development*, https://doi.org/10.1007/978-1-4842-5784-5_23

23.2 SqlConnection Class

The SqlConnection class defines, opens, and closes a connection to a SQL Server database. The ConnectionString property of a SqlConnection object provides the details of the SQL Server database that an application will utilize. Although a connection string can take many forms, the syntax we will use in this chapter is

```
Data Source=Computer Name\SQL Server Instance; Initial Catalog=Database Name;
    Integrated Security=SSPI
```

where the items in italics are modifiable. In this book, we will place our connection string in the Web.config file so that it can be modified in *one* place in the application yet can be *referred to* in *many* places in the application. Thus, if we need to install the database on a different computer, add the database to a different SQL Server instance,[1] or change the name of the database, we need only change the connection string in the Web.config file. The references to the connection string throughout the application need not be modified.

The ConnectionTimeout property indicates the amount of time an application should wait on a database connection attempt before terminating the attempt and generating an error. And finally, the SqlCredential property indicates the credentials (i.e., login ID and password) of a database connection. In this chapter, we will not require our application to provide special login credentials to access the database.

It is important to remember that once a connection to a database is opened, it is *not* automatically closed when an application is done with it. Thus, we must be careful to close any connections we have opened by invoking the SqlCommand class's Close (or Dispose) method. Table 23-1 shows some of the properties, methods, and events of the SqlConnection class.

---

[1]A SQL Server instance is a complete SQL Server *service* with its own databases, credentials, and so forth. A computer can have more than one SQL Server instance installed and running at one time.

Table 23-1. *Some of the properties, methods, and events of the SqlConnection class*

Class SqlConnection[2]

Namespace System.Data.SqlClient

Properties

ConnectionString	Gets or sets the string used to open a SQL Server database.
ConnectionTimeout	Gets the time to wait while trying to establish a connection before terminating the attempt and generating an error.
Credential	Gets or sets the SqlCredential object for this connection.

Methods

Close()	Closes the connection to the database. This is the preferred method of closing any open connection.
Open()	Opens a database connection with the property settings specified by the ConnectionString.

Events

InfoMessage	Occurs when SQL Server returns a warning or informational message.

Reference

```
https://msdn.microsoft.com/en-us/library/system.data.sqlclient.
sqlconnection(v=vs.110).aspx
```

---

[2]All property, method, and event descriptions were taken directly from Microsoft's official documentation. The event handler methods used to handle the events of this class were omitted to conserve space. See the reference for all of the methods of this class.

23.3 WebConfigurationManager Class

The WebConfigurationManager class provides access to the information in an application's Web.config file. In this chapter, we will need to access the connection string we defined in our Web.config file so that we can create a new SqlConnection object for opening and closing a connection to our SQL Server database. The syntax used to access a connection string that exists in the Web.config file is

```
WebConfigurationManager.ConnectionStrings["Connection String Name"].
ConnectionString
```

where the item in italics is the name of the connection string in the <connectionStrings> section of the Web.config file. Table 23-2 shows some of the properties, methods, and events of the WebConfigurationManager class.

Table 23-2. *Some of the properties, methods, and events of the WebConfigurationManager class*

Class WebConfigurationManager[3]

Namespace System.Web.Configuration

Properties

ConnectionStrings	Gets the Web site's connection strings.

Methods

(See reference.)

Events

(See reference.)

Reference

```
https://msdn.microsoft.com/en-us/library/system.web.
configuration.webconfigurationmanager(v=vs.110).aspx
```

---

[3]All property, method, and event descriptions were taken directly from Microsoft's official documentation. The event handler methods used to handle the events of this class were omitted to conserve space. See the reference for all of the methods of this class.

23.4 SqlCommand Class

The SqlCommand class executes SQL commands against a SQL Server database. A SqlCommand object contains several methods that we can use to retrieve and manipulate the data in a database. These include the ExecuteScalar method, the ExecuteReader method, and the ExecuteNonQuery method. The ExecuteScalar method retrieves the first column of the first row of the *result set* returned by a SQL query. Any additional columns and rows are ignored. This is the method of choice when we wish to determine whether or not at least one row of data is returned from a SQL query or when we wish to retrieve a single aggregate value (e.g., average, sum) from a SQL query. The ExecuteReader method loads a SqlDataReader object, which is a move-forward-only, read-only data structure that we can use to process the entire result set returned from a SQL query—one row at a time. And the ExecuteNonQuery method executes Insert, Update, and Delete commands. After SQL Server completes one of these operations, the number of rows affected by the operation is returned so that we can determine the status of the operation (e.g., successful, unsuccessful).

A SqlCommand object also contains a number of properties that we can use to describe the nature of the object. The CommandText property indicates the name of a stored procedure, the name of a table, or the name of a string that contains a SQL statement. The CommandType property indicates how the CommandText property is to be interpreted. This property can be set to *StoredProcedure*, *TableDirect*, or *Text* (the default). When the CommandType property is set to *StoredProcedure*, we set the CommandText property to the name of a stored procedure in the SQL Server database. Stored procedures are discussed later in this chapter. When the CommandType property is set to *TableDirect*, we set the CommandText property to the name of a table in the SQL Server database. And when the CommandType property is set to *Text*, we set the CommandText property to a string that contains a valid SQL command. The CommandTimeout property indicates the amount of time the application should wait while attempting to execute a SQL command before terminating the command attempt and generating an error. And finally, the Connection property associates the SqlCommand object with a previously created SqlConnection object. Table 23-3 shows some of the properties, methods, and events of the SqlCommand class.

Table 23-3. *Some of the properties, methods, and events of the SqlCommand class*

Class SqlCommand[4]

Namespace System.Data.SqlClient

Properties

CommandText	Gets or sets the Transact-SQL statement, table name, or stored procedure to execute at the data source.
CommandTimeout	Gets or sets the wait time before terminating the attempt to execute a command and generating an error.
CommandType	Gets or sets a value indicating how the CommandText property is to be interpreted.
Connection	Gets or sets the SqlConnection used by this instance of the SqlCommand.
Parameters	Gets the SqlParameterCollection.

Methods

ExecuteNonQuery()	Executes a Transact-SQL statement against the connection and returns the number of rows affected.
ExecuteReader()	Sends the CommandText to the Connection and builds a SqlDataReader.
ExecuteScalar()	Executes the query and returns the first column of the first row in the result set returned by the query. Additional columns or rows are ignored.

Events

StatementCompleted	Occurs when the execution of a Transact-SQL statement completes.

Reference

https://msdn.microsoft.com/en-us/library/system.data.sqlclient.
sqlcommand(v=vs.110).aspx

---

[4]All property, method, and event descriptions were taken directly from Microsoft's official documentation. The event handler methods used to handle the events of this class were omitted to conserve space. See the reference for all of the methods of this class.

23.5 SqlDataReader Class

The SqlDataReader class creates a move-forward-only, read-only object that holds the data retrieved by a SqlCommand object's ExecuteReader method. This object resembles a set of database table rows that we can read from (one row at a time) as if we were reading the rows from an actual table. To read a row of data from a data reader (and move to the next row of data), we invoke the Read method of the SqlDataReader object. Since a SqlDataReader object is a move-forward-only data structure, we cannot move to a previous row in the data reader once a row has been read. And since a SqlDataReader object is a read-only data structure, we cannot change the data in a data reader.

It is important to remember that a SqlDataReader object is *not* automatically closed when an application is done with it. Thus, we must be careful to close any data readers we have opened by invoking the SqlDataReader object's Close method. Table 23-4 shows some of the properties, methods, and events of the SqlDataReader class.

Table 23-4. *Some of the properties, methods, and events of the SqlDataReader class*

Class SqlDataReader[5]	
Namespace System.Data.SqlClient	
Properties	
(See reference.)	
Methods	
Close()	Closes the SqlDataReader object.
Read()	Advances the SqlDataReader to the next record.
Events	
(See reference.)	
Reference	
`https://msdn.microsoft.com/en-us/library/system.data.sqlclient.sqldatareader(v=vs.110).aspx`	

---

[5]All property, method, and event descriptions were taken directly from Microsoft's official documentation. The event handler methods used to handle the events of this class were omitted to conserve space. See the reference for all of the methods of this class.

Figure 23-1 shows an example of the SqlDataReader class. The SqlDataReader object in this example will hold the results of a query that returns a list of customers.

Notice at 01 that the System.Data namespace has been added to the list of using directives (which appears at the top of the code behind file) to obviate the need to specify the fully qualified name of the CommandType class (i.e., System.Data. CommandType) each time we want to use one of its enumerations—*StoredProcedure*, *TableDirect*, or *Text*.

Notice at 02 that the System.Data.SqlClient namespace has also been added to the list of using directives. This was done so we are not required to specify the fully qualified name of the SqlConnection class (i.e., System.Data.SqlClient.SqlConnection), the SqlCommand class (i.e., System.Data.SqlClient.SqlCommand), and the SqlDataReader class (i.e., System.Data.SqlClient.SqlDataReader) each time we want to use one of their respective properties or methods.

Notice at 03 that the System.Web.Configuration namespace has been added to the list of using directives to avoid the need to specify the fully qualified name of the WebConfigurationManager class (i.e., System.Web.Configuration. WebConfigurationManager) each time we want to use one of its properties.

Notice at 04–05 that we are constructing a SQL Select command. This command will return the last name, first name, middle initial, and phone number of every customer in the Customer table and will order those customers by last name, first name, and middle initial. As mentioned previously, the result of this query will be stored in a SqlDataReader object from which we will read and display each customer's data—one row at a time.

Notice at 06 that we are defining the network connection to our SQL Server database. As can be seen, this connection is defined in the *SportsPlay* connection string that resides in the <connectionStrings> section of our Web.config file.

Notice at 07–08 that we are creating a new SqlCommand object and readying it for execution by setting its Connection, CommandType, and CommandText properties.

Notice at 09–10 that we are opening the connection to our SQL Server database, creating a new SqlDataReader object, and loading it with the results of the Select command defined at 04–05.

Notice at 11 that we are retrieving the rows from the data reader using the Read method of the SqlDataReader object—while there are rows of data to be read. For each row of data that is returned from the data reader, we are appending the customer's last name, first name, middle initial, and phone number (along with some formatting punctuation and a new line escape sequence) to the Text property of the txtCustomers object.

Notice at 12–13 that we are closing both the data reader and the connection to the database as these are not done automatically.

Notice at 14 that we have added a <connectionStrings> section to our Web.config file as well as a connection string called *SportsPlay*. This connection string provides the details of the SQL Server database that will be used by the SqlConnection object at 06. See Chapter 20, titled "Database Design, SQL, and Data Binding," for a detailed description of this connection string.

The screenshot in the Result section of the figure shows the result of clicking the Display button to display the alphabetical listing of customers.

ASPX CODE

```
<asp:Label runat="server" Font-Bold="true" Text="Customers" /><br />
<asp:TextBox runat="server" ID="txtCustomers" Columns="50" Rows="5"
    TextMode="MultiLine" /><br />
<asp:Button runat="server" ID="btnDisplay" OnClick="btnDisplay_Click"
    Text="Display" />
```

CODE BEHIND

```
01   using System.Data;
02   using System.Data.SqlClient;
03   using System.Web.Configuration;

     protected void btnDisplay_Click(object sender, EventArgs e)
     {
         // Develop the SQL call.
04       String strSQL = "";
         strSQL = "SELECT LastName, FirstName, MiddleInitial, Phone ";
         strSQL += " FROM Customer ";
05       strSQL += "ORDER BY LastName, FirstName, MiddleInitial ";
         // Define the network connection to the SQL Server database.
06       SqlConnection objSqlConnection = new
             SqlConnection(WebConfigurationManager.
             ConnectionStrings["SportsPlay"].ConnectionString);
         // Create the SQL command object.
07       SqlCommand objSqlCommand = new SqlCommand();
         objSqlCommand.Connection = objSqlConnection;
         objSqlCommand.CommandType = CommandType.Text;
08       objSqlCommand.CommandText = strSQL;
         // Open the connection and execute the data reader.
09       objSqlConnection.Open();
10       SqlDataReader objSqlDataReader = objSqlCommand.ExecuteReader();
         // Retrieve each row and display in the text box.
```

Figure 23-1. *Example of the SqlDataReader class*

```
11        while (objSqlDataReader.Read())
          {
              txtCustomers.Text = txtCustomers.Text +
                  objSqlDataReader["LastName"].ToString() + ", " +
                  objSqlDataReader["FirstName"].ToString() + " " +
                  objSqlDataReader["MiddleInitial"].ToString() + " (" +
                  objSqlDataReader["Phone"].ToString() + ")\r";
          }
          // Close the data reader and the connection.
12        objSqlDataReader.Close();
13        objSqlConnection.Close();

      }
```

WEB.CONFIG CODE

```
14   <connectionStrings>
       <add name="SportsPlay"
           connectionString="Data Source=MATRBeasley-18\SQLEXPRESS;
           Initial Catalog=SportsPlay; Integrated Security=SSPI" />
     </connectionStrings>
```

RESULT

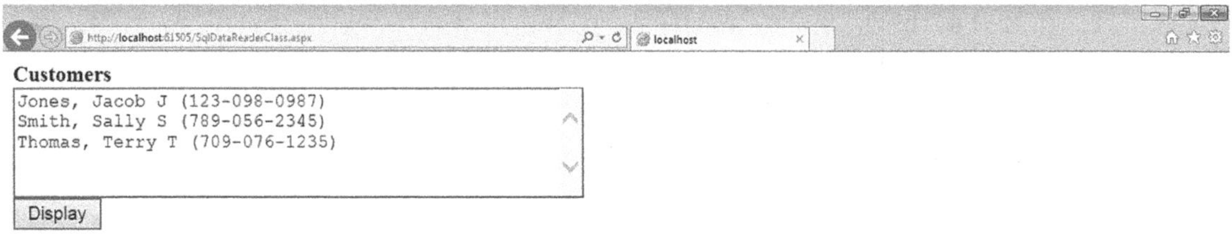

Figure 23-1.   *(continued)*

23.6 Non-parameterized Queries

It is often necessary to supply the Where clause of a SQL query with one or more input parameter arguments to limit the number of rows the query returns. One way to do this is by constructing and executing a *non-parameterized query*. A non-parameterized query is *programmatically* constructed in the code behind after the end user supplies the necessary input parameter arguments. To be more specific, a non-parameterized query is built at *runtime* by concatenating the Where clause of a SQL call with any inputs supplied by the end user.

One caveat should be stated right upfront regarding the construction and execution of non-parameterized queries: they can be very problematic from a security point of view. More on that in the next section of this chapter. Even though we would normally not want to utilize non-parameterized queries, we will discuss them here for two reasons. First, discussing them will help us illustrate the difference between non-parameterized and parameterized queries. And second, discussing them will help us spot non-parameterized queries in existing code so that we can correct the potential security risks.

Figure 23-2 shows an example of a non-parametrized query. This query is used to validate the login credentials of an employee.

Notice at 01 and 02 that the end user will be supplying an email address and password, respectively. These items will be used to construct our non-parameterized query.

Notice at 03 that the System.Data namespace has been added to the list of using directives (which appears at the top of the code behind file) so we don't have to specify the fully qualified name of the CommandType class (i.e., System.Data.CommandType) each time we want to use one of its enumerations—*StoredProcedure*, *TableDirect*, or *Text*.

Notice at 04 that the System.Data.SqlClient namespace has also been added to the list of using directives. This was done to obviate the need to specify the fully qualified name of the SqlConnection class (i.e., System.Data.SqlClient.SqlConnection), the SqlCommand class (i.e., System.Data.SqlClient.SqlCommand), and the SqlDataReader class (i.e., System.Data.SqlClient.SqlDataReader) each time we want to use one of their respective properties or methods.

Notice at 05 that the System.Web.Configuration namespace has been added to the list of using directives so we are not required to specify the fully qualified name of the WebConfigurationManager class (i.e., System.Web.Configuration. WebConfigurationManager) each time we want to use one of its properties.

Notice at 06–07 that we are constructing a *dynamic* SQL Select command using the email address and password supplied by the end user. Here, we are building the Where clause of the Select statement by concatenating it with the end user's email address and password.

Notice at 08 that we are defining the network connection to our SQL Server database. As can be seen, this connection is defined in the *SportsPlay* connection string that resides in the <connectionStrings> section of our Web.config file.

Notice at 09-10 that we are creating a new SqlCommand object and readying it for execution by setting its Connection, CommandType, and CommandText properties.

Notice at 11-13 that we are opening the connection to our SQL Server database, creating a new SqlDataReader object, loading it with the results of the Select command defined at 06-07, and attempting to retrieve a row from the data reader using the Read method of the SqlDataReader object. If a row is retrieved from the data reader, which indicates that the end user *was* found in the Employee table, we save his or her EmployeeID to a session variable (so we can identify who is logged in on subsequent pages) and display a welcome message. If a row is *not* retrieved from the data reader, which indicates that the end user was *not* found in the Employee table, we display an error message.

Notice at 14-15 that we are closing both the data reader and the connection to the database as these are not done automatically.

Notice at 16 that we have added a <connectionStrings> section to our Web.config file as well as a connection string called *SportsPlay*. This connection string provides the details of the SQL Server database that will be used by the SqlConnection object at 08. See Chapter 20, titled "Database Design, SQL, and Data Binding," for a detailed description of this connection string.

The first screenshot in the Result section of the figure shows the end user entering an *invalid* email address and password combination. The second screenshot shows the error message displayed as a result of entering the invalid combination. The third screenshot shows the end user entering a *valid* email address and password combination. And the fourth screenshot shows the welcome message displayed as a result of entering the valid combination.

ASPX CODE

```
      <asp:Label runat="server" Font-Bold="true" Text="Employee Login" />
      <br /><br />
      <asp:Label runat="server" Text="Message " />
      <asp:Label runat="server" ID="lblMessage" /><br /><br />
      <asp:Table runat="server">
          <asp:TableRow>
              <asp:TableCell>
                  <asp:Label runat="server" Text="Email Address" />
              </asp:TableCell>
              <asp:TableCell>
01                <asp:TextBox runat="server" ID="txtEmailAddress"
                      MaxLength="50" Width="240px" />
              </asp:TableCell>
          </asp:TableRow>
          <asp:TableRow>
              <asp:TableCell>
                  <asp:Label runat="server" Text="Password" />
              </asp:TableCell>
              <asp:TableCell>
02                <asp:TextBox runat="server" ID="txtPassword" MaxLength="10"
                      TextMode="Password" Width="240px" />
              </asp:TableCell>
          </asp:TableRow>
          <asp:TableRow>
              <asp:TableCell>
                  <asp:Button runat="server" ID="btnLogin"
                      OnClick="btnLogin_Click" Text="Login" />
              </asp:TableCell>
          </asp:TableRow>
      </asp:Table>
```

CODE BEHIND

```
03  using System.Data;
04  using System.Data.SqlClient;
05  using System.Web.Configuration;

    protected void btnLogin_Click(object sender, EventArgs e)
    {
        // Develop the SQL call.
06      String strSQL = "";
        strSQL = "SELECT EmployeeID, FirstName + ' ' + MiddleInitial + ' ' +
                    LastName AS FullName ";
        strSQL += " FROM Employee ";
        strSQL += "WHERE EmailAddress = '" + txtEmailAddress.Text + "' ";
```

Figure 23-2. *Example of a non-parametrized query*

```
07      strSQL += "  AND Password = '" + txtPassword.Text + "' ";
        // Define the network connection to the SQL Server database.
08      SqlConnection objSqlConnection = new
            SqlConnection(WebConfigurationManager.
            ConnectionStrings["SportsPlay"].ConnectionString);
        // Set up the SQL command object.
09      SqlCommand objSqlCommand = new SqlCommand();
        objSqlCommand.Connection = objSqlConnection;
        objSqlCommand.CommandType = CommandType.Text;
10      objSqlCommand.CommandText = strSQL;
        // Open the connection and execute the data reader.
11      objSqlConnection.Open();
12      SqlDataReader objSqlDataReader = objSqlCommand.ExecuteReader();
        // Attempt to retrieve the row from the table.
13      if (objSqlDataReader.Read())
        {
            Session["intEmployeeID"] =
                objSqlDataReader["EmployeeID"].ToString();
            lblMessage.ForeColor = System.Drawing.Color.Green;
            lblMessage.Text = "Welcome " +
                objSqlDataReader["FullName"].ToString() + "!";
        }
        else
        {
            lblMessage.ForeColor = System.Drawing.Color.Red;
            lblMessage.Text = "Invalid email address and password combination.
                Please try again.";
        }
        // Close the data reader and the connection.
14      objSqlDataReader.Close();
15      objSqlConnection.Close();

    }

WEB.CONFIG CODE

16  <connectionStrings>
      <add name="SportsPlay"
          connectionString="Data Source=MATRBeasley-18\SQLEXPRESS;
          Initial Catalog=SportsPlay; Integrated Security=SSPI" />
    </connectionStrings>
```

Figure 23-2. *(continued)*

RESULT

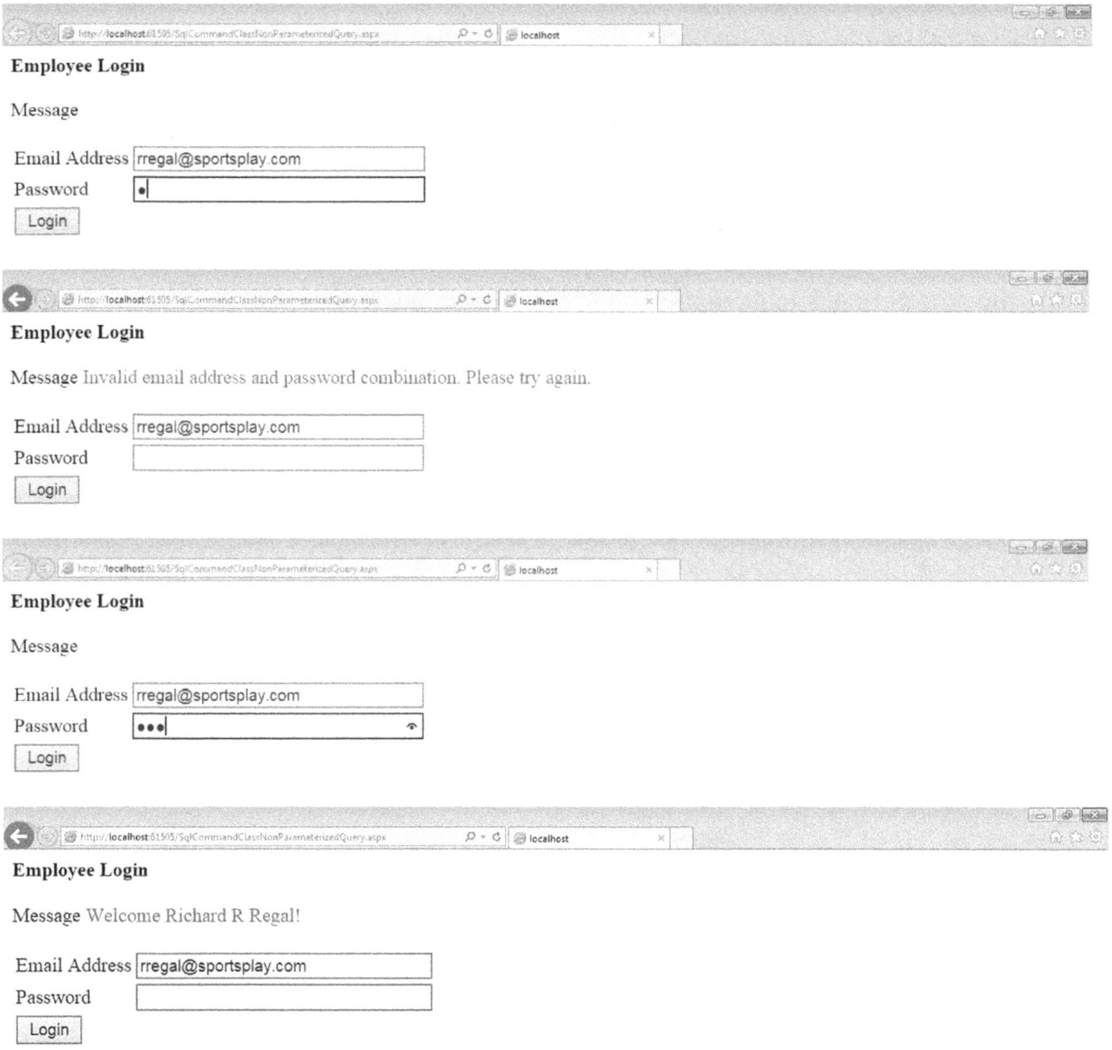

Figure 23-2. *(continued)*

23.7 Parameterized Queries

In the previous section, we discussed the concept of a non-parameterized query. We said that a non-parameterized query is *programmatically* constructed in the code behind after the end user supplies the necessary input parameter arguments. Although non-parameterized queries work, they present a potential problem in that they do not protect against a common security threat called *SQL injection*.

One type of SQL injection occurs when an end user with malicious intent enters (i.e., *injects*) SQL calls into the text box fields of a login page (e.g., an email address field and a password field) that permits him or her to gain access to the application's functionality. This works by tricking the application into thinking the end user has entered valid login credentials. Another type of SQL injection occurs when an end user enters a SQL call into a text box field that permits him or her to add data to the application's database (via a SQL Insert command), modify data in the application's database (via a SQL Update command), delete data from the application's database (via a SQL Delete command), modify the structure of a table in the application's database (via a SQL Alter command), remove a table from the application's database (via a SQL Drop command), or otherwise corrupt the data in the application's database. This works by tricking the application into executing SQL commands.

SQL injection works because when a SQL call is programmatically constructed (i.e., the SQL call is built at *runtime* by concatenating the parts of the SQL call with the end user's inputs), the SQL call is altered dynamically before it is submitted to the DBMS for execution. However, when a *parameterized query* is used, the SQL call is *statically* constructed (i.e., the SQL call is built at *design time* using predefined parameters). Thus, the SQL call is *not* altered dynamically before it is submitted to the DBMS for execution. So, when a parameterized query is used, a string intended to be used for SQL injection will *always* and *only* be interpreted as an input parameter argument to the SQL call.

As can be seen, it is important to construct parameterized queries (instead of non-parameterized queries) when developing software applications that make calls to a database. Before we can construct such queries in ASP.NET, we need to have a basic understanding of two additional classes—the SqlParameterCollection class and the SqlParameter class. These classes are discussed next.

23.7.1 SqlParameterCollection Class

The SqlParameterCollection class defines the collection of parameters associated with a SqlCommand object. The Add method of a SqlParameterCollection object adds a SqlParameter object to the SqlParameterCollection, whereas the AddWithValue method adds a SqlParameter object and its associated parameter value to the SqlParameterCollection object. Table 23-5 shows some of the properties, methods, and events of the SqlParameterCollection class.

Table 23-5. *Some of the properties, methods, and events of the*
SqlParameterCollection class

Class SqlParameterCollection[6]

Namespace System.Data.SqlClient

Properties

(See reference.)

Methods

Add(Object)	Adds the specified SqlParameter object to the SqlParameterCollection.
AddWithValue(String, Object)	Adds a value to the end of the SqlParameterCollection.

Events

(See reference.)

Reference

```
https://msdn.microsoft.com/en-us/library/system.data.sqlclient.
sqlparametercollection(v=vs.110).aspx
```

23.7.2 SqlParameter Class

The SqlParameter class defines a single parameter within a SqlParameterCollection
object. The Direction property of a SqlParameter object indicates whether a parameter
is input-only, output-only, bidirectional, or a value returned from a stored procedure.
The ParameterName property indicates the name of a parameter, and the SqlDbType
property indicates the data type of a parameter. SqlDbTypes include Bit, Char, Date,
Decimal, Float, Int, Money, NVarChar, SmallInt, Text, and TinyInt. Many other
SqlDbTypes are available as well. Table 23-6 shows some of the properties, methods, and
events of the SqlParameter class.

---

[6]All property, method, and event descriptions were taken directly from Microsoft's official
documentation. The event handler methods used to handle the events of this class were omitted
to conserve space. See the reference for all of the methods of this class.

Table 23-6. *Some of the properties, methods, and events of the SqlParameter class*

Class SqlParameter[7]

Namespace System.Data.SqlClient

Properties

Direction	Gets or sets a value that indicates whether the parameter is input-only, output-only, bidirectional, or a stored procedure return value parameter.
ParameterName	Gets or sets the name of the SqlParameter.
SqlDbType	Gets or sets the SqlDbType of the parameter.

Methods

(See reference.)

Events

(See reference.)

Reference

```
https://msdn.microsoft.com/en-us/library/system.data.sqlclient.
sqlparameter(v=vs.110).aspx
```

Figure 23-3 shows an example of a parametrized query. This query is used to validate the login credentials of an employee.

Notice at 01 and 02 that the end user will be supplying an email address and password, respectively. These items will be used to construct our parameterized query.

Notice at 03 that the System.Data namespace has been added to the list of using directives (which appears at the top of the code behind file) to avoid the need to specify the fully qualified name of the CommandType class (i.e., System.Data. CommandType) each time we want to use one of its enumerations—*StoredProcedure, TableDirect*, or *Text*.

---

[7]All property, method, and event descriptions were taken directly from Microsoft's official documentation. The event handler methods used to handle the events of this class were omitted to conserve space. See the reference for all of the methods of this class.

Notice at 04 that the System.Data.SqlClient namespace has also been added to the list of using directives. This was done so we don't have to specify the fully qualified name of the SqlConnection class (i.e., System.Data.SqlClient.SqlConnection), the SqlCommand class (i.e., System.Data.SqlClient.SqlCommand), and the SqlDataReader class (i.e., System.Data.SqlClient.SqlDataReader) each time we want to use one of their respective properties or methods.

Notice at 05 that the System.Web.Configuration namespace has been added to the list of using directives to obviate the need to specify the fully qualified name of the WebConfigurationManager class (i.e., System.Web.Configuration. WebConfigurationManager) each time we want to use one of its properties.

Notice at 06–07 that we are constructing a *static* SQL Select command. That is, we are coding the structure of our Select command *fully* using email address and password parameters, which are designated by the *at signs* (@). This way, the parameters supplied by the end user will *always* and *only* be interpreted as parameters for the SQL call's Where clause. So, for example, if an end user with malicious intent attempts to delete a table from the database by injecting a *Drop* command into the email address field of the page, the word "Drop" would simply be interpreted as an email address for lookup purposes.

Notice at 08 that we are defining the network connection to our SQL Server database. As can be seen, this connection is defined in the *SportsPlay* connection string that resides in the <connectionStrings> section of our Web.config file.

Notice at 09–10 that we are creating a new SqlCommand object and readying it for execution by setting its Connection, CommandType, and CommandText properties.

Notice at 11–12 that we are taking the email address and password supplied by the end user and adding them as input parameter arguments to our SqlCommand object. The @ signs in these lines of code correspond with the @ signs in the Where clause at 06–07.

Notice at 13–14 that we are opening the connection to our SQL Server database, creating a new SqlDataReader object, loading it with the results of the Select command defined at 06–07, and attempting to retrieve a row from the data reader using the Read method of the SqlDataReader object. If a row is retrieved from the data reader, which indicates that the end user *was* found in the Employee table, we save his or her EmployeeID to a session variable (so we can identify who is logged in on subsequent pages) and display a welcome message. If a row is *not* retrieved from the data reader, which indicates that the end user was *not* found in the Employee table, we display an error message.

Notice at 15–16 that we are closing both the data reader and the connection to the database as these are not done automatically.

Notice at 17 that we have added a <connectionStrings> section to our Web.config file as well as a connection string called *SportsPlay*. This connection string provides the details of the SQL Server database that will be used by the SqlConnection object at 08. See Chapter 20, titled "Database Design, SQL, and Data Binding," for a detailed description of this connection string.

The first screenshot in the Result section of the figure shows the end user entering an *invalid* email address and password combination. The second screenshot shows the error message displayed as a result of entering the invalid combination. The third screenshot shows the end user entering a *valid* email address and password combination. And the fourth screenshot shows the welcome message displayed as a result of entering the valid combination.

ASPX CODE

```
    <asp:Label runat="server" Font-Bold="true" Text="Employee Login" />
    <br /><br />
    <asp:Label runat="server" Text="Message " />
    <asp:Label runat="server" ID="lblMessage" /><br /><br />
    <asp:Table runat="server">
        <asp:TableRow>
            <asp:TableCell>
                <asp:Label runat="server" Text="Email Address" />
            </asp:TableCell>
            <asp:TableCell>
01              <asp:TextBox runat="server" ID="txtEmailAddress"
                    MaxLength="50" Width="240px" />
            </asp:TableCell>
        </asp:TableRow>
        <asp:TableRow>
            <asp:TableCell>
                <asp:Label runat="server" Text="Password" />
            </asp:TableCell>
            <asp:TableCell>
02              <asp:TextBox runat="server" ID="txtPassword" MaxLength="10"
                    TextMode="Password" Width="240px" />
            </asp:TableCell>
        </asp:TableRow>
```

Figure 23-3. *Example of a parametrized query*

```
    <asp:TableRow>
        <asp:TableCell>
            <asp:Button runat="server" ID="btnLogin"
                OnClick="btnLogin_Click" Text="Login" />
        </asp:TableCell>
    </asp:TableRow>
</asp:Table>
```

CODE BEHIND

```
03  using System.Data;
04  using System.Data.SqlClient;
05  using System.Web.Configuration;

    protected void btnLogin_Click(object sender, EventArgs e)
    {
        // Develop the SQL call.
06      String strSQL = "";
        strSQL = "SELECT EmployeeID, FirstName + ' ' + MiddleInitial + ' ' +
                        LastName AS FullName ";
        strSQL += " FROM Employee ";
        strSQL += "WHERE EmailAddress = @EmailAddress ";
07      strSQL += "   AND Password = @Password ";
        // Define the network connection to the SQL Server database.
08      SqlConnection objSqlConnection = new
            SqlConnection(WebConfigurationManager.
            ConnectionStrings["SportsPlay"].ConnectionString);
        // Set up the SQL command object.
09      SqlCommand objSqlCommand = new SqlCommand();
        objSqlCommand.Connection = objSqlConnection;
        objSqlCommand.CommandType = CommandType.Text;
10      objSqlCommand.CommandText = strSQL;
        // Define the input parameters.
11      objSqlCommand.Parameters.AddWithValue("@EmailAddress",
            txtEmailAddress.Text);
12      objSqlCommand.Parameters.AddWithValue("@Password",
            txtPassword.Text);
        // Open the connection and execute the data reader.
13      objSqlConnection.Open();
        SqlDataReader objSqlDataReader = objSqlCommand.ExecuteReader();
        // Attempt to retrieve the row from the table.
14      if (objSqlDataReader.Read())
        {
            Session["intEmployeeID"] =
                objSqlDataReader["EmployeeID"].ToString();
            lblMessage.ForeColor = System.Drawing.Color.Green;
            lblMessage.Text = "Welcome " +
                objSqlDataReader["FullName"].ToString() + "!";
        }
```

Figure 23-3. *(continued)*

```
         else
         {
             lblMessage.ForeColor = System.Drawing.Color.Red;
             lblMessage.Text = "Invalid email address and password combination.
                 Please try again.";
         }
         // Close the data reader and the connection.
15       objSqlDataReader.Close();
16       objSqlConnection.Close();

     }
```

WEB.CONFIG CODE

```
17  <connectionStrings>
      <add name="SportsPlay"
          connectionString="Data Source=MATRBeasley-18\SQLEXPRESS;
          Initial Catalog=SportsPlay; Integrated Security=SSPI" />
    </connectionStrings>
```

RESULT

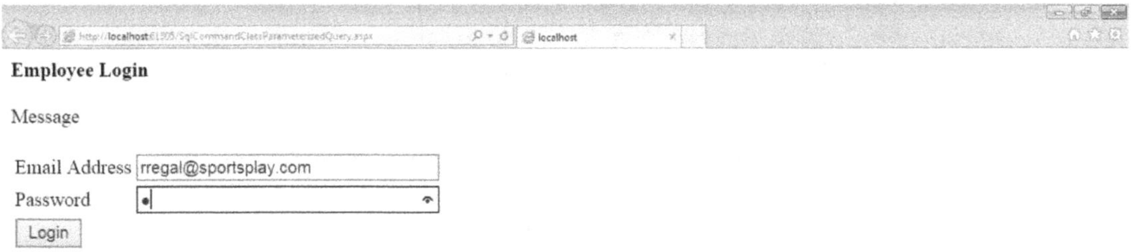

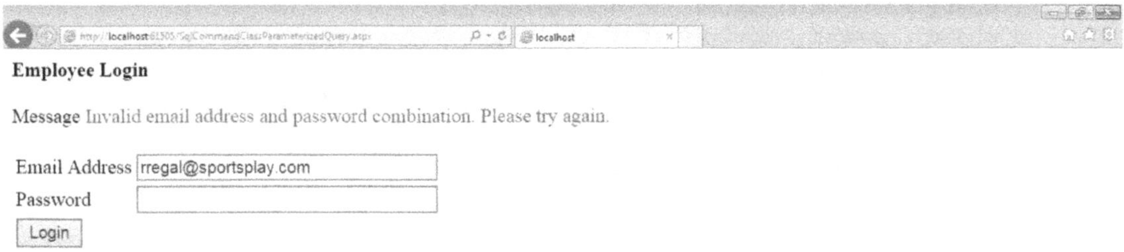

Employee Login

Message

Email Address rregal@sportsplay.com
Password
Login

Employee Login

Message Invalid email address and password combination. Please try again.

Email Address rregal@sportsplay.com
Password
Login

Figure 23-3. *(continued)*

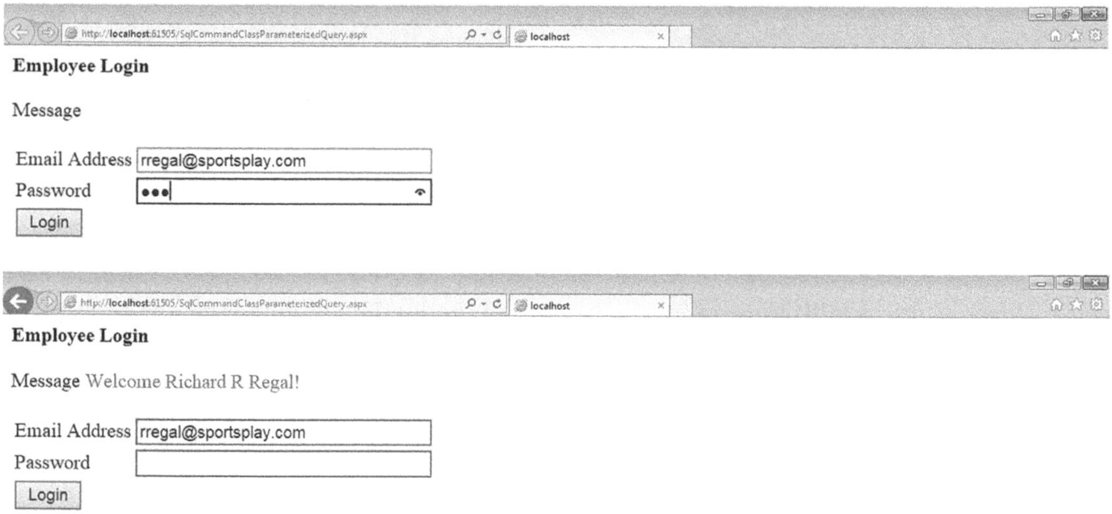

Figure 23-3. *(continued)*

23.8 Stored Procedures

A stored procedure is a standalone file that contains one or more SQL commands. Unlike the SQL commands we have seen so far (which were embedded in our Aspx and C# source code), the SQL commands in a stored procedure reside in a database on a database server. Like other software components, stored procedures can be called from other software components, can accept input parameters, can perform programming operations, can return output parameters, and can call other software components.

There are at least three advantages to storing SQL commands in stored procedures (as opposed to embedding them in source code). First, since stored procedures permit us to store SQL commands in one place (i.e., in a database), they eliminate duplicate code when the same SQL command must be executed from many locations. As can be imagined, this approach maximizes code reuse and makes changing a SQL command or group of SQL commands much more efficient as the change need only be made once. Second, since the SQL commands that reside in a stored procedure are parsed and optimized once (when they are created) and are compiled once (when they are used for the first time), they execute much faster than the SQL commands that are embedded in source code, which are parsed, optimized, and compiled every time they are used. And third, since the SQL commands that reside in a stored procedure are already on the database server, they produce less network traffic than the SQL commands that are embedded in source code because the latter must be sent to the database server from the application server via a network connection.

Of course, there are also advantages to embedding SQL commands in source code. First, when SQL commands are embedded in source code, it is easier for us to write, modify, and test our source code, since *all* of the source code (e.g., ASP.NET, C#, and SQL) is available in a single development application (e.g., Visual Studio). Thus, we need not switch between two development applications (e.g., Visual Studio and SQL Server Management Studio) when coding and testing. And second, when SQL commands are embedded in source code, we are able to step through the source code line by line to observe how a given SQL command is constructed on the fly—assuming we are using a modern IDE like Visual Studio.

The bottom line is that while both approaches have their advantages, neither approach is always better under all circumstances. Thus, it is a good idea to weigh the relative advantages of these approaches when making decisions about storing SQL commands in stored procedures or embedding them in source code.

Figure 23-4 shows an example of a SQL Server stored procedure that performs a query. This query is used to validate the login credentials of an employee.

Notice at 01 that this stored procedure is used by the SportsPlay database.

Notice at 02 the comment section of the stored procedure. This section indicates who wrote the procedure, when the procedure was created, and what the procedure does. If this procedure were to be modified, we would also indicate in this section who modified the procedure, when the procedure was modified, and what the nature of the modification was.

Notice at 03 the name of the stored procedure. As the name implies, this procedure will be used to log employees into the SportsPlay application.

Notice at 04–05 that we are defining two *input* parameters for the stored procedure—EmailAddress and Password. As can be seen, these parameters are preceded by at signs (@). Arguments for these parameters will be received from the code behind of the page that calls the procedure.

Notice at 06 the SQL Select statement that will be executed to validate an employee's login credentials, which are based on the email address and password he or she supplies. Notice in the Where clause of the statement the two items preceded by at signs (@). These items correspond directly to the input parameters defined previously.

SQL CODE

```
01  USE [SportsPlay]
    GO
    /****** Object: StoredProcedure [dbo].[EmployeeLogin]
    Script Date: xx/xx/20xx 2:48:26 PM ******/
    SET ANSI_NULLS ON
    GO
    SET QUOTED_IDENTIFIER ON
    GO
02  -- ==============================================
    -- Author:      Beasley, Robert E.
    -- Create date: 20xx-xx-xx
    -- Description: Check employee login credentials.
    -- ==============================================
03  ALTER PROCEDURE [dbo].[EmployeeLogin]

        -- Add the parameters for the stored procedure here.
04      @EmailAddress AS NVARCHAR(50),
05      @Password AS NVARCHAR(10)

    AS

    BEGIN

        -- SET NOCOUNT ON added to prevent extra result sets from
        -- interfering with SELECT statements.
        SET NOCOUNT ON;

        -- Insert statements for procedure here.
06      SELECT EmployeeID, FirstName + ' ' + MiddleInitial + ' ' + LastName
            AS FullName
          FROM Employee
         WHERE EmailAddress = @EmailAddress
           AND Password = @Password;

    END
```

Figure 23-4. *Example of a SQL Server stored procedure that performs a query*

Figure 23-5 shows an example of calling a stored procedure that performs a query. Note that the stored procedure that is called in this example is the same stored procedure just described (see Figure 23-4).

Notice at 01 and 02 that the end user will be supplying an email address and password, respectively.

Notice at 03 that the System.Data namespace has been added to the list of using directives (which appears at the top of the code behind file) so we are not required to specify the fully qualified name of the CommandType class (i.e., System.Data. CommandType) each time we want to use one of its enumerations—*StoredProcedure*, *TableDirect*, or *Text*.

Notice at 04 that the System.Data.SqlClient namespace has also been added to the list of using directives. This was done to avoid the need to specify the fully qualified name of the SqlConnection class (i.e., System.Data.SqlClient.SqlConnection), the SqlCommand class (i.e., System.Data.SqlClient.SqlCommand), and the SqlDataReader class (i.e., System.Data.SqlClient.SqlDataReader) each time we want to use one of their respective properties or methods.

Notice at 05 that the System.Web.Configuration namespace has been added to the list of using directives so we don't have to specify the fully qualified name of the WebConfigurationManager class (i.e., System.Web.Configuration. WebConfigurationManager) each time we want to use one of its properties.

Notice at 06 that we are defining the network connection to our SQL Server database. As can be seen, this connection is defined in the *SportsPlay* connection string that resides in the <connectionStrings> section of our Web.config file.

Notice at 07–08 that we are creating a new SqlCommand object and readying it for execution by setting its Connection property as usual. However, since we will be calling a stored procedure to validate the end user' login credentials, we are setting the CommandType property to *StoredProcedure* and the CommandText property to *EmployeeLogin*, which is the name of the stored procedure we will be executing (see Figure 23-4).

Notice at 09–10 that we are taking the email address and password supplied by the end user and adding them as input parameter arguments to our SqlCommand object.

Notice at 11–12 that we are opening the connection to our SQL Server database, creating a new SqlDataReader object, loading it with the results of the Select command defined in our stored procedure, and attempting to retrieve a row from the data reader using the Read method of the SqlDataReader object. If a row is retrieved from the data reader, which indicates that the end user *was* found in the Employee table, we save his or her EmployeeID to a session variable (so we can identify who is logged in on subsequent pages) and display a welcome message. If a row is *not* retrieved from the data reader, which indicates that the end user was *not* found in the Employee table, we display an error message.

Notice at 13–14 that we are closing both the data reader and the connection to the database as these are not done automatically.

Notice at 15 that we have added a <connectionStrings> section to our Web.config file as well as a connection string called *SportsPlay*. This connection string provides the details of the SQL Server database that will be used by the SqlConnection object at 06. See Chapter 20, titled "Database Design, SQL, and Data Binding," for a detailed description of this connection string.

The first screenshot in the Result section of the figure shows the end user entering an *invalid* email address and password combination. The second screenshot shows the error message displayed as a result of the invalid combination. The third screenshot shows the end user entering a *valid* email address and password combination. And the fourth screenshot shows the welcome message displayed as a result of the valid combination.

```
ASPX CODE

    <asp:Label runat="server" Font-Bold="true" Text="Employee Login" />
    <br /><br />
    <asp:Label runat="server" Text="Message " />
    <asp:Label runat="server" ID="lblMessage" /><br /><br />
    <asp:Table runat="server">
        <asp:TableRow>
            <asp:TableCell>
                <asp:Label runat="server" Text="Email Address" />
            </asp:TableCell>
            <asp:TableCell>
01              <asp:TextBox runat="server" ID="txtEmailAddress"
                    MaxLength="50" Width="240px" />
            </asp:TableCell>
        </asp:TableRow>
        <asp:TableRow>
            <asp:TableCell>
                <asp:Label runat="server" Text="Password" />
            </asp:TableCell>
            <asp:TableCell>
02              <asp:TextBox runat="server" ID="txtPassword"
                    MaxLength="10" TextMode="Password" Width="240px" />
            </asp:TableCell>
        </asp:TableRow>
        <asp:TableRow>
            <asp:TableCell>
                <asp:Button runat="server" ID="btnLogin"
                    OnClick="btnLogin_Click" Text="Login" />
            </asp:TableCell>
        </asp:TableRow>
    </asp:Table>
```

Figure 23-5. *Example of calling a stored procedure that performs a query*

CODE BEHIND

```
03   using System.Data;
04   using System.Data.SqlClient;
05   using System.Web.Configuration;

     protected void btnLogin_Click(object sender, EventArgs e)
     {
         // Define the network connection to the SQL Server database.
06       SqlConnection objSqlConnection = new
             SqlConnection(WebConfigurationManager.
             ConnectionStrings["SportsPlay"].ConnectionString);
         // Set up the SQL command object.
07       SqlCommand objSqlCommand = new SqlCommand();
         objSqlCommand.Connection = objSqlConnection;
         objSqlCommand.CommandType = CommandType.StoredProcedure;
08       objSqlCommand.CommandText = "EmployeeLogin";
         // Define the input parameters.
09       objSqlCommand.Parameters.AddWithValue("@EmailAddress",
             txtEmailAddress.Text);
10       objSqlCommand.Parameters.AddWithValue("@Password", txtPassword.Text);
         // Open the connection and execute the data reader.
11       objSqlConnection.Open();
         SqlDataReader objSqlDataReader = objSqlCommand.ExecuteReader();
         // Attempt to retrieve the row from the table.
12       if (objSqlDataReader.Read())
         {
             Session["intEmployeeID"] =
                 objSqlDataReader["EmployeeID"].ToString();
             lblMessage.ForeColor = System.Drawing.Color.Green;
             lblMessage.Text = "Welcome " +
                 objSqlDataReader["FullName"].ToString() + "!";
         }
         else
         {
             lblMessage.ForeColor = System.Drawing.Color.Red;
             lblMessage.Text = "Invalid email address and password combination.
                 Please try again.";
         }
         // Close the connection.
13       objSqlDataReader.Close();
14       objSqlConnection.Close();

     }
```

Figure 23-5. *(continued)*

WEB.CONFIG CODE

```
15   <connectionStrings>
       <add name="SportsPlay"
          connectionString="Data Source=MATRBeasley-18\SQLEXPRESS;
          Initial Catalog=SportsPlay; Integrated Security=SSPI" />
     </connectionStrings>
```

RESULT

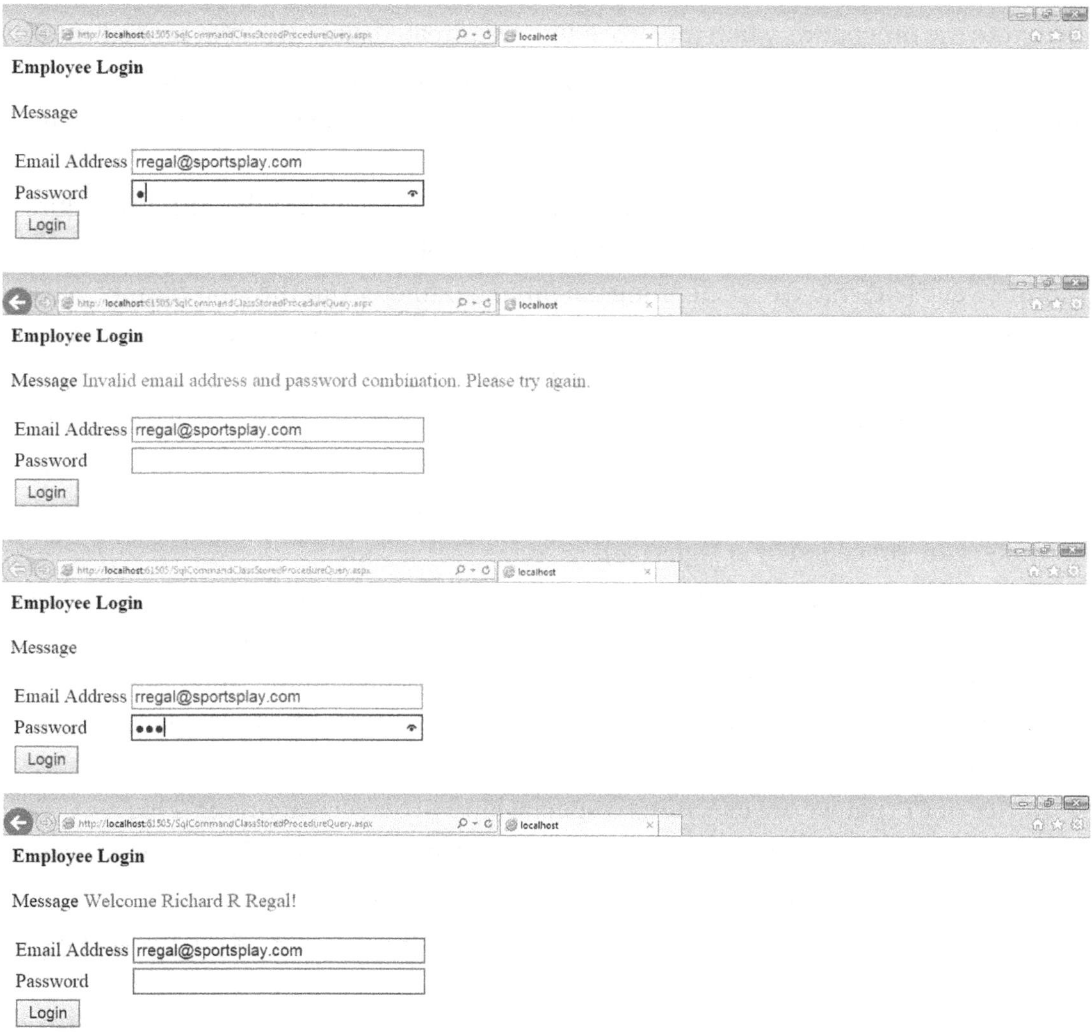

Figure 23-5. *(continued)*

Figure 23-6 shows an example of a SQL Server stored procedure that performs a non-query. This query is used to update an existing product in the Product table. Although this example illustrates an update procedure, all of the ingredients are present for an insert or delete procedure. Thus, creating those from the example shown should be relatively straightforward.

Notice at 01 that this stored procedure is used by the SportsPlay database.

Notice at 02 the comment section of the stored procedure. This section indicates who wrote the procedure, when the procedure was created, and what the procedure does. If this procedure were to be modified, we would also indicate in this section who modified the procedure, when the procedure was modified, and what the nature of the modification was.

Notice at 03 the name of the stored procedure. As the name implies, this procedure will be used to modify a product in the SportsPlay database.

Notice at 04–05 that we are defining ten *input* parameters for the stored procedure—Product ID through ReorderLevel. Arguments for these parameters will be received from the code behind of the page that calls the procedure. Notice as well that we are defining one *output* parameter for the stored procedure—RowCount. The argument for this parameter (i.e., the number of rows affected by the SQL call) will be returned to the code behind of the page that called the procedure. As can be seen, all of the procedure's parameters are preceded by at signs (@).

Notice at 06 the SQL Update statement that will be executed to modify an existing product in the Product table using the input parameter arguments supplied by the end user. Notice in the Set and Where clauses of the statement the ten items preceded by at signs (@). These items correspond directly to the input parameters defined previously.

Notice at 07 that we are executing a special kind of Select statement. This statement retrieves the number of rows affected by the previous SQL call and places that value in the RowCount output parameter. This information will be used in the code behind of the page that invoked the stored procedure to determine the success or failure of the update.

SQL CODE

```
01  USE [SportsPlay]
    GO
    /****** Object: StoredProcedure [dbo].[ProductModify]
    Script Date: xx/xx/20xx 10:54:44 AM ******/
    SET ANSI_NULLS ON
    GO
    SET QUOTED_IDENTIFIER ON
    GO
02  -- ===============================================
    -- Author:      Beasley, Robert E.
    -- Create date: 20xx-xx-xx
    -- Description: Update the product.
    -- ===============================================
03  ALTER PROCEDURE [dbo].[ProductModify]

        -- Add the parameters for the stored procedure here.
04      @ProductID AS INT,
        @CategoryID AS INT,
        @SupplierID AS INT,
        @Product AS NVARCHAR(50),
        @Description AS NVARCHAR(MAX),
        @Image AS NVARCHAR(50),
        @Price AS DEC(18,2),
        @NumberInStock AS TINYINT,
        @NumberOnOrder AS TINYINT,
        @ReorderLevel AS TINYINT,
05      @RowCount AS INT OUTPUT

    AS

    BEGIN

        -- SET NOCOUNT ON added to prevent extra result sets from
        -- interfering with SELECT statements.
        SET NOCOUNT ON;

        -- Insert statements for procedure here.
```

Figure 23-6. *Example of a SQL Server stored procedure that performs a non-query*

```
06        UPDATE Product
             SET CategoryID = @CategoryID,
                 SupplierID = @SupplierID,
                 Product = @Product,
                 Description = @Description,
                 Image = @Image,
                 Price = @Price,
                 NumberInStock = @NumberInStock,
                 NumberOnOrder = @NumberOnOrder,
                 ReorderLevel = @ReorderLevel
           WHERE ProductID = @ProductID;

07        SELECT @RowCount = @@ROWCOUNT;

      END
```

Figure 23-6. *(continued)*

Figure 23-7 shows an example of calling a stored procedure that performs a non-query. Note that the stored procedure that is called in this example is the same stored procedure just described (see Figure 23-6).

Notice at 01 that the ProductID will be entered into a TextBox control by the end user. Keep in mind that, in a real-world application, the ProductID would not likely be entered into a text box, since primary keys like this are meaningless to the end user (e.g., no one knows what ProductID 3712 represents). Instead, the ProductID would probably be set when the end user selects a meaningful option from some other control, like a DropDownList control.

Notice at 02 and 03 that the end user will be selecting a category and supplying a product name. As can be seen, several other inputs from the end user (i.e., supplier, description, image, price, number in stock, number on order, and reorder level) have been omitted for brevity.

Notice at 04 that the System.Data namespace has been added to the list of using directives (which appears at the top of the code behind file) to obviate the need to specify the fully qualified name of the CommandType class (i.e., System.Data. CommandType) each time we want to use one of its enumerations—*StoredProcedure, TableDirect,* or *Text*.

Notice at 05 that the System.Data.SqlClient namespace has also been added to the list of using directives. This was done so we are not required to specify the fully qualified name of the SqlConnection class (i.e., System.Data.SqlClient.SqlConnection), the

SqlCommand class (i.e., System.Data.SqlClient.SqlCommand), and the SqlDataReader class (i.e., System.Data.SqlClient.SqlDataReader) each time we want to use one of their respective properties or methods.

Notice at 06 that the System.Web.Configuration namespace has been added to the list of using directives to avoid the need to specify the fully qualified name of the WebConfigurationManager class (i.e., System.Web.Configuration. WebConfigurationManager) each time we want to use one of its properties.

Notice at 07 that we are defining the network connection to our SQL Server database. As can be seen, this connection is defined in the *SportsPlay* connection string that resides in the <connectionStrings> section of our Web.config file.

Notice at 08–09 that we are creating a new SqlCommand object and readying it for execution by setting its Connection property as usual. However, since we will be calling a stored procedure to update the product in the Product table, we are setting the CommandType property to *StoredProcedure* and the CommandText property to *ProductModify*, which is the name of the stored procedure we will be executing (see Figure 23-6).

Notice at 10–11 that we are taking the ProductID, CategoryID, SupplierID, Product, Description, Image, Price, NumberInStock, NumberOnOrder, and ReorderLevel supplied by the end user and adding them as *input* parameter arguments to our SqlCommand object.

Notice at 12 that we are also adding an *output* parameter to our SqlCommand object. This parameter will return the number of rows affected by the SQL Update command in the stored procedure.

Notice at 13–14 that we are opening the connection to our SQL Server database, executing the non-query defined in our stored procedure (i.e., the Update command), and checking our RowCount output parameter to determine how many rows of data were affected by the SQL call. If a single row of data was affected by the Update command, which indicates that the update *was* successful, we display a success message. If something other than a single row of data was affected by the Update command, which indicates that the update *was not* successful, we display an error message.

Notice at 15 that we are closing the connection to the database as this is not done automatically.

Notice at 16 that we have added a <connectionStrings> section to our Web.config file as well as a connection string called *SportsPlay*. This connection string provides the details of the SQL Server database that will be used by the SqlConnection object at 07. See Chapter 20, titled "Database Design, SQL, and Data Binding," for a detailed description of this connection string.

The screenshot in the Result section of the figure shows a product after it has been modified successfully.

```
ASPX CODE

    ⋮
    : (Code continues.)
    ⋮

    <asp:Label runat="server" Font-Bold="true" Text="Modify Product" />
        <br /><br />
    <asp:Label runat="server" Text="Message " />
    <asp:Label runat="server" ID="lblMessage" /><br /><br />

    <asp:Table runat="server">
        <asp:TableRow>
            <asp:TableCell>
                <asp:Label runat="server" Text="ProductID" />
            </asp:TableCell>
            <asp:TableCell>
01              <asp:TextBox runat="server" ID="txtProductID" />
            </asp:TableCell>
        </asp:TableRow>
        <asp:TableRow>
            <asp:TableCell>
                <asp:Label runat="server" Text="Category" />
            </asp:TableCell>
            <asp:TableCell>
02              <asp:DropDownList runat="server" ID="ddlCategory"
                    DataSourceID="sdsDropDownListCategory"
                    DataTextField="Category" DataValueField="CategoryID" />
            </asp:TableCell>
        </asp:TableRow>
        ⋮
        : (Code continues.)
        ⋮
        <asp:TableRow>
            <asp:TableCell>
                <asp:Label runat="server" Text="Product" />
            </asp:TableCell>
```

Figure 23-7. *Example of calling a stored procedure that performs a non-query*

```
                <asp:TableCell>
03                  <asp:TextBox runat="server" ID="txtProduct"
                        MaxLength="50" />
                </asp:TableCell>
            </asp:TableRow>
            ⋮
            ⋮ (Code continues.)
            ⋮
    </asp:Table>

    <asp:Button runat="server" ID="btnSave" OnClick="btnSave_Click"
        Text="Save" />
```

CODE BEHIND

```
04  using System.Data;
05  using System.Data.SqlClient;
06  using System.Web.Configuration;

    protected void btnSave_Click(object sender, EventArgs e)
    {

        // Define the network connection to the SQL Server database.
07      SqlConnection objSqlConnection = new
            SqlConnection(WebConfigurationManager.
            ConnectionStrings["SportsPlay"].ConnectionString);
        // Set up the SQL command object.
08      SqlCommand objSqlCommand = new SqlCommand();
        objSqlCommand.Connection = objSqlConnection;
        objSqlCommand.CommandType = CommandType.StoredProcedure;
09      objSqlCommand.CommandText = "ProductModify";
        // Define the input parameters.
10      objSqlCommand.Parameters.AddWithValue("@ProductID",
            txtProductID.Text);
        objSqlCommand.Parameters.AddWithValue("@CategoryID",
            ddlCategory.SelectedValue);
        objSqlCommand.Parameters.AddWithValue("@SupplierID",
            ddlSupplier.SelectedValue);
        objSqlCommand.Parameters.AddWithValue("@Product",
            txtProduct.Text);
        objSqlCommand.Parameters.AddWithValue("@Description",
            txtDescription.Text);
        objSqlCommand.Parameters.AddWithValue("@Image",
            txtImage.Text);
        objSqlCommand.Parameters.AddWithValue("@Price",
            txtPrice.Text);
        objSqlCommand.Parameters.AddWithValue("@NumberInStock",
            txtNumberInStock.Text);
        objSqlCommand.Parameters.AddWithValue("@NumberOnOrder",
            txtNumberOnOrder.Text);
```

Figure 23-7. (continued)

```
11      objSqlCommand.Parameters.AddWithValue("@ReorderLevel",
            txtReorderLevel.Text);
        // Define the output parameters.
12      objSqlCommand.Parameters.Add("@RowCount", SqlDbType.Int).Direction =
            ParameterDirection.Output;
        // Open the connection and execute the non-query.
13      objSqlConnection.Open();
        objSqlCommand.ExecuteNonQuery();
14      if ((Int32)objSqlCommand.Parameters["@RowCount"].Value == 1)
        {
            lblMessage.ForeColor = System.Drawing.Color.Green;
            lblMessage.Text = "Product successfully modified.";
        }
        else
        {
            lblMessage.ForeColor = System.Drawing.Color.Red;
            lblMessage.Text = "Product NOT successfully modified.
                Please report this message to....:";
        }
        // Close the connection.
15      objSqlConnection.Close();

    }
```

WEB.CONFIG CODE

```
16  <connectionStrings>
      <add name="SportsPlay"
          connectionString="Data Source=MATRBeasley-18\SQLEXPRESS;
          Initial Catalog=SportsPlay; Integrated Security=SSPI" />
    </connectionStrings>
```

Figure 23-7. *(continued)*

RESULT

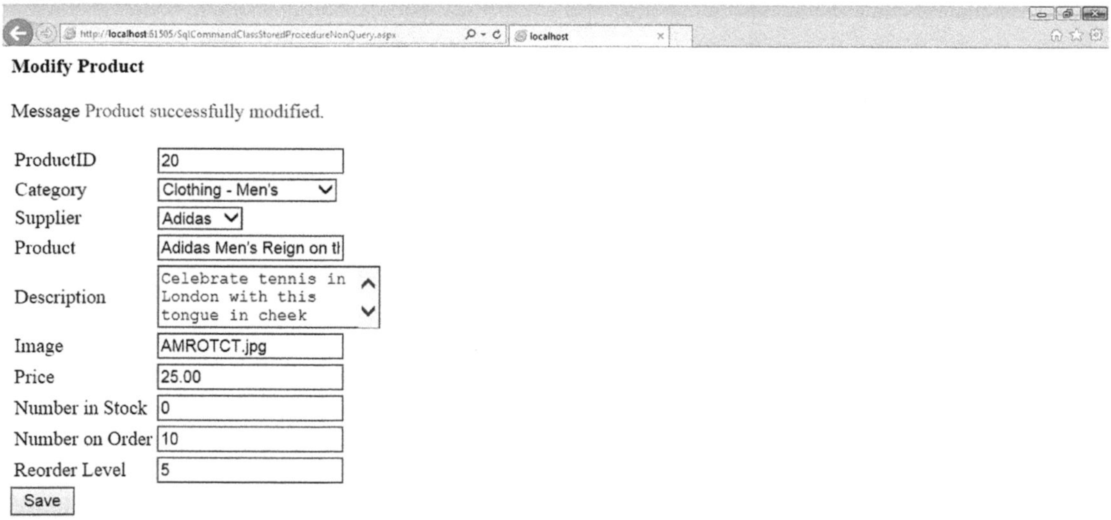

Figure 23-7. (continued)

PART VI

Additional Functionality

CHAPTER 24

Email Messaging

24.1 Introduction

Email messaging is the process of distributing written messages to computer users over a network. Although there are several email protocols in use today, the *Simple Mail Transfer Protocol* (SMTP) is the standard protocol for sending emails over the Internet. In fact, most of us use SMTP-based client-server email systems regularly for delayed, asynchronous, two-way communication with others.

The Simple Mail Transfer Protocol utilizes a *store-and-forward model* for data transmission. Within this model, the sender's email client *forwards* a message to the sender's email server. When the sender's email server receives the message, it *stores* the message until it is ready to pass the message on. When the sender's email server is ready, it *forwards* the message to an intermediate server. When the intermediate server receives the message, it *stores* the message until it is ready to pass the message on. When the intermediate server is ready, it *forwards* the message to another intermediate server. This process continues until the message arrives at the recipient's email server. At this point, the recipient's email server *stores* the message until the recipient's email client requests that the message be delivered. When the recipient's email client requests that the message be delivered, the recipient's email server *forwards* the message to the recipient's email client for display.

In this chapter, we will begin by installing an email server on our development machine so that we can test our Web applications that send email messages. This server, called Papercut, is a simplified SMTP server that receives and displays email messages without forwarding them to real recipients. Next, we will discuss the MailMessage class, which constructs the email messages we wish to send. And finally, we will examine the SmtpClient class. This class sends the email messages we have constructed to an SMTP server for forwarding for delivery.

489

© Robert E. Beasley 2020
R. E. Beasley, *Essential ASP.NET Web Forms Development*, https://doi.org/10.1007/978-1-4842-5784-5_24

24.2 Development Machine Email Server

Before we discuss the classes required for implementing email functionality, we need to install an email server on our development machine so that we can test our Web applications that send email messages. Although there are several SMTP servers available, we will download, install, and use *Papercut*. Papercut is a simplified SMTP server that receives and displays email messages without forwarding them to real recipients. Since the Papercut server only *displays* the email messages it receives (i.e., it doesn't *forward* them), we can safely test our email message code without cluttering the inboxes of real people. The Papercut server is available for free, and the *Papercut.Setup. exe* file can be downloaded and run from the GitHub Web site:

```
https://github.com/ChangemakerStudios/Papercut/releases
```

There are three things to remember when using the Papercut server. First, the Papercut server must be running to receive and display email messages. When the Papercut server is running, its icon will appear in the system tray. Second, when the Papercut server receives an email message, it will display a notification above the system tray. To view the email message, we can click the notification, or we can click the Papercut icon itself. And third, when we are ready to deploy our Web application to a real server, we will only need to modify our Web.config file to point to a real SMTP server so that our email messages can be forwarded to real recipients.

24.3 MailMessage Class

The MailMessage class constructs the email messages we wish to send. A MailMessage object has a number of properties that we can set when constructing an email message. The From property specifies the email address of the sender of the message. If the recipient replies to the message, the sender will be sent the reply. The ReplyToList property contains the collection of email addresses that will be sent the reply if the recipient replies to the message. The To property contains the collection of email addresses that will receive the message. The CC property contains the collection of email addresses that will receive a *carbon copy* of the message. The recipients of a carbon copy of the message *will be seen* by the other recipients of the message. The Bcc property contains the collection of email addresses that will receive a *blind carbon copy* of the message. The recipients of a blind carbon copy of the message *will not be seen* by the other recipients of the message. The Subject property specifies the subject line of the message. The Body property specifies the content of the message. The body of the message can contain text, images, hyperlinks, and so on. The IsBodyHtml property specifies whether or not the body of the message is in HTML form. If the IsBodyHtml property is set to *true*, any HTML markup (e.g., <br />, <b>, <i>) will be interpreted as such by the recipient's email client and will thus be used to format the message. If the IsBodyHtml property is set to *false*, any HTML markup will be interpreted as regular text by the recipient's email client and will thus be displayed as is. The Priority property specifies the urgency (i.e., low, medium, high) of the message. And finally, the Attachments property contains the collection of attachments we wish to send along with the message. Table 24-1 shows some of the properties, methods, and events of the MailMessage class.

Table 24-1. *Some of the properties, methods, and events of the MailMessage class*

Class MailMessage[1]

Namespace System.Net.Mail

Properties

Attachments	Gets the attachment collection used to store data attached to this email message.
Bcc	Gets the address collection that contains the blind carbon copy (BCC) recipients for this email message.
Body	Gets or sets the message body.
CC	Gets the address collection that contains the carbon copy (CC) recipients for this email message.
From	Gets or sets the from address for this email message.
IsBodyHtml	Gets or sets a value indicating whether the mail message body is in Html.
Priority	Gets or sets the priority of this email message.

(*continued*)

---

[1]All property, method, and event descriptions were taken directly from Microsoft's official documentation. The event handler methods used to handle the events of this class were omitted to conserve space. See the reference for all of the methods of this class.

Table 24-1. (*continued*)

ReplyToList	Gets or sets the list of addresses to reply to for the mail message.
Subject	Gets or sets the subject line for this email message.
To	Gets the address collection that contains the recipients of this email message.

Methods

(See reference.)

Events

(See reference.)

Reference

```
https://msdn.microsoft.com/en-us/library/system.net.mail.
mailmessage(v=vs.110).aspx
```

24.4 SmtpClient Class

The SmtpClient class sends the email messages we have constructed to an SMTP server for forwarding for delivery. To send an email message using the SmtpClient class, we must specify the name of the host email server and any required server credentials (i.e., username and password). As a general rule, we will specify these things in the Web. config file so that any changes to the host email server configuration can be made in one place. When a host email server requires credentials, the syntax used to identify the server and its associated credentials in the <system.net> <mailSettings> <smtp> section of the Web.config file is

```
<network host="Host Email Server" userName="Username" password="Password"
    port="Port Number" />
```

where the items in italics are the name of the host email server (e.g., mail.company.com, localhost), the username of the email account on the server, the password of the email account on the server, and the port number on the server, respectively. The port number may or may not be required. When a host email server does not require credentials, we need not include the entries for the username and password.

To send an email message to a host email server so that it can be forwarded for delivery, we use the Send method of an SmtpClient object. After an email message has been sent, and we are done with the SmtpClient object, we must make sure to invoke the Dispose method of the SmtpClient object. This method sends a *quit* message to the host email server, ends the TCP/IP connection to the server, and releases the memory resources used by the SmtpClient object. Table 24-2 shows some of the properties, methods, and events of the SmtpClient class.

Table 24-2. *Some of the properties, methods, and events of the SmtpClient class*

Class SmtpClient[2]

Namespace System.Net.Mail

Properties

Credentials	Gets or sets the credentials used to authenticate the sender.
Host	Gets or sets the name or IP address of the host used for SMTP transactions.
Port	Gets or sets the port used for SMTP transactions.

Methods

Dispose()	Sends a QUIT message to the SMTP server, gracefully ends the TCP connection, and releases all resources used by the current instance of the SmtpClient class.
Send(MailMessage)	Sends the specified message to an SMTP server for delivery.

Events

(See reference.)

Reference

https://msdn.microsoft.com/en-us/library/system.net.mail.
smtpclient(v=vs.110).aspx

---

[2]All property, method, and event descriptions were taken directly from Microsoft's official documentation. The event handler methods used to handle the events of this class were omitted to conserve space. See the reference for all of the methods of this class.

Figure 24-1 shows an example of the MailMessage and SmtpClient classes. These classes are being used to send the end user a forgotten password.

Notice at 01 and 02 that the end user will be entering his or her email address into a text box and clicking the *Send Password* button.

Notice at 03 that the System.Net.Mail namespace has been added to the list of using directives (which appears at the top of the code behind file). This was done so we are not required to specify the fully qualified name of the MailMessage class (i.e., System. Net.Mail.MailMessage), the SmtpClient class (i.e., System.Net.Mail.SmtpClient), and the MailAddress class (i.e., System.Net.Mail.MailAddress) each time we want to use one of their respective properties or methods.

Notice at 04–05 that we are saving the end user's full name and password to two string variables. As we will see in a moment, the values of these variables will be displayed in the body of the email message to personalize it and make it appear more professional.

Notice at 06–07 that we are building the email message using the MailMessage class. First, we are creating a new MailMessage object from the MailMessage class. Next, we are setting the From property of the message using a MailAddress object. In this case, we are setting the property to a "noreply" email address. Of course, we could have set the property to an active email address if that is what the application required. After that, we are adding the recipient's email address to the To property of the message using a MailAddress object. Notice that this email address is coming from the email address text box on the page. We are then setting the Subject property of the message so that the recipient will know the purpose of the message at a glance. Next, we are setting the Body property of the message. Notice that the end user's full name and password (both of which we saved previously) are being embedded in the message. Notice as well that we have included some HTML markup in the message. We are then setting the IsBodyHtml property of the message to *true* to indicate that the body of the email message is in HTML form. Thus, the HTML markup in the message will be interpreted as such by the recipient's email client, which will cause the message to be formatted according to our intentions.

Notice at 08–09 that we are creating a new SmtpClient object from the SmtpClient class, using that object to send the MailMessage object we just created to the SMTP server, and disposing of the SmtpClient object, which sends a *quit* message to the host email server, ends the TCP/IP connection to the server, and releases the memory resources used by the SmtpClient object.

Notice at 10 that we have specified the name of the host email server and port number in the <system.net> <mailSettings> <smtp> section of the Web.config file. This particular configuration permits us to send messages to the Papercut server on our development machine.

The first screenshot in the Result section of the figure shows the error message displayed as a result of entering an invalid email address when attempting to retrieve and send a password. The second screenshot shows the message displayed as a result of entering a valid email address when attempting to retrieve and send a password. And the third screenshot shows the email message displayed by the Papercut server.

ASPX CODE

```
        <asp:Label runat="server" Font-Bold="true" Text="Employee Login" />
        <br /><br />
        <asp:Label runat="server" Text="Message " />
        <asp:Label runat="server" ID="lblMessage" /><br /><br />
        <asp:Table runat="server">
            <asp:TableRow>
                <asp:TableCell>
                    <asp:Label runat="server" Text="Email Address" />
                </asp:TableCell>
                <asp:TableCell>
01                  <asp:TextBox runat="server" ID="txtEmailAddress"
                        MaxLength="50" Width="240px" />
                </asp:TableCell>
            </asp:TableRow>
            <asp:TableRow>
                <asp:TableCell>
                    <asp:Label runat="server" Text="Password" />
                </asp:TableCell>
                <asp:TableCell>
                    <asp:TextBox runat="server" ID="txtPassword" MaxLength="10"
                        TextMode="Password" Width="240px" />
                </asp:TableCell>
            </asp:TableRow>
            <asp:TableRow>
                <asp:TableCell>
                    <asp:Button runat="server" ID="btnLogin"
                        OnClick="btnLogin_Click" Text="Login" />
                </asp:TableCell>
                <asp:TableCell>
02                  <asp:Button runat="server" ID="btnSendPassword"
                        OnClick="btnSendPassword_Click" Text="Send Password" />
                </asp:TableCell>
            </asp:TableRow>
        </asp:Table>
```

Figure 24-1. *Example of the MailMessage and SmtpClient classes*

CODE BEHIND

```
    using System.Data;
    using System.Data.SqlClient;
    using System.Web.Configuration;
03  using System.Net.Mail;

protected void btnSendPassword_Click(object sender, EventArgs e)
{

    // Develop the SQL call.
    String strSQL = "";
    strSQL = "SELECT FirstName + ' ' + MiddleInitial + ' ' + LastName
                    AS FullName, Password ";
    strSQL += " FROM Employee ";
    strSQL += "WHERE EmailAddress = @EmailAddress ";
    // Define the network connection to the SQL Server database.
    SqlConnection objSqlConnection = new
        SqlConnection(WebConfigurationManager.
        ConnectionStrings["SportsPlay"].ConnectionString);
    // Set up the SQL command object.
    SqlCommand objSqlCommand = new SqlCommand();
    objSqlCommand.Connection = objSqlConnection;
        objSqlCommand.CommandType = CommandType.Text;
        objSqlCommand.CommandText = strSQL;
        // Define the input parameters.
        objSqlCommand.Parameters.AddWithValue("@EmailAddress",
            txtEmailAddress.Text);
        // Open the connection and execute the data reader.
        objSqlConnection.Open();
        SqlDataReader objSqlDataReader = objSqlCommand.ExecuteReader();
        // Attempt to retrieve the row from the table.
        if (objSqlDataReader.Read())
        {
            // Save the full name and password.
04          String strFullName = objSqlDataReader["FullName"].ToString();
05          String strPassword = objSqlDataReader["Password"].ToString();
            // Close the data reader and the connection.
            objSqlDataReader.Close();
            objSqlConnection.Close();
            // Build the email message.
06          MailMessage objMailMessage = new MailMessage();
            objMailMessage.From = new MailAddress("noreply@sportsplay.com");
            objMailMessage.To.Add(new MailAddress(txtEmailAddress.Text));
            objMailMessage.Subject = "Password Retrieval";
            objMailMessage.Body = "Dear " + strFullName + "," +
                "<br /><br />Please retain the following password as you
                will need it to login to the system.<br /><br />
                Password: <i>" + strPassword + "</i><br /><br />Thank you.";
```

Figure 24-1. *(continued)*

```
07          objMailMessage.IsBodyHtml = true;
            // Send the email message.
08          SmtpClient objSmtpClient = new SmtpClient();
            objSmtpClient.Send(objMailMessage);
09          objSmtpClient.Dispose();
            // Set the message.
            lblMessage.ForeColor = System.Drawing.Color.Green;
            lblMessage.Text = "Your email address was found, and your password
                was sent. Please check your email.";
        }
        else
        {
            // Close the data reader and the connection.
            objSqlDataReader.Close();
            objSqlConnection.Close();
            lblMessage.ForeColor = System.Drawing.Color.Red;
            lblMessage.Text = "Your email address was NOT found.
                Please check your email address for accuracy and try again.";
        }

    }
```

WEB.CONFIG CODE

```
    <system.net>
      <mailSettings>
        <smtp>
10          <network host="localhost" port="25" />
        </smtp>
      </mailSettings>
    </system.net>
```

RESULT

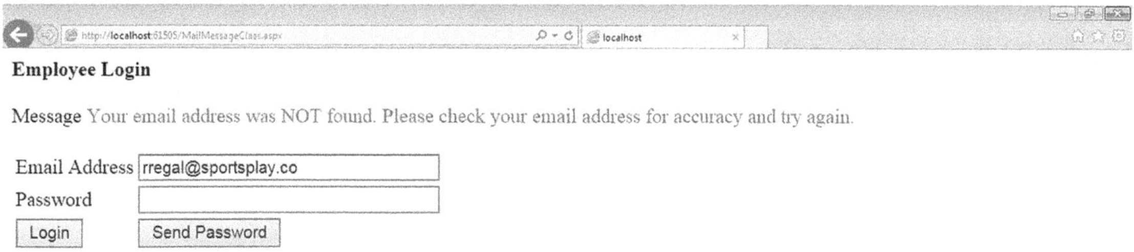

Employee Login

Message Your email address was NOT found. Please check your email address for accuracy and try again.

Email Address rregal@sportsplay.co
Password
Login   Send Password

Figure 24-1. *(continued)*

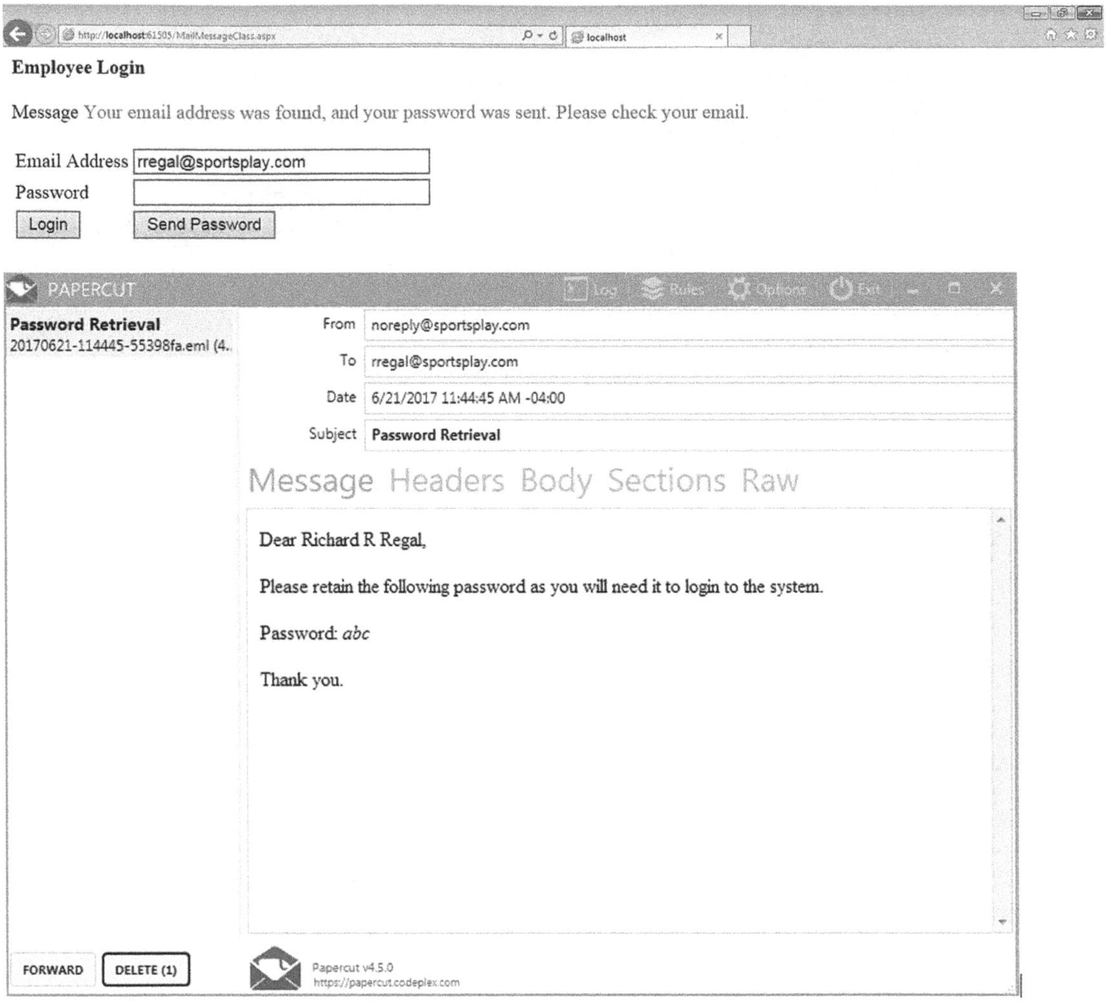

Employee Login

Message Your email address was found, and your password was sent. Please check your email.

Email Address [rregal@sportsplay.com]
Password   [   ]
[Login]   [Send Password]

PAPERCUT   Log   Rules   Options   Exit   –   □   ×

Password Retrieval
20170621-114445-55398fa.eml (4.

From   noreply@sportsplay.com
To   rregal@sportsplay.com
Date   6/21/2017 11:44:45 AM -04:00
Subject   **Password Retrieval**

Message   Headers   Body   Sections   Raw

Dear Richard R Regal,

Please retain the following password as you will need it to login to the system.

Password: *abc*

Thank you.

[FORWARD] [DELETE (1)]   Papercut v4.5.0
                                    https://papercut.codeplex.com

Figure 24-1. *(continued)*

CHAPTER 25

Ajax Programming

25.1 Introduction

Ajax (Asynchronous JavaScript and XML) is a collection of special script-based classes. These classes enable the client and the server to interact in such a way that only a *region* of a page is re-created, re-formatted, sent back to the client, and re-rendered in the client's browser. To understand how the Ajax classes work, we need to contrast the concepts of *synchronous postbacks* and *full-page rendering* with *asynchronous postbacks* and *partial-page rendering*.

A synchronous postback occurs when a page is sent to the server and processed (all of the server-side events are processed), *and* the *entire* page is re-created, re-formatted, sent back to the client, and re-rendered in the client's browser. Since the *entire* page is re-created, re-formatted, sent back to the client, and re-rendered in the client's browser, *full-page rendering* occurs. Synchronous postbacks can be *inefficient* for a few reasons. First, since the *entire* page is re-created, re-formatted, sent back to the client, and re-rendered in the client's browser, the server must perform some unnecessary processing when only a part of the page needs to be updated. Second, since the *entire* page is re-rendered in the client's browser, he or she must wait for the entire page to re-display before continuing their work on the page. And third, since the *entire* page is re-rendered in the client's browser, the top of the page is, by default, automatically re-aligned with the top of the browser when the page re-displays.[1] This can make for a frustrating experience since the end user may be required to scroll down the page to where he or she was when they submitted the page for processing. By default, the ASP.NET page model uses synchronous postbacks.

---

[1]This can be avoided by setting the maintainScrollPositionOnPostBack property of the <pages> tag to *true* in the <system.web> section of the Web.config file.

© Robert E. Beasley 2020
R. E. Beasley, *Essential ASP.NET Web Forms Development*, https://doi.org/10.1007/978-1-4842-5784-5_25

An asynchronous postback, on the other hand, occurs when a page is sent to the server and processed (all of the server-side events are *still* processed), *but* only a *part* of the page is re-created, re-formatted, sent back to the client, and re-rendered in the client's browser. Since only a *part* of the page is re-created, re-formatted, sent back to the client, and re-rendered in the client's browser, *partial-page rendering* occurs. Asynchronous postbacks can be more *efficient* for a few reasons. First, since only a *part* of the page is re-created, re-formatted, sent back to the client, and re-rendered in the client's browser, the server need not perform as much unnecessary processing when only a part of the page needs to be updated. Second, since only a *part* of the page is re-rendered in the client's browser, he or she need not wait for the entire page to re-display before continuing their work on the page. And third, since only a *part* of the page is re-rendered in the client's browser, the top of the page is not automatically re-aligned with the top of the browser when the page re-displays. This can make for a much less frustrating experience since the end user may not be required to scroll down the page to where he or she was when they submitted the page for processing.

Ajax classes are implemented in HTML, CSS, and JavaScript. Because of this, Ajax controls will not function properly in browsers that do not support scripting or have browser scripting disabled. In addition, some smartphones and other special devices may not support the use of Ajax controls. Thus, it is important that alternative non-Ajax code be in place when such devices may be used to access an application.

In this chapter, we will begin by looking at the ScriptManager class. This class manages a Web page's Ajax resources, including the automatic download of Ajax scripts that enable asynchronous postbacks and partial-page rendering. Next, we will discuss the Ajax extension classes, which are part of the .NET Framework, and add basic Ajax functionality to Web applications. And finally, we will consider the Ajax Control Toolkit. This toolkit is an open-source class library that we can use to enhance the interactivity and overall experience of the Web applications we develop.

25.2 ScriptManager Class

The ScriptManager class manages a Web page's Ajax resources. This management includes, among other things, the automatic download of Ajax scripts that enable asynchronous postbacks and partial-page rendering. A ScriptManager control *must* be included in a Page class that contains Ajax controls, and *only* one ScriptManager control can be included in a Page class. Table 25-1 shows some of the properties, methods, and events of the ScriptManager class.

Table 25-1. *Some of the properties, methods, and events of the ScriptManager class*

Class ScriptManager[2]
Namespace System.Web.UI
Properties
(See reference.)
Methods
(See reference.)
Events
(See reference.)
Reference
`https://msdn.microsoft.com/en-us/library/system.web.ui.` `scriptmanager(v=vs.110).aspx`

25.3 Extension Classes

The Ajax extension classes are part of the .NET Framework and add basic Ajax functionality to Web applications. The Ajax extension classes include the UpdatePanel class, the UpdateProgress class, and the Timer class. We will discuss the first two of these classes in this section. Together, they will permit us to exploit the use of asynchronous postbacks and partial-page rendering and will allow us to provide feedback to the end user with regard to the status of an asynchronous postback.

25.3.1 UpdatePanel Class

The UpdatePanel class defines a *page region* that will be asynchronously posted back to the server and re-rendered in the browser. Thus, this class is an essential part of the Ajax model. The ContentTemplate property of an UpdatePanel control defines the content of the update panel, which typically includes one or more server controls. More than one UpdatePanel control can be included in a single Page class, which permits us to define discrete regions on a page that can be posted back and re-rendered independently.

---

[2]All property, method, and event descriptions were taken directly from Microsoft's official documentation. The event handler methods used to handle the events of this class were omitted to conserve space. See the reference for all of the methods of this class.

When a page is first requested, all of the page regions (i.e., all of the UpdatePanel controls) on the page are rendered in the browser. However, when an individual page region (i.e., an individual UpdatePanel control) is requested, only that page region is re-rendered in the browser. An UpdatePanel control can be included in a MasterPage class or a content Page class, can be defined in a template control like a FormView control or a ListView control, or can be nested in another UpdatePanel control. We can also apply styles to an UpdatePanel control using CSS. Table 25-2 shows some of the properties, methods, and events of the UpdatePanel class.

Table 25-2. *Some of the properties, methods, and events of the UpdatePanel class*

Class UpdatePanel[3]

Namespace System.Web.UI

Properties

ContentTemplate   Gets or sets the template that defines the content of the UpdatePanel control.

Methods

(See reference.)

Events

(See reference.)

Reference

```
https://msdn.microsoft.com/en-us/library/system.web.ui.
updatepanel(v=vs.110).aspx
```

Figure 25-1 shows an example of the UpdatePanel class.

Notice at 01 the ScriptManager control, which automatically downloads the Ajax scripts necessary for asynchronous postbacks and partial-page rendering.

Notice at 02 the UpdatePanel control. This control defines the page region that will be asynchronously posted back to the server and re-rendered in the browser.

Notice at 03 the ContentTemplate property of the UpdatePanel control, which defines the content of the update panel. As can be seen, the contents of the update panel include a text box, a button, and a message label.

---

[3]All property, method, and event descriptions were taken directly from Microsoft's official documentation. The event handler methods used to handle the events of this class were omitted to conserve space. See the reference for all of the methods of this class.

Notice at 04 the event handler method that is invoked when the end user clicks the *Save* button. When this occurs, only the page region defined by the update panel will be re-created, re-formatted, sent back to the client, and re-rendered in the client's browser. The remainder of the page will not be updated.

The screenshot in the Result section of the figure shows the message displayed as a result of saving an email address. If we could have observed the behavior of the browser when the *Save* button was clicked, we would have noticed that the entire page was *not* re-rendered in the client's browser. In addition, we would have noticed the absence of the familiar "page flicker" that normally occurs during a synchronous postback.

ASPX CODE

```
01   <asp:ScriptManager runat="server" />

     <asp:Label runat="server" Font-Bold="true" Text="Email Address" /><br />

02   <asp:UpdatePanel runat="server" ID="uppEmailAddress">
03       <ContentTemplate>
             <asp:TextBox runat="server" ID="txtEmailAddress" /><br />
             <asp:Button runat="server" ID="btnSave" OnClick="btnSave_Click"
                 Text="Save" />
             <asp:Label runat="server" ID="lblMessage" />
         </ContentTemplate>
     </asp:UpdatePanel>
```

CODE BEHIND

```
04   protected void btnSave_Click(object sender, EventArgs e)
     {

         // The database call to save the email address would go here.
         // If successful, the following message would be displayed.
         lblMessage.ForeColor = System.Drawing.Color.Green;
         lblMessage.Text = "The email address was successfully saved.";

     }
```

RESULT

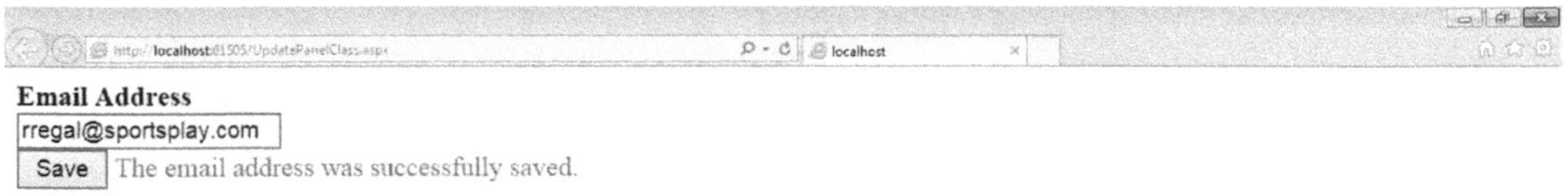

Figure 25-1. *Example of the UpdatePanel class*

25.3.2 UpdateProgress Class

The UpdateProgress class provides the end user with feedback regarding the progress of an asynchronous postback. It is the ProgressTemplate property of an UpdateProgress control that defines the control's content, which usually contains some kind of message asking the end user to wait while the process (i.e., the asynchronous postback) completes. When a page is initially rendered in the browser, the content in the ProgressTemplate property of the UpdateProgress control is *not* displayed. However, subsequent *asynchronous* postbacks may cause the content in the ProgressTemplate property to display.

To connect an UpdateProgress control to its associated UpdatePanel control, we set the AssociatedUpdatePanelID property of the UpdateProgress control to the ID property of the associated UpdatePanel control. If we wish to display the content in the ProgressTemplate property of an UpdateProgress control after a given amount of time (in milliseconds), we set the DisplayAfter property of the UpdateProgress control. By default, an UpdateProgress control will wait for 500 milliseconds (i.e., 0.5 seconds) before it displays the content defined in its ProgressTemplate property. We can also apply styles to an UpdateProgress control using CSS. Table 25-3 shows some of the properties, methods, and events of the UpdateProgress class.

Table 25-3. *Some of the properties, methods, and events of the UpdateProgress class*

Class UpdateProgress[4]	
Namespace System.Web.UI	
Properties	
AssociatedUpdatePanelID	Gets or sets the ID of the UpdatePanel control that the UpdateProgress control displays status for.
DisplayAfter	Gets or sets the value in milliseconds before the UpdateProgress control is displayed.
ProgressTemplate	Gets or sets the template that defines the content of the UpdateProgress control.

(continued)

---

[4]All property, method, and event descriptions were taken directly from Microsoft's official documentation. The event handler methods used to handle the events of this class were omitted to conserve space. See the reference for all of the methods of this class.

Table 25-3. (*continued*)

Methods
(See reference.)
Events
(See reference.)
Reference
`https://msdn.microsoft.com/en-us/library/system.web.ui.` `updateprogress(v=vs.110).aspx`

Figure 25-2 shows an example of the UpdateProgress class.

Notice at 01 the ScriptManager control, which automatically downloads the Ajax scripts necessary for asynchronous postbacks and partial-page rendering.

Notice at 02 the UpdatePanel control that defines the page region that will be asynchronously posted back and re-rendered in the browser.

Notice at 03 the UpdateProgress control. As can be seen, we have associated this control with the UpdatePanel control at 02 by setting the AssociatedUpdatePanelID property of the UpdateProgress control to the ID property of the UpdatePanel control. Notice as well that we have set the DisplayAfter property of the control to *2000*. This means that we want the UpdateProgress control to display if the asynchronous postback takes longer than 2,000 milliseconds (i.e., 2 seconds).

Notice at 04 the ProgressTemplate property of the UpdateProgress control. As can be seen, we have included a label in this template that displays a message asking the end user to wait for the asynchronous postback to complete.

Notice at 05 that we have included a line of code at the very bottom of the event handler method that is invoked when the end user clicks the *Save* button. This line of code was added to slow down the processing on the server—that is, to simulate a 5,000-millisecond (i.e., 5-second) response time. This line of code would not normally be included in such an event handler method, but it serves as a good example of how to test an UpdateProgress control.

The first screenshot in the Result section of the figure shows the message displayed as a result of the (artificial) delay in the progress of the asynchronous postback. The second screenshot shows the message displayed after the email address is saved.

ASPX CODE

```
01   <asp:ScriptManager runat="server" />

     <asp:Label runat="server" Font-Bold="true" Text="Email Address" /><br />

02   <asp:UpdatePanel runat="server" ID="uppEmailAddress">
         <ContentTemplate>
             <asp:TextBox runat="server" ID="txtEmailAddress" /><br />
             <asp:Button runat="server" ID="btnSave" OnClick="btnSave_Click"
                 Text="Save" />
             <asp:Label runat="server" ID="lblMessage" />
         </ContentTemplate>
     </asp:UpdatePanel>

03   <asp:UpdateProgress runat="server"
         AssociatedUpdatePanelID="uppEmailAddress" DisplayAfter="2000">
04       <ProgressTemplate>
             <asp:Label runat="server" Text="Please wait...." />
         </ProgressTemplate>
     </asp:UpdateProgress>
```

CODE BEHIND

```
     protected void btnSave_Click(object sender, EventArgs e)
     {

         // The database call to save the email address would go here.
         // If successful, the following message would be displayed.
         lblMessage.ForeColor = System.Drawing.Color.Green;
         lblMessage.Text = "The email address was successfully saved.";
         // Slow down processing on the server to simulate a 5 second
         // response time.
05       System.Threading.Thread.Sleep(5000);

     }
```

RESULT

Figure 25-2. *Example of the UpdateProgress class*

25.4 Ajax Control Toolkit

The *Ajax Control Toolkit* is an open-source class library that is built on top of the basic Ajax functionality provided by the .NET Framework.[5] This class library contains over 30 classes that can be used to enhance the interactivity and overall experience of the Web applications we develop. All of the classes in the Ajax Control Toolkit can be used "out of the box" and require no knowledge of the Ajax extension classes (discussed earlier) or JavaScript (discussed in Chapter 26, titled *"JavaScript Programming"*).

The classes in the Ajax Control Toolkit can be divided into *Ajax control classes* and *Ajax control extender classes*. Control classes are used to create standalone (i.e., self-contained) ASP.NET server controls, whereas control extender classes are used to extend or enhance the behavior of standard ASP.NET server controls. The control classes in the Ajax Control Toolkit include the Accordion class and the AjaxFileUpload class. The control extender classes in the Ajax Control Toolkit include the BalloonPopupExtender class, the CalendarExtender class, the ModalPopupExtender class, and the PasswordStrength (extender) class. Although there are many more classes than these in the Ajax Control Toolkit, we will limit our discussion to these six. Together, they will give us a good feel for how to use the Ajax Control Toolkit to further exploit the use of asynchronous postbacks and partial-page rendering. The interested reader is encouraged to explore the use of the other classes in the Ajax Control Toolkit on his or her own.

25.4.1 Installing the Ajax Control Toolkit

Before the classes in the Ajax Control Toolkit will work, we need to install the toolkit in our development environment (i.e., Visual Studio). Installing this toolkit makes available all of the Ajax scripts necessary for using the Ajax controls and Ajax control extenders. If the Ajax Control Toolkit has not been installed, an error will occur when a page containing an Ajax Control Toolkit class is requested. To install the Ajax Control Toolkit

1. Navigate to `www.devexpress.com/Products/ajax-control-toolkit/`.

2. Click *Download*.

3. Follow the installation directions.

---

[5]The Ajax Control Toolkit is the result of a joint effort between Microsoft and the ASP.NET Ajax community. The Toolkit is currently managed by DevExpress—a software organization that specializes in the development of GUI classes, including Ajax classes for ASP.NET.

Once the Ajax Control Toolkit is installed, its classes will appear in the Visual Studio Toolbox. There is no need to reinstall the Toolkit for each new application we create as the installation results in the Toolkit being installed in Visual Studio itself. For demos of all of the controls and control extenders in the Ajax Control Toolbox, see https:// ajaxcontroltoolkit.devexpress.com/.

When creating a new project *after* the Ajax Control Toolkit has been installed, we *may* need to add the Toolkit's assembly reference to the project. To do this

1. Open the Solution Explorer.

2. Right-click *References.*

3. Select *Add Reference....*

4. Click *Browse....*

5. Locate the AjaxControlToolkit.dll file.

6. Select the file.

7. Click *Add.*

8. Make sure that the AjaxControlToolkit.dll file is checked in the Reference Manager.

9. Click *OK* to close the Reference Manager.

By default, the Aspx tag prefix for the Ajax Control Toolkit is *ajaxToolkit*. Although it is not necessary to do so, we will create a shorter tag prefix (i.e., *act*) that looks similar to the *asp* tag prefix we are used to (for readability and standardization purposes). To do this, all we must do is add a reference to the new tag prefix in the <system.web> <pages> <controls> section of the Web.config file. Figure 25-3 shows the Web.config file with the *act* (Ajax Control Toolkit) tag prefix reference.

```
WEB.CONFIG CODE

<system.web>
  <pages theme="Theme1">
    <controls>
      <add tagPrefix="act" assembly="AjaxControlToolkit"
          namespace="AjaxControlToolkit" />
    </controls>
  </pages>
</system.web>
```

Figure 25-3. *Web.config file with the act (Ajax Control Toolkit) tag prefix reference*

25.4.2 Control Classes

The Ajax Control Toolkit control classes are used to create standalone (i.e., self-contained) ASP.NET server controls. These classes include the Accordion class and the AjaxFileUpload class. Although there are many more control classes than these in the Ajax Control Toolkit, we will limit our discussion to these two as they will sufficiently illustrate the use of such classes to further exploit the use of asynchronous postbacks and partial-page rendering.

25.4.2.1 Accordion Class

The Accordion class displays an expandable/collapsible collection of panes that can be used by an end user to display information one pane at a time. The AccordionPane property of an According control defines the header and content areas of a *child pane* within the accordion's pane collection. The ContentCssClass property indicates the default CSS class used to format the content areas of the accordion's child panes. The FadeTransitions property indicates whether or not a fade effect will be used when transitioning from one accordion pane to another. The HeaderCssClass property indicates the default CSS class used to format the header areas of the accordion's child panes. The Panes property contains the collection of child accordion panes. And finally, the TransitionDuration property indicates the length of time it will take to transition from one accordion pane to another. By default, this transition is 500 milliseconds (i.e., 0.5 seconds). Table 25-4 shows some of the properties, methods, and events of the Accordion class.

Table 25-4. *Some of the properties, methods, and events of the Accordion class*

Class Accordion[6]

Namespace NA

Properties

AccordionPane	A child pane in the Accordion.
ContentCssClass	The CSS class used to format the content area of the control.
FadeTransitions	Whether or not to use a fade effect when transitioning between selected Accordion Panes. The default is false.
HeaderCssClass	The CSS class used to format the header area of the control.
Panes	A collection of child panes in the Accordion.
TransitionDuration	Length of the transition animation in milliseconds. The default is 500.

Methods

(See reference.)

Events

(See reference.)

Reference

```
https://ajaxcontroltoolkit.devexpress.com/Accordion/Accordion.aspx
```

Figure 25-4 shows an example of the Accordion class.

Notice at 01 the ScriptManager control, which automatically downloads the Ajax scripts necessary for asynchronous postbacks and partial-page rendering.

Notice at 02 the Accordion control. As can be seen, we have set the ContentCssClass property of the control to *AccordionContent* to indicate the default CSS class selector used to format the *content* areas of the accordion's child panes. This class selector can be seen at 07. Similarly, we have set the HeaderCssClass property to *AccordionHeader* to indicate the default CSS class selector used to format the *header* areas of the accordion's child panes. This class selector can be seen at 08. Note that the class selectors can contain other CSS formatting declarations as well. We can also see that we have set the FadeTransitions property to *true* to indicate that we want to use a fade effect when

---

[6]See the reference for all of the properties, methods, and events of this class.

transitioning from one accordion pane to another. In addition, we can see that we have set the TransitionDuration property to *1000* to indicate that we want the control to take 1,000 milliseconds (i.e., 1 second) to transition from one accordion pane to another.

Notice at 03 the Panes property of the Accordion control, which contains the collection of child accordion panes. In this example, there are three accordion panes.

Notice at 04 the AccordionPane property of the Accordion control. This property defines the header and content areas of a *child pane* within the accordion's pane collection. These areas are seen at 05 and 06, respectively.

The first screenshot in the Result section of the figure shows the first child pane of the Accordion control being displayed. This child pane is automatically displayed by default. The second screenshot shows the result of clicking the header area of the second child pane.

ASPX CODE

```
01  <asp:ScriptManager runat="server" />

    <asp:Label runat="server" Font-Bold="true" Text="Product" /><br />

02  <act:Accordion runat="server" ID="accAccordion"
        ContentCssClass="AccordionContent" HeaderCssClass="AccordionHeader"
        FadeTransitions="true" TransitionDuration="1000">
03      <Panes>
04          <act:AccordionPane runat="server">
05              <Header>
                    <asp:Label runat="server" Text="Prince Tour Elite Junior
                        25 Racquet" />
                </Header>
06              <Content>
                    <asp:Label runat="server" Text="This 100% graphite junior
                        racquet features Prince's Extreme String Pattern
                        technology for explosive power and spin. Its 25 inch
                        length is great for kids ages 8-9. Price: $85." />
                </Content>
            </act:AccordionPane>
            <act:AccordionPane runat="server">
                <Header>
                    <asp:Label runat="server" Text="Prince Lightning 110" />
                </Header>
```

Figure 25-4. *Example of the Accordion class*

```
            <Content>
                <asp:Label runat="server" Text="Perfect for beginner and
                    intermediate level players in search of power and
                    comfort. There's also plenty of spin for bringing the
                    ball down on target. Head size: 110in². Length: 27.5
                    inch. String Pattern: 16x19. Price: $75." />
            </Content>
        </act:AccordionPane>
        <act:AccordionPane runat="server">
            <Header>
                <asp:Label runat="server" Text="Prince Textreme Warrior
                    100" />
            </Header>
            <Content>
                <asp:Label runat="server" Text="This fast and very spin
                    friendly racquet offers amazing feel and plenty of
                    pop. Although perfectly weighted for intermediates,
                    the Warrior 100 has near universal appeal. Head size:
                    100in². Length: 27in. String Pattern: 16x18. Price:
                    $199." />
            </Content>
        </act:AccordionPane>
    </Panes>
</act:Accordion>
```

CSS CODE

```
07  .AccordionContent
    {
        background-color: white;
        font-size: small;
    }

08  .AccordionHeader
```

Figure 25-4. *(continued)*

```
{
    background-color: lightgray;
}
```

RESULT

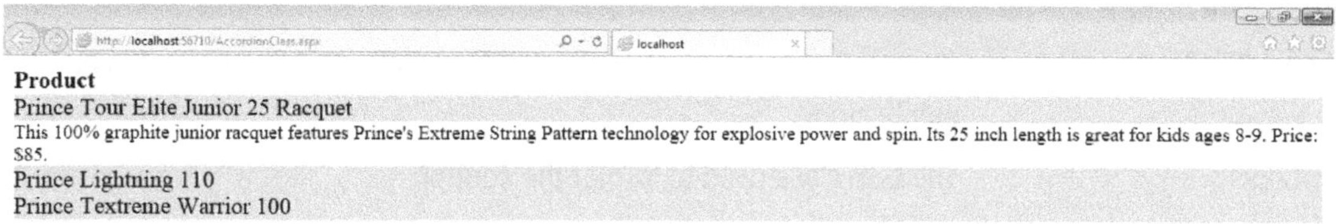

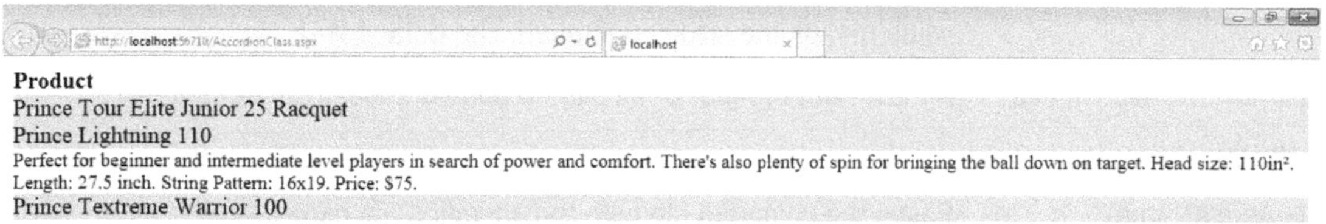

Product
Prince Tour Elite Junior 25 Racquet
This 100% graphite junior racquet features Prince's Extreme String Pattern technology for explosive power and spin. Its 25 inch length is great for kids ages 8-9. Price:
$85.
Prince Lightning 110
Prince Textreme Warrior 100

Product
Prince Tour Elite Junior 25 Racquet
Prince Lightning 110
Perfect for beginner and intermediate level players in search of power and comfort. There's also plenty of spin for bringing the ball down on target. Head size: 110in².
Length: 27.5 inch. String Pattern: 16x19. Price: $75.
Prince Textreme Warrior 100

Figure 25-4. *(continued)*

25.4.2.2 AjaxFileUpload Class

The AjaxFileUpload class displays a control that can be used by an end user to upload files to the server. This control is often used instead of the FileUpload control provided by the .NET Framework as it is more user-friendly, performs file uploads asynchronously, and contains more sophisticated features. When a file to be uploaded is selected, an AjaxFileUpload control temporarily stores the file in a temporary folder on the Web server's hard drive. Then, when the SaveAs method of the control is invoked, the file is copied to its permanent location on the Web server's hard drive (i.e., the location specified in the code behind), and the temporary file is deleted from the temporary folder on the Web server's hard drive.

The AllowedFileTypes property of an AjaxFileUpload control indicates the types of files (as indicated by their file extensions) that are allowed to be uploaded. The CssClass property indicates the CSS class used to format the control. The MaxFileSize property indicates the maximum size (in kilobytes) that a file can be to be uploaded by the control. If the size of a file to be uploaded should be unlimited, this property should be set to a nonpositive integer. The MaximumNumberOfFiles property indicates the maximum number of files that can selected and uploaded at one time. The SaveAs method saves an uploaded file to its permanent location on the Web server's hard drive. And finally, the UploadComplete event is raised when the file upload is complete. Table 25-5 shows some of the properties, methods, and events of the AjaxFileUpload class.

Table 25-5. *Some of the properties, methods, and events of the AjaxFileUpload class*

Class AjaxFileUpload[7]	
Namespace NA	
Properties	
AllowedFileTypes	A comma-separated list of allowed file extensions. The default is an empty string.
CssClass	The CSS class used to format the control.
MaxFileSize	The maximum size of a file to be uploaded in Kbytes. A nonpositive value means the size is unlimited. The default is 0.
MaximumNumberOfFiles	A maximum number of files in an upload queue. The default is 10.
Methods	
SaveAs(fileName)	Saves the uploaded file with the specified file name.
Events	
UploadComplete	An event raised when the file upload is complete.
Reference	

https://ajaxcontroltoolkit.devexpress.com/AjaxFileUpload/AjaxFileUpload.aspx

Figure 25-5 shows an example of the AjaxFileUpload class.

Notice at 01 the ScriptManager control, which automatically downloads the Ajax scripts necessary for asynchronous postbacks and partial-page rendering.

Notice at 02 the AjaxFileUpload control. As can be seen, we have set the AllowedFileTypes property of the control to *gif,jpg,png* to indicate that only .gif, .jpg, and .png files are allowed to be uploaded. We have also set the CssClass property to *AjaxFileUpload* to indicate the default CSS class selector used to format the control. This class selector can be seen at 06. Note that the class selector can contain other CSS formatting declarations as well. In addition, we have set the MaxFileSize property to *1000* to indicate that the largest file that can be uploaded is 1000KB (i.e., 1MB). We have also set the MaximumNumberOfFiles property to *1* to indicate that only one file can be selected and uploaded at a time. And finally, we have set the OnUploadComplete property to *afuImage_UploadComplete* to indicate the event handler method that will be invoked *after* the end user selects a file to be uploaded and clicks the *Upload* button.

---

[7]See the reference for all of the properties, methods, and events of this class.

Notice at 03 the UploadComplete event handler method that will be invoked after the end user selects a file to be uploaded and clicks the *Upload* button.

Notice at 04 that we are programmatically constructing the *full* path of the file to be saved to the server. First, we are using the PhysicalApplicationPath property of the HttpRequest class to get the physical file system path of the application's root directory. Using this property permits us to get the path of the application's root directory without having to hard code it. This way, if we install the application on another server (or in a different location on the same server), the path to the application's root directory is always correct. Second, we are concatenating the application's root directory with its Images subdirectory. And third, we are concatenating the result of that concatenation with the name of the file to be saved. As can be seen, the name of the file to be saved is passed to the event handler method via the AjaxFileUploadEventArgs class—the alias of which is e.

Notice at 05 that we are using the SaveAs method of the AjaxFileUpload control to permanently save the file on the server in the desired location.

Notice at 07 that we have added a reference to the AjaxFileUploadHandler in the <system.webServer> <handlers> section of the Web.config file. If we do not include this entry in the Web.config file, the AjaxFileUpload control will not work.

The first screenshot in the Result section of the figure shows the AjaxFileUpload control before a file has been selected for upload. Notice that the end user can drop a file into the control or select one by clicking the *Select File* button. Clicking the *Select File* button results in a *Choose File to Upload* dialog that the end user can use to locate and select the desired file. The second screenshot shows the control after a file has been selected for upload. Notice that the upload is now *pending* and that the control is awaiting further instructions from the end user. At this point, the end user can remove the file from the list of pending files by clicking the *Remove* button, or he or she can permanently upload the file to the Images folder by clicking the *Upload* button. Finally, the third screenshot shows the control after the file has been permanently uploaded to the Images folder.

ASPX CODE

```
01  <asp:ScriptManager runat="server" />

    <asp:Label runat="server" Font-Bold="true" Text="Product Image" /><br />
    <asp:Label runat="server" Text="Please select a product image and click
        Upload." /><br />
02  <act:AjaxFileUpload runat="server" ID="afuImage"
        AllowedFileTypes="gif,jpg,png" CssClass="AjaxFileUpload"
        MaxFileSize="1000" MaximumNumberOfFiles="1"
        OnUploadComplete="afuImage_UploadComplete" />
```

CODE BEHIND

```
03  protected void afuImage_UploadComplete(object sender,
        AjaxControlToolkit.AjaxFileUploadEventArgs e)
    {
        // Save the file to the specified location.
04      String strFilePath = Request.PhysicalApplicationPath + "Images\\" +
            e.FileName;
05      afuImage.SaveAs(strFilePath);

    }
```

CSS CODE

```
06  .AjaxFileUpload
    {
        background-color: lightgray;
    }
```

WEB.CONFIG CODE

```
    <system.webServer>
      <handlers>
07      <add name="AjaxFileUploadHandler" verb="*"
            path="AjaxFileUploadHandler.axd"
            type="AjaxControlToolkit.AjaxFileUploadHandler,
            AjaxControlToolkit" />
      </handlers>
    </system.webServer>
```

Figure 25-5. *Example of the AjaxFileUpload class*

RESULT

Figure 25-5. *(continued)*

25.4.3 Control Extender Classes

The Ajax Control Toolkit control extender classes are used to extend or enhance the behavior of standard ASP.NET server controls. These classes include the BalloonPopupExtender class, the CalendarExtender class, the ModalPopupExtender class, and the PasswordStrength (extender) class. Although there are many more control extender classes than these in the Ajax Control Toolkit, we will limit our discussion to these four as they will sufficiently illustrate the use of such classes to further exploit the use of asynchronous postbacks and partial-page rendering.

25.4.3.1 BalloonPopupExtender Class

The BalloonPopupExtender class displays a graphic that can be used by an end user to get additional information about a standard ASP.NET server control. A BalloonPopupExtender control can contain content of any kind, including text and images. The BalloonPopupControlID property of a BalloonPopupExtender control indicates the ID of the Panel control that contains the balloon popup's content. The BalloonStyle property indicates the type of balloon popup (i.e., cloud, custom, or rectangle) to be displayed. The DisplayOnMouseOver property indicates whether or not the balloon popup should be displayed when the end user hovers over the associated ASP.NET server control. If this property is set to *true*, the balloon popup will be displayed when the end user *hovers over* the associated server control. If it is set to *false*, the balloon popup will be displayed when the end user *clicks* the associated server control. The TargetControlID property indicates the ID of the ASP.NET server control that the BalloonPopupExtender control extends. And finally, the UseShadow property indicates whether or not to display a drop shadow when displaying the balloon popup. A drop shadow gives the balloon popup a more three-dimensional look. Table 25-6 shows some of the properties, methods, and events of the BalloonPopupExtender class.

Table 25-6. *Some of the properties, methods, and events of the BalloonPopupExtender class*

Class BalloonPopupExtender[8]

Namespace NA

Properties

BalloonPopupControlID	The ID of the control to display.
BalloonStyle	Optional setting specifying the theme of balloon popup. Default value is Rectangle.
DisplayOnMouseOver	Optional setting specifying whether to display balloon popup on the client onMouseOver event. Default value is false.
TargetControlID	The ID of the control that the extender extends.
UseShadow	Optional setting specifying whether to display shadow of balloon popup or not.

(continued)

[8]See the reference for all of the properties, methods, and events of this class.

Table 25-6. *(continued)*

Methods

(See reference.)

Events

(See reference.)

Reference

`https://ajaxcontroltoolkit.devexpress.com/BalloonPopup/BalloonPopup.aspx`

Figure 25-6 shows an example of the BalloonPopupExtender class.

Notice at 01 the ScriptManager control, which automatically downloads the Ajax scripts necessary for asynchronous postbacks and partial-page rendering.

Notice at 02 the ASP.NET TextBox control we are extending. When the end user hovers over this text box, the balloon popup will display.

Notice at 03 the BalloonPopupExtender control. As can be seen, we have set the BalloonPopupControlID of the control to *panPrice* to indicate the ID of the Panel control that contains the balloon popup's content. This panel is shown at 04. Notice as well that we have set the BalloonStyle property to *Cloud* to indicate the type of balloon popup to be displayed. We have also set the DisplayOnMouseOver property to *true* to indicate that we want the balloon popup to be displayed when the end user hovers over the associated TextBox control. In addition, we have set the TargetControlID property to *txtPrice* to indicate the ID of the ASP.NET server control that the BalloonPopupExtender control extends. And finally, we have set the UseShadow property to *true* to indicate that we want the balloon popup to include a drop shadow when it displays.

Notice at 04 the Panel control. This control contains the content that will be displayed when the BalloonPopupExtender control becomes visible. In this case, the panel contains a label with some instructions for the end user regarding what he or she should enter into the associated text box. Notice as well that we have set the CssClass property of the control to *BalloonPopupExtenderPanel* to indicate the default CSS class selector used to format the control. This class selector can be seen at 05. Note that the class selector can contain other CSS formatting declarations as well.

The screenshot in the Result section of the figure shows the result of hovering over the price text box. Notice how helpful a balloon popup extender can be when specific instructions are required for inputting data.

ASPX CODE

```
01   <asp:ScriptManager runat="server" />

     <asp:Label runat="server" Font-Bold="true" Text="Price" /><br />
02   <asp:TextBox runat="server" ID="txtPrice" />
03   <act:BalloonPopupExtender runat="server" BalloonPopupControlID="panPrice"
         BalloonStyle="Cloud" DisplayOnMouseOver="true"
         TargetControlID="txtPrice" UseShadow="true" />
04   <asp:Panel runat="server" ID="panPrice"
         CssClass="BalloonPopupExtenderPanel">
         <asp:Label runat="server" Text="Please enter a price between $0 and
             $100." />
     </asp:Panel>
```

CSS CODE

```
05   .BalloonPopupExtenderPanel
     {
         background-color white;
         font-size: medium;
     }
```

RESULT

Figure 25-6. *Example of the BalloonPopupExtender class*

25.4.3.2 CalendarExtender Class

The CalendarExtender class displays a monthly calendar that can be used by an end user to select a date. A CalendarExtender control is attached to an ASP.NET TextBox control and thus extends the text box. In terms of appearance, a calendar extender displays a *header* section that includes the month, year, and links for moving backward and forward to previous and future months, a *body* section that includes headings for the days of the week and an array of selectable days, and a *footer* section that displays today's date. By clicking the title section of the control, the end user can select other months or other years directly. By default, a calendar extender displays the current month of the current year.

520

The appearance and behavior of an Ajax CalendarExtender control is, in many ways, superior to that of an ASP.NET Calendar control. For example, an ASP.NET Calendar control takes up significantly more room on a page than an Ajax CalendarExtender control. And, unlike an Ajax CalendarExtender control, an ASP.NET Calendar control *always* performs an auto postback when a date is selected, which can be very annoying when such behavior is not required. On the other hand, unlike an ASP.NET Calendar control, an Ajax CalendarExtender control *cannot* be used to select a range of dates (e.g., an entire week, an entire month).

The CssClass property of a CalendarExtender control indicates how the control should be formatted. A CalendarExtender control is highly customizable via several predefined CSS class selectors. The interested reader should see the reference at the bottom of Table 25-7 for more information on these class selectors. The FirstDayOfWeek property indicates which day (i.e., Monday, Tuesday, Wednesday, Thursday, Friday, Saturday, or Sunday) should be displayed in the leftmost column of the calendar. The SelectedDate property indicates the date that the calendar extender should be initialized to or the date that was selected by the end user. The TargetControlID property indicates the ID of the TextBox control that the calendar extender extends. And finally, the TodaysDateFormat property indicates how the date (i.e., today's date) that is displayed in the footer section of the calendar extender should be formatted. Table 25-7 shows some of the properties, methods, and events of the CalendarExtender class.

Table 25-7. *Some of the properties, methods, and events of the CalendarExtender class*

Class CalendarExtender[9]

Namespace NA

Properties

CssClass	The CSS class used to format the control.
FirstDayOfWeek	The first day of the week. The default value is Sunday.
SelectedDate	The date that the calendar is initialized with.
TargetControlID	The ID of the control that the extender extends.
TodaysDateFormat	A format string used to display today's date. The default value is MMMM d, yyyy.

(*continued*)

---

[9]See the reference for all of the properties, methods, and events of this class.

Table 25-7. *(continued)*

Methods

(See reference.)

Events

ClientDateSelectionChanged   A script that is executed when a new date is selected.

Reference

`https://ajaxcontroltoolkit.devexpress.com/Calendar/Calendar.aspx`

Figure 25-7 shows an example of the CalendarExtender class.

Notice at 01 the ScriptManager control, which automatically downloads the Ajax scripts necessary for asynchronous postbacks and partial-page rendering.

Notice at 02 the ASP.NET TextBox control we are extending. When the end user clicks this text box, the calendar extender will display, and the end user can select a date.

Notice at 03 the CalendarExtender control. As can be seen, we have set the TargetControlID property to *txtDate* to indicate the ID of the TextBox control that the calendar extender extends. Notice as well that we have set the CssClass property of the control to *CalendarExtender* to indicate the default CSS class selector used to format the control. This class selector can be seen at 04.

Notice at 04 that the *CalendarExtender* class selector has been defined as an *ajax calendar container*. This indicates that the class selector contains one or more *predefined* child class selectors (see the reference at the bottom of Table 25-7) and their associated formatting declarations.

Notice at 05 and 06 that the child class selectors are the *ajax calendar title* class selector (for formatting the title of the calendar extender) and the *ajax calendar footer* class selector (for formatting the footer of the calendar extender), respectively. Note that the class selectors can contain other CSS formatting declarations as well.

The first screenshot in the Result section of the figure shows the result of clicking the order date text box. Notice that the background color of the calendar extender is light gray, whereas the background color of the title and footer is dark gray. These were set in the CSS code. Notice as well that the current date is April 17, which can be seen in the footer of the calendar extender. The second screenshot shows the result of selecting a different date—April 10.

ASPX CODE

```
01   <asp:ScriptManager runat="server" />

     <asp:Label runat="server" Font-Bold="true" Text="Order Date" /><br />
02   <asp:TextBox runat="server" ID="txtDate" />
03   <act:CalendarExtender runat="server" ID="caeDate"
         CssClass="CalendarExtender" TargetControlID="txtDate" />
     <asp:Label runat="server" ID="lblDate" />
```

CSS CODE

```
04   .CalendarExtender .ajax__calendar_container
     {
         background-color: lightgray;
         color: black;
     }

05   .CalendarExtender .ajax__calendar_title
     {
         background-color: darkgray;
         color: black;
     }

06   .CalendarExtender .ajax__calendar_footer
     {
         background-color: darkgray;
         color: black;
     }
```

RESULT

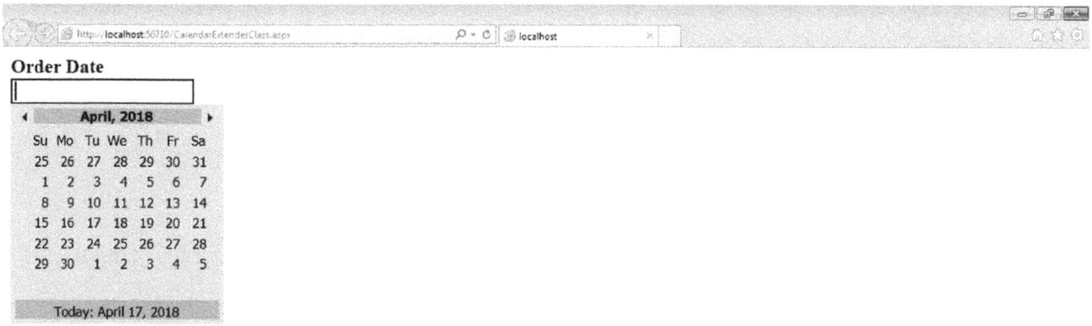

Figure 25-7. *Example of the CalendarExtender class*

25.4.3.3 ModalPopupExtender Class

The ModalPopupExtender class displays a panel that can be used by an end user to acknowledge a message or make a decision. A ModalPopupExtender control behaves like a *modal dialog* in that it does *not* permit the end user to interact with other parts of the page until he or she dismisses the modal popup extender. A modal popup extender is always displayed on top of its associated page and is, by default, centered on it. Once a button on a modal popup extender is clicked, the control is dismissed, and the event handler method of the button clicked (if any) is executed to perform the desired processing. A ModalPopupExtender control can contain any of the ASP.NET server controls that are permitted inside a Panel control.

The BackgroundCssClass property of a ModalPopupExtender control indicates how the background of the control should be formatted. This property is often used to "gray out" the associated page while the end user gives his or her attention to the modal popup extender. The DropShadow property indicates whether or not a drop shadow should be added to the modal popup extender to give it a more three-dimensional look. The PopupControlID property indicates the ID of the panel to display that contains the content of the modal popup extender. And finally, The TargetControlID property indicates the ID of the ASP.NET server control that the modal popup extender extends. Table 25-8 shows some of the properties, methods, and events of the ModalPopupExtender class.

Table 25-8. *Some of the properties, methods, and events of the ModalPopupExtender class*

Class ModalPopupExtender[10]	
Namespace NA	
Properties	
BackgroundCssClass	A CSS class to apply to the background when the modal popup is displayed.
DropShadow	Set to True to automatically add a drop shadow to the modal popup.
PopupControlID	ID of an element to display as a modal popup.
TargetControlID	The ID of the control that the extender extends.

(continued)

---

[10]See the reference for all of the properties, methods, and events of this class.

Table 25-8. *(continued)*

Methods

(See reference.)

Events

(See reference.)

Reference

https://ajaxcontroltoolkit.devexpress.com/ModalPopup/ModalPopup.aspx

Figure 25-8 shows an example of the ModalPopupExtender class.

Notice at 01 the ScriptManager control, which automatically downloads the Ajax scripts necessary for asynchronous postbacks and partial-page rendering.

Notice at 02 the ASP.NET Button control we are extending. When the end user clicks this button, the modal popup extender will display, and the end user can select a shipper.

Notice at 03 the ModalPopupExtender control. As can be seen, we have set the BackgroundCssClass property of the control to *ModalPopupExtenderBackground* to indicate the default CSS class selector used to format the control. This class selector can be seen at 07. Note that the class selector can contain other CSS formatting declarations as well. We have also set the DropShadow property to *true* to indicate that we want the modal popup extender to include a drop shadow when it displays. In addition, we have set the PopupControlID property to *panSelectShipper* to indicate the ID of the Panel control that contains the modal popup extender's content. This panel is shown at 04. And finally, we have set the TargetControlID property to *btnSelectShipper* to indicate the ID of the ASP.NET server control that the ModalPopupExtender control extends.

Notice at 04 the Panel control. This control contains the content that will be displayed when the ModalPopupExtender control becomes visible. In this case, the panel contains a label that includes some instructions for the end user regarding what he or she should do, three radio buttons, and two buttons. As can be seen, we have set the CssClass property of the control to *ModalPopupExtenderPanel* to indicate the default CSS class selector used to format the control. This class selector can be seen at 08. Note that the class selector can contain other CSS formatting declarations as well.

Notice at 05 the event handler method that is invoked when the end user clicks the *Select* button. If the end user chooses a shipper, a message is displayed indicating which shipper he or she selected. If the end user does not choose a shipper, an appropriate message is displayed.

Notice at 06 the event handler method that is invoked when the end user clicks the *Cancel* button. When the end user clicks the *Cancel* button, an appropriate message is displayed.

The first screenshot in the Result section of the figure shows the page before the *Select Shipper* button is clicked. The second screenshot shows the result of clicking the *Select Shipper* button and choosing the *UPS* option on the modal popup extender. And finally, the third screenshot shows the result of clicking the *Select* button on the modal popup extender.

ASPX CODE

```
01   <asp:ScriptManager runat="server" />

     <asp:Label runat="server" Font-Bold="true" Text="Order" /><br />
     <asp:Label runat="server" Text="OrderID 16756" /><br />
02   <asp:Button runat="server" ID="btnSelectShipper" Text="Select Shipper" />
     <asp:Label runat="server" ID="lblShipper" />
03   <act:ModalPopupExtender runat="server"
         BackgroundCssClass="ModalPopupExtenderBackground" DropShadow="true"
         PopupControlID="panSelectShipper"
         TargetControlID="btnSelectShipper" />
04   <asp:Panel runat="server" ID="panSelectShipper"
         CssClass="ModalPopupExtenderPanel">
         <asp:Label runat="server" Text="Please select a shipper." /><br />
         <asp:RadioButton runat="server" ID="radUSPS" GroupName="Shipper"
             Text="USPS" /><br />
         <asp:RadioButton runat="server" ID="radUPS" GroupName="Shipper"
             Text="UPS" /><br />
         <asp:RadioButton runat="server" ID="radFedEx" GroupName="Shipper"
             Text="FedEx" /><br />
         <asp:Button runat="server" ID="btnSelect" OnClick="btnSelect_Click"
             Text="Select" />
         <asp:Button runat="server" ID="btnCancel" OnClick="btnCancel_Click"
             Text="Cancel" />
     </asp:Panel>
```

Figure 25-8. *Example of the ModalPopupExtender class*

CODE BEHIND

```
05  protected void btnSelect_Click(object sender, EventArgs e)
    {

        lblShipper.ForeColor = System.Drawing.Color.Green;
        if (radUSPS.Checked)
        {
            lblShipper.Text = "You have selected USPS as your shipper.";
        }
        else if (radUPS.Checked)
        {
            lblShipper.Text = "You have selected UPS as your shipper.";
        }
        else if (radFedEx.Checked)
        {
            lblShipper.Text = "You have selected FedEx as your shipper.";
        }
        else
        {
            lblShipper.ForeColor = System.Drawing.Color.Red;
            lblShipper.Text = "You have not selected a shipper.
                Please try again.";
        }

    }

06  protected void btnCancel_Click(object sender, EventArgs e)
    {

        lblShipper.ForeColor = System.Drawing.Color.Red;
        lblShipper.Text = "You have not selected a shipper.
            Please try again.";
    }
```

CSS CODE

```
07  .ModalPopupExtenderBackground
    {
        background-color: gray;
        opacity: 0.7;
    }
```

Figure 25-8. *(continued)*

```
08   .ModalPopupExtenderPanel
     {
         background-color: lightgray;
         border-color: black;
         border-style: solid;
         border-width: 1px;
         height: 115px;
         padding-left: 10px;
         padding-top: 10px;
         width: 155px;
     }
```

RESULT

Figure 25-8. *(continued)*

25.4.3.4 PasswordStrength Class

The PasswordStrength (extender) class displays the strength of a password as it is being entered into a text box and thus can be used by an end user to create more secure passwords. A PasswordStrength control extends an ASP.NET TextBox control. We define the strength criteria of a password in the properties of a PasswordStrength control. As the end user enters a password, the PasswordStrength control displays, by default, *nonexistent, very weak, weak, poor, almost OK, barely acceptable, average, good, strong, excellent*, or *unbreakable*. However, these descriptions can be customized via the TextStrengthDescriptions property of the control.

The DisplayPosition property of the PasswordStrength class indicates where a PasswordStrength control should be displayed relative to the TextBox control that it extends (i.e., above left, above right, below left, below right, left side, or right side). The MinimumLowerCaseCharacters property, the MinimumNumericCharacters property, the MinimumSymbolCharacters property, and the MinimumUpperCaseCharacters property indicate the minimum number of these characters necessary to fully satisfy the security requirements of a password. The PreferredPasswordLength property indicates the preferred length of a password. The StrengthIndicatorType property indicates whether the strength indicator displays text or a bar indicator. The latter requires the use of an associated CSS class. The TargetControlID property indicates the ID of the TextBox control that the PasswordStrength control extends. And finally, the TextCssClass property indicates the CSS class used to format the control when the StrengthIndicatorType property is set to *Text*. Table 25-9 shows some of the properties, methods, and events of the PasswordStrength class.

Table 25-9. *Some of the properties, methods, and events of the PasswordStrength class*

Class PasswordStrength[11]

Namespace NA

Properties

DisplayPosition	Positioning of the strength indicator relative to the target control.
MinimumLowerCaseCharacters	Minimum number of lowercase characters required when requiring mixed case characters as part of your password strength considerations.
MinimumNumericCharacters	Minimum number of numeric characters.
MinimumSymbolCharacters	Minimum number of symbol characters (e.g., $ ^ *).
MinimumUpperCaseCharacters	Minimum number of uppercase characters required when requiring mixed case characters as part of your password strength considerations.
PreferredPasswordLength	Preferred length of the password.
StrengthIndicatorType	Strength indicator type (Text or BarIndicator).
TargetControlID	The ID of the control that the extender extends.
TextCssClass	CSS class applied to the text display when StrengthIndicatorType=Text.
TextStrengthDescriptions	List of semicolon separated descriptions used when StrengthIndicatorType=Text (Minimum of 2, maximum of 10; order is weakest to strongest).

Methods

(See reference.)

Events

(See reference.)

Reference

```
https://ajaxcontroltoolkit.devexpress.com/PasswordStrength/PasswordStrength.aspx
```

---

[11]See the reference for all of the properties, methods, and events of this class.

Figure 25-9 shows an example of the PasswordStrength class.

Notice at 01 the ScriptManager control, which automatically downloads the Ajax scripts necessary for asynchronous postbacks and partial-page rendering.

Notice at 02 the ASP.NET TextBox control we are extending. As the end user enters a password into this text box, the password strength extender will display the strength of the password with respect to the password strength criteria specified.

Notice at 03 the PasswordStrength control. As can be seen, we have set the DisplayPosition property of the control to *RightSide* to indicate that the password strength message should be displayed to the right of the password text box. We have also set the MinimumLowerCaseCharacters property, the MinimumNumericCharacters property, the MinimumSymbolCharacters property, and the MinimumUpperCaseCharacters property to *1* to indicate the minimum number of these characters necessary to fully satisfy the security requirements of the password. In addition, we have set the PreferredPasswordLength property to *10* to indicate the preferred length of a password. Note that this is the *preferred* length of a password. The length of a password is *not* enforced by this property. We have also set the StrengthIndicatorType property to *Text* to indicate that we want the strength indicator to display as text—not as a bar indicator. We have also set the TargetControlID property to *txtPassword* to indicate the ID of the TextBox control that the PasswordStrength control extends. And finally, we have set the TextCssClass property to *PasswordStrengthText* to indicate the default CSS class selector used to format the control. This class selector can be seen at 04. Note that the class selector can contain other CSS formatting declarations as well.

The screenshot in the Result section of the figure shows the result of entering a password that is deemed "average" by the standards we set in the properties of the PasswordStrength control.

ASPX CODE

```
01   <asp:ScriptManager runat="server" />

     <asp:Label runat="server" Font-Bold="true" Text="Password" /><br />
02   <asp:TextBox runat="server" ID="txtPassword" MaxLength="10"
         TextMode="Password" Width="240px" />
03   <act:PasswordStrength runat="server" DisplayPosition="RightSide"
         MinimumLowerCaseCharacters="1" MinimumNumericCharacters="1"
         MinimumSymbolCharacters="1" MinimumUpperCaseCharacters="1"
         PreferredPasswordLength="10" StrengthIndicatorType="Text"
         TargetControlID="txtPassword" TextCssClass="PasswordStrengthText" />
     <br />
     <asp:Button runat="server" ID="btnSave" OnClick="btnSave_Click"
         Text="Save" />
```

CSS CODE

```
04   .PasswordStrengthText
     {
         background-color: red;
         color: yellow;
     }
```

RESULT

Figure 25-9. *Example of the PasswordStrength class*

CHAPTER 26

JavaScript Programming

26.1 Introduction

JavaScript is a sophisticated, general-purpose, object-oriented, interpreted programming language originally developed by Netscape Communications Corporation for building Web applications that require *client-side processing* (i.e., processing that occurs in the browser).[1] In addition, JavaScript is a *non-type-safe programming language*. This means that an invalid operation on an object (e.g., adding a string value to an integer value) will *not* be detected at *design time* (i.e., when the source code is parsed and compiled) but will be detected at *runtime* (i.e., when the operation is executed). However, before an invalid operation occurs during execution, JavaScript will *attempt* to convert the objects (i.e., operands) of the operation to types that are compatible with the operation so that the operation can be executed without causing a program crash. For example, the operation x = "abc" + 123 would *not* throw a type error during execution (and thus cause the program to crash) even though *abc* is a string and *123* is an integer. This is because JavaScript can (and will) convert the *123* to a string before the concatenation occurs. Anyone familiar with C, C++, Java, or similar language will have little difficulty learning JavaScript with its familiar curly bracket style.

In this chapter, we will begin by looking at browser compatibility and the importance of testing the applications we develop with JavaScript using all of the browsers we expect our end users to use. We will then discuss the *script element*. A script element contains a script tag (<script>) and an associated end script tag (</script>) and defines an area in a .aspx file that contains JavaScript code or points to an external file that contains JavaScript code. Next, we will discuss the JavaScript function, which contains one or more JavaScript statements and either performs a function (i.e., a task that returns a value) or performs a procedure (i.e., a task that *does not* return a value). After that, we

---

[1]Although JavaScript was initially designed to execute exclusively in Web browsers, it can now be executed on Web servers, in desktop applications, and in runtime environments.

© Robert E. Beasley 2020
R. E. Beasley, *Essential ASP.NET Web Forms Development*, https://doi.org/10.1007/978-1-4842-5784-5_26

will examine the HTML Document Object Model. This model is the standard object model and application programming interface for HTML documents that will permit us to access the HTML elements that are rendered in the browser. And finally, we will look at a number of JavaScript function examples. These examples will illustrate the use of the JavaScript programming language to perform some commonly required client-side tasks. Although there are many more aspects of the JavaScript programming language than we will discuss in this chapter, we will learn enough to give us a good feel for how to use JavaScript to perform client-side processing. The interested reader is encouraged to explore the JavaScript programming language in more detail on his or her own.

26.2 Browser Compatibility

All modern Web browsers (e.g., Internet Explorer, Chrome, Firefox) permit the execution of JavaScript code via their own built-in JavaScript interpreters. Since a given Web browser has its own JavaScript interpreter, it may or may not support all of the JavaScript functionality defined in the *ECMAScript Language Specification*.[2] The purpose of the *ECMAScript Language Specification* is to standardize the JavaScript programming language across all of the JavaScript interpreter implementations. Although JavaScript is the most commonly used implementation of the *ECMAScript Language Specification*, other commonly used implementations are JScript (i.e., Microsoft's dialect of the ECMAScript standard used in Internet Explorer), V8 (i.e., Google's dialect of the ECMAScript standard used in Chrome), and SpiderMonkey (i.e., Mozilla's dialect of the ECMAScript standard used in Firefox).

Since browser compatibility is an important attribute of a robust Web application, it is important that we thoroughly test the applications we develop with JavaScript using all of the browsers we expect our end users to use. It is also important to remember that JavaScript will *not* function in a browser that does not support scripting. Nor will it function in a browser that has browser scripting disabled. Thus, we should code our pages so that they remain useable in the absence of the features provided by JavaScript. A good technique for ensuring this is called *progressive enhancement*. Progressive enhancement requires that we code the pages of an application so that they work well in the *absence* of JavaScript and then enhance those pages so that they work well in the *presence* of JavaScript. This way, an application that makes use of JavaScript will work properly whether or not a given browser permits the execution of JavaScript code.

---

[2]ECMA stands for the European Computer Manufacturers Association.

26.3 Script Elements

A script element contains a script tag (<script>) and an associated end script tag (</script>). A script element either defines an area in a .aspx file that contains JavaScript code, or it points to an external file (via the URL specified in the script element's src property) that contains JavaScript code. Although we will focus on the former approach in this chapter, the latter approach is helpful when there are JavaScript functions or procedure that must be performed in many places within a single Web application or across multiple Web applications. So, instead of writing a segment of JavaScript code to perform a function or procedure and then copying that code to many places, we can write a single JavaScript function or procedure, save it in a JavaScript file, and then call that function or procedure as needed. That way, when a change to the logic of the JavaScript code is required, we need only make the change in one place.

Figure 26-1 shows an example of a script element. As we will soon see, we place the JavaScript code we write between the <script> tag and the associated </script> tag. Keep in mind that we can place a script element anywhere in a .aspx file. However, our standard practice will be to place script elements at the *bottom* of our .aspx files.

```
ASPX CODE

<script type="text/javascript">
</script>
```

Figure 26-1. *Example of a script element*

26.4 Functions

A JavaScript function contains one or more JavaScript statements and either performs a function (i.e., a task that returns a value) or performs a procedure (i.e., a task that *does not* return a value). A properly constructed JavaScript function begins with the word *function* (in lower case) and is followed by the name of the function, a left parenthesis, a comma-separated list of parameters (if any), a right parenthesis, a left curly bracket, one or more JavaScript statements, and a right curly bracket.

When a parameter argument is a *primitive data type* (e.g., string, integer, decimal number), it is passed *by value*. This means that a *copy* of the argument is passed by the *calling* function to the *called* function. Thus, if the value of the argument is modified in the called function, only the copy of the argument is modified. The associated argument value in the calling function is left untouched. When a parameter argument is an *object* (i.e., a collection of properties and methods), it is passed *by reference*. This means that a *reference* to the object's memory location is passed by the *calling* function to the *called* function. In this scenario, if the object is modified in the called function, the modification will be present in the calling function as well.

All of the variables declared *inside* a JavaScript function are *local* in scope. Thus, they can only be accessed and/or manipulated by the code in that function. All of the variables declared *outside* a JavaScript function, on the other hand, are *global* in scope. Thus, they can be accessed and/or manipulated by the code in any function. Keep in mind that the use of global variables can lead to unintended results, since multiple functions can access and modify such variables independently. For this reason, the use of global variables is usually discouraged.

26.5 HTML Document Object Model

The HTML Document Object Model (DOM) is the object model and application programming interface standard for HTML documents. In this model, all of the HTML elements on a page are represented as objects, and each of these objects can contain properties, methods, and events. Each time an HTML page is loaded into a Web browser, an *HTML document object* is created that represents the page and its collection of HTML elements. It is the presence of this object that permits us to *programmatically* (via JavaScript) add new HTML elements to a page, modify existing HTML elements on a page, and delete existing HTML elements from a page.

One of the methods of the HTML document object that we will make heavy use of in this chapter is the *getElementById* method. This method permits us to retrieve an individual HTML element in a page by referring to its unique ID property. The invocation of this method takes the form

```
document.getElementById(HTML Element ID)
```

where *HTML Element ID* is the unique ID of the HTML element that we wish to access and/or manipulate in the client via JavaScript.

Notice that the getElementById method refers to an *HTML element* in a page. However, we typically don't code HTML elements when developing ASP.NET Web applications. Instead, we code *ASP.NET server controls*. The thing to keep in mind is that *all* of the ASP.NET server controls on a page are translated to their equivalent HTML elements by the server before the server sends the page back to the browser for rendering. Thus, in the browser, there are no ASP.NET server controls per se—just their equivalent HTML elements. So, the question becomes: How do we refer to an ASP. NET server control by its ID property in JavaScript if only its equivalent HTML element resides in the document object? The answer is: We set the ClientIDMode property of the ASP.NET server control to *Static*. When we do this, the HTML element in the document object is given the *same* ID as the ASP.NET server control (e.g., ddlState, radBasic, txtLastName) when the ASP.NET server control is translated to its equivalent HTML element. This makes it very easy for us to know the name of the HTML element we wish to access and/or manipulate in the client via JavaScript.

As we write JavaScript code, it is important to remember that a JavaScript function will not execute if even the smallest syntax error occurs (e.g., declaring a function with the word *Function* instead of *function*). This can make JavaScript difficult to debug. Thus, it is important to code and test carefully before deploying an application that includes JavaScript.

26.6 Examples

For the remainder of this chapter, we will learn from looking at some JavaScript examples. These examples will illustrate the use of the JavaScript programming language to perform some commonly required client-side processing tasks. Since JavaScript is so similar to C# in terms of its structure and syntax, only a few examples are necessary to illustrate the basics of the language. In the sections that follow, we will learn about assignment operations, confirm dialogs and alert messages, control property manipulation, date and time display, and iterative operations.

26.6.1 Assignment Operations

In this section, we will learn how to assign values to control properties. Figure 26-2 shows an example of a JavaScript function that sets shipping information.

Notice at 01 and 02 the txtBillingLastName control and the ddlBillingState control, respectively. These controls are associated with the person to be billed. As can be seen, the ClientIDMode properties of these controls are set to *Static* so that we can refer to the equivalent HTML elements by their ASP.NET server control IDs in the JavaScript code.

Notice at 03 the chkSameAsBilling control. This control indicates whether or not the shipping information should be the same as the billing information. As can be seen, the onClick property of this control is set to *SetShippingInformation()*. This is the name of the JavaScript function that will be executed when the chkSameAsBilling control is clicked.

Notice at 04 and 05 the txtShippingLastName control and the ddlShippingState control, respectively. These controls are associated with the person to receive the shipment. As can be seen, the ClientIDMode properties of these controls are set to *Static* so that we can refer to the equivalent HTML elements by their ASP.NET server control IDs in the JavaScript code.

Notice at 06 and 20 the script tag and its associated end tag. Together, these tags define the area in the .aspx file that contains the page's JavaScript code.

Notice at 07 the SetShippingInformation function that is executed when the chkSameAsBilling control at 03 is clicked.

Notice at 08 that we are checking to see if the chkSameAsBilling control has been checked. If it has been checked, we are setting the shipping fields to their corresponding billing fields. If it has not been checked, we are setting the shipping fields to their default values.

Notice at 09 that we are setting the value of the txtShippingLastName control to the value of the txtBillingLastName control.

Notice at 10 that we are creating a local object called ddlBillingState and assigning it the HTML element of the same name. This will permit us to refer to the HTML element in shorthand form.

Notice at 11 that we are creating a local variable called strBillingSelectedValue and assigning it the value of the billing state selected by the end user.

Notice at 12 that we are creating a local variable called strBillingSelectedText and assigning it the text of the billing state selected by the end user.

Notice at 13 that we are setting the value of the ddlShippingState control to the value in the strBillingSelectedValue variable.

Notice at 14 that we are setting the text of the ddlShippingState control to the text in the strBillingSelectedText variable.

Notice at 15 that we are setting the value of txtShippingLastName control to its default (i.e., blank).

Notice at 16 that we are creating a local object called ddlShippingState and assigning it the HTML element of the same name. This will permit us to refer to the HTML element in shorthand form.

Notice at 17 that we are setting the value of the ddlShippingState control to its default (i.e., IN).

Notice at 18 that we are setting the text of the ddlShippingState control to its default (i.e., Indiana).

Notice at 19 that we are ending the execution of the JavaScript function.

The first screenshot in the Result section of the figure shows the billing information fields as entered by the end user. The second screenshot shows the result of *checking* the checkbox to make the shipping information fields the same as their corresponding billing information fields. And the third screenshot shows the result of *unchecking* the checkbox to set the shipping information fields back to their default values.

ASPX CODE

```
<asp:Label runat="server" Font-Bold="true" Text="Step 3 - Billing and
    Shipping Information" /><br />

<asp:Table runat="server">
    <asp:TableRow>
        <asp:TableCell>
            <asp:Table runat="server" >
                <asp:TableRow>
                    <asp:TableCell>
                        <asp:Label runat="server" Font-Bold="true"
                            Text="Billing Information" />
                    </asp:TableCell>
                </asp:TableRow>
                <asp:TableRow>
                    <asp:TableCell>
                        <asp:Label runat="server" Text="Last Name" />
                    </asp:TableCell>
                    <asp:TableCell>
                        <asp:TextBox runat="server"
                            ID="txtBillingLastName"
                            ClientIDMode="Static" />
                    </asp:TableCell>
                </asp:TableRow>
                ⋮
                ⋮ (Code continues.)
                ⋮
                <asp:TableRow>
                    <asp:TableCell>
                        <asp:Label runat="server" Text="State" />
                    </asp:TableCell>
                    <asp:TableCell>
                        <asp:DropDownList runat="server"
                            ID="ddlBillingState"
                            ClientIDMode="Static">
                            <asp:ListItem Value="IL" Text="Illinois" />
                            <asp:ListItem Value="IN" Text="Indiana"
                                Selected="True" />
                            <asp:ListItem Value="KY" Text="Kentucky" />
                            <asp:ListItem Value="OH" Text="Ohio" />
                            <asp:ListItem Value="MI" Text="Michigan" />
                        </asp:DropDownList>
```

01

02

Figure 26-2. *Example of a JavaScript function that sets shipping information*

```
                    </asp:TableCell>
                </asp:TableRow>
                ⋮
                ⋮ (Code continues.)
                ⋮
            </asp:Table>
        </asp:TableCell>
        <asp:TableCell>
            <asp:Table runat="server" >
                <asp:TableRow>
                    <asp:TableCell ColumnSpan="2">
                        <asp:Label runat="server" Font-Bold="true"
                            Text="Shipping Information" />
                        (<asp:CheckBox runat="server"
                            ID="chkSameAsBilling"
                            ClientIDMode="Static" Font-Size="Medium"
                            onClick="SetShippingInformation()"
                            Text="Same as Billing" />)
                    </asp:TableCell>
                </asp:TableRow>
                <asp:TableRow>
                    <asp:TableCell>
                        <asp:Label runat="server" Text="Last Name" />
03                  </asp:TableCell>
                    <asp:TableCell>
04                      <asp:TextBox runat="server"
                            ID="txtShippingLastName"
                            ClientIDMode="Static" />
                    </asp:TableCell>
                </asp:TableRow>
                ⋮
                ⋮ (Code continues.)
                ⋮
                <asp:TableRow>
                    <asp:TableCell>
                        <asp:Label runat="server" Text="State" />
                    </asp:TableCell>
                    <asp:TableCell>
05                      <asp:DropDownList runat="server"
                            ID="ddlShippingState"
                            ClientIDMode="Static">
                            <asp:ListItem Value="IL" Text="Illinois" />
                            <asp:ListItem Value="IN" Text="Indiana"
                                Selected="True" />
                            <asp:ListItem Value="KY" Text="Kentucky" />
                            <asp:ListItem Value="OH" Text="Ohio" />
                            <asp:ListItem Value="MI" Text="Michigan" />
                        </asp:DropDownList>
                    </asp:TableCell>
                </asp:TableRow>
```

Figure 26-2. (continued)

```
            ⋮
          ⋮ (Code continues.)
            ⋮
            </asp:Table>
          </asp:TableCell>
      </asp:TableRow>
  </asp:Table>
  <asp:Button runat="server" ID="btnNext" Text="Next" />
```

JAVASCRIPT CODE

```
06   <script type="text/javascript">

07       function SetShippingInformation() {

08           if (document.getElementById("chkSameAsBilling").checked) {
                 // Set the shipping information.
09               document.getElementById("txtShippingLastName").value =
                     document.getElementById("txtBillingLastName").value;
                 ⋮
               ⋮ (Code continues.)
                 ⋮
10               var ddlBillingState =
                     document.getElementById("ddlBillingState");
                 var ddlShippingState =
                     document.getElementById("ddlShippingState");
11               var strBillingSelectedValue =
                     ddlBillingState.options[ddlBillingState.selectedIndex].
                     value;
12               var strBillingSelectedText =
                     ddlBillingState.options[ddlBillingState.selectedIndex].
                     text;
13               ddlShippingState.options[ddlShippingState.selectedIndex].
                     value = strBillingSelectedValue;
14               ddlShippingState.options[ddlShippingState.selectedIndex].
                     text = strBillingSelectedText;
                 ⋮
               ⋮ (Code continues.)
                 ⋮
             }
             else {
                 // Clear the shipping information.
15               document.getElementById("txtShippingLastName").value = "";
                 ⋮
               ⋮ (Code continues.)
                 ⋮
16               var ddlShippingState =
                     document.getElementById("ddlShippingState");
```

Figure 26-2. *(continued)*

```
17                 ddlShippingState.options[ddlShippingState.selectedIndex].
                      value = "IN";
18                 ddlShippingState.options[ddlShippingState.selectedIndex].
                      text = "Indiana";
                   ⋮
                   ⋮ (Code continues.)
                   ⋮
              }
19           return;

         }

20   </script>
```

RESULT

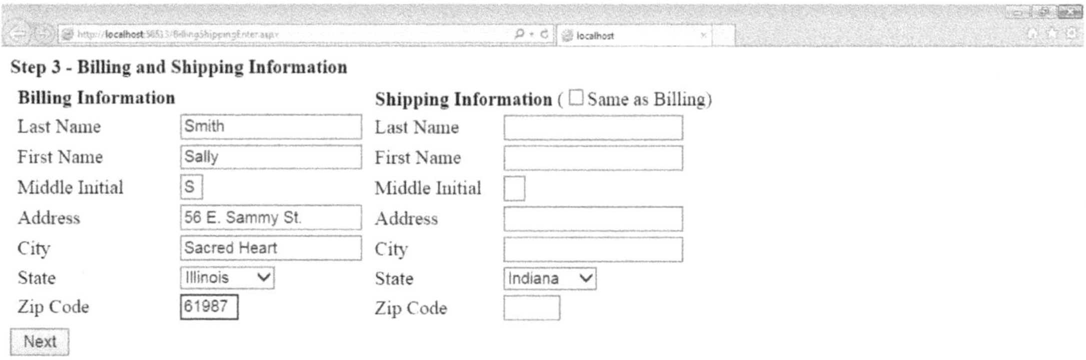

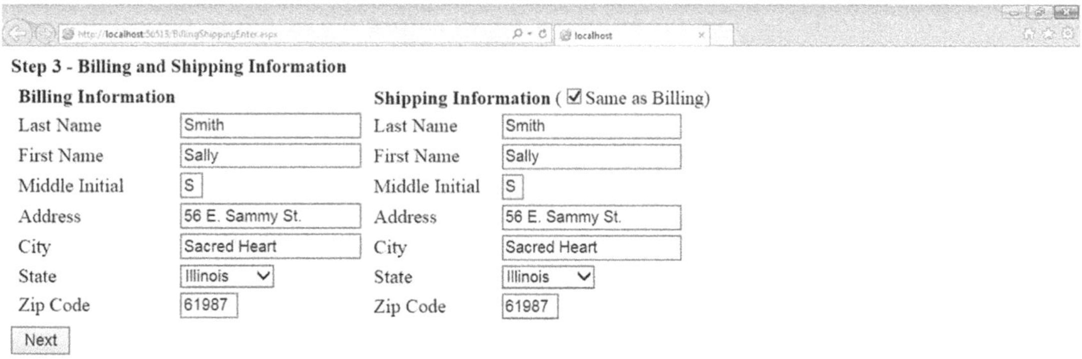

Figure. 26-2 *(continued)*

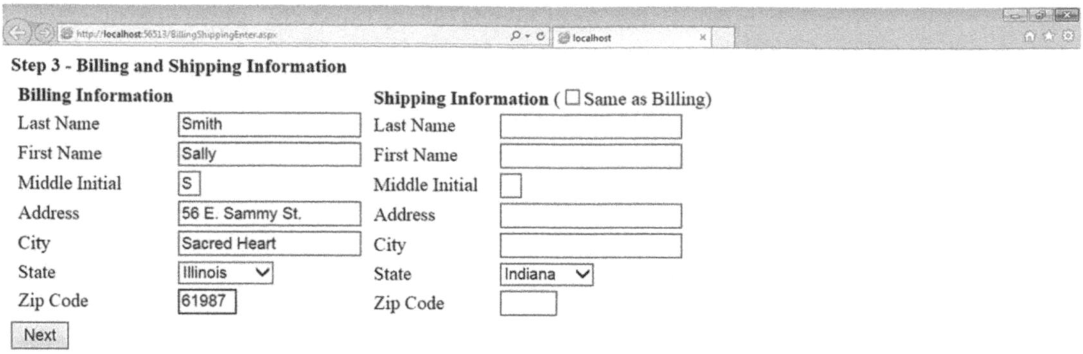

Figure 26-2. *(continued)*

26.6.2 Confirm Dialogs and Alert Messages

In this section, we will learn how to display confirm dialogs and alert message. Figure 26-3 shows an example of a JavaScript function that confirms the modification of an email address.

Notice at 01 the txtEmailAddress control that contains the email address to be modified.

Notice at 02 the btnModify control. As can be seen, the ClientIDMode property of this control is set to *Static* so that we can refer to the equivalent HTML element by its ASP.NET server control ID in the JavaScript code. We can also see that the OnClientClick property of the control is set to *return ConfirmModification()*. The *return* part of this property indicates that the called JavaScript function will return a value to the control. The *ConfirmModification()* part of the property indicates the name of the JavaScript function that will be executed when the btnModify control is clicked.

Notice at 03 and 10 the script tag and its associated end tag. Together, these tags define the area in the .aspx file that contains the page's JavaScript code.

Notice at 04 the ConfirmModification function that is executed when the btnModify control at 02 is clicked.

Notice at 05 that we are creating a local variable called booConfirm. As can be seen by how this variable is named, the intent of the variable is to contain a Boolean value.

Notice at 06 that we are displaying a *confirm* dialog and then assigning to the booConfirm variable either *true* (if the end user selects OK) or *false* (if the end user selects Cancel).

Notice at 07 that we are checking to see if the end user has selected OK or Cancel. If he or she has selected OK, we are displaying an *alert* message indicating that the email address will be changed. In addition, we are returning *true* to the btnModify control so that the page will be posted back to the server and the code at 09 will be executed. If the end user has selected Cancel, we are displaying an alert message indicating that the email address will *not* be changed. We are also returning *false* to the btnModify control so that the page will *not* be posted back to the server and the code at 09 will *not* be executed.

The first screenshot in the Result section of the figure shows the result of clicking the Modify button on the page. As can be seen, this displays the confirm dialog with its two options—OK and Cancel. The second screenshot shows the result of clicking the OK button on the confirm dialog, which displays an alert message stating that the email address will be changed. When the OK button on this dialog is clicked, the dialog will be dismissed, the page will be posted back to the server, and the code required to update the email address will be executed. And finally, the third screenshot shows the result of clicking the Cancel button on the confirm dialog, which displays an alert message stating that the email address will *not* be changed. When the OK button on this dialog is clicked, the dialog will be dismissed, but the page will *not* be posted back to the server. Thus, the code required to update the email address will *not* be executed.

ASPX CODE

```
   <asp:Label runat="server" Font-Bold="true" Text="Email Address" /><br />
01 <asp:TextBox runat="server" ID="txtEmailAddress" /><br />
02 <asp:Button runat="server" ID="btnModify" ClientIDMode="Static"
       OnClick="btnModify_Click"
       OnClientClick="return ConfirmModification();" Text="Modify" />
```

JAVASCRIPT CODE

```
03 <script type="text/javascript">

04     function ConfirmModification() {

05         var booConfirm;
06         booConfirm = confirm("Are you sure you want to modify your email
               address? Click OK to change it. Click Cancel to leave it the
               same.");
07         if (booConfirm) {
               alert("Your email address will be changed.");
               return true;
           }
           else {
               alert("Your email address will NOT be changed.");
               return false;
           }

       }

08 </script>
```

CODE BEHIND

```
09 protected void btnModify_Click(object sender, EventArgs e)
   {

       // The code for saving the email address to the database
       // would go here.

   }
```

Figure 26-3. *Example of a JavaScript function that confirms the modification of an email address*

RESULT

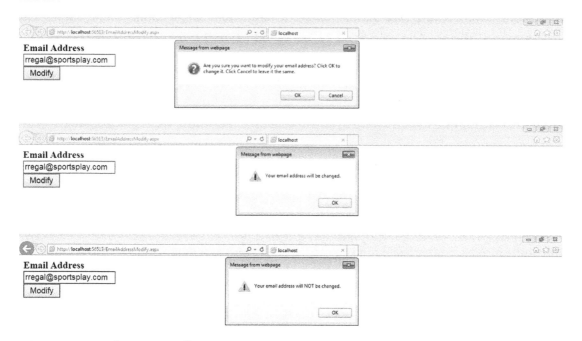

Figure 26-3. *(continued)*

26.6.3 Control Property Manipulation

In this section, we will learn how to manipulate control properties. Figure 26-4 shows an example of a JavaScript function that selects and deselects shippers and displays a message.

Notice at 01 the chkAll control. When this control is clicked, all of the other checkboxes on the page will be checked or unchecked depending on the current value of the control's Checked property. Also notice that the OnClick property of the control is set to *CheckAll()*. This indicates the name of the JavaScript function that will be executed when the chkAll control is clicked.

Notice at 02–05 the chkFedEx, chkUPS, chkUSPS, and lblMessage controls, respectively. As can be seen, the ClientIDMode properties of these controls are set to *Static* so that we can refer to the equivalent HTML elements by their ASP.NET server control IDs in the JavaScript code.

Notice at 06 and 09 the script tag and its associated end tag. Together, these tags define the area in the .aspx file that contains the page's JavaScript code.

Notice at 07 the chkAll function that is executed when the chkAll control at 01 is clicked.

Notice at 08 that we are checking to see if the chkAll control is checked. If the chkAll control is checked, we are checking the other three checkboxes and disabling them so that they cannot be manipulated by the end user. In addition, we are setting the innerText property of the lblMessage control to an appropriate message. If the chkAll control is *not* checked, we are unchecking the other three checkboxes and enabling them so that they can be manipulated by the end user. In addition, we are setting the innerText property of the lblMessage control to an appropriate message.

The first screenshot in the Result section of the figure shows the four checkbox controls before a shipper has been selected. The second screenshot shows the result of checking the *Any* checkbox. As can be seen, the three shippers have been checked and disabled indicating that the shipment should be sent via the cheapest shipper. And finally, the third screenshot shows the result of unchecking the *Any* checkbox and selecting two individual shippers indicating that the shipment should be sent via the cheapest selected shipper.

ASPX CODE

```
   <asp:Label runat="server" Font-Bold="true" Text="Shipper" /><br />
01 <asp:CheckBox runat="server" ID="chkAll" ClientIDMode="Static"
       onClick="CheckAll();"
       Text="Any (Cheapest Shipper)" /><br />
02 <asp:CheckBox runat="server" ID="chkFedEx" ClientIDMode="Static"
       Text="FedEx" /><br />
03 <asp:CheckBox runat="server" ID="chkUPS" ClientIDMode="Static"
       Text="UPS" /><br />
04 <asp:CheckBox runat="server" ID="chkUSPS" ClientIDMode="Static"
       Text="USPS" /><br />
   <asp:Button runat="server" ID="btnContinue" OnClick="btnContinue_Click"
       Text="Continue" />
05 <asp:Label runat="server" ID="lblMessage" ClientIDMode="Static" />
```

JAVASCRIPT CODE

```
06 <script type="text/javascript">

07     function CheckAll() {

08         if (document.getElementById("chkAll").checked) {
               document.getElementById("chkFedEx").checked = true;
               document.getElementById("chkUPS").checked = true;
               document.getElementById("chkUSPS").checked = true;
               document.getElementById("chkFedEx").disabled = true;
               document.getElementById("chkUPS").disabled = true;
               document.getElementById("chkUSPS").disabled = true;
               document.getElementById("lblMessage").innerText = "Your order
                   will be sent by the cheapest shipper.";
           }
           else {
               document.getElementById("chkFedEx").checked = false;
               document.getElementById("chkUPS").checked = false;
               document.getElementById("chkUSPS").checked = false;
               document.getElementById("chkFedEx").disabled = false;
               document.getElementById("chkUPS").disabled = false;
               document.getElementById("chkUSPS").disabled = false;
               document.getElementById("lblMessage").innerText = "Your order
                   will be sent by the cheapest selected shipper.";
           }

       }

09 </script>
```

Figure 26-4. *Example of a JavaScript function that selects and deselects shippers and displays a message*

RESULT

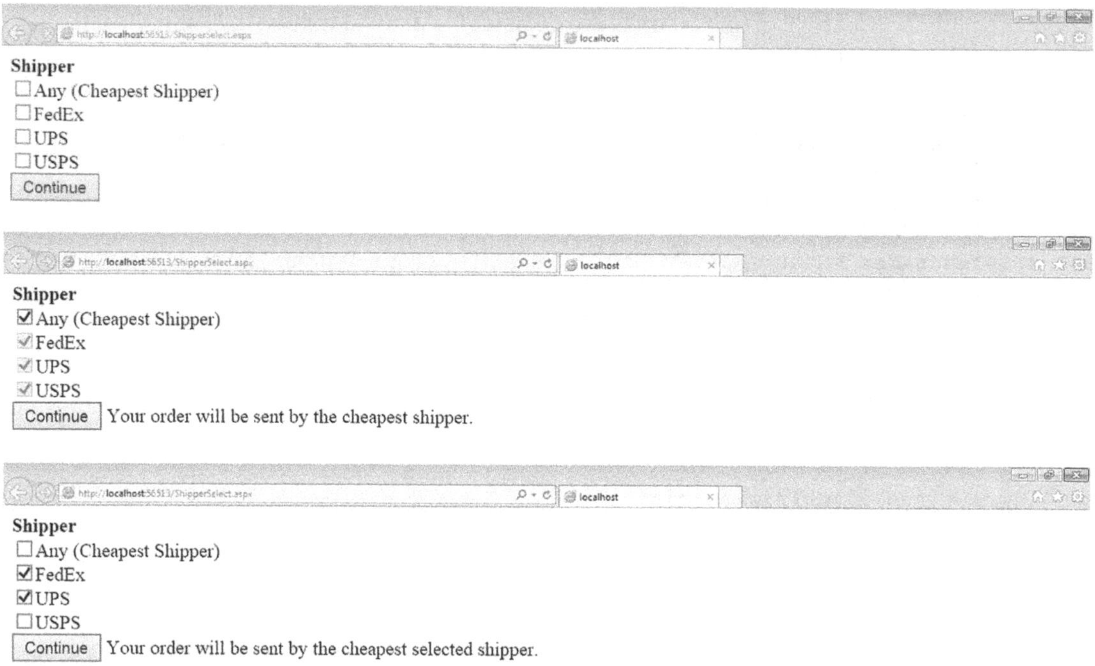

Figure 26-4.   *(continued)*

26.6.4 Date and Time Display

In this section, we will learn how to display a running date and time. This date and time will be displayed inside a label and will be updated every second. Figure 26-5 shows an example of a JavaScript function that displays a running date and time inside a label.

Notice at 01 the HTML body element of the page. As can be seen, the onload property of this element is set to *StartClock()*. This indicates the name of the JavaScript function that will be executed when the body of the page is loaded into the browser.

Notice at 02 the lblDateTime control. The ClientIDMode property of this control is set to *Static* so that we can refer to the equivalent HTML element by its ASP.NET server control ID in the JavaScript code.

Notice at 03 and 10 the script tag and its associated end tag. Together, these tags define the area in the .aspx file that contains the page's JavaScript code.

Notice at 04 the StartClock function that is executed when the body of the page is loaded into the browser.

Notice at 05 that we are immediately calling the UpdateClock function when the StartClock function is executed. This sets into motion the continually updating date and time.

Notice at 06 the UpdateClock function, which displays and updates the date and time displayed in the label on the page.

Notice at 07 that we are creating a new Date object called objDate from the Date class. Note that this automatically retrieves the current date and time from the client's operating system.

Notice at 08 that we are getting the locale-sensitive (e.g., language-sensitive) date and time from the objDate object, concatenating them, and assigning the result to the innerText property of the lblDateTime control.

Notice at 09 that we are calling the UpdateClock function again after waiting 1,000 milliseconds (i.e., 1 second). As can be seen, this creates an infinite loop that redisplays the date and time in the label every one second.

The screenshot in the Result section of the figure shows the date and time as they are displayed in the date/time label on the page. If we were able to view the page in real time, we would see the date and time update every second.

ASPX CODE

```
01  <body onload="StartClock()">

    <asp:Label runat="server" Font-Bold="true" Text="Date/Time" /><br />
02  <asp:Label runat="server" ID="lblDateTime" ClientIDMode="Static" />
```

JAVASCRIPT CODE

```
03  <script type="text/javascript">

04      function StartClock() {

05          UpdateClock();

        }

06      function UpdateClock() {

07          var objDate = new Date();
08          document.getElementById("lblDateTime").innerText =
                objDate.toLocaleDateString() + ' ' +
                objDate.toLocaleTimeString();
09          setTimeout('UpdateClock()', 1000);

        }

10  </script>
```

RESULT

Date/Time
7/8/2017 10:32:22 AM

Figure 26-5. *Example of a JavaScript function that displays a running date and time inside a label*

26.6.5 Iterative Operations

In this section, we will learn how to perform iterative operations (i.e., repeating operations, looping operations). Figure 26-6 shows an example of a set of JavaScript functions that modify the product information in a drop-down list.

Notice at 01 the HTML body element of the page. As can be seen, the onload property of this element is set to *SaveProductOptions()*. This indicates the name of the JavaScript function that will be executed when the body of the page is loaded into the browser.

Notice at 02–04 the radBasic, radPlus, and radDeluxe controls, respectively. When these controls are clicked, the prices of the items in the drop-down list at 05 will be modified. Notice that the onClick properties of these controls are set to *UpdateProductPrice()*. This indicates the name of the JavaScript function that will be executed when these controls are clicked. Also notice that a parameter value of *Basic*, *Plus*, or *Deluxe* is passed to the function depending on the radio button that is selected. Notice as well that the ClientIDMode properties of these controls are set to *Static* so that we can refer to the equivalent HTML elements by their ASP.NET server control IDs in the JavaScript code.

Notice at 05 the ddlProduct control. As will be seen, the prices of the items in this drop-down list will be modified to reflect the end user's selection with regard to the selected package—*Basic*, *Plus*, or *Deluxe*.

Notice at 06 and 11 the script tag and its associated end tag. Together, these tags define the area in the .aspx file that contains the page's JavaScript code.

Notice at 07 the SaveProductOptions function that is executed when the body of the page is loaded into the browser. In this function, we are creating a new array object from the Array class that contains three elements. We are then saving the three product options in the drop-down list to the array so that we can restore them to their original values when necessary (i.e., when a different radio button is selected). This function is only invoked once.

Notice at 08 the UpdateProductPrice function that is executed when one of the radio buttons is selected. In this function, we are using a switch structure to identify the type of package the end user has selected—Basic, Plus, or Deluxe. If the end user has selected the *Basic* package, we are calling the RestoreDropDownListOptions function to restore the options in the drop-down list to their original values. If the end user has selected the *Plus* package, we are calling the RestoreDropDownListOptions function to restore the options in the drop-down list to their original values, defining an upcharge of $10,

553

and calling the UpdateDropDownListOptions function with the upcharge to increase the prices of the items displayed in the drop-down list. If the end user has selected the *Deluxe* package, we are calling the RestoreDropDownListOptions function to restore the options in the drop-down list to their original values, defining an upcharge of $40, and calling the UpdateDropDownListOptions function with the upcharge to increase the prices of the items displayed in the drop-down list.

Notice at 09 the RestoreDropDownListOptions function. In this function, we are looping through the elements of the array to restore the options in the drop-down list to their original values.

Notice at 10 the UpdateDropDownListOptions function. As can be seen, this function receives an upcharge value from the UpdateProductPrice function at 08. In this function, we are looping through the items in the product drop-down list and modifying their associated prices. Within the loop, we are getting the product from the drop-down list and placing it into a product string that is easy to modify, locating and extracting the original price of the product in the string, computing the new price of the product and formatting it, replacing the old price with the new price, and replacing the product in the drop-down list with the modified product string.

The first screenshot in the Result section of the figure shows the product drop-down list with the *Basic* product package selected (the default). The second screenshot shows the result of clicking the drop-down list to view the product options. Notice the options in the drop-down list and their respective prices. The third screenshot shows the result of selecting the *Plus* product package and clicking the drop-down list to view the modified product options. Notice that the prices in the drop-down list have been increased by $10. And finally, the fourth screenshot shows the result of selecting the *Deluxe* product package and clicking the drop-down list to view the modified product options. Notice that the prices in the drop-down list have been increased by $40.

ASPX CODE

```
01  <body onload="SaveProductOptions()">

    <asp:Label runat="server" Font-Bold="true" Text="Product Package" /><br />
02  <asp:RadioButton runat="server" ID="radBasic" Checked="true"
        ClientIDMode="Static" GroupName="Package"
        onClick="UpdateProductPrice('Basic');"
        Text="Basic (Racquet Only)" />
        <br />
03  <asp:RadioButton runat="server" ID="radPlus" ClientIDMode="Static"
        GroupName="Package" onClick="UpdateProductPrice('Plus');"
        Text="Plus (Racquet and Strings) + $10" /><br />
04  <asp:RadioButton runat="server" ID="radDeluxe" ClientIDMode="Static"
        GroupName="Package" onClick="UpdateProductPrice('Deluxe');"
        Text="Deluxe (Racquet, Strings, and Bag) + $40" /><br />
05  <asp:DropDownList runat="server" ID="ddlProduct" ClientIDMode="Static">
        <asp:ListItem Value="PTEJ25R"
            Text="Prince Tour Elite Junior 25 Inch Racquet ($85.00)" />
        <asp:ListItem Value="PL110"
            Text="Prince Lightning 110 ($75.00)" />
        <asp:ListItem Value="PTW100"
            Text="Prince Textreme Warrior 100 ($199.00)" />
    </asp:DropDownList><br />
    <asp:Button runat="server" ID="btnContinue" OnClick="btnContinue_Click"
        Text="Continue" />
```

JAVASCRIPT CODE

```
06  <script type="text/javascript">

07      function SaveProductOptions() {

            // Save the product options in the drop down list to an
            // array so that they can be restored to their original
            // values when necessary.
            strProductOptionsArray = new Array(3);
            ddlProduct = document.getElementById("ddlProduct");
            for (var i = 0; i < ddlProduct.length; i++) {
                strProductOptionsArray[i] = ddlProduct.options[i].text;
            }

        }
```

Figure 26-6. *Example of a set of JavaScript functions that modify the product information in a drop-down list*

```
08      function UpdateProductPrice(strPackageType) {

            switch (strPackageType) {
                case "Basic":
                    RestoreDropDownListOptions();
                    break;
                case "Plus":
                    RestoreDropDownListOptions();
                    var decUpcharge = 10.00;
                    UpdateDropDownListOptions(decUpcharge);
                    break;
                case "Deluxe":
                    RestoreDropDownListOptions();
                    var decUpcharge = 40.00;
                    UpdateDropDownListOptions(decUpcharge);
                    break;
            }

        }


09      function RestoreDropDownListOptions() {

            // Restore the options in the drop down list to
            // their original values.
            for (var i = 0; i < ddlProduct.length; i++) {
                ddlProduct.options[i].text = strProductOptionsArray[i];
            }

        }


10      function UpdateDropDownListOptions(decUpcharge) {

            for (var i = 0; i < ddlProduct.length; i++) {
                // Get the product from the drop down list and place
                // it into a product string that is easy to modify.
                var strProduct = ddlProduct.options[i].text;
                // Locate and extract the original price.
                var intIndexStart = strProduct.lastIndexOf("($")
                var intIndexEnd = strProduct.lastIndexOf(")")
                var decPriceOld = Number(strProduct.substring(intIndexStart +
                    2, intIndexEnd))
                // Compute the new price and format it.
                var decPriceNew = decPriceOld + decUpcharge;
                var decPriceNewFormatted = "$" + decPriceNew.toFixed(2);
                // Replace the old price with the new price.
                strProduct = strProduct.substring(0, intIndexStart) + "(" +
                    decPriceNewFormatted + ")";
```

Figure 26-6. (continued)

```
        // Replace the product in the drop down list with the
        // modified product string.
        ddlProduct.options[i].text = strProduct;
    }

}
```

11   `</script>`

RESULT

Figure 26-6. *(continued)*

Index

A

Adding a cascading style sheet file, 333
Adding a Classes folder, 268
Adding a MasterPage class, 305
Adding a non-static C# class, 268
Adding a Page class, 32
Adding a Page class with a MasterPage, 309
Adding a SiteMap class, 345
Adding a skin file, 325
Adding a static C# class, 273
Adding a theme, 323
Advanced Research Projects Agency
       Network (ARPANET), 3
Ajax
    accordion class, 509
    Ajax Control Toolkit, 507
    AjaxFileUpload class, 513
    BalloonPopupExtender class, 518
    CalendarExtender class, 520
    control classes, 509
    control extender classes, 517
    extension classes, 501
    installing the Ajax Control Toolkit, 507
    ModalPopupExtender class, 524
    PasswordStrength class, 529
    ScriptManager class, 500
    UpdatePanel class, 501
    UpdateProgress class, 504

Ajax programming, 499
Apache HTTP server, 5
Application layer, 3
Application server, 6
Arithmetic
       operations, 193
Arithmetic operators, 194
Array class, 222
Array operations, 221
As Clause, 367
ASP.NET and C# Programming, 21
AspNet.ScriptManager.jQuery, 101
ASP.NET Server tags, 36
Assembly, 8
Assignment operations, 125
Assignment operators, 130
Asynchronous postbacks, 499
Attributes, 362

B

Banker's rounding, 156, 202
Base class, 14
BaseValidator class, 101
Basic server controls, 39
Breadcrumb, 343
Break statement, 180
Business logic, 7
Button class, 45

C

Calendar class, 59
Cascading style sheet files, 332
Cast, 133
Cast operator, 149
C# Class, 267
CheckBox class, 63
Child class, 14
Class design, 266
Class diagram, 10
Classes, 8
Classes and objects, 10
Class selectors, 332
Client application, 5
Client-based state maintenance, 282
Client host, 5
Clients, 4
Client-server model, 4
Client-side processing, 533
Client-side validation, 115
Close tag, 36
Code behind database operations, 449
Code behind directives, 308, 311
Code behind file, 33
Code points, 126
Code redundancy, 14
Code reuse, 14
Code units, 126
Cohesion, 266
Collection operations, 241
Common Language Runtime (CLR), 8
Common type system, 8
CompareValidator class, 105
Compound assignment operators, 131
Concatenations, 183
Constant declarations, 130
Constructor methods, 14

Content pages, 303
Content placeholder, 303
Continue statement, 180
Control class, 18
Control operations, 161
Control parameters, 381
Conversion operations, 145
Convert class, 153
Cookie parameters, 381
Cookies, 284
Copy area end, 403, 428
Copy area start, 403, 428
Coupling, 266
Css selectors, 332
Custom C# classes, 265
Custom subsetting criterion, 386, 392
CustomValidator class, 114

D

Database administration, 365
Database design, SQL, and Data binding, 359
Database management
                system (DBMS), 359
Database schema, 360
Database server, 6
Database usage, 365
DataBoundControl class, 379
Data control language, 365
Data definition language, 365
Data manipulation language, 365
Data models, 359
DataPager class, 441
Data pages, 441
Data query language, 365
Data source, 395, 420
Data source control, 397, 421

Data validation controls, 99
Date and time operations, 207
Date formatting, 213
Date parsing, 214
Date-related methods, 212
Date-related properties, 211
DateTime structure, 208
Decision structures, 164
Declarative programming languages, 365
Default skins, 325
Design time, 21
Destructor methods, 14
Development machine email server, 490
DivideByZeroException class, 137
Domain, 127
.NET Framework, 8
Do-While Structure, 175
DropDownList class, 90
Dynamic menu, 349
Dynamic web pages, 4

E

ECMAScript Language Specification, 534
Element selectors, 332
Email messaging, 489
Encapsulation, 13
Encoded URL, 289
End tag, 36
Entity integrity, 363
Enumerations, 133
Equality operators, 162
Escape sequences, 184
Event handler methods, 11
Events, 13
Exception, 134
Exception class, 135
Exception handling, 134

Exception helper, 134
Execution plan, 366

F

File class, 254
File system operations, 253
File transfer protocol (FTP), 3
FileUpload class, 68
Filters, 386
Footer, 312
For-Each structure, 178
Foreign key, 363
FormatException class, 138
Format specifiers, 213, 218
Form parameters, 381
FormView class, 395
For structure, 176
Fourth generation programming
    language, 364
403 Error, 37
404 Error, 347
Framework class library, 8
From clause, 366
Full-Page rendering, 499
Full path, 254

G

Google chrome, 5
Gregorian calendar, 208
Group By Clause, 367

H

Having clause, 367
Header, 312
HTML document object, 536

HTML elements, 332
HTML tags, 36
HTTP request, 6
HTTP response, 6
HttpSessionState class, 296
HyperLink class, 71
Hypermedia, 3
Hypertext links, 29
Hypertext markup language (HTML), 6, 29
Hypertext transfer protocol (HTTP), 3

I

Identifier, 29
Identifier naming standards, 29
If-Else-If structure, 168
If-Else structure, 167
If structure, 164
ImageButton class, 74
Image class, 72
ImageMap class, 77
Imperative programming languages, 364
IndexOutOfRangeException class, 139
Information hiding, 13
Inheritance, 14
Instance, 11
Integrated development environment (IDE), 22
Internet Information Services (IIS), 5
Internet Information Services Express (IIS Express), 22
IP addresses, 6
Iterative structures, 174

J, K

JavaScript
    assignment operations, 538
    browser compatibility, 534
    confirm dialogs and alert messages, 544
    control property manipulation, 547
    date and time display, 550
    examples, 537
    functions, 535
    HTML Document Object Model, 536
    iterative operations, 553
    script elements, 535
JavaScript programming, 533
Join operation, 371

L

Label class, 40
LinkButton class, 82
LinkedList class, 246
ListBox class, 92
ListControl class, 87
ListItem class, 89
ListView class, 420
Literal, 130
Logical operators, 163

M

MailMessage class, 490
Maintaining the state of a data structure, 301
Managed code, 8
MasterPage class, 303
Master page directive, 306
Master pages, 303
Master type directive, 316
Math class, 201
Mathematical rounding, 202
Members, 9
Menu class, 349

Menu Cursor, 351

Methods, 12

Microsoft Intermediate Language, 8

Microsoft Internet Explorer, 5

Microsoft SQL Server, 359

Microsoft SQL Server Management Studio, 359

More Server Controls, 59

Mozilla Firefox, 5

Multiple exceptions, 142

Multiple-Row Database Table Maintenance, 419

N

Named skins, 325

Namespace, 10

Narrowing conversions, 148

Naturally-occurring subsetting criterion, 386, 392

Navigation, 343

Nested-If structure, 169

NextPreviousPagerField class, 442

Non-parameterized queries, 458

Non-persistent cookies, 285

Non-static classes, 10, 265

Non-type-Safe programming language, 533

NuGet package, 101

NumericPagerField class, 445

O

Object class, 17

Object-orientation concepts, 9

One-dimensional arrays, 224

Open tag, 36

Oracle iPlanet Web Server, 5

Order By clause, 367

Order of precedence and associativity, 197

Original_{0}, 401, 426

OverflowException class, 141

P

Packets, 3

Packet switching, 3

Page class, 30

Page development, 29

Page directive, 33

Page region, 501

Paging controls, 441

Panel class, 94

Papercut, 490

Parameterized queries, 463

Parent class, 14

Parentheses, 199

Partial-page rendering, 499

Path, 254

Persistent cookies, 285

PostBack, 80

Primary key, 362, 363

Profile parameters, 381

Progressive enhancement, 534

Projects, 24

Properties, 12

Protected void, 35, 308

Public partial class, 35, 311

Q

Query optimizer, 366

Query plan, 366

Query string parameters, 381

Query strings, 289

Queue class, 244

R

RadioButton class, 65
RangeValidator class, 107
RectangleHotSpot class, 78
Reference types, 125
Referential integrity, 363
RegularExpressionValidator class, 110
Relational database, 359
Relational database management system
    (RDBMS), 359
Relational operators, 162
Relationships, 363
Relative path, 254
Render, 39
RequiredFieldValidator class, 103
Reserved words, 365
Result set, 453
Reuse, 266
Root directory, 254
Route parameters, 381
Run time, 21
Runtime error, 134

S

Script Manager, 100
Script Manager package, 101
Select clause, 366
Select parameters, 387
Separation of concerns, 34
Server, 4
Server application, 4
Server-based state maintenance, 294
Server host, 4
Server-side validation, 115
Session, 5
Session ID, 294
Session object, 294

Session parameters, 381
Sessions, 294
Session state, 294
Session timeout, 295
Simple assignment operators, 131
Simple Mail Transfer Protocol, 3, 489
Single-Row Database Table
    Maintenance, 395
SiteMap class, 344
Skin files, 325
SmtpClient class, 492
Solution Explorer, 24
Solution file, 32
Solutions, 24
SortedList class, 250
SqlCommand class, 453
SqlConnection class, 450
SqlDataReader class, 455
SqlDataSource
    Connection strings, 383
    Data-bound control filtering, 386
    Data-bound control population, 384
    Filtering with control parameters, 386
    Filtering with session parameters, 392
SqlDataSource class, 380
SQL injection, 463
SqlParameter class, 465
SqlParameterCollection class, 464
Stack class, 242
Starting a new project, 23
Start page, 36
Start tag, 36
Stateless, 281
State maintenance, 281
Static classes, 10, 265
Static menu, 349
Static Web pages, 4
Store-and-forward model, 489

Stored procedures, 471
String class, 186
String operations, 183
Structure, 208
Structured Query Language (SQL), 364
    Delete Statement, 378
    Insert Statement, 374
    Select Statement, 366
    Update Statement, 377
Surrogate pairs, 126
Switch structure, 171
Switch-Through structure, 173
Synchronous postbacks, 499

T

TableCell class, 54
Table class, 52
TableRow class, 53
Tables, 361
Tags, 29
TCP/IP, 3
Telnet, 3
Templates, 395, 420
TextBox class, 43
Themes, 323
Ticks, 208
Time formatting, 218
Time-related methods, 216
Time-related properties, 216
Toolbox, 39
TreeView class, 353

Try-Catch-Finally structure, 137
Two-dimensional arrays, 231
Types, 125
Type safe, 146
Type-safe programming language, 21

U

Unicode characters, 126
Uniform Resource Locator, 29
Using directives, 35
UTF-16, 126

V

ValidationSummary class, 117
Value types, 125
Variable declarations, 127
Verbatim literals, 186
View state, 282
Visual Studio, 22

W, X, Y, Z

Web address, 29
Web Application Development, 3
Web browsers, 5
WebConfigurationManager class, 452
WebControl class, 19
Where clause, 367
While structure, 174
Widening conversions, 145

CPSIA information can be obtained
at www.ICGtesting.com
Printed in the USA
LVHW050409221122
733775LV00006B/305